BETWEEN
WORLDS

BETWEEN WORLDS

Access to Second Language Acquisition

DAVID E. FREEMAN
&
YVONNE S. FREEMAN

Heinemann
Portsmouth, NH

Heinemann
A division of Reed Elsevier Inc.
361 Hanover Street
Portsmouth, NH 03801–3912
Offices and agents throughout the world

The authors and publisher wish to thank those who have generously given permission to reprint borrowed material:

Figures 5-1 and 5-2 were originally published in *The Rainbow Collection* by Santillana Publishing Co. Copyright © 1984 by Santillana Publishing Co. All rights reserved. Reprinted by permission.

Excerpts from Diane Larsen-Freeman and Michael Long in *An Introduction to Second Language Acquisitions Research* edited by C. N. Candlin. Copyright 1991. Published by Longman Group Ltd. Reprinted by permission.

Acknowledgments for borrowed material continue on page 366, which constitutes an extension of the copyright page.

Library of Congress Cataloging-in-Publication Data

Freeman, David E.
　　Between worlds : access to second language acquisition / David & Yvonne Freeman.
　　　　p.　cm.
　　Includes bibliographical references and index.
　　ISBN 0-435-08819-X
　　1. Second language acquisition.　I. Freeman, Yvonne S.　II. Title.
　P118.2.F74　1994
　418'.0071—dc20

　　　　　　　　　　　　　　　　　　　　　　　　　　　　　94-15010
　　　　　　　　　　　　　　　　　　　　　　　　　　　　　CIP

Editor: Dawn Boyer
Editorial and production services: Camden Type 'n Graphics
Text design: Connie Leavitt
Cover design: Joyce Weston

Front cover photographs: Katie Bausch-Ude, Elaine Poser, and Bunny Rogers.
Interior photographs: Kay Armijo, Elaine Poser, Katie Bausch-Ude, Kelly Austin, and
　Lurette C. Kerr.

Printed in the United States of America on acid-free paper
99 98 97 96 95 94　HP　1 2 3 4 5 6 7 8 9

We dedicate this book to our daughters,
Mary and Ann, who have provided us with
very personal lessons about acquiring a
second language and learning to live between worlds.

CONTENTS

ACKNOWLEDGMENTS

This book is a result of our experiences with teachers who are committed to improving the lives of their students. Our examples come from classes where creative teachers provided access to language for all their students. We wish to acknowledge the teachers with whom we have worked and especially the following outstanding educators whose work we share in this book: Maureen Anderson, Gayleen Aoki, Loretta Aragón, Kay Armijo, Katie Bausch-Ude, Laura Beery, María Blancas, Sharon Borgstadt, Jackie Brown, Alicia Cabello, Pauline Castañeda, Carolina Cervantes, Pat Cheek, Roxanne Claassen, Paulette Clement, Darrin Cook, Evelyn Crews, Lonna Deeter, Kathy DerMugredechian, Rusty DeRuiter, Cándida Dillon, Mary Durazo, David East, Joan Ellis, Jeannette Erickson, Stacey Esraelian, Steve Ewert, Jean Fennacy, Linda Friberg, Linda Gage, Roberta Gentes, Toni Gerbrandt, Tammy González, Melissa Greer, Genaro Guerrero, Kari Hayworth, Joan Heinrichs, Shelly Hernández, Georgia Hill, Kathy Houghton, Gaylene Joe, Jane Jones, Lurette Kerr, Charlene Klassen, Ellen Kunz, Maryann Lambarén, Mike Lebsock, Xueguang Lian, Debbie Manning, Lisa Marasco, Miriam Marquardt, Eva Mauch, Terri Mejorado, Marjorie Miller, Cheryl Milligan, Xe Moua, Sandy Neilsen, Sam Nofziger, Roxie Pires, Elaine Poser, Brigeen Radoicich, Denise Rea, Michael Roberts, Bunny Rogers, Jill Rojas, Dan Sands, Herb Scott, Yolanda Shahbazian, Henrietta Siemens, Kathy Smith, Pam Smith, Joyce Swisher, Lea Tafolla, Kathy Thompson, Rhoda Toews, Patty Trask, Yvette Vásquez, Kristene Vaux, Lori Wilson, Vince Workmon, Marta Yoshimura, and Denette Zaninovich.

In addition, we would like to thank our editor, Dawn Boyer, who encouraged and supported us throughout this project, overcoming obstacles created by having to work with authors who move between worlds.

INTRODUCTION

What more can you expect of me? Now you want me to attend a series of inservices on second language acquisition and cross-cultural communication! It's true that every year I have more students who don't speak English, but if I just use the whole language techniques I've been learning, my students will soon be speaking English. A whole language curriculum is meaningful and has purpose for all students. I'm giving my students what they need.

These words were spoken by Mrs. Johnson, a conscientious teacher with ten years of experience. There have been many changes at her school site during the last five years, and she has made the effort to keep up. When the district switched from the traditional basal reader series to the literature-based program, she attended the district workshops. When her grade level decided to try process writing, she read the same professional books her colleagues were reading and planned with them as they each implemented a writers workshop. When her colleagues started integrating curriculum and organizing around themes, Mrs. Johnson met with the other teachers at her level to make plans and order new materials.

Mrs. Johnson believes that she understands language, teaching, learning, and curriculum. She is convinced that if she gives her students extensive experience with quality literature, offers them authentic opportunities for writing, and involves them in inquiry-based content area study, all her students, including her second language students, will soon be speaking, reading, and writing English. She has already invested considerable time and energy in updating her professional preparation for teaching, and she is confident that what she does in her classroom is good for all her students.

Although Mrs. Johnson is right in many ways, the students in her classroom are much more diverse than the students she taught a few years ago. The approach she is taking does not address the specific needs of her second language learners. While it is very important that English learners be encouraged to participate in the kinds of authentic activities Mrs. Johnson is providing, their academic success depends on many factors inside and outside the classroom. Students learning in a new language and in a new culture have unique needs. In a school like Mrs. Johnson's, the students and the teachers are worlds apart—almost literally. It is critical that teachers, resource specialists, paraprofessionals, administrators, teacher educators, parents, and the general public understand that many elements interact to influence the school performance of students who are acquiring English as another language.

Rejecting Single-Cause Explanations

Certainly, no magic formula will ensure the academic success of any group of students, and while this book offers examples of practices that have proved effective with a variety of students, we are aware that each learning situation is different. What works in one classroom may not apply down the hall, much less in another part of the country. We hope, however, that by identifying and discussing the social and psychological factors that impact students who are learning academic content in their second or third languages, we can help professionals like Mrs. Johnson to examine their programs and their classroom practices to ensure that they are providing what is best for all their students.

The approach we develop here recognizes that any student's second language development and academic content learning are the result of many interacting forces. No one factor determines success or failure for a particular student or group of students. Yet, in the past, some educators have relied on single-cause explanations to account for students' progress. For example, some have focused on English proficiency. However, learning English is not the only key to academic achievement. English proficiency, by itself, does not determine success or failure. Cummins (1989) expresses this clearly:

> Understanding why and how minority students are failing academically requires that educators dig a little deeper than superficial linguistic mismatches between home and school or insufficient exposure to English. Underachievement is not caused by lack of fluency in English (pp. 33–34).

Even when lack of English is not seen as the cause of failure, the students themselves or their backgrounds are sometimes blamed. Such single-cause explanations are often based on social or cultural stereotypes. For example, some teachers might say that Hispanic students lack motivation, so they do not do well in school, but that Asians get good grades because they are influenced by high parental expectations. We would like to suggest that the question of school success and failure is much more complex than most people think.

Throughout this book we will examine the different worlds, the different contexts in which English language learners find themselves, but we do this with an important goal. We want to identify the factors within those contexts that influence learning and suggest specific ways that teachers can enrich the context for their students to provide them with opportunities to develop both language and academic content knowledge. By eliminating the myth of single causes for failure, educators can expand the potential for learning for the diverse students in our schools.

In our discussion we refer to the Contextual Interaction Model proposed by Cortés (1986). Cortés identifies various influences from both the societal context and the school context that determine student success. He explains how the different influences interact in complex ways and how changes in any one area can affect the entire system. Student success is influenced by the perceptions their family, their community, and their schools have of them and of education; by their socioeconomic status; by politics at local and national levels; by the history of their ethnic or language groups, including the treatment they have received by the mainstream society; by their background knowledge and experiences, including previous education; by the view of learning, and language learning in particular, that their teachers hold; by the approach to curriculum students experience in the classroom; by the way their teachers and peers respond to them; and by their own expectations of what education should be like. These factors from both the societal and the school contexts interact to influence student success or failure.

Between Worlds: Access to Second Language Acquisition

The title for this book, *Between Worlds,* reflects our conviction that providing the best education for second language students requires that as we plan educational experiences, we take into account factors from two worlds, the school and the larger society. In a sense, school is a place that is between two worlds for all students. Students entering school are leaving the smaller world of their home and entering the larger world of their community. For English language learners, these two worlds are often very different. In school, language minority students are often taught by teachers like Mrs. Johnson whose only experience has been with students from mainstream society. Despite the curriculum changes she has made in the past five years, Mrs. Johnson belongs to this mainstream world, and her attitudes and values are shaped by this world. Mrs. Johnson and other teachers like her benefit from examining their attitudes and values and also by considering the values and attitudes that their second language learners bring to school. By doing this they can help all their students fully experience the best of both worlds.

Some students are unable to move successfully between worlds because they never fully enter the mainstream school community. They are marginalized by the instruction they receive and the attitudes they encounter. Eventually, many of them drop out or are pushed out of school. Unfortunately, these students are often not able to succeed in school or return to their home community. They may be in a state of cultural ambivalence, not really accepted at school or at home. When this happens, increasing numbers of students turn to alternate communities, such as gangs. Rather than experiencing the best of both worlds, they cannot participate fully in either one.

Other students succeed in school, but in the process they become alienated from their home community. These are students who enter school as monolingual Spanish or Korean speakers and leave school as monolingual English speakers. They are unable to communicate with family and friends in the home community. These students may reject their heritage language and culture in order to become part of the mainstream. Rather than experiencing the best of both worlds, they simply trade one world for another.

For second language students to benefit from both their worlds, schools must provide experiences that enable them to do just that. Effective school programs take into account factors from both the school and the societal contexts in planning curriculum for language minority students. Accordingly, we have organized this book around these two contexts. We begin by looking at factors in one world, the school, because these are the factors over which teachers have the most immediate control. We then examine factors that impact schooling from the other world, the society, including teachers' and students' values and attitudes. In the last section of this book we discuss ways teachers can bring these two worlds together and transform their practice through research that takes both worlds, school and society, into account.

We have chosen *Access to Second Language Acquisition* as the subtitle for this book because we believe that a number of different psychological and social factors interact to permit or deny students access to the acquisition of a new language. However, the subtitle also has another purpose. We hope that this book gives all those involved with second language learners access to language learning theories and effective classroom practice. We hope to bring the theories alive for the readers of this book by providing numerous examples of classroom practice. Educators who understand these theories and their implications can provide all English learners with access to their new language.

In addition, teachers have the responsibility for developing not only language, but also academic content. We provide a number of examples that demonstrate that language is learned best when students are focused on content area studies rather than on aspects of language itself. We learn language as we use language for a variety of purposes. This is true for students in mainstream classes as well as those in ESL (English as a second language) or foreign language classes. As Halliday (1984) has pointed out, students can learn language as they learn through language.

Who Is This Book For?

We are teacher educators, and the idea of writing this book came to us as we taught a course called Language Acquisition and Cross-Cultural Communication. The teachers in our graduate program needed a text that described different theories of language acquisition and also provided examples for putting theory into practice. In addition, as we worked with teachers in schools, we were reminded daily that teaching second language learners involves much more than an understanding of theory, methods, and materials. We realized that this text needed to address social and cultural factors that influence students' learning. This book reflects our attempts to meet these goals. Our examples come from our own experiences and those of teachers who are working with a wide variety of second language learners of different ages in different settings. It is our hope that other teacher educators might find this book useful in courses dealing with learning theory, second language acquisition, and social and cultural factors that influence learning. These courses could be part of a preservice program for prospective teachers or part of a program for teachers wishing to continue their professional development.

However, we do not intend that the audience for this book be restricted to people taking formal coursework or to designated ESL or bilingual teachers. We hope that mainstream teachers like Mrs. Johnson will also find this book useful. In fact, we wrote this book with several possible audiences in mind. One audience includes teachers, counselors, paraprofessionals, and others who work with second language students and who wish to continue their own professional development through independent reading. As student populations change and increasing numbers of second language students enter our schools, it is important for all the professionals working with these students to be knowledgeable about current theories of language acquisition and aware of the social and cultural factors that influence students' academic performance. We have presented explanations of theory and examples of successful classroom practice that should clarify many of these issues. We encourage educators who are not taking formal courses to find one or two others who will also read this book and then meet in pairs or small groups to reflect on the ideas that are presented.

We have also written this book for school administrators. Administrators provide leadership in curriculum, and they support the efforts of classroom teachers. School demographics have changed radically. In many schools, language minority students have become the numerical majority. For administrators to carry out their role, they need to be aware of the psychological and social factors that influence the academic performance of second language students as well as their curriculum needs.

Finally, we have written this book for parents and for community members interested in school improvement. Parents and other community members play a key role in the academic success of language minority students. We discuss in some detail ways in which the social context of schooling influences the educational context. We also describe successful programs that involve parents and other community members. Second language students can succeed when home and school work together to provide them access to the best possible education. We hope that parents and other members of the general public will find the examples and explanations here helpful as they increase their own involvement in programs to improve schooling for all students. We have written this book with these different audiences in mind to bring together the worlds that influence English language learners.

At the end of each chapter we have included a section we call Applications. These applications are not intended as end-of-chapter tests or exercises that must be completed for a grade. Instead, they are invitations to explore in more detail the concepts raised in the chapter. We hope they will help readers apply the ideas to their own experiences with second language learners. We believe that people learn by doing, and the applications ask readers to do something with what they have read or to read related material. We have asked our own students to try these activities, and they have reported that the applications enabled them to relate the concepts being studied more directly to their own teaching. Since we also believe that learning takes place in social interaction, we have suggested that the activities be completed in pairs or small groups. With our students, this sharing has led not only to the expansion of ideas, but also to the building of a supportive community.

Our earlier book, *Whole Language for Second Language Learners,* focused on different methods that have been used to teach English as a second language. In that book we outlined a series of principles that constitute our orientation toward teaching and learning. This orientation is holistic and learner centered. We included a number of examples of classroom practice to illustrate these principles. In the present book, we shift from a focus on methods to a consideration of the process of language acquisition. However, we retain the same basic orientation toward teaching and learning and again attempt to illustrate that orientation with specific classroom examples.

Terminology

Since we are writing for readers with a variety of backgrounds, we feel it is important to clarify certain terms. We will briefly define these terms here rather than within the text of the chapters where definitions would break the flow of ideas. Several terms relate to whole language classroom practice. These may be new to some of our readers. Readers familiar with whole language may wish to skip to the next section.

Whole Language Terms

In many whole language classrooms, teachers use *authentic materials,* which are materials used for real purposes outside the classroom. For example, teachers may bring into class magazines, newspapers, advertisements, or promotional materials. In addition, whole language teachers use a wide variety of literature books for reading rather than anthologies of carefully selected and edited readings published by textbook companies. Whole language classrooms provide a *print-rich environment*. Besides authentic books and magazines in the classroom library, *environmental print*, such as posters, signs, and writing, surrounds the students. Sometimes these print resources are published commercially, but more often they are produced by the students themselves.

For beginning readers, whole language teachers try to choose *predictable books*. In books such as *The Little Red Hen*, a language pattern is repeated throughout the story. ("Who will help me _____ ?" asked the little red hen. "Not I," said the cat. "Not I," said the dog. "Not I," said the goose. "Then I shall do it myself!" said the little red hen.) Books are also predictable books even when there are no repeated language patterns if the pictures support the words on the page, if the story line is one that allows the reader to predict what will happen next in the story, or if the book is written by an author students have read before.

Often teachers will use predictable stories produced in *big books,* oversized books that the whole class can see as the teachers *track* by moving their hands under the print as they read the words. Predictable reading materials can also be produced by the students. In *language experience* students write stories by dictating to their teacher who acts as a scribe. These stories are then predictable because the students themselves helped to compose them.

Whole language teachers often encourage beginning writers to get their ideas down on paper even if their spelling is not yet conventional. Beginning writers use *invented spelling* that reflects their growing understanding of the sound/letter system of the language they are learning. Often teachers allow invented spelling in daily journals where students write about their experiences and interests. These teachers encourage conventional spelling for more formal writing, such as the publication of books or stories. This writing, which usually has a broader audience than just the teacher and the student, may be produced through *writers workshop,* a process writers go through that may include writing *rough drafts, conferencing* with the teacher and other students about the writing, *revising* the writing for organization and content, and, finally, *editing* for details such as spelling and punctuation. Though writers may do all of the above in producing a final product, they often do not. The writing process is cyclical rather than a series of prescribed steps, and writers may skip parts of the process, do them in a different order, or even abandon a piece they are working on altogether to start writing something completely different.

Terms to Describe Students

In addition, we wish to comment on terminology we use to refer to the students we write about in this book. It is always difficult to choose a descriptive term for any group because the words used may, in fact, label or limit the people in that group (Wink 1993). For example, the frequently used label for non-English speakers, LEP (limited English proficient) focuses attention on what students cannot do. All of us have limited (or no) proficiency in a number of languages.

In the past, we have referred to students in our schools who do not speak English as their first language as "second language learners" or "bilingual learners." We use these terms to make the point that they already have another language, and English is an additional language. However, we have become uncomfortable with using these terms since we are very aware that many English language learners are, in fact, adding a third, fourth, and even fifth language to their repertoire. Therefore, the terms "bilingual learners" and "second language learners" might also be seen as limiting.

There are only so many ways of describing any population of students. We will try to be specific when possible, but there may be times when we use the above terms inaccurately to refer to the whole population of students learning English. At times we use these terms to avoid undue repetition of more accurate terms such as "English learners," PEP (Potentially English Proficient) students, or ESL students. We also do not want to overuse more awkward, longer expressions such as "nonnative speakers of English" or "students for whom English is not a first language."

Organization of This Book

The basic question we explore in this book is "How can teachers provide students who are between worlds access to second language acquisition and to the content area knowledge they need for academic success?" To answer this big question, we raise a series of smaller questions. In the first section of the book, "Inside the Classroom," we consider questions from the school context. Then, in the second section, "Outside the Classroom," we consider questions from the societal context. The final section, "Back In Again," suggests ways educators can bring the world of mainstream school society and the world of English language learners together through classroom-based research.

The first eight chapters focus on the school context. Chapter 1 poses the questions, "Who are our English language learners, and what factors influence their school performance?" In this chapter, we present a series of case studies of English learners to provide specific examples for the research and theory developed in later chapters. Chapter 2 asks "What influences how teachers teach?" Here we consider how beliefs, theories, and practice all influence teaching. We look in detail at the changes one teacher has experienced in moving from an eclectic to a principled approach. Chapter 3 raises the question, "How does learning take place in explorer classrooms?" In this chapter we explain what explorer classrooms are, and we develop a general theory of how students learn. In Chapter 4 we turn to second language issues and ask "What do we acquire when we acquire a language?" This question is more complex than it appears, and the answer has important implications for teaching second language students. Chapter 5 then follows with the question, "What are the principal theories of second language acquisition?" In this chapter we review second language acquisition theories and develop a view of second language acquisition that is consistent with the general view of learning presented in Chapter 3.

In Chapters 6, 7, and 8, we further develop the idea of teaching as exploration by presenting classroom examples of explorer teachers putting acquisition theory into practice. Chapter 6 asks "How do explorer teachers provide all their students with access to second language acquisition?" The question for Chapter 7 is "How do explorer teachers focus on learners and build on their strengths?" And Chapter 8 centers on "How do explorer teachers celebrate students' first languages and cultures?"

In the next five chapters we turn to the societal context for education. In Chapter 9 we ask, "How do community attitudes and the politics of English Only affect bilingual students?" Chapter 10 investigates the questions, "What influences student and teacher attitudes?" We continue to focus on attitudes in Chapter 11, "How do teachers recognize and resolve value conflicts?" Chapter 12 asks "How can teachers develop an intercultural orientation?" Chapter 13 discusses the important role of parents. We ask, "How can schools involve parents?"

In the last section of the book, we suggest ways to bring the two worlds together. Our question is "How can teachers improve their practice through classroom-based research?" We suggest that when teachers investigate factors that impact their students in both the school and the societal context, then teachers can modify their practices and help students who are between two worlds succeed in both their worlds.

In each of the three sections, we present current theory and provide examples of teachers working effectively with second language students. We hope that this information will be useful to teachers, counselors, paraprofessionals, administrators, parents, and others involved in the education of language minority students. We are aware that no easy answers to the questions we are raising exist, but we are convinced that all students benefit when educators working with them are aware of current research and effective classroom practice.

We began this introduction with a quote from Mrs. Johnson. In answer to her question "What more can you expect of me?" we would say that we hope that she would want to know all that she possibly could about the different factors that affect all her students including her second language learners. Her background in whole language will allow her to provide strong support for her new students. However, these students are from a world very different from her own. Because of their language and cultural backgrounds, their needs may vary from those of her mainstream students of the past. If Mrs. Johnson is aware of second language acquisition theories, sociocultural influences on bilingual learners, and the effective practices of other teachers working with diverse populations, she can better provide her students who are between worlds access to second language acquisition.

INSIDE
THE
CLASSROOM

CHAPTER ONE

Who Are Our English Language Learners, and What Factors Influence Their Academic Performance?

To begin exploring one world—the school context—we present a series of case studies of English learners. These case studies provide a concrete basis for the content of this book because the research, theory, and practice described here are intended to help educators respond in an informed way as they work with second language issues. Each case study is based on a real student, a real situation, and a real school setting. Some of the case studies were conducted by teachers studying second language acquisition in the graduate education program at our college. These teachers focused on one of their own students, and they analyzed that student's success or failure. Other case studies presented here are based on our own reading or our personal experiences with second language students. We have chosen examples that represent students from kindergarten through college, and adults. We have included students with different educational, cultural, and linguistic backgrounds.

While we realize that no two students are alike and that no two students have the same needs, there are commonalities among learners that help us as educators approach our teaching in a more informed way. Here, we describe seven different English as a second language learners who have studied in our schools. After each case study, we list several of the factors that may have influenced that student's success or failure. We ask readers to compare these students and their situations to English learners with whom they have worked, and to think about the differences and similarities in the factors that may have influenced them. Our focus in this and the following seven chapters is on the world of the school. However, we recognize that the school context exists within the broader societal context and that different combinations of factors from both these worlds may determine academic success or failure in any particular case. It is important that we, as educators, be aware of the different forces involved and consider them as we work to provide our students who are between worlds access to second language acquisition and content area knowledge.

Eugenia

Eugenia is a five-year-old in a bilingual kindergarten in a small rural community in the Central Valley of California. Both her parents have worked on farms for several years. In the past, during seasonal work times, they would leave their children in Mexico, and the mother would find work in California while the father would travel as far as Idaho for job opportunities. Neither parent speaks English, and neither has had much formal education. Eugenia's mother attended school for seven years and her father for three in rural Mexican schools.

Eugenia was born a United States citizen in a Central Valley city in the apartment of a family friend. Her mother was afraid to go to a hospital since she was an illegal alien. Shortly after Eugenia's birth, her parents became legal residents under the recent amnesty laws for migrant laborers who have worked in the United States over a period of years. Since then the whole family has lived together in the small farming town where her parents both work at a canning factory. Their apartment complex is located near the school, so Eugenia and her brothers and sisters can easily walk there.

Eugenia has had a very positive year in kindergarten. She and her other Hispanic classmates love their teacher, Cándida, an energetic Puerto Rican woman who was raised in New York City. Cándida uses Spanish for most of the school day, although the children also sing, read big books, play games, and recite poetry in English. In Cándida's classroom literacy development is encouraged in social interaction. The playhouse, which doubles as a store, includes paper, pencils, and lots of cans and boxes so the children can "take orders" and "prepare meals."

Cándida found Eugenia to be an enthusiastic learner from the first day of school when her parents introduced themselves and offered to help whenever something was needed. At first the parents were concerned about Cándida's language-teaching philosophy. One of their high school sons, who had recently dropped out of school, had had several negative experiences in bilingual classrooms. However, Cándida was able to explain to them why she would teach Eugenia in Spanish and how building a strong first language base would help Eugenia in English in the future. Because Cándida speaks Spanish and has shown an interest in them and their child, Eugenia's parents come to the school frequently and have even asked for help in filling out government forms. Cándida has shown respect for them and understands that they want to do the best they can for their child.

Eugenia has thrived in Cándida's classroom. She loves to play and participate in collaborative activities, but she also spends a lot of time reading predictable books in both Spanish and English. Even before she came to school, she could write the letters of her name, and now, at the classroom writing center, she is writing readable messages in Spanish using invented spelling. Because the class does language experience charts, class books, and lots of brainstorming, Eugenia is comfortable with writing and experiments with writing for different purposes.

Cándida believes that Eugenia will succeed in school. "She is lucky enough to have a supportive and caring home environment," Cándida explains, "which will help her weather academic difficulties or disappointments and tolerate and defeat racism and expectations of failure. She has strong self-esteem."

Perhaps Cándida is optimistic because she sees her Hispanic children when they first come to school, and she, herself, has such a strong belief in them. In her own words, Cándida describes why she feels she can work well with her students.

> I believe that being a Latina from the South Bronx helps me understand my kids not only linguistically, but also philosophically. I know the challenges that face these children, but I also know that if someone cares, their chances for success are great. Obstacles such as teacher prejudice and home/school discontinuities have not been a problem for me because I was a child like Eugenia and the other kids in my room, and I know their experience. I enjoy my kids and their families, and I feel like I am at home.

Analysis—Eugenia

Cándida is giving Eugenia a positive start. Several different factors seem to be contributing to Eugenia's success. Other factors present in this situation may or may not contribute to problems in her future.

At this point Eugenia is doing well. She has a very supportive family and teacher in a rural, small school setting. Her parents are eager for her to succeed and willing to help her in any way they can. Her teacher, a Hispanic herself, is sensitive to the needs of both Eugenia and her parents. In addition, her teacher is giving Eugenia the kind of curriculum she needs, including first language support, a print-rich classroom environment, opportunities for social interaction, and experiences with meaningful literacy activities.

However, other influences may affect Eugenia in the future. As her teacher points out, many Hispanic children suffer in school from teacher and community prejudice and home/school discontinuities. Eugenia's parents are farm workers without education or English skills. They will not be able to help her with her academic studies as she moves into more complex content in the intermediate grades. Though they are now in the United States legally, the uncertainty and transience of the past and their socioeconomic status may keep them from being as confident as they need to be in dealing with schools. An older brother has already encountered problems and dropped out of school while the parents watched helplessly. Eugenia's teacher is optimistic, but her experiences as a New York City Puerto Rican do not really give her the same background as her students. We have hope for Eugenia, but we must look at both the positive and negative influences that might affect her in the coming years.

Eugenia is experiencing academic success at this point because she has support from both her parents and her teacher. The next case study describes a student who also has strong parental support but is experiencing academic difficulties in a good whole language classroom.

Robert

Sharon, a second-grade teacher in an inner-city school in California's Central Valley, chose Robert, a Hmong student, for her case study. His family has been in the United States since 1980. Robert's father was a soldier in Laos when the communists took over during the Vietnam War, so he had to leave the country or face death (Bliatout, Downing, Lewis, and Yang 1988). He fled to a refugee camp in Thailand to avoid the persecution he knew would result from his having assisted the United States military. He met and married Robert's mother in the camp. Since he had a brother living in the United States, the couple was fortunate enough to be sponsored to come to live in Tennessee within only seven months. They spent their first two years in Memphis and then decided to leave Tennessee to join relatives in California.

Both of Robert's parents value education and have high expectations for their children. Both have attended adult ESL classes in an attempt to become more proficient in English. Robert's father had ten years of formal schooling in Laos where the language of instruction was Laotian. He is also fairly unusual because he is able to read and write Hmong. The Hmong have only had a written language system with a Romanized Practical Alphabet since the 1950s when it was developed by missionaries (Bliatout et al. 1988). Even though many Hmong are interested in becoming literate and afternoon classes are beginning to be established to teach the written language, only a few can read and write Hmong. Robert's father spends time at home trying to teach his children literacy in their native language.

Robert is the second youngest in his family of six children. The oldest is in sixth grade, and the youngest in kindergarten. Robert also has several cousins who attend the same school. All family members, including the extended family, support one another whenever possible.

When tested this year in second grade with the Idea Oral Language Proficiency Test (IPT), one of several classification instruments used with second language learners to determine English proficiency, Robert scored a level B, which means that he is considered a non-English speaker. This is the same classification he had in kindergarten and first grade.

Robert only reads books with very limited text and only writes words he can copy from the board or charts. He is quiet in large group settings, and also in small groups or in one-on-one situations with adults and people he does not know well. In cooperative learning activities with peers, he does contribute, especially when he is assured that he may use his native language as well as English. When given a choice, Robert always does math activities or art. In fact, during Sustained Silent Reading (SSR) time, Robert usually chooses books about drawing techniques.

Robert's most enjoyable time at school is recess. He not only plays with students in his own class, but also with a wide range of children at the school. Sharon reported that he is "always right in the middle of whatever is going on. He does not seem to be quiet or shy with his friends." Robert uses both Hmong and English freely in these informal settings.

Sharon is concerned about Robert and blames his lack of progress in part on his past instruction. "I feel Robert's oral language has not grown much in the past two years," Sharon explains. "The kindergarten and first grades at my school are really part-to-whole curriculum." Sharon has made her teaching in English as comprehensible as possible and has tried to draw on Robert's interests and strengths, giving a special emphasis to several kinds of art projects. However, she is concerned that she has no Hmong instructional services for him except for a few audio- and video-taped stories.

Sharon has encouraged her principal to start a parent ESL program on her campus that would include Hmong literacy. This program would not only help the adults with English and native language literacy, but could also lead to a Hmong literacy program for Hmong children at the school. In addition, Sharon hopes that she can encourage parent volunteers to help students with their primary language development.

In the meantime, Sharon hopes that she can engage Robert in learning in her classroom, and she encourages him to use language in a wider variety of settings.

> I am giving him lots of opportunities to give output without being verbal. He is able to draw, paint, and copy print from his environment. I am giving him lots of oral language. I try to make my lessons and stories very comprehensible by using lots of visual cues such as real experiences, pictures, maps, graphs, charts, and other realia.

Perhaps Sharon's curriculum plans will make a difference for Robert, but many other factors may also influence how well he will do in school in the future.

Analysis—Robert

According to standardized tests, Robert is behind his classmates and has, in fact, made no progress in English since kindergarten. Only very limited first language support exists for him at school. Robert's kindergarten and first-grade experiences were not positive. He did not do well in a structured, part-to-whole curriculum. He seems afraid to interact in classroom large-group activities and is not yet reading or writing much at all.

Robert is from a large family, and his parents are Hmong refugees who have suffered the trauma of war and displacement. The family has moved from Southeast

Asia and also relocated within the United States. Robert now attends an inner-city school that is struggling to meet the needs of its diverse student body. Immigrant children are influenced by the city surroundings, including problems with crime, drugs, and gangs. All of these factors may be contributing to Robert's lack of school success.

Robert's mother and father, however, are supportive, and they attend school to learn English themselves. His father is unusual because he had ten years of schooling in Laos and reads and writes Laotian and Hmong. He is teaching his children to read and write their first language, and this serves as a positive example that may contribute to Robert's future success. At Robert's school in the past, second language students came primarily from Hispanic backgrounds. The school is struggling to find ways to meet the needs of Southeast Asian students. For example, the school may start an adult Hmong literacy program. This could prepare Hmong adults to provide tutoring in different content areas in Hmong at the school.

Although Robert is not working at the same level as his peers, he has a teacher this year who has discovered his interest in art and especially drawing. Because of her encouragement, he is beginning to show an interest in books and literacy. His teacher also uses small cooperative groups and this encourages Robert to speak in class. Robert is well adjusted socially and interacts in English and Hmong on the playground. Although Robert is not doing well in school now, all these factors may contribute to his eventual academic success.

In the next case study, we look at another student whose cultural background differs from that of both the mainstream students and the typical second language population of the school.

Sharma

Rhoda, a fifth-grade teacher in an elementary school in a rural farming community, describes her first impression of her Punjabi student, Sharma.

> She walked into my fifth-grade classroom and smiled at me with warm, giving brown eyes. Her dark brown hair was neatly braided, and she politely introduced me to her mother and her baby sister. The woman's traditional Indian silk was embroidered in rich primary colors setting off her beautiful olive skin. In accented English she asked for a few moments of my time. She asked that I arrange for the school's Punjabi aide to spend time with her daughter so she would not fall behind the rest of the class. I was intrigued by this caring mother and wanted to know more about her soft-spoken daughter.

As Rhoda gathered information for her case study, she learned a great deal about Sharma.

Sharma's parents moved to the largest city in the central farming valley of California shortly before Sharma was born. They had moved because family members already in California had promised them better jobs and more money in America than they could earn managing their small farm in India. However, only five months after Sharma's birth, she sent back to live in India with an aunt because Sharma's mother and father both worked, and they could not afford a baby sitter. Six months later, her parents gave up trying to make ends meet in the United States and returned to their farm in India.

Although their middle-class life in India was comfortable, Sharma's parents were concerned when, at age five, Sharma had to attend the primitive rural school near their home. Her parents, who had both gone through the rigid Indian school system and passed the difficult tests for high school graduation, wanted a better education for Sharma. They moved back to California, this time buying a small trailer home in a rural farming community.

Sharma's parents now both work. Her father works on local farms and her mother in a local packing plant. Both speak English, but they use Punjabi with Sharma and her two younger sisters, who were also born in California after the second move to this country.

Sharma and her sisters dress in western clothing for school and make an effort to fit into the activities in which the other students participate. Her parents are willing to allow their children to give up some of their traditions because they see this as necessary for school success. They believe in hard work and have high academic expectations for their children. On weekends the girls go to the local Sikh temple to develop their first language abilities and to learn about their Sikh religion. In addition, the whole family participates in Punjabi festivals and games.

Sharma has attended the same rural school from kindergarten through fifth grade except for a six-month period during fourth grade when the family lived in the state of Washington. Though the school has a bilingual program for Spanish speakers, only limited primary language support is available for Punjabi students. The school has a strong whole language curriculum, so all of Sharma's teachers have emphasized reading a variety of children's literature, writing for authentic purposes, and organizing curriculum around themes.

In fifth grade Sharma is an active member of her classroom community. She especially seeks out friends among Caucasians in her class. Her social English is animated and full of the same idioms used by her peers. She tends to avoid contact with other newer and less proficient Punjabi students, although she is willing to be helpful with information about India or to support the newcomers when asked.

Sharma is categorized as proficient in English by the Bilingual Syntax Measure (BSM), the test the school uses to determine the English proficiency of second language students. However, Rhoda has noticed that the language of some content area texts is a challenge to Sharma, and Sharma, on her own, looks for resource books, pictures, and charts to help make sense of some of the more difficult content.

Rhoda hopes that Sharma will continue to study her native language so that she will develop that resource as she progresses in English. First language instruction is minimal at school, but her family has found an outside source of support. Sharma seems well adjusted and able to move from the culture of the school to that of her home. Her teachers have enhanced her self-esteem because they have encouraged her to value her home culture. However, recently she has begun to have questions about how this will affect her. Rhoda explained this concern: "Even though she has a strong self-image, she still has questions about how a more traditional cultural image can reflect on her. This may be the beginning of the cultural struggles specific to adolescents who are already experiencing self-conscious social episodes" (Elkind 1967—in Scarcella 1990). Rhoda summarizes her concerns about Sharma's future.

Although Sharma has had some advantages other language minority students have not had, she still has a problem with not being able to work to her potential because of lagging academic language development (Cummins 1989). As she continues to be exposed to comprehensible input, and continues to develop academic language, concepts will become less cognitively demanding. Because Sharma does not have a strong background in reading and writing Punjabi, it would appear that her primary language needs continued support. Teachers should continue to appreciate new Punjabi students for who they are and model this acceptance to their classroom communities. They should allow them to speak out of their personal experience so students like Sharma can understand that "traditional" Punjabis have as much value as their Americanized counterparts.

Analysis—Sharma

Many factors have influenced and will continue to influence Sharma's progress in school. Her parents are both educated and speak English well when compared with other immigrants. On the other hand, because of their jobs, their socioeconomic status is not high. The family has experienced financial stress in the past and for this reason has had to move often. They presently live in a small farming community with a history of little tolerance for immigrants, especially for immigrants from a culture so different from the mainstream American culture. Teachers at the school have little understanding of the Punjabi culture and customs.

The family maintains their home language and culture even in this country; yet, they want Sharma and their other two children to succeed academically in a society that is very different from their own. Their expectations for their children are very high, almost demanding. Sharma must do well in a competitive school system but also be a traditional Punjabi girl. This creates a struggle for Sharma, and she even avoids social contact with Punjabi students who have recently arrived.

Sharma seems to be thriving despite these possible problems. She is in a school that has prepared teachers to support second language students by providing staff development in the areas of second language acquisition, bilingual education, and whole language. Though no teachers speak Punjabi, a Punjabi-speaking aide works with those students who need first language support. Sharma's parents are quick to seek assistance from the school when they think their daughter needs it. Sharma herself interacts freely with her Anglo peers and seems well adjusted socially. Sharma presently is able to function in both the Punjabi home context and the school context. It remains to be seen if she will continue to be able to do this successfully.

The next case study involves an adolescent whose life has even more contrasts than Sharma's. Functioning well in the different contexts he deals with daily is a challenge difficult for most educators to imagine.

Juan Medina

Brimner in his book, *A Migrant Family,* tells and depicts through photographs the poignant, true story of Juan Medina. Juan is a twelve-year-old migrant boy who represents approximately half a million immigrant school-age children in the United States. He was born in Mexico and now lives in California. Juan has also lived in several other states where his family has found work, including Indiana, Illinois, and Iowa. His family is here legally. Presently, he is living with his mother, stepfather, two younger brothers, and his baby sister in Encinitas, a coastal community in southern California near San Diego. The family has found housing in a temporary migrant camp along a major highway. Brimner describes the scene.

> The hillside above the road is dotted with expensive houses that have red-tiled roofs and electric gates. But Juan's house, like those of the 300 other people in the camp, doesn't have a red-tiled roof. Here, houses are built of salvaged plywood. Orange or blue sheets of plastic make do for roofs (p. 9).

According to Brimner, there are over two hundred migrant camps in the San Diego area alone. Although the state of California has health and safety regulations, only about forty camps are registered and meet minimum standards.

The shelter that Juan and his family share has a dirt floor and two plywood platforms for the two mattresses on which the six family members sleep. No electricity or gas are available, so the cooking is done on an outside fire. A water faucet and portable toilets are set up for the workers across the highway next to the Jobs Center that provides information about work and workers' rights. However, workers and their families have to be careful crossing the busy road to get to the facilities. Cars speed by despite official highway signs reading "Entering Pedestrian Accident Area Next 8 Miles." Several people have been killed by speeding motorists.

Juan knows that this temporary, uncomfortable camp cannot be considered home for long. Rumors have circulated around the camp that people in the expensive houses above the camp have complained about the camp, and county authorities may order the camp destroyed. Other camps have been bulldozed, and the migrant workers living in them were left with only what they were wearing and what they could salvage.

Attitudes of others toward migrant workers are usually negative. Juan is hurt by Anglo slurs. When he hears himself referred to as a "wetback," he asserts, "We have papers. We have a right to be here. Who are we hurting?" (p. 17). He points out that "They want us to work. And they want us to disappear" (p. 18).

As often as he can, Juan attends a local junior high school. He keeps to himself except for a few friends from the camp. The migrant children are well aware of the attitudes of the rest of the community toward them. Juan remembers the time the mother of one of the girls riding his same school bus spit on him because she didn't want him near her daughter.

Juan's academic progress has been slow. He has attended school so sporadically that he has learned only a little English. At this school, subjects such as science and history are taught in Spanish, which helps him understand these content areas. He also has a two-hour block of English and gets extra help from tutors and migrant family aides. Despite this extra help, Juan finds it hard to keep up. When migrant students move frequently, schools have a difficult time keeping track of them and meeting their different needs. Statistics show that in some parts of California, over seventy percent of the migrant children do not finish high school.

When Juan returns home from school one day, he finds that his camp has been bulldozed. All the people recover what they can and, by the end of the week, establish a new camp in another section of the same region. Even though this camp is closer to a market, it is a two-mile hike to drinking water, toilets, and the central Jobs Center.

The life of the migrant family seems incredibly hard, though Juan's stepfather asserts it is better than it would be in Mexico. "Here," he says, "I have hope—if not for me, then for my children" (p. 24). Brimner's book ends with Juan and his brother starting out early in the morning toward school. Juan says, "I have missed too much. Too much" (p. 39). The reader wonders if Juan is not right. Juan and other migrant children have tremendous odds to overcome if they ever are to succeed in school.

Analysis—Juan

Juan's present school situation has great potential. He is receiving content area instruction in his first language. This allows him to develop academic concepts, and this knowledge, acquired in Spanish, will transfer to English. At the same time, he also has a two-hour block of English daily and receives extra help from aides and migrant tutors. However, Juan can't take advantage of any of these benefits if he is prevented from attending school on a regular basis. Already, Juan feels he has "missed too much."

Despite a positive school context, factors beyond the school will probably spell academic failure for Juan. He speaks little English. He has not received education consistently in his primary language, so he has not developed the content area knowledge required for school success. He has no permanent residence and is likely to move away from his present school soon. He has also experienced the negative attitudes from the parents of some of his classmates.

Research by Collier (1989) has shown that for older learners like Juan, chances of school success are poor even when socioeconomic factors are favorable. The students in Collier's study came from middle- or upper-class homes where parents were well educated. Nevertheless, students in her study who entered U.S. schools at the high school level with limited English proficiency could not reach the fiftieth percentile on standardized tests in content areas in the time remaining before high school graduation because reaching the norm takes seven to ten years. As a result, many older second language students drop out before completing school. This will probably be the case for Juan, who also faces pressure to work and earn money for his family.

Schooling for students who are children of migrant workers is difficult, but so is schooling for immigrant students living in urban areas. The next case study describes a teenager trying to succeed in school and facing a number of different pressures.

Tou

Kathy, a junior high school English teacher, chose Tou for a case study because while he was typical of other junior high school students she had, he was also unusual. In describing her choice she explained that Tou "typified many of my rather academically apathetic, immature boy students." The population at Kathy's school is approximately seventy-five percent Hispanic, ten percent Asian, eight percent African American and seven percent Caucasian. Like many of Kathy's students, Tou tested well below the fiftieth percentile on reading and struggled academically. Kathy explained that his lack of a "grasp of basic writing conventions was similar to the majority of my students."

Tou's academic achievement was similar to that of many of Kathy's other students, but in other ways Tou was different. Kathy described some of his problems.

> As the year progressed, it became increasingly clear that Tou was one of my more uninvolved learners. He worked with a variety of others in the class, but he could not

find a partner he was comfortable with. Other students complained about him and he responded even more defensively by acting out his frustrations in class. Tou was not generally well liked. His small stature and immaturity certainly contributed to this unpopularity. I witnessed several instances of racial slurs aimed at Tou and the isolation that ensued. The normal adolescent self-doubt and low self-esteem combined with the hostility he encountered daily seemed a certain formula for failure.

Tou is the youngest of seven children in a refugee Hmong family. He is now an eighth grader in an inner-city school. Most of the students at his school are from low-income families. Many of the parents are unemployed laborers or refugees on welfare.

Tou was born in a refugee camp in Thailand but spent only a few months there. After his birth, his family lived briefly in Hawaii and then moved to its present location. Now, at age fourteen, he lives with his father and two of his older brothers who are married with children. His mother is living with a daughter and her family in another city several hours away. This situation is an extremely sensitive one that is not discussed, but it is disturbing to Tou and the rest of the family.

The family came to the United States with the hope of finding not only freedom but also a better life. Economic and emotional problems, however, have kept them from achieving their goals. Tou's father, a farmer in Laos, does not speak English, is not literate in Hmong, and does not have any job skills appropriate for his inner-city neighborhood. One sister and her immediate family moved to Georgia in hopes of finding a better job for themselves and work for other family members. Kathy wrote how important this move was to the extended family. "His (Tou's) dad will visit when they get settled and the hope is that there will be work for everyone, and Mom, Dad, and the family will all be together again—a wish fervently held by Tou."

Tou was Kathy's student for seventh-grade English. Kathy worked with three other content area teachers. She and the math, science, and social science teacher worked with one group of students. This "Explorer Team" shared curriculum ideas to try to better meet the needs of their students.

Although Tou was an extremely reluctant participant in most class activities at first, Kathy was able to engage him during a unit developed around folktales. He read independently, and, with a partner, wrote a story about a young child getting a puppy of his very own. This more positive behavior in English was reflected in his other classes, too. He ended the first semester "on a definite upbeat." He seemed to be proud of the work he was doing and was given an award for effort and improvement at the end-of-semester assembly.

However, after the eight-week break (the school is on a year-round schedule, so students have an eight-week break and a four-week break instead of the traditional summer vacation), his previous achievements seemed to be forgotten. He began a pattern of frequent absences, and his behavior changed. Kathy became really concerned:

> He often would come to school toward the middle of the week and then start his weekend early—kind of a two day school week, five day weekend model! When he was there, his anti-social behavior was more obvious, and students began to ask me not to seat them close to Tou.

This behavior eventually led to an emotional conference with Tou's father. During the conference a Hmong-speaking aide translated the father's words. He told of his hopes and dreams, of what America meant to him, and of his aspirations for his children. He told how one older brother had dropped out of high school because of involvement in gang activity and how worried he was that Tou was following the same failed path. Everyone except Tou was in tears by the end of the conference. The effect on Tou was not clear.

After that conference, Kathy saw that there was a change in Tou's behavior, though not a transformation. "Truthfully, it was old-fashioned parental hovering, teacher monitoring, and weekly progress reports sent home requiring Dad's signature that kept Tou in school the last two months of school." His teachers and father did manage to get him through, and he was promoted to eighth grade, an event Kathy explained as "not life-long success exactly but an achievement nonetheless."

This year Kathy and the other teachers in their Explorer Team have been working on an experiment in their school. They are teaching the same group of students during their eighth-grade year that they worked with in seventh grade. The teachers have seen that for most students of middle school age, the stability of working with the same classroom community and teachers over an extended period of time is extremely rewarding. Unfortunately, Tou seems to be an exception. While his work in eighth grade has been passing, and while he has functioned well within the safe, familiar environment of the Explorer Team classrooms, outside of class, he has been in weekly fights with students of other ethnic groups. There is strong suspicion that he is part of a Hmong gang.

A few months ago, Tou was given a "social transfer" to a different junior high school in the district. It is unclear whether he was transferred because school officials were concerned about the trouble he was getting into or if the transfer was requested by his father in the hope that a change of schools would give Tou a new start. Just recently Tou was transferred back to Kathy's school, but not back to Kathy's class-room. Kathy told us he was put directly into Opportunity, a class that is like a continuation school where students are given one last chance to make it. Kathy summarized her concerns for Tou and students like him at the end of her case study.

> This case study made me sadly aware that my students are all individuals with diverse and complicated needs and that I can never hope to solve them all. Just my one-on-one interviews with Tou and my special efforts to talk at least briefly with him every day pointed up that all my students need that attention. I feel stretched to the limit.

Analysis—Tou

As Kathy points out, Tou's situation is a complex one. Many negative factors are at work, and they appear to be outweighing the efforts his father and his teachers are making to help him succeed. Tou is the youngest in a large family that is caught in a struggle to survive in a new and challenging culture, a culture that has little in common with their own. The home situation for Tou is not a happy one. His parents are separated, a situation that has been very unusual in the Hmong culture in the past (Bliatout et al. 1988), and is a source of embarrassment now. He lives with his father, who does not speak English and cannot find work. Older siblings either did not get schooling or had trouble in school. One brother has a history of gang membership. Tou does not see many examples of success in his family.

In his large inner-city junior high school, Tou is like many students who are involved in gang activity and have social and economic problems. He is not well liked even among Hmong students. Though he doesn't fight other Hmong students, he does get into frequent fights before and after school with students from other ethnic minority groups. In the classroom, he is a loner and does not work well with others. He frequently cuts classes.

Tou's school situation was an unusually good one during seventh grade. His teachers formed a team to work more effectively with students who needed continuity and caring. They made an effort to get to know students and support their learning with meaningful curriculum. They even decided to keep the same group together for more than one year to provide more support and avoid discontinuity. However, this change came too late for Tou. When he was moved to a new school in eighth grade and that did not work, he was switched to Opportunity, the school within a school that provides a last chance. One fears that this change will not be enough for him. In fact, Kathy told us that the caring teacher for that Opportunity class works very hard with students, but that it is well known that he spends more time at his students' funerals than any other type of event. Students in Opportunity have lost hope and many commit suicide or are killed during family violence or in gang warfare.

The students in the next description are also refugees. However, they come from a different part of the world with very different backgrounds. The factors affecting their lives have led to a more positive outcome.

José Luis, Guillermo, and Patricia

We first met these three teenagers in 1984 less than a week after they arrived in Tucson, Arizona, from El Salvador. A few days before they flew to Tucson, they had watched as their father, an important military official, was assassinated in front of their home in San Salvador. The three had narrowly escaped being arrested and probably murdered themselves. In fact, sixteen-year-old Guillermo had two bullet wounds in his leg when he arrived in this country. Their stepmother in El Salvador distanced herself from the three teens for her own safety and that of a two-year-old daughter, who was their stepsister. José Luis, Guillermo, and Patricia, alone in a country that had suddenly become hostile, sought asylum with their aunt, a fellow doctoral student and friend of ours at the university. Through that connection, we often had the opportunity to spend time with these remarkable teens over the next six years. We maintain contact to the present.

Although they had studied English at private bilingual schools in San Salvador, their comprehension of and conversation in English was extremely limited when they first arrived. Despite this, their aunt, a dedicated academic herself, was anxious to get them into school and working toward school success. All three were enrolled in a local high school almost immediately and admonished by their aunt that they must do well in all their subjects. She warned them that there was no time to be wasted and that she would not tolerate irresponsibility.

The aunt, who had an older, ailing husband, found them an apartment near her and supported the three financially the best she could. They also received some sporadic financial help from aging grandparents in El Salvador. Therefore, the teenagers were soon almost entirely on their own, trying to cope with a new culture and language. Each handled the situation in a different way.

The oldest, José Luis, was seventeen and felt responsible for the other two. He also felt somehow responsible for not having saved his father and wrestled with that guilt. He studied day and night, smiling little, and taking almost no time for any relaxation. English was a struggle for him, and he spent hours with a dictionary, translating his textbooks and studying for tests. Classes in algebra, calculus, and physics were less linguistically demanding, so he soon concentrated on them as a possible specialization. He graduated from high school with a President's Award for excellent academic scholarship just two years after arriving.

Guillermo responded in a totally different way to his new surroundings. He was the social one of the three. He worked hard to make friends and joined high school clubs almost immediately. He talked to anyone who would try to understand him and soon became involved in school government. His grades were not extremely high, but he studied enough in high school to earn a B− average and qualify to attend the university.

Patricia depended more on our family for emotional and personal support at first. At thirteen, she was the youngest of the three and the only female. Her aunt wanted her to be responsible for the cooking and cleaning of the apartment the three siblings shared, but those responsibilities and the adjustment to the new language and culture were often too much for her. Her brothers seemed to understand, but they also insisted that she be part of the threesome. She studied and made friends, but in some ways was the most affected by the move and the loss of her father. English probably came faster to Patricia than to her brothers. She spent more time with our family, and our two younger daughters helped introduce her to customs and fads in the United States.

The three teens and their aunt became involved in our church shortly after their escape from El Salvador. The church family was especially important when they applied for asylum in this country. At that time, refugees from El Salvador had to prove their lives were endangered to be granted asylum. Even though they had newspaper articles about the assassination of their father, it was difficult to prove the danger to the three children. When the hearing for their asylum was held, church members even took time off from work to attend. That show of support impressed the judge and probably was instrumental in the judge's positive report to the federal government.

All three children eventually attended the university and are still studying there. José Luis completed his B.S. in engineering with honors. He is presently finishing his master's degree. Guillermo is studying engineering and international economics. He continues his interest in politics. He has served on the university's student government several times and spent one summer as an aide to a senator in Washington, D.C. Patricia has studied as a premed student. She is presently in charge of a chemical laboratory at the university and is considering whether to continue her studies in medical research or to enter medical practice.

After almost ten years in this country, the three recently went back to El Salvador for a visit. It was the first time they felt they could do so safely. The trip was very traumatic for all three, and they still struggled with fears of being harmed. The trip turned out to be a good one, and they were able to visit some friends and family. They now consider the United States home. They probably will not return to El Salvador to live, despite intentions to do so when they first arrived.

Analysis—José Luis, Guillermo, and Patricia

Certainly the three teenagers faced overwhelming obstacles when they came to this country. Their only relative here was an aunt who had never had children and who had her own personal responsibilities including the care of a sick husband, graduate studies, and teaching. The three young people had to learn to live on their own almost from the beginning. Money was tight and had to be budgeted, something the three had never had to do before.

The trauma of their father's assassination was difficult to cope with, and the three rehashed the scene and what might have been many times. They were immediately enrolled in a public school where they had to deal with the academic work in English, and establish their own identities apart from the other Hispanics at their school. They were not Mexican, and their past was very different from almost all the other students.

That past was probably what helped them the most. They were from an important family in El Salvador. Their relatives, including their aunt, knew high government officials, including former presidents. They had pride in their past and a strong sense of their worth. They had attended good private schools in San Salvador and had traveled to the United States and Europe. Although they did not speak and understand English well, they had studied some English grammar and did have a strong background in Spanish language and literature.

Once they arrived in Tucson, they found different kinds of support. Their aunt provided the money for the basics of living, and they received some funds from family in El Salvador. Eventually, with the encouragement of their aunt and others, they earned academic scholarships. They did not have to depend on welfare. They also had emotional and social support from people in the community. Our family often did things with them on weekends, delighting in introducing them to American culture and advising them about schooling and finances. The church provided another important support. They had weekly and sometimes biweekly contact with Americans with whom they had the chance to use English for real purposes. Their past experiences in El Salvador, their aunt's academic expectations, their social interactions with an American family, and the support from a church community placed José Luis, Guillermo, and Patricia in different contexts that influenced them positively.

The teens were self-confident and had a strong desire to succeed. At first all three planned to return to El Salvador to help rebuild their country and reclaim their land and property. For that reason both boys went into engineering, and Patricia studied medicine. While this goal faded, it gave them all a reason for their studies and a reason to work hard from the very beginning. As they achieved academic success, they were encouraged to continue.

The final description is of two adult learners who had, in some ways, a similar background to the adolescents from El Salvador. However, as adults with a family, the factors that influenced them were different from those that influenced José Luis, Guillermo, and Patricia.

Chham and Navy

Chet Chham, his aging parents, his wife, and his two children arrived in the United States in late spring of 1975, very shortly after the fall of Phnom Penh. They were sent by a Catholic relief agency to a coastal town in far northern California. Chham and his wife were part of a large group of Vietnamese and Cambodian refugees who came to Yvonne's daytime ESL class the following September. These refugees were in the first wave to arrive in the area after the Vietnam War, and their stories were incredible. Since then stories from these and other refugees from Southeast Asia have been widely reported (Bliatout et al. 1988; Criddle and Mam 1987; Ouk, Huffman, and Lewis 1988).

Chham and his wife, Navy, were part of Cambodia's educated elite. Over five thousand people attended their wedding in Phnom Penh in a ceremony that lasted over three days. Navy's father was the Minister of Education, and Chham's father was a high military official. When Phnom Penh fell to the Khmer Rouge, Chham, a military officer, knew he and his family would be killed if they remained, so he arranged their departure for the United States. In a matter of a few days, they became refugees dependent on relief agencies in a country whose language, religion, and culture were foreign.

Chham and Navy were lucky. They found employment quickly. He took a job in a lumber mill, and she found work as a hotel maid. His parents were too old to work, but they were able to take care of the two elementary-aged children when they were not in school. Whenever their work schedule allowed it, both Chham and Navy attended ESL classes. They were fluent in Khmer and French, but their English was too limited for them to attend the local junior college at first.

Once here, they faced adjustments beyond finding work. These included being dependent on government aid, having to learn English, and adapting to a new culture. In addition they were attending school with other refugees from different cultural and social backgrounds. Students in the ESL classes included farm laborers from Mexico, Portuguese fishermen from the Azores, refugees from Central America, wives of college students from the Middle East, exchange students from Japan, restaurant owners from Korea, as well as other Southeast Asian refugees. Perhaps the students that made school adjustment the most difficult were the ones from closest to home. In the same classroom there was a Vietnamese Army general, Vietnamese peasants, and Cambodian peasants. Historically, these groups of people have either been enemies or, at least, have had no social contact. In ESL classes they sat next to one another and struggled together to learn English.

Chham and Navy never showed any negative reactions to the situation at school. In fact, they were always cheerful contributors to class discussion, school programs, and collective celebrations, including meals. They seldom looked back, but instead planned ahead. Chham knew he needed to go on to junior college, and he and his wife explored different possible majors. Navy soon found herself pregnant with a third child, so she and her mother began taking in sewing. They specialized in sewing dresses for Cambodian celebrations such as weddings.

When news of the genocide in his country began to leak out (Criddle and Mam 1987; Ouk, Huffman, and Lewis 1988), Chham found living in the United States more painful. He once told Yvonne about a close friend who had decided to return to Cambodia to try to find his wife and children. This emotional story was a tragic one because Chham had little hope of ever seeing his friend again. This, of course, brought home to him the tragedy of his many lost friends and family members, not to mention the loss of his country. The news of the genocide was the beginning of the serious organization of Cambodian families in the area and throughout California. Periodic meetings were held, and Chham was one of the leaders. He and his contemporaries realized that if their culture was to be maintained, it would have to be done outside Cambodia.

Throughout all the adjustments and the taking on of new responsibilities, Chham and Navy continued to attend adult ESL classes faithfully. They studied when they could and brought questions and problems to class. A major concern was for their children's schooling. They asked about the public school system and were careful to communicate as best they could with the schools. They knew their children needed English and American culture, but they did not want them to forget their own heritage. They made sure that holidays and important festivals were celebrated in a traditional way, and they worked to teach their children their first language at home. Still, they worried as their children became more and more Americanized in what seemed to them a short time. When a teenage niece wanted to pick her own Cambodian husband instead of marrying the one the family had chosen for her, a major Cambodian community meeting was held. The customs were changing too quickly, and it was hard for everyone to adapt.

We eventually moved and lost touch with the family. Almost twenty years have gone by. Recently, however, we read a newspaper account of a Cambodian gathering in a town not far from their city. We were both concerned to read that two former Cambodian military men got into an argument about how that war some twenty years ago had been fought. In a fit of anger one man shot the other. He killed a man named Chet Chham. It is probably not the same person we knew since the name is a common one, but those military men had undoubtedly had experiences similar to those of our former student. The tragedy of living through the war, escaping, coming to this country, surviving the trauma of adjustment, and then dying in an argument over the past is an irony difficult to contemplate.

Analysis—Chham and Navy

Like the teenagers from El Salvador, Chham and Navy came to this country with a strong sense of who they were. Their families were important members of Cambodian society, and Chham and Navy had expectations of raising their children as they had been raised. Both attended private schools in Cambodia and had also studied in France. Chham was at the height of his military career when the war changed their lives completely.

Overnight, Chham, Navy, their children, and his parents had to leave almost everything behind and flee to the United States. In many ways, they were among the lucky refugees. They flew into California and quickly found jobs and a place to live. They had a strong educational background and expected to attend school to learn the English language and to become familiar with American culture.

However, many difficulties surfaced. Though they never complained, the change from having five thousand people attend their wedding to working as a laborer in a lumber mill and a maid in a hotel must have been very difficult for the couple. Chham's parents were completely lost in this country and refused to leave their small house or have anything to do with the new, and, to them, hostile world outside their home. Their children attended public schools and seemed to do well, but they became "Americanized" almost overnight. The children were losing their first language and their culture.

The news of the genocide of Cambodians was a terrible blow. Suddenly, Cambodians in this country had to band together or lose any national identity. This often caused conflict with younger Cambodians who wanted to live like Americans and forget the past. Chham had to help settle several conflicts that involved arranged marriages.

Meanwhile, the ESL classes provided still another challenge. The adult students came from many different backgrounds. While Yvonne tried to highlight the positive aspects of the diversity in her class, it was not easy for people from different social and economic classes as well as from different political perspectives to study together. The students responded well, but their differences created an added tension they had to deal with daily.

In addition, it was difficult for Chham and Navy to meet basic needs. When Navy became pregnant, there was not only another child to care for but also the necessity for her to find different work. The job at the lumber mill became less steady. In addition, Chham had trouble finding a course of study he could complete in a short time at the local junior college.

We have lost contact with Chham and his family, so we don't know their present circumstances. We hope the story in the newspaper was not about our friend. We have known many other refugees who came here as adults and while some have adjusted and are living fairly well, the past still haunts many. Questions of what might have been are left unanswered.

Exploring the Factors That Lead to School Success or Failure

Analysis of these case studies reveals a number of factors in both the school and societal contexts that affect the lives of English learners. In the following chapters we will consider these factors in more detail, beginning with those from the world of the school. We know that teachers are working with many different students, often under difficult circumstances. Throughout this book, though, we want readers to keep the stories of real second language learners, like the students we have described here, foremost in their minds. We will refer to these real examples, as well as others, as we discuss the different factors that have influenced and continue to influence students who are between worlds. We hope that by drawing on research, theory, and successful practice we can provide readers with a better understanding of the factors that contribute to academic success or failure for their second language learners.

Applications

1. Choose two of the case studies described in this chapter. Compare and contrast the factors that have influenced, are influencing, and may influence school success for each. Discuss your comparisons in pairs or in a small group.

2. Choose one of the students discussed in the case studies that reminds you of a second language learner you know. Compare and contrast the factors that affect the schooling of both. Discuss your comparison in pairs or in a small group.

3. In small groups choose a case study described here or a second language learner you know. On butcher paper or an overhead, list the factors that seem to predict school success and those that seem to limit success in each case. Share your results with the large group, and combine your lists to make a composite list of positive and negative factors.

4. Choose a second language learner who seems to be especially successful in school or one that seems to be struggling. Interview that student and/or family members to try to determine what factors might be influencing school performance. Before the interview, compile a list of possible questions with others and discuss culturally appropriate ways of approaching the interview.

5. For an excellent picture of the new students entering our schools, read *Crossing the Schoolhouse Border* (see references). The appendix contains a good list of interview questions. You might also wish to read Brimner's book about Juan, *A Migrant Family,* and/or *Voices from the Fields: Children of Migrant Farmworkers Tell Their Stories* (Atkin 1993). Atkin's book also presents stories of the children of migrant farm workers. It is a valuable resource for teachers and could also be read by students to promote discussion about immigrants.

6. For further reading about case studies, see D. Freeman and Y. Freeman, 1990, Scarcella, 1990, in the references.

CHAPTER TWO

What Influences
How Teachers Teach?

W hen we visit classes in different schools and at different grade levels with different student populations, we see teachers using a variety of techniques and methods to help their students learn English and academic content. This variation is not surprising. In fact, even within the same school and at the same grade level with a similar student population, teachers differ considerably in how they teach. Why is this?

We continue our exploration of factors in the world of the school by turning from a description of second language students to look at their teachers. The basic question we wish to explore here is "What influences how teachers teach?" A number of factors seem to be at work, and these help to account for the variation in classroom practices we have observed. For one thing, teachers have been students themselves, and often the way they teach reflects the way they were taught. In addition, teachers have studied teaching methods, and those studies may affect how they teach. Teachers are influenced by their colleagues and the administrators with whom they work. Sometimes, teachers use new techniques in their classrooms because they have heard about them in the teachers' lounge or during a staff development session. If teachers change schools or grade levels, they are exposed to additional ideas from new colleagues and these ideas affect their practice. In some schools, the materials that are available (or required) for teachers to use have a strong influence on their teaching. Finally and perhaps most importantly, the kinds of students teachers encounter and the view teachers have of learners influences what they do in the classroom. A teacher's practice, then, changes over time in response to new experiences, new studies, new materials, and new types of students (see Figure 2-1).

We begin by telling the story of one teacher to illustrate the factors that can change a teacher's practice. We will then discuss the relationships between teachers' beliefs, theories, and practices. We also distinguish between a teacher's orientation and the approach or methods and techniques a teacher employs. We conclude by identifying different images of learners a teacher may hold. We hope that our discussion will help our readers reflect on their own beliefs and practices. Greater awareness of why we teach the way we do can help us adopt a principled orientation and make any changes necessary for providing the best education for all our students.

We begin to answer the question, "What influences how teachers teach?" with Yvonne's story. She has moved through different stages of understanding about how

Past Experience	Educational Experience	Colleagues/ Administrators	Changes in Teaching Situation	Materials
Teach as we were taught	Teach as we were taught to teach	Teach as others teach, or as we are required to teach	Adjust teaching to new school or level or new students	Teach using available or required materials

Figure 2-1 Influences on how teachers teach

language is learned and how language and content might be taught. Her experiences provide a context for the ensuing discussion of the factors involved in developing a principled orientation toward teaching.

The Story of an Eclectic Teacher Becoming Principled

Yvonne studied several different languages in high school and college. Her four years of high school Latin were taught through a grammar translation method where students memorized grammar rules and vocabulary and carefully translated great works such as *The Odyssey* and *The Iliad* from Latin to English. The study of Latin was considered a good scholarly exercise that would provide a base for English vocabulary development, but there was never any consideration that knowledge of the Latin language might be useful outside the Latin class.

As a high school junior, Yvonne, who at the time had no intention of ever becoming a teacher, decided to study Spanish. Students in her Spanish class studied less grammar and vocabulary than in the Latin class. Instead, they memorized dialogues that they practiced and recited. The most memorable and enjoyable activities in the Spanish class were learning and performing the Mexican Hat Dance and singing songs in Spanish. Yvonne continued her study of Spanish at the junior college. The advanced Spanish Yvonne studied there was tedious with grammar tests and long hours spent repeating drills in the language laboratory.

It wasn't until she went to the university as a junior majoring in Spanish that it dawned on Yvonne that there was more to language learning than memorizing rules and taking tests. Her Spanish grammar class was going well but she was put into a Spanish literature class with an instructor who only lectured in Spanish! For the first three weeks of class, she was limited to writing three sentences of notes because the language seemed to fly by her unintelligibly. She knew something had to be done, so she made plans to go to Mexico that summer.

The Mexican summer experience was a turning point in her Spanish proficiency. Yvonne's train trip to Guadalajara gave her the opportunity to put the language she had learned to real use. She was amazed when her carefully formed sentences were understood and somewhat shaken when rapid answers came shooting back. She stayed with a family while she studied in Guadalajara, and because she had the strongest Spanish language background, she soon found herself the language negotiator for the other three college students living with the family. Her success with the family, a brief romantic interlude, and exciting weekend travel excursions convinced Yvonne she had found her niche. Her interest in the Spanish language and the Latin culture led naturally to her decision to become a Spanish teacher.

Yvonne enrolled in a "cutting edge" teacher education program. In just one year, students in this program got both a teaching credential and a master's degree in education. Teacher training included videotaped microteaching sessions that allowed student teachers to view their performance and critique their lessons. Methodology classes presented the latest techniques of leading different kinds of audiolingual drills. These techniques were based on a behaviorist view of learning. In fact, one of her education methods professors was considered a national and international language teaching expert. Yvonne accepted the idea that learning, and especially language learning, consisted of forming habits. All her own language instruction had assumed that kind of a model. In her classes, students had memorized dialogues, and teachers had corrected errors quickly. Yvonne and her classmates had repeated their lines as their cheerleading teachers led them rapidly through carefully selected language pattern exercises. Yvonne's teacher education classes prepared her to teach as she had been taught.

She received her credential and landed a job in an inner-city high school. Despite all her preparation, her first teaching position was a real eye opener. She was teaching five classes a day of Spanish One. Her ALM Spanish One book included lesson after lesson of dialogues and drills. Her students hated what they called the "boring repetition" and the "stupid dialogues." Yvonne was devastated! She wanted her students to love speaking Spanish as much as she did! She remembered her positive experiences in Mexico but had forgotten how bored she had been when forced through similar drills.

Faced with 150 resisting and restless high school students each day, Yvonne began to look closely at the lines from the dialogues that the students were repeating. Instinctively, without really knowing what she was doing, she began to change the dialogues to make them more relevant, so "A mí no me gustan las albóndigas" (I don't like meatballs) became "A mí no me gustan las hamburguesas con cebolla" (I don't like hamburgers with onion), and the students could talk about what *they* really didn't like. She even gave her students choice in what they were practicing. Yvonne wanted her students to realize that Spanish is a language that real people use for real purposes. She invited some friends visiting from Mexico to her class. The students prepared and asked questions they wanted to know about teenagers in Mexico. That class period was one of the best of the year.

The classroom context for learning was improving. However, contexts interact, and what goes on outside the classroom may have a great impact on curriculum. Yvonne soon found herself in trouble on two very different fronts. In the first place, the department chair discovered that Yvonne was giving students vocabulary lists with words that were not part of the department curriculum and was encouraging students to create their own dialogues. The problem, of course, was that the students were not always saying things correctly and were undoubtedly learning some incorrect Spanish. The department chair, a strong advocate of ALM, did not want students to develop bad language habits. In the second place, as she attempted to use more authentic Spanish with her students, Yvonne realized that she had not learned enough "real" Spanish to truly help her students say everything they wanted to say.

Yvonne decided to find an opportunity to improve her Spanish proficiency. She and her adventurous husband, a high school English teacher, decided they should live abroad, so they both found teaching jobs at an American school in Colombia, South America. Yvonne found herself with absolutely no background for her teaching job. Educated as a high school Spanish teacher, she was assigned to teach fifth grade in South America using curriculum from the United States. Some of her students spoke English as a foreign language and would never visit the United States. Others were native speakers of English whose parents expected them to attend college in the United States.

Like many teachers faced with a difficult assignment for which she was not prepared, Yvonne relied heavily at first on the textbooks the school provided. Basal readers from the United States as well as social studies and science textbooks were the center of her curriculum. Again, however, she found herself responding to her students. Many of the basal reading stories were boring or completely unrelated to the students' interests and needs. The social studies and science texts were almost impossible for the students to read and understand. Though nontextbook materials were not easy to find, Yvonne centered much of what she and the students did around projects, stories, and discussions. Since most of the teachers in the school were experiencing the same problems, they shared ideas about what worked for their students.

The teaching couple returned to the United States after a year, more fluent in Spanish. Yvonne's husband found a job teaching high school in a small city, but there were no high school Spanish jobs. When a local welfare agency in their new town called to ask if she would volunteer to teach English to Spanish-speaking adults, Yvonne decided to try it. Her first class of students included two Mexican women with no previous schooling and a college-educated couple from Bolivia. With no materials— not even paper or pencils—and diverse students, Yvonne, in desperation, asked the students what English they wanted and needed to learn. Starting with any materials she could get, including props, maps, pamphlets, and resource guides, Yvonne soon found herself teaching thirty to forty adults daily on a variety of topics, including nutrition, shopping, community services, child care, and geography.

Yvonne's class became a part of the public school's adult education program, and Yvonne began teaming with another teacher who also loved teaching adult ESL. The two collaborated daily, making up skits, writing songs, organizing around themes, and creating a community with students who came from Mexico, Central America, South America, Northern and Eastern Europe, the Middle East, Japan, Korea, and Southeast Asia.

Though Yvonne had come a long way from having students memorize dialogues and do drills, she was still uncomfortable about what she should be doing to teach language. She and her team teacher, a previous high school English teacher, often would pull out traditional grammar sheets and do a part of their daily lesson with some of those exercises "to be sure the students understood the structure of the language." When those lessons seemed to go nowhere, especially with adults who had little previous schooling, the grammar books were dropped in favor of books with stories and discussion questions. However, the readings seldom related to student needs and experiences, so the two teachers kept returning to skits, songs, and discussions and projects created around relevant themes.

Yvonne and her partner also had an additional experience that stretched them in new directions and strengthened their conviction that language learning was more than memorizing grammatical rules and repeating pattern drills. The two were asked to teach as adjunct instructors in an intensive English program at the local university. A large group of Japanese college students had arrived, and although these students had extensive background in English grammar and vocabulary, they understood and spoke little English. Initially, the Japanese students resisted classroom activities that were not carefully organized around grammar exercises, but Yvonne and her partner worked hard to get the students to take the risk to speak English in class and in the community. Several of the Japanese students came to appreciate the stress on using English for real purposes and began to attend the adult ESL classes as well as the university classes.

After she had taught the Japanese students for two years and the adults for nine, Yvonne and her husband decided they would like to teach abroad again, taking their children along. They moved to Mexico City where new learning and teaching experiences awaited them. They first taught professional adults English in a large language institute. The institute was moving away from using a textbook based on audiolingual methodology to a new series centered on a notional functional approach, so both Yvonne and her husband learned about teaching language communicatively around functions such as apologizing, giving directions, or making introductions.

Since their teaching schedule did not fit the school schedule for their young children, Yvonne left her job with adults and began teaching fifth grade at the bilingual school her daughters attended. The school was typical of most private schools in Mexico City. The student body for the kindergarten through sixth grade had about five thousand students. The playground was a huge expanse of cement with no trees or play equipment of any kind. Classrooms had one chalkboard in the front of the room with a raised platform for the teacher's desk. There was one bulletin board, decorated monthly by the teacher and checked by the supervising administrator. Desks were bolted in rows filling up the entire room.

The school where Yvonne taught had classes of only forty students. This school was popular because of the small class size. Other schools had sixty or more in a classroom. Yvonne soon learned that most parents in Mexico City, if they could scrape together any money, sent their children to a private school such as this because public schools had larger classes and fewer materials.

At this bilingual school one half of the day was taught in Spanish and one half in English. The English curriculum was centered around basal readers and textbooks from the United States, as it had been in Colombia, and the Spanish curriculum around Mexican government texts. The school required teachers to follow the textbook-based curriculum carefully. All assignments involved copying and memorizing. Students' needs were viewed only in terms of passing the textbook or government tests that were administered by the school monthly. Discipline was strict. Students stood up to answer questions and were not to speak otherwise.

Fortunately, the administration of this school discovered Yvonne had a master's degree in education, a very high degree among Mexican teachers at schools like this. Many elementary teachers in Mexico have little training beyond high school. After teaching a month of the regimented fifth-grade curriculum, Yvonne found herself the administrator in charge of the English curriculum for twenty-three teachers. She began to reflect on how many times she had found herself in positions she was unprepared for and yet how similar her conclusions were each time. Again, she wondered how meaningful the curriculum was for the students. If the Mexican students were studying at a bilingual school so that they could learn to read, write, and speak English, were the United States textbooks appropriate? Should they be reading in basal readers about blonde, blue-eyed Americans going to an American birthday party or going ice skating in snowy weather? Would they really learn English when their teachers rarely allowed them to speak English, or any language, in class and when the teachers rarely spoke to them in English or Spanish?

Yvonne encouraged the teachers to center their curriculum around themes of possible interest to children of various ages. She collected stories and information related to celebrations, science topics, and biographies of famous people that seemed to lend themselves to language use and content learning. She encouraged teachers to involve students in drama and music using English songs and plays. She helped teachers write plays for their students and tried to encourage conversation activities. However, all of this was done on a limited basis as the school requirements were stringent and any activities beyond preparing students for tests were considered frills.

After two years of teaching in Mexico City, Yvonne and her husband moved back to the United States where her husband began graduate study, and she took a position teaching senior composition and freshman English at a private high school. The composition class was organized around a packet of materials that students were to follow carefully, completing assignments at their own pace with no class discussion. The freshman English class curriculum included short stories, a library unit, *Romeo and Juliet,* and a grammar book written in England. Again, Yvonne looked at her students, this time all native speakers of English, and wondered about teaching to their interests and needs. In this situation, unlike the Mexico situation or the high school Spanish situation, the English department chairperson was flexible and sympathetic to deviations from the set curriculum. Before the year was over, Yvonne had students in the composition class meeting in groups, having whole-class discussions, writing joint compositions, and sharing their writing. She largely ignored the grammar book for the freshman, had them write and edit their own compositions, and encouraged discussion of their reading. Before teaching *Romeo and Juliet,* Yvonne planned with another freshman English teacher to have their students view the movie *West Side Story,* which provided them with valuable background for the Shakespearean play.

However, Yvonne did not feel that all her previous experiences were best utilized by teaching English to high school students, so the following year she went back to graduate school herself and worked as a graduate teaching assistant in the Spanish department. Her graduate work included both a second master's degree, this time in English as a second language, and doctoral work in education. In her ESL program she studied second language acquisition theory and second language teaching methods. Many of the writers advocated a communicative approach to teaching language. She was especially impressed by the work of Krashen (1982) who differentiated between acquisition and learning, a distinction that made sense to Yvonne because of her own language learning and teaching experiences.

While her ESL work was interesting, it was her doctoral work that really challenged Yvonne to think seriously about learning and teaching and the relationship between the two. She began studying about language learning with a focus on the development of second language literacy. As she read the work of Ferreiro and Teberosky, Y. and K. Goodman, Halliday, Graves, Kolars, Heath, Lindfors, Piaget, Smith, and Vygotsky, Yvonne began to make connections among all her language learning and teaching experiences and the theories she was studying. She realized two things: First, what she was learning about made sense because of what she had experienced in her own language learning and her many teaching jobs. Second, she realized that much classroom practice was not consistent with current theory.

As she studied, Yvonne made her beginning college Spanish classes her laboratory. With her first-year classes, she talked about how children learn language, how language is acquired naturally in a risk-free environment, and how language must have meaning and purpose for learners. Students wrote in Spanish daily in their journals, and she responded in writing. Students read current articles of interest to them, working in groups to interpret the Spanish. Students learned Spanish in the course of investigating themes such as friendship, professions, and dating customs. One of the most successful projects was a pen pal exchange of letters between students in different college classes. Yvonne realized that students would devote more energy to writing a nongraded assignment—a letter for a peer—than writing a theme in Spanish for the instructor to grade!

After graduation, Yvonne and her husband found positions at a small college. Yvonne now works with teachers of second language learners. Each day she is confirmed in her beliefs that teaching must be geared to student needs and that learning occurs when students are interested in the topic they are studying. Yvonne has learned many lessons through her experiences, but perhaps the most important of these is one she came to late in her teaching career: Theory informs practice, and reflection on practice can shape a teacher's working theory. Yvonne, like most teachers, began with an eclectic view. She used whatever seemed to work. By reflecting on her practice in the light of theory, Yvonne was able to move away from eclecticism and develop a more principled orientation toward her teaching.

Theories of Learning

Knowledge of learning theory can inform a teacher's practice. In the next chapter we present a synthesis of the theories that represent our current understanding of learning theory. We believe that there is a unity in the learning process and that our discussion of learning in general applies to language learning. First, however, to set a context for the discussion of learning theory and to continue our investigation of what influences how teachers teach, we will discuss the relationships among teachers' beliefs, theories, and practices. We then distinguish among a teacher's orientation and the approach—the methods and techniques—the teacher uses to implement his or her beliefs. We conclude by considering three different images of learners teachers may hold. These images reflect different beliefs about how people learn and affect how teachers teach.

Beliefs, Practices, and Theory

A number of methods have been developed to teach second languages. These methods reflect different beliefs about how people learn language. Some well-known methods are the Grammar-Translation Method, the Direct Method, Suggestopedia, Community Language Learning, the Natural Approach, the Silent Way, and Sheltered English. We have described and discussed these methods from a whole language perspective in another book (Freeman and Freeman 1992a). Appendix A includes a list of resources that describe in detail various second language teaching methods that have been widely used.

A teacher might try out one or more of these methods. Teachers, however, are generally not in a position to experiment. They only gain experience with a variety of methods if they change schools or if the school where they teach adopts a new program. This is what happened to Yvonne. And each time she tried a different method, she adjusted it depending on what seemed to meet her students' needs. It wasn't until she began to study learning theory that she devised a framework for evaluating the methods she had used. At this point, she had an opportunity to consider the theory that supported each method and to make choices for her teaching practice based on a particular set of beliefs about how people learn rather than on established practices or a collection of materials.

Sumara (1993), a teacher educator, writes about his experience with Michelle, an exemplary fourth-grade teacher who adopted a holistic stance because whole language principles "best facilitated the kind of teacher she wanted to be" (p. 137). Through his work with Michelle and other classroom teachers in collaborative research, Sumara has become convinced that a primary strength of the whole language movement is its attentiveness to action and that this emphasis on practice enables teachers to help their students. He quotes Novak (1971) who said, "It is not true that faith, creed convictions come first and then action. It is rather true that we are already acting long before we are clear about our ultimate convictions" (p. 45).

Certainly, for Yvonne and many other teachers, Novak's and Sumara's conclusions ring true. Yvonne, like many mainstream teachers, followed traditional practices, teaching her students as she was taught. She went through different experiences on her way to developing a principled orientation to her teaching. As teachers find that certain activities seem to work with students, they may read about the theory that supports their new practices and gradually develop an orientation that they can apply consistently throughout their teaching day.

Watson (1993) and Crowley (1993) have explored the relationships between teachers' beliefs, practices, and theories. They have found that teachers change in the ways described above. While some teachers change over time through a variety of experiences, other teachers start with a strong theory base as a result of reading during their teacher education classes and then, when they begin to teach, work little by little to make their practice consistent with their theory. Whether teachers start with theory or with practice, what is important is developing a consistency among underlying beliefs about learning, knowledge of theory, and particular classroom activities. This consistency marks the difference between a teacher who is principled and one who is eclectic.

Beliefs

Watson (1993) points out that teachers, even eclectic teachers, do have beliefs, but some are examined beliefs and others are unexamined. For example, teachers may believe that direct phonics instruction is essential for students to learn to read. When questioned about this belief, those teachers who answer, "Everyone knows you need to know the sounds of the letters before you can say the words" are probably teachers whose beliefs are unexamined. On the other hand, teachers who have examined their beliefs explain that they teach phonics in context because they understand from what they have learned about the reading process that graphophonics (sound–letter relationships) is only one of the cueing systems that readers use as they construct meaning from text.

Practices

Teachers also adopt certain practices. Their practices may be borrowed from other people. For example, they may discuss literature studies with a colleague and then try literature studies in their own class. Practice is also borrowed if the idea is taken from something the teacher has read. Some materials are accompanied by a teacher's guide that gives suggestions for lessons. Whether the initial idea comes from another teacher or from some written materials, it is borrowed as long as the teacher is just experimenting with it. At some point, teachers own their practices, usually as the result of adapting them for their particular situation.

Theory

Finally, the research by Watson and Crowley suggests that teachers do have a theory about learning. For example, teachers may hold a theory that learning occurs when students work together in cooperative groups. Theories may be active or inactive. If the theory is active, the teacher is consciously aware of it and tests it out against practice and belief. The tensions among beliefs, theories, and practice give rise to inquiry. Professional teachers make their classrooms the arenas where they explore the most effective ways to promote learning for all their students. They examine their beliefs, own their practice, and revise their theory of learning in light of evidence taken from specific classroom experiences.

Joan, a special education resource teacher in a county office of education, has recently begun classes in second language methodology. As she reads about and experiences different ways of learning, she is adjusting her own understanding of what promotes language learning. After reading about the importance of social interaction, Joan wrote the following:

> The whole concept of learning taking place in social interaction is so clearly emphasized in this class. My thoughts and ideas are really expanded by working with the others in my literature group and my method group. Being able to bounce ideas around, problem solve, and come up with conclusions together just promotes additional learning by all of us.
>
> I recently volunteered in an ESL class for adults where they used recitation activities a lot. In thinking about it now, the glaring problem was that people weren't talking to each other. They all worked in workbooks. Very little social interaction. I realize the need for reading and writing but these were not authentic in any way, nor did they support the oral communication (which was only with the teacher).

Teachers can develop a consistency among beliefs, practice, and theory by examining and analyzing their beliefs and making their theory active. In Chapter 14 we will return to this idea of teachers as researchers in their own classrooms.

Orientation, Approach, and Technique

When we talk about becoming principled, we are really talking about developing practices consistent with our beliefs about language, learning, teaching, and curriculum. Anthony (1965) has made a useful distinction among three terms: approach, method, and technique. In describing second language teaching, Anthony defines an approach as "a set of correlative assumptions dealing with the nature of language and the nature of language teaching and learning" (p. 5). For Anthony, an approach is an "article of faith" (p. 5) or a philosophy, "something which one believes but cannot necessarily prove" (p. 5). A method, for Anthony, is "an overall plan for the orderly presentation of language material" (p. 6). The method might be seen as the syllabus or the long-term way of organizing curriculum. Finally, a technique is "a particular trick, stratagem, or contrivance used to accomplish an immediate objective" (p. 7).

We have found it useful in discussions about teaching to distinguish these different levels. Our goal is to help teachers make choices that result in congruence among the levels. Although Anthony's distinctions are useful, we prefer not to equate our set of beliefs with our approach. Rather, our beliefs form our orientation toward teaching. Zapata (personal communication) has pointed out that *approach* more properly refers to a method of putting beliefs into action. How teachers approach teaching a certain group of students depends on their ideas about teaching and learning. Teachers may use particular techniques to implement their approach. Thus, we prefer to use the terms *orientation*, *approach*, and *technique* to refer to these three levels. In Chapter 12 we will describe in more detail what Cummins (1989) calls an intercultural orientation.

Using an analogy with religion might make these distinctions clearer. With a religion, one adopts a set of beliefs about the nature of a god or gods and the relationship between that god and people. Different religions—Christianity, Judaism, Hinduism, Islam—hold different beliefs about these issues. We might say that these religions constitute different orientations. Within each orientation there may be different approaches to worship or methods of worshiping. For example, within Christianity each denomination, such as Catholics, Presbyterians, Episcopalians, Baptists, and Mennonites, organizes its church in a certain way and stresses different aspects of the faith. Each denomination, then, is similar to a method, in that there is an accepted long-term plan about how to carry out the faith. Finally, there are techniques that may or may not cross over denominations. All the Christian churches above, for example, sing hymns which is a common technique of worship. Some techniques are different. Catholics and Episcopalians kneel more often during a service than Baptists.

Without really being aware of it, Yvonne began her career as a Spanish high school teacher with a certain set of beliefs. She believed that language learning involved habit formation and that practice and memorization would result in language learning. She used the audiolingual method, which was consistent with this orientation. In fact, her department chairperson insisted she use only ALM materials from a textbook and not allow students to create their own dialogues because they might "develop bad language habits." The department chair wanted the method to be pure and true to her beliefs. The techniques Yvonne used included memorization of dialogues and practice of language structures in controlled drills. However, she also used some techniques that were not consistent with her method, such as allowing the students to create their own interview questions and encouraging uncontrolled discussion on topics not included in the textbooks.

Although we prefer to use different terms, Anthony's distinctions still seem useful as we consider the best way to provide students who are between worlds with access to second language acquisition and to teach them language through content. In particular, we would agree with Anthony that "techniques must be consistent with a method, and therefore in harmony with an approach [or orientation] as well" (p. 7). The danger is in developing a grab bag of techniques that do not fit into a consistent method or in following parts of several different methods that are not in harmony with your basic beliefs about curriculum, language, learning, and teaching. The grab bag orientation can lead to unprincipled eclecticism.

Yvonne, for example, found herself repeatedly struggling to follow the curriculum and materials she was given and also trying to meet students' needs. She was uncomfortable drilling students or teaching isolated grammar because she did not see how it was helping her students learn language. On the other hand, those techniques seemed to be accepted ways to teach language, and she did not know why she was uncomfortable. Other teachers talked confidently about doing "what works" and that seemed to be good advice. Yvonne used a variety of techniques but didn't totally trust her own instincts. After she had had a variety of teaching experiences and also had begun to read theory, Yvonne was able to develop a more consistent and principled orientation to teaching.

It is not always possible to determine a teacher's orientation simply by observing her techniques. For example, a whole language teacher who structures the class around themes using literature and process writing may teach a minilesson on capital letters. That same lesson might also be taught by a teacher using a traditional grammar approach to language teaching. The technique, the lesson on capital letters, could be observed in classrooms of teachers with two quite different orientations. The first teacher teaches the minilesson because she has seen that students do not use capitals correctly in their writing, while the second teacher teaches capitals on a particular day because that is the point in the curriculum where capitals are to be taught.

Our beliefs about language, about how people learn, and about how we should teach all form our orientation. While our ideas are not fixed and while they change as we continue to learn and study, they guide the methods and techniques we use. At any given time we strive for consistency at the three levels: orientation, approach, and technique. At the level of our basic beliefs, eclecticism reflects a lack of well thought through principles. However, at the level of technique a principled teacher may be eclectic. The minilesson on capital letters may be chosen by either a whole language teacher or a more traditional teacher.

In the same way, either teacher might read a story to the class, but for different purposes. The first teacher might read it so that students can enjoy and discuss the story, relate it to their own lives, and develop language as they respond in discussion and writing. The traditional teacher might read the story because it can help her teach a grammar point. If the story contains many examples of the past tense, for example, students might be asked to rewrite the story changing all the verbs to the present tense.

Many language teachers work in a school that has adopted a method and the materials that go with it. It is important to understand, however, that methods are based on certain beliefs about language, teaching, and learning. Take the audiolingual method, for example. A teacher who adopts this method gets a long-term plan, usually in the form of a textbook. The book includes a set of techniques. Students memorize dialogues, the teacher leads pattern practice drills, and so on. The book is based on beliefs about learning taken from behavioral psychology (language is habit learned through repetition) and structural linguistics (language patterns are more important than individual vocabulary items; patterns can be learned inductively).

When a teacher follows a method, then the techniques and the basic beliefs are thrown in at no extra charge. It's a package deal, much like the basal reading programs. And, as with the basals, the teacher may end up playing the role of technician, delivering instruction someone else (or a team of "experts") has devised. If we start by adopting a method, we really leave the answer to the question, "How can we provide our students with access to second language acquisition?" in someone else's hands.

Since teachers are professionals rather than technicians, they reflect on their practice as they refine their beliefs about teaching. They make their own decisions. They know that in order to teach language effectively, they must understand both language and learning. They move away from eclecticism and develop a principled orientation to language, learning, teaching, and curriculum.

Theories of Learning—Images of the Learner

A teacher's orientation may affect the way the teacher views students. Lindfors (1982) suggests three ways teachers may look at learners. These three images of the learner correspond to three different theories of learning. The first image is of the student as a plant. In this view, the teacher provides students with all they need in order to learn, in order to "grow." This traditional image is reflected in the word "kindergarten" (garden of children) and in the often-used description of a student as a "late bloomer." The assumption is that if the teacher provides the needed information, the student will bloom with new knowledge. As Lindfors observes, the limitation of the plant image is that "we are not simply well adapted for getting watered . . . we are well adapted for actively making sense of language as we interact meaningfully with others in a language-filled world" (p. 146).

This leads Lindfors to propose a second image, the builder. "In the builder image, the child acts on his or her environment . . . constructing his or her own meanings, interpretations, understandings, and expressions from abundant and diverse encounters with people and objects" (p. 146). Lindfors points out two problems with the builder image. First, the learner is seen as acting on, rather than interacting with, people and objects. Second, the meanings the learner constructs are seen as permanent. This view contradicts the belief that as we learn concepts or language our understandings need to be open to revision in light of new experiences.

The third image is that of the explorer, an image that is "at one and the same time active, healthy, interactive, and dynamic" (p. 148). Lindfors cautions that the difficulty with creating explorer classrooms is that schools and teachers most often view students as performers instead of explorers. "The goal has traditionally been that children will demonstrate what they know and can do, rather than that they will explore in order to know and do better as they go along" (p. 148). In explorer classrooms students ask questions, they initiate investigations, they are involved in diverse experiences, they constantly interact, and they engage in meaningful activity.

Barnes (1990) presents a similar idea. He points out that language in the classroom can be used for either presenting ideas or for exploring them. "Exploratory talk often occurs when peers collaborate on a task, when they wish to talk it over in a tentative manner, considering and rearranging their ideas" (p. 50). Traditional classes are places where language is often presentational, but learning occurs when language is exploratory. A curriculum that engages students in exploratory learning requires a view of the learner as an explorer rather than as a plant or builder.

These three images of the learner reflect three different views of learning: behaviorist, cognitive, and transactional. Behaviorism is based on the belief that learning is the result of the environment acting on the learner (Harste, Woodward, and Burke 1984). Learners are seen as passive, waiting for teachers or materials to give them what they need to learn. A cognitive view, on the other hand, assumes an active learner who constructs knowledge by acting on the environment. These two views, which correspond to Lindfors' images of plant and builder, have triggered a debate over the relative influences of nurture and nature. Behaviorists, such as Skinner (1957), emphasize the role of outside influences, of nurture, on learning, while cognitivists like Piaget (1955) stress the importance of inner factors, of nature.

Lindfors' explorer image represents a third possibility, that both inner and outer forces are equally important in the learning process. Instead of seeing students as plants who passively wait to be fed information, teachers can view students as explorers who actively try to make sense of the world. Instead of conceiving of students as builders who take what they learn and construct fixed knowledge, teachers can look at students as explorers who continually revise their understandings as they live through and reflect on new experiences.

Explorers act on the environment and, at the same time, they are affected by the environment. Exploration involves choice. When explorers come to a river, for example, they have choices to make. They might change their course, try to wade across, or build a bridge. Further, any expedition needs a leader, a coexplorer, so both the teacher and the students are active participants in the process of learning.

Gayleen, a first-grade teacher of first and second language learners, provides a perfect example of a teacher exploring her understanding of how best to teach her students. Questions she raised in a graduate class also showed how a teacher, in this case Yvonne, and a student can be colearners. Recently, Gayleen saw a demonstration of some jazz chants (Graham 1979). Because Gayleen has had several graduate courses in reading and writing process, she questioned where jazz chants fit into her understanding of learning:

> I would like some of your input about jazz chants. (We listened to a few last week.) I wonder what the goals of these chants are? I feel they are a bit staged, stilted, and part to whole. Some I feel seem to parallel those practice dialogs, yet they seem to be used quite frequently. I'd like to be sure I understand the uses before I decide whether they fit into my understanding of the way children/adults acquire language.

Gayleen is an explorer as she works to ensure that her practice fits the theory of learning that she holds. She sees her college instructors as colearners with her, and they, in turn, respond to her exploration. In fact, Gayleen's questions helped both Gayleen and Yvonne come to understand exactly how jazz chants do fit into informed practice. Yvonne had to think through her response to Gayleen:

> You're right on! Many *are* practice dialogues. I'd like to see people use them only to get their own students playing with language and rhythm-writing their own. Remember, you have a bit more understanding than many other people in this class because of classes you have taken and your classroom experience! I see jazz chants as a technique I'd use sparingly and only in certain circumstances. (For example, I saw them used in the English as a foreign language setting with elementary students as an alternative to boring, meaningless memorized monologues for their parent show. They chose and choreographed the chants they wanted to do.)

We use Dewey and Bentley's (1949) term "transaction" to describe the view of learning that explorers experience. Rosenblatt (1978) took their term and applied it to what happens when we read. We might better understand these images of the learner by looking at different views of the reading process. One view of reading is that the reader is passive (a plant) and simply receives the message written by the author. A second view is that the reader is active (a builder) and reconstructs the message the author has encoded in the text. Rosenblatt suggests that neither of these views is entirely correct. Instead, she argues that readers construct a mental text as they read. Readers transact with the written text, and the meaning they construct depends on their background experiences and the purposes for reading they bring to the text. The written text is changed into different mental texts by different readers.

The text acts on the reader as well. As a result of their reading, readers change. They don't simply interact with a text and come away (mentally) the same as before they read it. Instead, they transact with the text. " 'Transaction' designates, then, an ongoing process in which the elements or factors are, one might say, aspects of a total situation each conditioned by and conditioning the other" (p. 17). A reader changes the text, and the text changes the reader, just as an explorer changes the wilderness and the wilderness changes the explorer.

An example might help make the idea of transaction a bit clearer. In one course that our graduate students take, they read various novels about ethnic groups in California. *Rain of Gold* (Villaseñor 1991), is a particularly popular one. However, different teachers read it differently. For example, Toni, a Hispanic who experienced discrimination in California schools as she grew up, read the book with interest comparing the characters to her own family members. She came away from the experience of reading the book with a new sense of pride in who she was and where she had come from. She intends to share that pride in who she is with her own Hispanic students. Judy, an Anglo from an affluent family in a small farming community, was amazed to read about the background of the book's characters. She had never before thought of the field laborers as people with dignity, pride, and an important history. Judy now views the Mexican-American students in her classroom as well as those in the Hispanic community in general with a new respect. Reading *Rain of Gold* changed both Toni and Judy as they transacted with the text. Both now view their own teaching and their students differently because of their experience reading the book.

When we ask "What influences how teachers teach?" we often find the answer in the images of learners and views of learning that teachers hold. Figure 2-2 summarizes information about the images of the learner.

Yvonne's story shows how teachers change in response to new experiences and how their view of their students also changes in this process. Yvonne first followed a method that caused her to view her students as plants. Her audiolingual lessons

Image	Role of Learner	View of Learning	Influence on Learning
Plant	Passive	Behaviorist	Environment acts on learner.
Builder	Active	Cognitive	Learner acts on environment.
Explorer	Active	Transactional	Environment acts on learner, and learner acts on environment.

Figure 2-2   Images of the learner

provided the nurture her students required in the form of drills and dialogues. She soon moved to a different view. With her adult ESL students, for example, she began to see her role as one of providing interesting materials and activities through which they could construct knowledge. She was still in control, but the students played a much more active role in their learning. They were builders, not plants. Now Yvonne sees her teacher/students as explorers, and, with them, she investigates different aspects of teaching and learning second languages. She may be the expedition leader, but she does not pretend to have all the answers as she and her students pursue topics of inquiry together.

Yvonne is what Allwright (1993) calls an "exploratory teacher." He explains that exploratory teaching is a "potentially productive way of integrating research and pedagogy" (p. 125). He suggests that teachers "should try exploiting the already familiar and trusted classroom activities as ways of exploring the things that puzzle teachers and learners about what is happening in their own classrooms" (p. 125). If, for example, students appear to dislike group work, the teacher could ask the students why they dislike it. In this way, teachers can improve their practice by becoming researchers in their own classrooms. Allwright views research as the driving force for teacher development, and teacher development as the driving force for research progress. We will return to Allwright's idea of exploratory teaching in Chapter 14 because we believe that classroom research is the best way to develop context specific responses to the puzzles that teachers face. At this point, though, we wish to emphasize that both the teacher and the students are colearners in an explorer classroom.

These three images of the learner, then, correspond to different views of learning. Both our role as teachers and our relationship to our students can change depending on the image we hold. If we see students as plants, our job is to transmit knowledge to them. If we see students as builders, we provide the raw materials they can use for their buildings. But, if we see students as explorers, we recognize that they can pose problems and raise questions, and that during our joint investigations, we can construct knowledge together (Wells and Chang-Wells 1992).

We will return to these images of the learner when we look at theories of second language acquisition (SLA), but first we develop in some detail a view of learning that helps account for the learning that takes place in explorer classrooms for students between worlds.

Applications

1. Think about a language class you have taken or taught. (If you cannot identify a second language class, a first language reading, writing, literature, or language arts class is fine.) Try to identify the orientation of the teacher, the method, and some of the techniques used to teach that class. Discuss this in pairs or groups.

2. Read back over the different experiences of the teacher described at the beginning of the chapter. Do any of her experiences make you think of something you have experienced with teaching or learning? Discuss this with a partner or in a small group.

3. In a small group, brainstorm some classroom activities and assignments that are common to your present or future teaching situation. What image of the learner do those assignments reflect? Plant? Builder? Explorer?

4. Interview a teacher who has had at least ten years of teaching experience. (Use yourself if you have taught for several years.) What has influenced that teacher's curriculum decisions? What are your conclusions about how that teacher views learners? Does he or she generally view learners as plants? As builders? As explorers? Before the interview, brainstorm possible interview questions with a group.

CHAPTER THREE

How Does Learning Take Place in Explorer Classrooms?

*I*f teachers view themselves and their students as explorers, they create classroom experiences where learning takes place as the class reads, writes, and talks while investigating topics of interest. In these classes, students learn both content and language as they answer big questions that interest them. We continue our investigation of the world of the school by presenting a model that helps to account for the learning that takes place in explorer classrooms.

A Model of Learning

One general model of learning, consistent with the explorer image, has been developed by Cochrane, Cochrane, Scalena, and Buchanan (1984). These authors identify six steps involved in learning:

1. demonstration
2. intent
3. self-concepting—taking a risk
4. learning through doing
5. feedback
6. integration

Demonstrations

According to Cochrane et al., learning begins with a demonstration. For people to learn something, they must first observe someone else doing it. A demonstration could be as simple as hearing someone speaking another language. A demonstration may or may not be intentional, because the person providing it may not even be aware that he or she is demonstrating something. In this respect, demonstrations differ from modeling, which is a more conscious act that many teachers use as a technique.

The relationship of the learner to the demonstrator is also important. If the person providing the demonstration is significant to the learner, the learner is more apt to pay attention to the demonstration. For example, if older brothers or sisters speak and interact in another language, they provide important demonstrations for younger siblings, giving the younger children the desire to speak and understand the second language as well.

Intent

We are constantly surrounded by demonstrations, but we only attend to some of them. For example, many teenagers see their parents cleaning or cooking, but they pay very little attention. In order for learning to take place, according to Cochrane et al., learners must form the intent to learn. In other words, as the result of the demonstration, learners must decide that they would like to be able to do the same thing. It is not enough for teenagers to see their parents cleaning the house. Unless the teens form the intent to clean the house, they will not learn how. Many parents of teenagers are amazed when they discover that their children have no idea about how to do some chores around the house that they have seen their parents do many times.

Self-concepting

The next step in learning is self-concepting. For the intent to become reality, learners must be able to conceive of themselves as actually doing something. We could watch someone skydiving, but unless we can picture ourselves jumping from that plane, we will not learn to skydive. Self-concepting, then, involves the willingness to take a risk. As we weigh the likelihood of failure or success and the benefits of completing an act, we decide whether or not to even try. In the case of skydiving, we may see an unnecessarily high possibility of failure, and we may see no particular purpose for jumping, so we decide not to take the risk.

Learning can be short-circuited at any stage. If no one provides a demonstration, we won't form the intent to learn. If we decide that the risks of trying are too high or that the rewards for success are too low, we can't imagine ourselves ever doing the activity. This is why many teachers strive to create a classroom where students can take risks. In the English language classroom, students receive demonstrations from English speakers, but whether or not students are willing to try to speak English in class depends on the risk involved and the benefits the students believe are attached to learning English.

Learning by Doing

Cochrane et al. also emphasize the fact that people learn by doing. As the authors point out, people learn to read by reading, and they learn to write by writing. Second language students learn English or any other language by using that language. However, it is important to make a distinction here between learning by doing something meaningful or just practicing a teacher-imposed activity. When we practice, we are preparing to do something for someone else that will be tested in the future. On the other hand, when we *do* something, we do it for a real purpose now because we are interested in it. That helps explain why Yvonne had difficulty learning Spanish in her Spanish classes in the United States but learned a great deal of Spanish when she went to live in Mexico. Her Spanish classes were only seen as preparation, but living in Mexico provided opportunities for meaningful language use. The challenge is to find ways to make language classes places for meaningful learning. That is why we advocate teaching language through content. Students learn language more easily when the focus is on meaningful content than when the focus is on the grammar of the new language.

Feedback

In the process of doing, our learning continues in response to the feedback we receive. The feedback in situations out of school comes quite naturally. If we try to use a new language as we buy an item in a store, we get feedback from the clerk, who either understands what we are asking for or has no idea of what we want. In schools, feedback may come in several different forms, and the form of the feedback may affect the course of the learning. If an ESL teacher responds to students' questions by correcting the grammar, students may learn to focus on linguistic form. If the teacher criticizes the students' pronunciation as they try to use a new language, the students may decide the risk of speaking is too great to continue trying to use the language.

Ann, a college student who had a great deal of experience speaking Spanish, including two periods of her life when she lived in Mexico, complained recently about an incident in her advanced Spanish conversation class. Her Spanish professor kept interrupting her and correcting a grammar point during a discussion. She explained, "When he interrupted me for the third time, I refused to say another word. The frustrating thing was that I really was interested in the topic and wanted to say something. If this is how it's going to be every time, I think I'm going to hate that class." On the other hand, if the teacher responds to the content of the question, the student may focus on the communicative function of the new language.

Integration

Feedback helps learners refine the hypotheses they are making. As they do so, learners continually integrate their new knowledge into what they have already learned. For example, a student learning English may decide that all past-tense verbs are formed by adding "ed" to the base verb form. If English learners hear a verb like "go" used in the past tense—"Yesterday, I went to school"—they must refine their hypothesis about past-tense verb formation in English and integrate this new knowledge (some verbs are irregular) into their existing knowledge.

Teachers need to be aware that the demonstrations they provide may lead students to incorrect hypotheses. For example, teachers sometimes present the progressive tense by speaking aloud as they perform certain actions. "I am walking to the board. I am writing my name. I am turning toward the class." Despite the teacher's good intentions, one group of second language students we observed concluded that English speakers use progressive tense when they want to think aloud about what they are doing. As this example shows, it is important to embed language use in authentic contexts.

Traditional language classes are seldom places where students can explore language. Teachers may provide demonstrations of correct language usage, but they seldom provide demonstrations of authentic language use. As a result, students do not form the intent to learn, do not take the risks involved, and do not learn by doing, by speaking the language, at least they do not speak outside the confines of the language classroom.

Yvonne discovered the importance of authentic language use in her high school Spanish classes. When she invited her Mexican friends to visit her classes, she created an explorer classroom. She and her students prepared questions for the visitors ahead of time. As the Mexican visitors answered the questions, they provided important demonstrations—real people use this language for real reasons. The atmosphere was risk free. Yvonne's students asked questions because they were interested in finding out the answers, and in the process they used Spanish for authentic communication. They were learning by doing.

In the same way, when Yvonne had her college Spanish students write pen pal letters to another class, she created another situation where students learned through doing as they used language for real purposes. In her adult ESL classes, Yvonne's students read in English to find shopping bargains or to plan trips to visit relatives in other cities. In each case, students learned language when they used language to meet their real-life needs.

Demonstrations, Engagement, and Sensitivity

Smith (1983) has developed a theory of learning that is compatible with that of Cochrane et al. (1984). Smith identifies three steps necessary for learning to occur: demonstrations, engagement, and sensitivity. The first step is the same. Learners must be provided with demonstrations. The second step, engagement, involves forming an intent, accepting the risks, and learning through doing and receiving feedback. Smith defines the third step; sensitivity, as "the absence of any expectation that learning will not take place or that it will be difficult" (p. 105). Sensitivity is necessary for students to engage and to continue learning by doing.

Clearly, teachers play an important role in providing demonstrations and in creating classroom communities where students feel free to risk and engage in learning. Effective teachers also show sensitivity. They constantly assure students that learning is not going to be difficult. They continually express their faith in their students as learners. In explorer classrooms, students and teachers get caught up in the excitement of learning.

Rusty, who was teaching in a summer school program for English learners, relates how he created a risk-free environment where Jessica was able to engage in writing:

> In this ELD [English language development] summer school program, it has been neat to see the self-confidence grow in all the kids that I have the privilege of having in my classroom. As I look at the past four weeks, we have worked harder on the belief of "Yes, I can," than on anything else.
>
> Jessica came up to me early in the first week and whispered that she couldn't write yet (during writers workshop) because she hadn't learned how to read (and she was going into third grade). I convinced her that she either could or would before the week was out. We have done a lot of singing/chanting, choral reading, buddy-up reading, and individual reading. I also wrote specific poems using each of the kid's names which we have done choral reading with, and it was remarkable what that has done for them—kind of like seeing their name in lights!
>
> During the last hour we have some aides come into our classroom and work with us. The students decided that they wanted to read their own poem to the aides. Jessica spent each afternoon with her barely bilingual grandmother, one of the aides, who helped her each day. I thought Jessica was going to burst with pride when she finished reading and everybody in the class clapped for her. And of course, now she is "writing," too! Sometimes she forgets what she wrote when we do author's chair, but she goes for it with gusto anyway. It is amazing what believing in yourself can do.

It's also obvious that Jessica believed in herself because of Rusty's sensitivity. He created a risk-free classroom where Jessica and the other students never expected that learning would not take place and never thought that learning would be difficult.

Guillermo, one of the case study students described in Chapter 1, provides a good example of Smith's three stages of learning. Before coming to the United States, he had many demonstrations of success from the influential people around him who had traveled extensively and spoke at least two languages. Once he arrived in the United States, he saw that his aunt was finishing a Ph.D. program at a large university. This demonstration showed him that it was possible to succeed in this country through education.

From the first day of school, he engaged in learning English. He made friends with English-speaking American peers, and he soon joined clubs. He never hesitated to talk to his teachers or other English-speaking adults or to ask questions. Though he did not receive straight A's in academic work, he became an accepted part of the English-speaking community while he was still learning English. Because of the sensitivity of those around him, it never occurred to Guillermo that he might not learn English or succeed academically. He knew he would go to college and graduate. In addition, others around him, including his aunt, our family, and the people from the church, trusted him to succeed. Once in college he not only did well in his coursework but also was so outgoing and active in student affairs that he received one of only two invitations to work in Washington, D.C., with a state senator during the summer.

Joining the Club

In his more recent work, Smith (1988) has used the metaphor of joining a club to describe the process people go through as they learn something new. We might see the club as the context in which the learning process can most easily occur. Guillermo literally joined school clubs, but he also joined the English-speakers' club. Learning occurs in clubs for the following reasons:

1. It is meaningful. (We ignore things that are meaningless.)
2. It is useful. (We ignore things that don't serve our purposes.)
3. It is continual and effortless. (We stay in the club once we are learning and are not aware of the roles we play as club members.)
4. It is incidental. (We do not focus on what we are learning but on what we are doing as we accomplish our purposes.)
5. It is collaborative. (We draw on the expertise of other club members to help us accomplish our purposes.)
6. It is vicarious. (We learn from others without effort if they are the kind of people we admire and we want to do what they do.)
7. It is risk free. (We are accepted into a club. Clubs are safe places for learning.)

In explorer classrooms, teachers and students form clubs as they pose and answer questions about topics of interest. Language learners in these classrooms use their new language as they engage in meaningful inquiry. Their focus is not on the language but on using the language to accomplish their purposes.

Cambourne and Turbill (1988) have developed a set of conditions for learning to write that are similar to Smith's description of learning in a club: Teachers immerse students in written language, provide demonstrations of how print is used, and hold high expectations for their students. The students on their part assume responsibility for their learning, attempt to approximate adult models of writing, have many opportunities to write, and receive meaning-centered, relevant responses to their writing. Cambourne and Turbill comment, "If all these conditions are present in the classroom to a relatively high degree, then such a classroom may be labelled as a 'process writing' setting, or, for that matter, a 'process-oriented' setting" (p. 6). In Smith's terms, these classrooms are writing clubs.

We often say that the best way to learn a new language is to live in the country where that language is spoken. Certainly, going to France to learn French could be seen as joining the French-speakers' club. In France, French is meaningful and useful. Learning is continuous, incidental, and vicarious. Of course, whether or not the learning is risk free depends on how other club members (native French speakers) respond. In fact, the key to learning is acceptance into the club, and just going to a country may not result in club membership at all. Some Americans live abroad, but they spend all their time with other Americans, forming their own community within the foreign country, and as a result they don't learn the language spoken there. We have to want to join a club, and club members must be accepting for learning to take place.

Taking a French class could also be a step toward joining the French-speakers' club. The same factors would affect learning in a classroom. The difference between going to France and taking a French class is that the class has an officially designated teacher. Smith describes the teacher's responsibility as twofold: being sure that clubs exist and that no student is excluded from them. In the case of literacy clubs, Smith says, "In simple terms, this means lots of collaborative and meaningful reading and writing activities, the kinds of things that are often characterized as extras, reward or even 'frills'" (p. 15). In a French class, this would mean that the students are hearing and using French for purposes that are meaningful and interesting to them in a risk-free environment.

Clubs are places where learning takes place during social interaction. Smith takes a transactional view of learning. When we join a club, we change the club and the club changes us. Learning is an ongoing and dynamic process of exploration. Smith's metaphor for learning as joining a club challenges traditional views of teachers transmitting information or of students gathering information and building knowledge. Instead, club members acquire knowledge as they interact with one another. Gee has developed a theory of learning similar to Smith's concept of clubs, but Gee's theory can be applied more directly to learning languages.

Discourses

Gee (1990, 1992) claims that learning involves entering into Discourses (which he writes with a capital D). A discourse involves "ways of talking, acting, interacting, valuing, and believing, as well as the spaces and material 'props' the group uses to carry out its social practices" (1992, p. 107). Discourses in a society are "owned and operated" by a particular group of people who are accepted as members and who play certain roles. Students in a junior high classroom, for example, may be part of different discourse groups—the most important of which is probably their peers—and their behavior, speech, and values are determined by that group. In fact, during difficult teen years, the conflicts among peer discourse, classroom discourse, and home discourse may cause serious problems. These different discourses interact in complex ways and strongly affect school success. For example, the peer discourse may not value school success, and some students may actively discourage their friends from doing homework or answering questions in class. Teachers are aware of (and sometimes frustrated by) the demands imposed on their students by different discourses.

How do people learn the rules of a discourse and thus gain membership in it? Gee suggests that entrance into a discourse is a matter of enculturation. "Discourses are not mastered by overt instruction . . . but by enculturation into social practices through scaffolded and supported interaction with people who have already mastered the Discourse" (p. 114). We acquire, or pick up naturally, the ways of speaking, acting, dressing, and so on that are characteristic of a particular discourse by associating with people who belong to that discourse. We are changed as the result of becoming part of a discourse, and once we are accepted into the discourse, we can change it, too. If "the 'style' with which I carry out a recognizable act 'catches on' with others" (p. 111), then the manner of acting in that discourse changes.

For example, when Yvonne went to Mexico, then to Colombia, and returned to Mexico again, she learned more than the Spanish language. In each setting, she entered the discourse of the people with whom she lived and worked. She learned how to ask for things, how to respond, and what not to talk about. She learned how to dress, what things people valued, and what they thought was unimportant. Since she was an American living in another culture, she did not conform to all the practices of the discourses she entered. As she took part in different discourses, her perspective as an American helped broaden and change the views of the people in those discourses. They accepted some of her customs, values, and ideas, and modified some of their own.

When Yvonne became the English director at the Mexican elementary school, she gave workshops for the teachers on ways to create more interactive, student-centered classes. This school, like many others in Latin America, put great value on student presentations. Parents were invited, and students dressed up to act out some event and recite their lines. Parents spent a great deal of money on the costumes, and teachers devoted hours to preparing students for the presentations.

Often, these presentations were shows for the parents rather than real learning opportunities for the students. During her workshops, Yvonne demonstrated for the teachers ways they could change the assemblies by involving the students more fully and exploring topics of interest. For example, Yvonne had one class study nutrition and then make up costumes, skits, and songs around the theme of good health. Students dressed up as candy and sang about "Three Bad Things" to the tune of "Three Blind Mice" before being chased off the stage by other students dressed up as toothbrushes and a tube of toothpaste. The parents still enjoyed the presentation, but now the students learned about health as they used English.

Yvonne was working in one discourse, one way of doing things. She was able to change that discourse by adding her own ideas about teaching and learning. She did not try to replace one discourse with another. Instead, she found subtle ways of modifying the dominant discourse. This allowed her to present a different view of language, teaching, learning, and curriculum that the Mexican teachers could use and that the parents could accept.

Gee's idea of a discourse seems very similar to Smith's conception of a club. Both Smith and Gee view learning as something that happens naturally and without conscious awareness as people associate with others who are club or discourse members. Both writers stress the role of social interaction in learning. Thus, the explorer image of the learner fits Gee's theory as well as Smith's since Gee stresses that new members of a discourse can change the discourse as well as be changed by it. In this respect, Gee also takes a transactional view of learning.

By stressing social aspects of learning, Gee and Smith differ from both behavioral and cognitive psychologists who view learning as something done by an individual acting alone. For the behaviorist, learning occurs as individuals respond to stimuli. For the cognitive psychologist, learning happens when individuals construct meaning by acting on the environment. Piaget and Vygotsky are two psychologists who have helped us understand how it is that learners construct meaning.

Piaget's Experiential View

Piaget spent a great deal of time observing young children at play as they developed concepts. His descriptions of assimilation and accommodation, decentering, and his distinction between adult and child concepts have led us to view learning differently.

Piaget believed that learners must have concrete experiences in order to form concepts. For Piaget, the role of language is to express the things we already understand. In part, Piaget's view of language resulted from his concern that much teaching is verbal rather than experiential and that words are often used to introduce a concept that children are not ready to learn because they lack the necessary experiences. As a result, children may be able to answer questions about a topic without really understanding that topic.

The process of developing concepts occurs only as learners have a variety of experiences. Students learning about fractions might start with some whole, a cake for example, and then cut it into pieces. This experience could be the basis for a discussion of how fractions represent the parts of a whole. The problem with much teaching, from Piaget's perspective, was the lack of concrete experiences such as this. Some math teachers might simply write fractions on the board, talk about them, and then start having students perform operations (adding, dividing, and so forth) with the numbers. According to Piaget, the words of explanation and the abstract number operations are not enough for students to really develop concepts. Students might perform the exercises correctly, but they usually do not understand what mathematical concept lies behind the operation.

Assimilation and Accommodation

Piaget explains the process of concept development as one of assimilation and accommodation. He maintains that learners change new experiences to make them fit in with their present concepts, and they change their concepts as they add new experiences.

For example, Yvonne had a certain view of teaching when she took her first job. It was based on her own experience as a learner and on the teachers she had observed. As she taught and studied, she came into contact with other teachers and with other ideas about teaching. She adapted these new ideas to fit her schemas, her notions of teaching, and as the new ideas came in, they changed her view. The way she views teaching and learning now is much different from when she began her career.

Decentering

Piaget also pointed out the importance of decentering or looking at experiences from a variety of perspectives. He noted that young children are egocentric. They are limited to a single point of view. As they mature and have more experiences, they can take on additional points of view and gain new understandings. In this process, they develop the ability to abstract out of their experience certain characteristics of objects or experiences and form categories. For example, a child might develop the concept of bicycle as a vehicle with two wheels (as opposed to a three-wheeled tricycle). As children get older and have experience with more kinds of bikes, they may categorize them differently (three-speed vs. ten-speed, or mountain bikes vs. street bikes). As children see new kinds of bikes, their concept of bikes changes. In fact, as their children grow up, parents may develop still other ways of categorizing bikes (more or less expensive).

When people learn additional languages, they can also move away from a single point of view. They can decenter and take on new ways of understanding language. Knowing two languages allows a person to step outside the framework imposed by a language and see it differently by comparing it with other languages. This helps explain why many people only learn English grammar when they study a foreign language. It is only at that point that they can step outside English and see it from a different perspective.

Adult/Child Concepts—Ferreiro and Teberosky

Another potential problem with instruction is that it may assume that children's concepts are the same as adults' concepts. Ferreiro and Teberosky (1982), two Piagetian scholars, asked students to carry out a series of tasks with words and numbers to try to get at what children thought was "for reading" when they entered school. Ferreiro and Teberosky discovered that young children thought something was for reading if it had enough letters (usually at least four) and a variety of letters. Their Spanish-speaking subjects thought that common words such as "el" or "la" (the) were not for reading, nor were words that commonly appear in stories for young readers, such as "oso" (bear).

Y. Freeman and Whitesell (1985) replicated this experiment with English-speaking preschoolers and found the same results. Because they are surrounded by environmental print, children develop a concept of what is for reading and what is not for reading before starting school. Beginning reading materials in both Spanish and English, on the other hand, often use short words with repeated letters. Adults might think that these short words would be easier for children to read. By investigating children's concepts rather than relying on adult concepts, teacher researchers can better adapt instruction to build on what students bring to the learning situation.

Vygotsky's Social View of Learning

The views of Vygotsky, the Soviet psychologist, differ in some important ways from those of Piaget. Vygotsky (1981) saw language as a tool for developing thought and believed that all learning is social:

> Any function in the child's cultural development appears twice, or on two planes. First it appears on the social plane, and then on the psychological plane. First it appears between people, as an interpsychological category, and then within the child as an intrapsychological category (p. 163).

Vygotsky has suggested three different concepts that might help us understand better how learning happens: the Zone of Proximal Development, mediation, and scientific concepts.

Zone of Proximal Development

For learning to take place, instruction must occur in a student's Zone of Proximal Development, which Vygotsky (1978) defines as "the distance between the actual developmental level as determined by independent problem solving and the level of potential development as determined through problem solving under adult guidance or in collaboration with more capable peers" (p. 86). According to Vygotsky, learning results when we talk with someone else, an adult or a more capable peer, in the process of trying to solve a problem.

Mike provides us an excellent example of how he works in his students' Zone of Proximal Development during literature studies in his fourth-grade classroom. Mike works in an inner-city school, and many of his students are second language learners. He believes that literature studies, which we describe in detail in Chapter 12, are important for his students' learning. It is clear that Mike has found ways to support his students' learning:

> I continue to explore this exciting concept of Literature Study. Students self-select books and then meet in book groups to determine how many pages to read each day to complete the reading within a time frame I decide. The students are then invited to read, as a group, with a partner(s) or by themselves.
>
> As students read, I float about, keeping anecdotal records of things students might be doing to make meaning from their texts. I have also joined in with groups as they have read, or even read with a group to provide some support and demonstrations of ways to approach reading and talk about it. Students are also encouraged to have a shared reading arrangement where they periodically stop and just do a "quick talk" with a partner about what they think is going on in their reading or to ask for clarification. This is to support the meaning making process.
>
> I do wander in and out of groups and will ask them what they are finding, and then offer some direction as to things that I would like for them to be on the lookout for in the text. I base my comments on the kind of interests I see the readers having. I also will have readers give regular response (though not always written) on their reading. I want to get a look at how they are transacting with text.

It is important to note that Mike is not the only one in the classroom helping students move within their Zones of Proximal Development. The way literature studies are organized in Mike's classroom, peers help each other understand and learn too.

Mediation

The role of the teacher is one of mediation, to use Vygotsky's term. A teacher (or other adult or more capable peer) mediates experience by helping the learner make sense out of it. The teacher asks questions or points out certain aspects of a situation. Mike helped his students mediate their learning through literature as he provided demonstrations, joined groups and asked questions, and encouraged "quick talks" when students were struggling with the texts they were reading.

Vygotsky also recognized the role that tools have in mediating experience and aiding learning. For example, in ancient times people tied knots in ropes to aid memory and help them count. A major insight of Vygotsky's was that language, both written and spoken, can also serve as a (psychological) tool that can mediate experiences and facilitate learning. Even when we are alone, we use the language of others (the words we have heard or read) to help us make sense of what is going on around us, to mediate our experiences. For example, teachers often tell us that something they read the night before really helped them understand what was happening the next day in their classroom. Another example of a psychological tool is the advice of parents or grandparents that we remember years later as we make important decisions in our lives.

Spontaneous and Scientific Concepts

Like Piaget, Vygotsky recognized the importance of experience in learning. He pointed out that schools are places where students' experiences can be organized into categories. Vygotsky differentiated between spontaneous and scientific concepts. Spontaneous concepts, like "brother," are acquired in the normal process of living. Scientific concepts, such as "brotherhood," are learned at school. Scientific concepts are ways to organize experience into the categories created by a particular society. In this way, learning in school is seen as a process of socialization.

Vygotsky and Luria gave adults who had not received formal schooling pictures of objects such as a hammer, a saw, a log, and a hatchet and asked which one didn't fit. These adults would say that all of them were needed. You need a hatchet to chop down a tree, a saw to cut it into logs, and a hammer to pound nails into the logs. A similar group who had received schooling, would pick out the log as different. In order to pick out the log, the adults had to operate on an abstract category (three of these things are tools) rather than on the functional properties of the objects. In the same way, presented with pictures of a bird, a rifle, a dagger, and a bullet, the first group argued that you needed all of them (the bullet goes into the rifle to shoot the bird, and you use the knife to cut it up), and the second group said the bird was different because the other three were weapons. Both groups had developed the same spontaneous concepts, but only those who had gone to school had developed the categories that allowed them to separate one item out as different.

Often, teachers are not aware that they operate at these abstract levels. However, learning may be difficult for students when teachers deal with abstractions and present scientific concepts before the students have had the concrete experiences needed to develop spontaneous concepts. Learning may also be difficult for students who come from social systems that consider different aspects of objects important and have different ways of categorizing experience.

When we lived in Venezuela, we had to learn to categorize many things in new ways in order to make sense of our world there. For example, the cuts of meat in Venezuela are different from those of the United States. When we arrived, we looked for familiar cuts such as chuck roasts, sirloin steaks, or short ribs. What we saw at the butcher shops was a confusing array of unfamiliar, fairly large pieces of meat. They had names such as "solomo," "pulpa negra," or "chocozuela." Since the meat was cut differently, these words could not be translated into English equivalents. In order to buy meat, we had to choose one of the large pieces and then ask for it to be cut into smaller pieces. These smaller pieces had names such as "milanesa," which still did not correspond to the cuts with which we were familiar. Learning to buy meat was difficult because we had to learn not only new vocabulary but also new ways of categorizing experience.

Even when students have had concrete experiences, they may not learn abstract concepts unless they see a purpose. We had a purpose for learning about meat in Venezuela. In school sometimes, purpose is not that obvious. Native speakers of a language, for example, may be required to study grammar. But they may not understand why they are carrying out grammar exercises. After all, they can already use the language to communicate. These students have concrete experience with their language, and the teacher is attempting to help them develop categories such as noun or verb to organize this experience. However, students won't learn abstract concepts until they see a purpose for learning them.

In David's graduate class in linguistics, he tries to give the teachers some purpose for studying language. The students learn to classify words as nouns, verbs, and so on in the process of completing a morphology project. They work on this project in teams. Each team analyzes a sample of words from a science text and a second sample from student writing. Their purpose is to investigate differences between the two samples and to decide whether they can increase students' vocabulary by teaching vocabulary directly. To complete their investigation, they need to use terms like "noun" and "verb." However, they learn these abstract concepts and the terms used to label them as they attempt to answer questions about teaching vocabulary. They learn the linguistics terms because those terms serve a purpose for them.

For second language learners, the study of grammar is a prime example of working at an abstract level. Many students have a great deal of difficulty completing exercises that ask them to identify or manipulate the parts of speech in a sentence. Second language learners whose instruction focuses on grammar are faced with a difficult task. They are trying to move from a very abstract level of grammatical analysis to the concrete experience of using a language to communicate rather than moving from concrete experiences toward an understanding of abstract categories.

Some students may be good at doing the grammar, but those same students may be unable to carry out basic communication in a second language. If the goal of language teaching is to help students use the language to communicate, grammar instruction is not the place to start. In fact, a focus on grammar can seriously inhibit language learning as the example of Ann in her advanced conversation class showed. Instead, when teaching involves students in using language to answer questions of interest, learners develop both a new language and new concepts.

Piaget's ideas of assimilation and accommodation help explain how learners form concepts. His research has shown that children move through a process of decentering that allows them to take different perspectives and focus on different attributes of objects to form categories. Vygotsky's ideas of spontaneous and scientific concepts explain the role of school knowledge in learning. Further, his concepts of mediation and the Zone of Proximal Development seem consistent with a transactional view of learning and an image of the learner as an explorer. For this reason, Piaget's and Vygotsky's theories of learning complement those of Cochrane, Smith, and Gee by explaining what is going on as people learn by doing and receiving feedback.

The Role of the Teacher

We have said that the teacher's role is one of mediation. How can teachers mediate learning? Cazden (1992) offers three different ways a teacher can support language learning. The teacher can provide scaffolding, modeling, or direct instruction.

Scaffolding

The idea behind scaffolding comes from Vygotsky, who said that we learn as we are supported by adults or more capable peers. What we can first do with their help, we can later do alone. An appropriate metaphor for this kind of adult assistance is the scaffold. A scaffold supports a building during its construction and then is taken down once the building is completed. Cazden defines a scaffold as "a temporary framework for construction in progress" (p. 103). A teacher, for example, might ask a student who has written a composition to expand on a certain point, to provide more information to support an argument. The teacher's questions provide the scaffold that allows the writer to move beyond what he or she produced by working alone. A native speaker might ask a nonnative speaker to rephrase or clarify a request, and in the process the nonnative speaker might start to develop the conventional forms needed for communication in the new language.

Marjorie, a fourth-grade teacher whose classroom has many second language learners, uses buddy partners and cooperative techniques with her students. She has found that she can use other students as "teachers" and all students are able to progress. In a response to some reading in a graduate ESL methods course, Marjorie explained how students can provide a scaffold for one another:

> It's been interesting to watch the interaction this last week as my class has been reading the book *The Real Thief* by Stieg. One group of three girls has especially caught my eye. One of the girls is one of my top students academically, having been on the honor roll all year. The other two girls have been in the United States for about two years, and their independent reading level would be considered preprimer. As a team, all three are able to read and *enjoy* the book, even though many of the words are difficult. As one of the "lower" students reads along, every fourth or fifth word she stops and asks "Ab tsi?" ("What?" in Hmong). The "top" student explains and on they move. It has been especially important for the "lower" students to feel a part of the total class and not just be shunted off to the side for a separate reading group because their language development is "not ready" for what the others are reading. They love belonging! I love having all my students feel they are successful students!

Another kind of scaffolding occurs when the teacher or a peer provides a structure with slots to be filled in by the student. Teachers will, for example, read predictable stories to children and leave pauses for the children to fill in words using the language pattern. This approach is more controlled than the scaffolding Marjorie describes.

Another example of controlled scaffolding, called reciprocal teaching, has been developed by Palinscar (1986). During reading sessions, teachers ask a series of questions designed to help students make predictions, generate questions, give summaries, and clarify ideas. Teachers then instruct students in how to ask these same kinds of questions. Eventually, students take on the role of teacher and ask other students the questions. Reciprocal teaching involves students in teaching one another. The questions serve as scaffolds that help students understand what they are reading.

Goldenberg (1991) has developed a kind of scaffolding he calls instructional conversations. Instructional conversations are carefully orchestrated class discussions that give the appearance of casual conversations. There are five instructional elements in an instructional conversation and five conversational elements. The instructional elements include a thematic focus, activation of background knowledge, direct teaching of skills or concepts when necessary, promotion of complex language, and an attempt to have students provide a rationale for their statements. The conversational elements involve few "known-answer" questions—a responsiveness to student contributions, connected discourse, a challenging atmosphere, and general participation. The elements that constitute an instructional conversation are woven together by a skillful teacher. Goldenberg compares these elements to colors woven into a cloth:

> While particular elements can be picked out and identified—just as threads of different color can be picked out and identified on a cloth—instruction and conversation are woven into a seamless whole. The conversation is instructional, and the instruction is conversational (p. 9).

Scaffolds support learners by providing a structure or support they can rely on to build their competence. One role for a teacher is to provide scaffolds or to create situations where students can do this for each other. However, there is a danger that the intentions of the learner may be ignored. A scaffold should help learners do what they are trying to do. This is different from a scaffold that helps learners do what the teacher wants them to do. Searle (1984) suggests that teachers should always be asking "Who's building whose building?"

Modeling

A second kind of adult assistance is provided by modeling. Modeling, something a teacher can do with an entire class, is an intentional action by the teacher. In this respect, models differ from demonstrations, which may not be intentional. If teachers read a book, they are providing a demonstration for their students, showing that they value reading, but they may not even be aware that they are providing that demonstration. However, if teachers want to help students understand directionality in reading, they might decide to model directionality by reading a big book and moving their finger under the print to indicate left-to-right movement. In doing this, a teacher models one aspect of reading. Models provide students with data they can use to construct their own understanding. Cazden (1992) comments that "we must remember that the child's task is to acquire an underlying structure: imitation of the model itself does not suffice. The texts we supply are examples to learn from, not samples to copy" (p. 107).

Direct Instruction

Finally, teachers can support learning through direct instruction. In direct instruction, "the adult not only models a particular utterance but directs the child to say or tell or ask" (p. 108). A parent might say "Bye-bye" and wave to a friend when leaving and then tell the child, "Say 'bye-bye.'" Children's television host, Mr. Rogers, used direct instruction frequently: "Boys and girls, this is a crayon. Can you say 'crayon'?"

As Cazden says, "direct instruction seems to focus on two aspects of language development: appropriate social language use and correct vocabulary" (p. 108). Direct instruction might occur in an ESL lesson in which students first practice introductions. The teacher has three students come to the front of the class to model the correct form:

Mary: Albert, this is Bill.

Albert: Nice to meet you.

Bill: Nice to meet you, too.

Then the teacher divides the students into groups of three to practice introductions, telling them to rotate the roles so every student gets to play each part.

Modeling and direct instruction characterize second language teaching methods such as the audiolingual method that make extensive use of drills. First the teacher models a language pattern and then presents students with sentences that follow the model. Students fill in slots in the pattern with the appropriate word. For example, in a substitution drill a teacher might begin a sequence with "The ball is red" and then give a cue word, "blue." The students should then follow the pattern and put the new word in the slot, "The ball is blue."

Direct instruction, then, involves both modeling and directed practice of particular aspects of language. Yvonne used direct instruction and modeling frequently in her high school Spanish teaching. Though she tried to make practice and short dialogues relevant to students, she decided what structures and vocabulary students were to practice, she modeled the correct pronunciation and intonation, and then students practiced by repeating or working in pairs.

Direct instruction, modeling, and scaffolding may all have a place in an approach based on a transactional model of learning. These are all ways teachers can help mediate learning. However, a teacher who tries to establish an explorer classroom would deemphasize direct instruction and modeling and only use these techniques in response to observed student needs. For example, a teacher might give direct instruction during a minilesson on quotation marks if she has noticed that a group of her students are having difficulty with writing conversations. Or, she might consciously model the kinds of questions students could ask one another in peer writing conferences if students are having difficulty responding to one another's writing. In these cases, the teacher bases her instruction on her observations of her students and her knowledge of language, teaching, learning, and curriculum.

Coming to Know—Personal Invention and Social Convention

Cochrane, Smith, Gee, Piaget, and Vygotsky provide us with complementary perspectives on the learning process that help clarify what we mean when we refer to learning as a transaction and to the learner as an explorer. We would like to add to this picture one other compatible theory of learning. Goodman, Smith, Meredith, and Goodman (1987) write that "Learning conceived as coming to know through the symbolic transformation and representation of experience, involves three phases of mental activity" (p. 98). These three phases are perceiving, ideating, and presenting.

Perceiving is "that first contact through the eyes, ears, nose, or skin with an object or event that people are drawn to or select from the vast complex that surrounds them at any one time and place" (p. 99). All learning begins with the learner noticing something. The awareness may come as the result of a demonstration (intentional or unintentional), and what is perceived may reinforce or challenge existing beliefs and knowledge.

The second phase of coming to know is ideating. "The moment that individuals begin to talk and to think about what they have perceived, the phase of ideating has begun" (p. 102). We form ideas out of our perceptions in the course of talking with others who help mediate the experience for us. The new ideas must be integrated into our current understanding. As we add new concepts, our present concepts are changed through the processes Piaget (1955) has called assimilation and accommodation.

Feedback occurs during the final phase of coming to know, presentation. "After people have conceptualized a perceived event, they then give their conceptions back to the world to be tested against the notions of others" (p. 116). Presentation is important because it makes private concepts public and triggers feedback. When second language students try to communicate in their new language, their presentation allows others to respond in ways that show students whether or not they have used their new language effectively.

Maureen recently described a simple activity that helped her adult ESL students improve their pronunciation by providing them with feedback. Although Maureen's students were not hesitant to talk, they had difficulty understanding one another's English. Maureen asked the students to tape some of their discussions. Then she asked individual students to listen to themselves as they talked. She reported that many of her students were very surprised at how they sounded. They realized that their pronunciation was difficult to understand. The feedback provided by the tape helped them make changes in the way they talked.

Yvonne went through the three phases Goodman et al. (1987) describe as she tried to find the best way to teach her students in different situations. She watched others teach and then thought and studied about teaching in her teacher education classes. After perceiving and ideating, she presented her audiolingual lessons. She received feedback that helped her realize that the method was not working for her students. She tried some new approaches including making dialogues more meaningful and using interview techniques. When students actually did these things, she could evaluate how they worked. Through the many different teaching situations she found herself in, Yvonne continually went through the process of perceiving (This is not working), ideating (What can I do to improve this situation?), and presenting (I will try this and see how students respond).

Personal Invention and Social Convention

Presentations ensure that coming to know involves social activity. Vygotsky viewed learning as a process of internalizing social experience. He emphasized the role of social forces working on the individual. Goodman and Goodman (1990), however, argue that "language [and other aspects of learning] is as much personal invention as social convention" (p. 231). The Goodmans present a view of learning that recognizes both the effects of social forces and the efforts of the individual learner. "Human learners are not passively manipulated by their social experiences; they are actively seeking sense in the world" (p. 231). Social interaction is crucial. Individuals present their personal inventions to a social group that provides feedback the learner can use to shape the inventions to conform, to some degree, with social conventions. We see this process occur when young children begin to write and invent spellings for the words they use. Over time, if children are exposed to lots of print, their spellings change, moving steadily toward conventional usage. The key is to achieve a balance between the two forces of invention and convention. The Goodmans compare invention and convention with the centripetal and centrifugal forces that keep a satellite rotating around the earth. Both forces are needed to keep the satellite in orbit. In the same way, in classrooms, if students are allowed to write any way they wish, they may produce spellings no one can read. On the other hand, if teachers insist on correct spelling, some students may choose not to write at all.

Yvonne has tried out new ways of teaching, and these are her personal inventions. However, social conventions constrain the kinds of inventions she is likely to try. She can't bribe her students to study by offering them large amounts of money. Sometimes the social conventions are so strong that they discourage teachers from personal invention. Their students may respond negatively or not at all to things they try. Teachers may be intimidated by coworkers or administrators. On the other hand, some social convention is appropriate. While teachers need freedom to be creative, they also have the responsibility not to disturb other teachers' classes.

When second language learners try to communicate in their new language, they often invent structures or words based on what they know about the language. For example, many students learning Spanish use "Yo gusto" instead of the irregular, conventional form "Me gusta" for "I like" since other verbs add "o" to form the first-person singular.

Yvonne's Venezuelan friends were amused when she used "coliflor," the word for cauliflower, to refer to a hummingbird. Two conventional words are "colibri" or "chupaflor," and Yvonne seems to have combined these in her invention. In cases like this, when second language learners' inventions depart too far from social conventions, the feedback provided by native speakers helps learners seek a new way to express themselves. In the process, they learn a new language. They become part of the English (or French or Spanish) speakers' club. And they retain club membership so long as their personal inventions don't violate conventional club rules.

Conclusion—Learning as Exploration

Together, the theories presented here provide support for adopting a transactional view of learning and an explorer image of the learner. The different theorists we have discussed all view learning as an active process of constructing meaning in collaboration with others. We have developed this general view of learning in some detail to provide a context for our discussion of the different theories of second language learning in the following chapters. We will evaluate those theories by considering how consistent they are with the view of learning that we have developed here because we believe that learning a second language is only one instance of the more general process of learning.

Applications

1. Think of something you have learned to do. For example, have you learned to speak a second language, to play a musical instrument, or to build something? Relate the six steps of learning that Cochrane et al. propose to your own experience. Do your experiences fit what the theorists have suggested? Discuss this with a partner.

2. Smith defines sensitivity as "the absence of any expectation that learning will not take place or that it will be difficult." Can you think of any situation in which you were prevented from learning because of someone else's lack of sensitivity? Write about it and then share in a group.

3. Gee discusses the idea that people are members of different discourse groups. Try to identify some of the discourse groups you are part of and identify characteristics of each group. Share with a partner. Think about a second language learner you know. What are some of the different discourse groups that students might belong to? Discuss.

4. Think back to a learning experience where someone helped you to succeed. How does your experience fit in with Vygotsky's idea of a Zone of Proximal Development? Share your experience with others.

5. Cazden describes scaffolding, modeling, and direct instruction. Think of examples of each that you have done or have seen done with second language learners. Share the examples in a small group.

6. While learners are creative, their learning is controlled by people and situations that surround them. In a small group, brainstorm some examples of how social conventions influence inventions. Share your ideas with the larger group and discuss the implications invention and social convention have for teaching.

CHAPTER FOUR

What Do We Acquire When We Acquire A Language?

*I*n our discussion of the world of the school, we have reviewed different theories of how people learn to create a context for our discussion of how people learn languages, and particularly how people learn second languages. Our contention is that language learning is a specific example of a more general process, and that any theory of language learning we hold must be consistent with our beliefs about learning in general.

In this chapter we consider just what it is that people acquire when they acquire a language. The answer to this question may seem simple enough at first, but in fact, human languages are complex, and language, thought, and culture are interrelated.

Kinds of Competence

Different linguistic theories have given different answers to the question, "What do we acquire when we acquire a language?" Both linguists and language teachers have attempted to answer the question by identifying the kinds of competence people attain as they develop a new language. These include grammatical, pragmatic, and communicative competence.

Grammatical Competence

In the United States, at least, most of the current research in linguistics is based on the work of Noam Chomsky, who has attempted to develop a theory of language that describes particular languages. From these descriptions he hopes to abstract common properties that would constitute a universal grammar.

> Chomsky seeks to attain two parallel, interrelated goals in the study of language—namely to develop (i) a Theory of Language and (ii) a Theory of Language Acquisition. The Theory of Language will concern itself with what are the defining characteristics of natural (i.e. human) languages and the Theory of Language Acquisition with the question of how children acquire their native language(s). Of the two, the task (i) of developing a Theory of Language is—in Chomsky's view—logically prior to task (ii) of developing a Theory of Language Acquisition, since only if we know what language is can we develop theories of how it is acquired (Radford, 1981).

Chomsky's studies of language have led him and others working within his linguistic framework to advance the claim that humans are genetically equipped with language-specific knowledge. Chomsky refers to this knowledge as Universal Grammar (UG). We have what Chomsky calls a Language Acquisition Device (LAD), or an innate ability to acquire languages quickly and easily. To make an analogy with computers, Chomsky's claim might be that humans are born with built-in hardware (the LAD) that allows them to run a number of different kinds of software (human languages) if they are programmed properly.

For Chomsky, "a grammar of a language is a model of the linguistic competence of the fluent native speaker of the language" (p. 2). Grammatical competence includes knowledge of syntax, phonology, and semantics—that is, it allows a person to put words in the right sequence (syntax), to pronounce and comprehend words (phonology), and to derive meaning from what others say (semantics).

We want to emphasize that grammatical competence is not conscious knowledge. It is not the ability to put commas in the right place or to use "different from" instead of "different to." Those are matters of usage related to specific varieties of English, particularly standard written English. Grammatical competence from a linguistic perspective includes the semantic knowledge that "The dogs bit the man" means something different from "The man bit the dogs."

Grammatical competence also includes the phonological knowledge that the plural "s" on dogs is pronounced with a "z" sound, and the syntactic knowledge that "The the bit dogs man" is not an acceptable arrangement of words. This knowledge is implicit, not conscious, for most speakers. They can use the language to communicate, but they can't explain the rules they are using.

Chomsky's work attempts to describe what it is that speakers of a language, such as English, know that allows them to both comprehend a language and speak the language so native speakers can understand. He believes that people develop grammatical competence because of their innate disposition to acquire language:

> The main argument . . . is that without some endowment (first or second) language learning would be impossible because the input data are insufficiently "rich" to allow acquisition ever to occur, much less to occur (so uniformly and so quickly) in about five years for child language, and especially not if the child (or adult) were only equipped with general inductive learning procedures with which to attempt to make sense of that input (Larsen-Freeman and Long, p. 228).

A consideration of what happens as children acquire languages provides support for Chomsky's claim. Caretakers, for example, generally respond to the truth value of an utterance—what the child says—rather than to the correctness of the grammar. So, if a child says, "I goed to see my friend," a caretaker might respond with "When did you go?" or "Who did you see?" but not with "You mean you *went* to see your friend." Young children's grammar is seldom corrected. In addition, there are no negative examples in adult speech that children can use for inductive learning to take place. Children would need to be able to contrast grammatical and ungrammatical utterances to decide which is right, but they aren't exposed to such incorrect examples. Adults don't produce sentences like "I goed to see the movie yesterday" that they then label as incorrect.

We should add here that we are not only talking about developing standard English. Children acquire the grammar of the variety of the language they hear. In some dialects a sentence like "I don't have no money" would be acceptable. In schools, students may be exposed to and may acquire additional languages or additional varieties of one language. However, Chomsky's point is that children must figure out how language works without ever hearing negative examples that are set up clearly to contrast with positive examples.

Chomsky explains children's ability to hypothesize rules based on positive evidence alone with the assumption that children begin with a restricted idea of what is possible in a grammar and only add other possibilities if they hear positive examples. To take an example from White (1987), many languages require that prepositions precede noun phrases as in (2a), but prohibit ending a sentence with a preposition as shown in (2b).

2(a) With which friend does Dorothy live?
  (b) Which friend does Dorothy live with?

Chomsky would explain this by saying that children begin by assuming that only sentences like (2a) are acceptable. If they speak a language like English, however, they receive positive evidence that sentences such as (2b) are also correct (at least in most dialects). On the other hand, a child learning Spanish would never hear sentences that are the equivalent of (2b). A sentence like "¿Cuál amigo vive Dorothy con?" would not be grammatical in any dialect of Spanish, so Spanish-speaking children would never get positive evidence to that effect, and there would be no need for them to alter the initial assumption that prepositions always precede nouns.

One interesting finding is that second language learners seem to begin with restricted or conservative assumptions about a new language rather than transferring rules from the first language to the second. White, for example, found that English speakers learning French did not assume that sentences like (2b) were acceptable in French, and hearing no evidence to the contrary, they never produced those kinds of sentences even though the structure is permissible in English.

Chomsky has provided us with new understandings of the structure of our language, but some of his assumptions about language acquisition have been challenged. For example, he believes that children learn language quickly and that most learning is complete by age five. However, a number of studies have shown that much of the syntax of English is not learned until later adolescence. Also, Chomsky argues that certain syntactic principles must be innate because otherwise there would be no way for someone to learn them. This assumption has also been questioned. As Larsen-Freeman and Long point out, "General cognitive strategies and notions, such as conservative hypothesis-formation, developmental sequences based on cumulative complexity, and avoidance of discontinuity, are being used to reanalyze certain aspects of Universal Grammar" (pp. 236–237). The preposition examples show how a child might begin with a conservative hypothesis and then develop a more complex one based on language he or she hears, but without any innate sense of linguistic structure.

Competence and Performance

Chomsky also distinguishes between competence and performance. A speaker's competence may differ from his or her actual performance at any given time. Performance errors may result from a speaker's being nervous, tired, bored, uninterested, rebellious, and so forth. For example, ten-year-old Francisco, educated in both Mexico and the United States, understands, speaks, reads, and writes English well despite having an accent. When he arrives at a new school, his teacher first tries to engage him in friendly conversation and then calls on him to answer questions. He responds haltingly because he is nervous and is unaccustomed to the informal classroom atmosphere. Based on his performance, his teacher assumes Francisco understands and speaks very little English. Actually, his competence in English is much greater than his performance would suggest.

We can see another example of the difference between competence and performance in one school with a large number of African-American students. Since the students spoke only black dialect in school, teachers assumed that these students needed to be drilled on standard English in order to speak correctly and to read texts written in standard English. One day a teacher discovered that these students could speak "standard" English, but they chose not to. The teacher overheard the students imitating their teachers' standard accents perfectly to make fun of them when the students thought no teachers were around. These students had the competence to speak standard English but did not show it by their everyday performance. This also shows that factors outside the classroom can influence students' classroom actions. These students experienced peer pressure to speak black vernacular English (to enter that discourse), so attempts to change the variety of language they spoke by drilling them on standard English were not likely to succeed.

Pragmatic Competence

Chomsky's work has focused primarily on describing aspects of grammatical competence, but he also recognizes that linguistic competence includes pragmatic competence. For Chomsky, "Pragmatics is concerned with the role played by nonlinguistic information, such as background knowledge and personal beliefs in our use and interpretation of sentences" (Chomsky in Radford, 1981, p. 3).

Smith (1983) points out that language can serve three functions: the referential function, which speakers use to get and give basic information; the expressive function, which speakers use to show their attitude toward what they are saying (perspective taking); and the integrative function, which speakers use to mark their social identity (using different varieties of language for social purposes). Speakers of a language need grammatical competence for the referential function. The expressive and integrative functions require pragmatic competence.

Gee (1988) explains the expressive function: "When we speak, we do not just talk about the world . . . we take a particular perspective or viewpoint on the information we communicate" (p. 204). We reveal our viewpoints, our attitude, by stressing certain words, by pausing, even by choosing from among synonyms those words that carry the emotional tone we wish to communicate. Even with a simple sentence such as "I like cake," we can change the meaning by stressing different words. Stressing "I," for example, can set us in opposition to someone else (my wife hates it). Choosing "like" rather than "love" allows us to show a different attitude toward what we are saying. Finally, stressing "cake" might set us apart from someone who prefers cookies or pie. When we acquire a language, then, we acquire not only the ability to communicate certain ideas, but also ways to express our attitudes toward those ideas.

Gee also explains what is meant by the integrative function of language, which is the ability to vary language for social reasons. This is what the African-American students who spoke black vernacular in class but spoke standard English to make fun of their teachers were able to do. Gee suggests that two forces motivate language use. These are "the desire for status in regard to whatever reference group(s) one admires and the desire for solidarity with those one views as peers" (p. 212). By speaking black vernacular in class, the African Americans chose solidarity over their teachers' attempts to have them use a variety of English that might improve their status (at least from the teachers' perspective). Smith's idea of "clubs" fits in here. As part of joining a club, we learn to use the variety of English that the other club members use. The African-American students who spoke black vernacular were signaling their club membership through their choice of a particular variety of English.

Since languages give speakers options—different ways to say the same thing—second language learners must be aware of the social effects of choosing one way of saying something over another if they seek status and/or solidarity. Proficient language users are able to change from more to less formal registers depending on their audience and purpose for speaking. Language variation to mark social class can include changes in syntax, vocabulary, or pronunciation. While we were in Venezuela we noticed that our maid spoke more rapidly and dropped many endings when speaking with members of her family. At first we thought she was speaking more slowly and clearly to us because we were foreigners. However, when Venezuelan professors came to our home, we realized that she dropped her dialect when speaking to people she perceived to be of a higher social status. A tension always exists between solidarity and status. In classrooms, teachers should realize that asking students to speak or write a certain way has definite social consequences for them. At times solidarity with their peers may be more important than academic achievement.

Part of what we acquire when we acquire a new language is the ability to choose language that reflects status or solidarity in appropriate ways. For example, when we taught at the university in Mérida, Venezuela, many of our interactions with other professors and with students took place in Spanish. Our grammatical competence allowed us to communicate, but we did not always choose the right variety of language to achieve either status or solidarity. The relationship in Latin America between students and professors is different from the relationship we have with our graduate students in the United States. In Venezuela professors maintain a position of such high respect that students do not expect their professors to treat them like friends. We came to realize that in interactions with students we needed to remain rather formal and even demanding if we wished to keep their respect as well as the respect of the other professors with whom we worked. This meant that the kind of language we used with students had to be different from the language we used with other professors.

Acquiring a second language, then, may entail a good deal more than learning a new set of words, how to pronounce them, and how to arrange them in correct sequences. Gee concludes, "The approach I am taking here sees second language learning as a form of enculturation since learning a language . . . necessarily involves learning the perspectives and identities as well as the ways of displaying them, that a culture allows and values" (p. 220).

Francisco, for example, who had grammatical competence, had only recently arrived in this country. He lacked pragmatic competence. He needed to understand how language worked in his new classroom and what was expected of him before he could really use all aspects of English competently.

Communicative Competence

Background knowledge and personal beliefs lead speakers to take certain attitudes toward what they say and to vary their language to fit the social situation. The ability to choose socially appropriate language constitutes an important part of what Hymes (1970) refers to as communicative competence. Hymes argues, "The ability to speak competently not only involves knowing the grammar of a language, but also knowing what to say to whom, when, and in what circumstances" (Hymes, in Scarcella and Oxford 1991, p. 68).

A number of methods of teaching a second language have been designed to move students beyond grammatical competence. Communicative teaching has as its goal the development of communicative competence, which Larsen-Freeman (1986) defines as "being able to use the language appropriate to a given social context" (p. 131):

When we communicate, we use the language to accomplish some function, such as arguing, persuading, or promising. Moreover, we carry out these functions within a social context. . . . It is through the interaction between speaker and listener (or reader and writer) that meaning becomes clear. The listener gives the speaker feedback as to whether or not he understands what the speaker has said (p. 123).

We became more aware of the importance of helping students develop communicative competence while living in Venezuela. Both of us speak Spanish well enough to communicate (we have grammatical competence), but at times we found ourselves lacking in communicative competence. For example, in Mérida there is a very popular bakery where many people go to get fresh breads, rolls, and pastries. At certain times of the day, the long counter of the bakery has people crowded two or three deep. We found ourselves avoiding these busy times because we had trouble getting the attention of the clerks. The orderly rules for taking turns that applied in the United States didn't apply at the bakery.

On one occasion Yvonne waited helplessly twenty minutes as people came, called out their orders to the clerks, and left with their purchases. Finally, a man noticed how long she had been standing there, and he called to the clerk to help the señora. Yvonne knew what words to use, she could understand the Spanish, but she simply could not call out her order aggressively as had all the Venezuelans who came and went. She lacked the communicative competence needed to buy bread in that situation.

Canale and Swain (1980) have expanded the definition of communicative competence to include grammatical competence, sociolinguistic competence, discourse competence, and strategic competence. Grammatical competence, the knowledge of the linguistic code itself, is what most second language teaching methods have focused on.

Sociolinguistic Competence

Sociolinguistic competence is the ability to say the right thing in a certain social situation. This is hard enough in one's first language, and developing sociolinguistic competence in a second language is even more difficult. A professor friend of ours from Venezuela came to study with us in California. We took trips with her along the coast and to Yosemite with the dean of our graduate school and his wife. Our Venezuelan friend was very impressed with the incredibly beautiful views and continually exclaimed, "Oh, my God! That's so beautiful!" In Spanish, "Dios mío" ("My God") is a very mild expression, so she thought nothing of the direct translation. However, coming from this sophisticated professor in that company, the words sounded completely wrong. In other settings with other people, there would be nothing unusual about her words. One of the problems for second language learners, especially for adults, is that teachers will seldom explain sociolinguistic gaffes. However, students benefit when teachers help them develop both grammatical and sociolinguistic competence.

A second example from Spanish is the word *epa*. In Venezuela, that expression is used to get someone's attention. However, one must be careful not to use the word in certain social situations. It's fine, for example, for college students to use it to get a friend's attention around campus, but if a female in a nice restaurant used the expression to summon a waiter, it would be considered very rude. Of course, there are hundreds of examples like this in every language, and as educators working with second language learners, we should be sensitive to our students when they know the words but use them inappropriately.

Widdowson (1978) points out, "The learning of a language, then, involves acquiring the ability to compose correct sentences. That is one aspect of the matter. But it also involves acquiring an understanding of which sentences, or parts of sentences, are appropriate in a particular context" (p. 3). Widdowson refers to the knowledge of how to compose correct utterances as "usage," and understanding how to use those expressions correctly in various social contexts as "use." This distinction between usage and use is similar to the distinction between grammatical and sociolinguistic competence.

Second language users need both grammatical and communicative competence to function in a new language community. Teachers can help students gain both kinds of competence. To some degree, the audiolingual method helped students develop sociolinguistic competence through role play and dialogues, but the situations often were contrived and designed primarily to teach a grammar point.

When teaching adult ESL, Yvonne and her teaching partner, Jean, helped students develop language for the situations they would encounter every day. The teachers and students carried out role plays for buying groceries at the supermarket, going to the doctor, applying for jobs, and communicating with teachers. These role plays created a social context for language use and students developed sociolinguistic competence.

Discourse Competence

A third component of communicative competence is discourse competence. Speech or writing can't be a set of separate sentences, no matter how grammatically correct they might be. The discourse has to hang together and make sense. A competent language user knows how to keep a conversation going. This includes starting a conversation, entering a conversation when others are speaking, contributing to a conversation, and ending a conversation. In addition, discourse competence includes the ability to express ideas through different genres of writing.

In her early teaching, Yvonne often had students write exercises that consisted of sets of unrelated sentences, usually focusing on some grammatical point. A typical exercise required students to change all the sentences from present to future tense. These kinds of exercises didn't take discourse competence into account. In contrast, while teaching adult ESL Yvonne had her students write letters and skits. In this process, the students produced oral and written texts that were logically connected. These activities helped the students develop discourse competence.

A method of teaching second languages that is particularly well suited to developing discourse competence is problem posing. In this method, students identify problems they face at home or in the workplace and then plan social action to remedy the problems. The interactive focus of problem posing makes it possible for students to develop discourse competence. Students have to talk together and also use written language for a variety of functions as they pose and solve problems.

Kathy, who teaches ESL to high school students from a variety of language backgrounds, uses problem posing to help her students develop discourse competence. She describes some of the activities her students have been involved in:

> In my ESL classes students have done participatory research, gathering information to present about the problems they have chosen to work with. Each group presentation has been videotaped and critiqued by students. Each project had to answer the questions: What did we want to know? How did we get the information? What did we find out? What are we doing about this problem?

One year groups chose drugs and gangs as two of their main concerns. They gathered information on these subjects from the library, the newspaper, and from fellow students. Then they invited a group called House of Hope to come and speak to the class. This group works with gang members, helping them to find jobs and get back into school. They invited Roosevelt High School graduates who were in college and successfully working toward their goals to come and tell how they had dealt with these problems as newcomers at Roosevelt.

We wrote a grant for Drug Free School Zone money, used the money to have T-shirts made with a message, and gave them away. The message on the T-shirts was "Crackdown on Drugs." It displayed a fist breaking down a brick wall. That T-shirt became the most popular T-shirt on campus that year. The basketball team ordered the shirts for everyone on the team. My students went to the elementary school down the street and talked to students in all fifth- and sixth-grade classes and gave away free T-shirts to the elementary school kids in those classes.

As Kathy's students gather information and present ideas orally and in writing, they develop their communicative competence, and especially their discourse competence. They work together as they learn how to present persuasive messages that hold together and make sense to others.

Strategic Competence

Canale and Swain point out that communicative competence also includes strategic competence. Second language learners develop strategies to communicate more effectively and to remedy problems caused by communication breakdowns. A number of strategies have been identified. Speakers may paraphrase if they are not sure of a word. While in Venezuela, Yvonne often found herself paraphrasing when talking to the maid about different kitchen objects and foods. When looking for the missing spatula she asked for "the white thing that has rubber on the end to clean out the bowl," and when describing a fruit drink as opposed to pure juice, she asked for "the juice that you add water and sugar to."

Another strategy language learners use is to make up a word to describe something in hopes that the person they are talking to will supply the word. Wells and Chang-Wells (1992) recorded a conversation in which Marilda employs this strategy by coining the word "windfinder" for weather vane. She could also paraphrase by referring to the weather vane as "the thing that helps us see which way the wind is blowing."

A third strategy is transfer. This might involve using the structure of the primary language with English words. For example, a Spanish speaker might say, "I have a book red," following Spanish syntax and putting the adjective after the noun. Learners also use the strategy of inserting a primary language word into an English sentence, "I have a *libro* red." In addition, direct translation is often common. ESL student teachers we worked with in Venezuela would ask, "Do you *use* a sweater or a bathing suit at the beach?" They translated directly from Spanish (*usar*—to wear). Language learners may also directly ask for assistance, "How do you say 'libro' in English?" Or they may try acting out the word, hoping the other person will supply it.

A fourth type of strategy that many second language learners use is avoidance. They may avoid a topic because they don't feel competent to talk about it in the target language, or they may stop in the middle of an explanation or story because the linguistic demands are simply too great. Cohen and Olshtain (1993) describe examples of avoidance during an experiment in which second language speakers had to make requests in different social situations. For example, one student began a sentence "I don't have any exc-" and stopped because, as he reported, he wasn't sure how to pronounce the "x" sound. In another case, a student wanted to explain that she was late to a meeting because the bus did not come, but she couldn't think of how to say that in English, so she changed her message to "I missed the bus."

Strategies such as paraphrasing, circumlocution, transfer from the primary language, and avoidance help second language learners communicate in a new language. Successful language learners develop a number of such strategies, but it is important for teachers to be aware of the ones students are using. In some cases, students need additional strategies, so they can continue to develop language proficiency. For example, if students always rely on the teacher for the words or spellings they need, they may not develop the ability to produce the needed language independently. On the other hand, if students avoid certain words or topics, teachers may want to consider activities where students would find a functional use for those topics and that language.

When we acquire a language, we acquire grammatical competence, pragmatic competence, and communicative competence. This expanded view of what language learners acquire when they acquire a language has led to teaching methods, such as problem posing, that involve using language for real communication. In fact, becoming competent in a new language is best viewed as a process of learning about and becoming part of a new culture. In this process, students learn a new language, new ways of thinking, and new ways of looking at the world. We might say that what we acquire when we acquire a new language is a new world view and a new way to talk about that world view.

Language, Thought, and Culture

The Hmong people provide a good example of how acquiring a new language also entails acquiring a new world view. Hmong speakers who come to the United States from Southeast Asia move not only physically but also across time. Their nomadic, agrarian society uses only hand tools, so many Hmong who come to America must try to understand a highly technological society. This involves learning new words for new concepts and a new way of viewing the world. Farming in the Central Valley of California is very different from farming in Laos. In California, farmers use a variety of machines and chemicals to help them produce their crops. Hmong farmers may have to rethink the whole idea of farming. In Laos, where the Hmong practiced slash-and-burn agriculture, they moved frequently. In California, they must cope with the idea of the ownership of land. Acquiring English is just one part of a process that enables the Hmong to see and talk about the world in a different way.

In some cases, immigrants, such as the Hmong, retain certain ways of acting and thinking, even if they learn English. In English there are a great number of different family names. People with the same last names can't be assumed to be part of the same families. Our name is Freeman, but we are not related to any of the other Freemans in our city. In contrast, there are only eighteen to twenty Hmong clan names. In North America these clan names serve as last names. For the Hmong, clan membership is important. If Hmong people travel to a city where they have never been before, they need only to look up their clan name in the phone book. A phone call is all that is needed to find food and lodging for the night even though they may be complete strangers to the family they call. Hmong people may acquire English and still retain their own concept of family names.

We become aware of the connections among language, thought, and culture when we travel or live abroad. In Venezuela we soon learned that people use different expressions to describe the various ways to serve coffee. If one is offered *un café*, one usually gets fairly strong, sugared coffee in a tiny cup. This is a social custom and everywhere one goes, one gets offered un café. In fact, it is socially important both to offer and to accept coffee because the small cup of coffee is an excuse for conversation. In the morning one usually drinks *café con leche*, which is half hot milk and half coffee. At restaurants after a meal one orders coffee by the amount of coffee and milk. *Marrón* is coffee with a little bit of milk, while *guayoyo* has more milk but not as much as café con leche. In Venezuela where coffee beans are grown, there are lots of ways to prepare and talk about the drink. For us, learning about coffee involved learning both language and culture.

Even commonplace occurrences like issuing and receiving invitations vary from one culture to another. After one month in Venezuela, we were feeling a bit hurt because we had not received any social invitations to homes despite the fact people were friendly at work. Several people had mentioned to us that we should stop by sometime, but we waited for a specific invitation with a time and day. Luckily, we had a talk with a sociolinguist who was also new to Mérida. She also felt isolated so decided to ask students in a course how *la visita* (the social visit) was done in this town. The local people explained that it is the obligation of the newcomer to visit first and that what we considered a casual comment had really been a definite invitation. She also discovered that if we, in turn, wanted people to visit us, we would need to specifically say, "Come by sometime and see where we live." That way people would feel free to visit us as newcomers. We needed to look at invitations in a new way to understand the social environment in which we lived.

When we acquire a new language, then, we may also acquire at least some aspects of a new culture. Do we also acquire new ways of thinking? The idea that language shapes thinking was advanced most forcefully by Whorf (1956), who wrote, "The background linguistic system (in other words, the grammar) of each language is not merely a reproducing instrument for voicing ideas but is itself the shaper of ideas" (p. 212). Whorf supports his hypothesis that language shapes thought by pointing out that different languages slice up reality in different ways. For example, languages have different numbers of basic color words, and they divide up the color spectrum at different points using these words. A person who learns a particular language learns a set of words that helps him or her see the world in a certain way.

Another example comes from Spanish where the grammatical structure of saying "I lost it"—"Se me perdió—or "I broke it"—"Se me quebró"—literally translates "It lost itself" and "It broke itself." The *me* in each construction is incidental as if the speaker is suggesting that "I just happened to be there." In the strong Whorfian view, one could say that because Spanish speakers express themselves in this way, in their culture people never take the blame for anything.

Whorf's hypothesis of linguistic determinism argues strongly that our language determines our world view. This hypothesis has been discounted by most linguists. It is probably more accurate to say that languages reflect what is important to their speakers than to say that a language determines how speakers perceive reality. Eskimos may have more words for snow than we do, but this does not imply that they see snow differently. Instead, it suggests that snow is important to them (just as it is important to English-speaking skiers, who also have an extensive set of terms to describe various snow conditions). Nevertheless, there is a link between language and thinking, and learning a new language does, to some extent, involve new ways of looking at the world. Hakuta (1986), for example, has found that bilinguals are more flexible than monolinguals in problem solving and have certain cognitive advantages because of their ability to take different perspectives on the world.

Language, culture, and thought are all interrelated. When someone acquires a new language, that person—to some degree at least—is entering a new culture and adopting a new way of looking at and thinking about the world. As a result, theories of second language acquisition need to encompass a number of factors if they are to account for the process people go through as they learn a new language. Current theories of second language acquisition are based on research from different fields including linguistics, psychology, sociology, and neurolinguistics.

Kinds of SLA Research: Psycholinguistic, Sociolinguistic, Neurolinguistic

Research in second language acquisition has been carried out from different perspectives. Psycholinguists look for insights into SLA from linguistics and psychology. They examine the system of language the learner is developing. This system is referred to as the learner's interlanguage. An interlanguage falls somewhere between the learner's native language and the target language.

Psycholinguists use evidence from errors to determine learners' strategies. For example, if someone produces a form like "goed," the strategy might be overgeneralization of the past tense rule to an irregular verb. Seliger (1988) identifies these three major questions of psycholinguistics:

1. How does the learner develop his or her second language system? What are thought to be the processes involved?
2. What role does previous knowledge, such as the first language, play in second language acquisition?
3. What psychological characteristics contribute to successful second language acquisition? Are there good learners and bad learners? (p. 20)

A second perspective on SLA, sociolinguistic research, looks at the effects of culture on language acquisition. Beebe (1987) lists these major questions that sociolinguists attempt to answer:

1. Is interlanguage variation systematic or random and, if systematic, according to what social variables does it vary?
2. Does the learner's interlanguage change over time?
3. What is the role of sociolinguistic transfer in L2 development?
4. What is the nature of L2 communicative competence?
5. What is the "cause" of variation in interlanguage? (pp. 3–4)

Neurolinguistic research is a newer field, and the results of this research have not yet been extensively applied to second language teaching. However, neurolinguists have made advances in their understanding of how the brain works to process language. These are some of the questions that neurolinguists are attempting to answer:

1. Where in the brain are first and second languages located?
2. What are the ways that languages with different characteristics are represented in the brain?
3. Is there a critical period for second language acquisition?

All three areas, psycholinguistics, sociolinguistics, and neurolinguistics, have contributed to an understanding of SLA.

Theoretical and Applied Research

Research in SLA can be either theoretical or applied. Examples of theoretical research would be a study of the natural order of acquisition of morphemes or a study of the relationship between intelligence and language aptitude. A theoretical researcher, for example, might develop a theory that the effects of reading in the second language will be reflected in students' second language writing. The researcher might then look at the writing of second language learners for evidence of the effects of reading. As Krashen (1985) observes, "Purely theoretical research does not have a direct impact on the second language classroom but adds to our knowledge of how second languages are acquired" (p. 46).

Applied research, in contrast, "attempts to answer practical problems directly without recourse to theory" (p. 47). An example of applied research would be a study that compares two methods of language teaching to see which method results in greater proficiency. For example, a researcher could have students read and write, setting up different ways of organizing the reading and writing. Some students would read, discuss, and write. Others would read and then write with no discussion. By looking at the student writing from the two groups, the researcher could determine if the discussion improved the quality of the writing, thus giving teachers some specific ideas to help students in their second language writing. This sort of research could be done without reference to any particular theory of learning.

Krashen suggests that both theoretical and applied research form the basis for SLA theory. A theory of second language acquisition must fit the findings of theoretical research, but "a valid theory must also be consistent with the results of applied research" (p. 47). In other words, both kinds of research are necessary in the formation of SLA theory. Further, "methodology in second language teaching is related to second language theory, not directly to research" (p. 47). Attempts to apply research directly have not been productive. As Krashen says, "I made this error several years ago when I suggested that the natural order of acquisition become the new grammatical syllabus" (p. 47). Instead, SLA theory acts to mediate between research and practice. Teachers can benefit from the knowledge they gain in their daily practice. "Methodologists are missing a rich source of information, however, if they neglect theory" (p. 48). Further, "without theory, there is no way to distinguish effective teaching procedures from ritual, no way to determine which aspects of a method are and are not helpful" (p. 52).

Theory and Research in the Classroom

A knowledge of SLA theory, then, allows a teacher to reflect on and to refine day-to-day practice. At the same time, daily activities help shape theory. Earlier we discussed the differences between orientation, approach, and technique. Now we can say that our orientation constitutes our working theory. Our orientation is a set of beliefs about language, teaching, learning, and curriculum, and we test our practice (our methods and techniques) against these beliefs. At the same time, as we reflect on our daily practice, we constantly test the beliefs that constitute our orientation. For this reason, we see teachers as teacher researchers who use their own classrooms to test out their ideas about language, teaching, learning, and curriculum.

Conclusion

We began this chapter by asking what it is that people acquire when they acquire a second language. Some methods of teaching a second language are based on the assumption that what people acquire is a set of words and the grammatical rules needed for comprehending and producing language with those words. These methods have the aim of helping students develop grammatical competence. However, an expanded notion of competence includes both grammatical and pragmatic competence. It is pragmatic competence that allows language users to show their attitude toward what they are hearing or saying and allows them to use different varieties of the language with different social groups.

In addition, when we acquire a language, we acquire communicative competence. In Hymes' words, speakers need to know what to say to whom and in what situations. For that reason, communicative competence includes sociolinguistic competence. Since conversations or written pieces have to hold together, speakers also need to develop discourse competence, the ability to put sentences and longer sections of oral and written text together in a way that makes sense. Finally, language learners need strategies that allow them to communicate when their linguistic resources are limited, so they also need to develop strategic competence. In fact, since language, thought, and culture are closely intertwined, learning a new language may also involve new ways of thinking and new ways of viewing the world.

Research into the process involved in acquiring a language has come from three different perspectives: psycholinguistic, sociolinguistic, and neurolinguistic. This research may be either theoretical or applied. Theories of second language acquisition are based on both kinds of research. A teacher's theory of SLA helps form that teacher's orientation toward teaching second language students. In the next chapter we review the principal theories of SLA that have been developed, and we consider the view of learning and the image of the learner a teacher whose orientation is formed by each type of theory would hold.

Applications

1. Early in this chapter we talked about the difference between "performance" and "competence" and gave a couple of different examples. Can you think of some examples in your own learning or in the learning of students you work with where performance did not reflect competence? Discuss this with a small group.

2. Communicative competence includes the ability to use language that is appropriate for the social situation. Have you been in any situations where you used a second language in ways that you later discovered were not appropriate? Share these with classmates.

3. Second language learners develop a number of strategies like paraphrasing, transfer, and avoidance. Think back about your own use of a second language. Did you use any of these strategies? Or you might think of strategies you have noticed your students using. List some examples to share.

4. Whorf's theory of linguistic determinism suggests that people's language determines their world view. While this theory is questioned by some, there were some examples given in the chapter that point to the relationship of language and thought. Can you think of any examples where language differences might influence how people view the world? Discuss this with a partner.

5. The difference between theoretical and applied research is that one is based on theory and the other does not take theory into account. Can you think of some research you would like to do in SLA? Would your research be theoretical or applied? Discuss this with a small group.

CHAPTER FIVE

What Are the Principal Theories of Second Language Acquisition?

To be most helpful to our English language learners in the world of school, we must have a good understanding of the different theories of second language acquisition. Larsen-Freeman and Long (1991) divide SLA theories into three general types: environmentalist, nativist, and interactionist. Books that provide further discussion of SLA are listed in Appendix B.

Environmentalist Theories

According to Larsen-Freeman and Long:

> Environmentalist theories of learning hold that an organism's nurture, or experience, are of more importance to development than its nature, or innate contributions. Indeed, they will typically deny that innate contributions play any role at all other than that of providing the animal with the internal structure which environmental forces can proceed to shape (p. 249).

Environmentalist theories are associated with behaviorist and neobehaviorist views of learning. The psychological theories of Skinner (1957) and other behaviorists formed the theoretical base for methods of second language teaching, such as the audiolingual method. Although this method is still extremely popular, its theoretical foundation has been largely discredited. Chomsky's (1959) review of Skinner showed quite clearly the difficulties of applying behaviorist stimulus-response models to human language learning.

Recently, psychologists have proposed a neobehaviorist model of learning called connectionism. Gee (1992), for example, describes how a computer in a submarine can be programmed to distinguish between rocks and mines. This computer model uses parallel distributed processing (PDP). The input sonar signal is analyzed. Different weights are assigned to various components of the signal as it goes through a network consisting of several layers. In the end, the computer decides whether the signal is coming from a rock or a mine and does so in a consistent manner. One important feature of PDP systems is that they are self-correcting. The weights given to the different parts of the input system and the strengths of the connections are adjusted so that, in time, the computer interprets the signal accurately nearly all the time. (Of course, with real submarines and real mines, the computer could not afford a long learning period.)

Connectionism holds that environmental, and not innate, influences allow learning to take place. Thus far, applying connectionist theory to language learning has been unsuccessful. When Pinker and Prince (1988) attempted to create a connectionist computer model that would teach the correct formation of past-tense verbs, the computer produced errors that were not similar to those made by children acquiring their first language. The machine could not even be programmed to consistently predict one isolated aspect of grammar, past tenses. (For a critique of connectionist models of reading, see Murphy 1991.)

Connectionist models of learning continue to be researched in hopes of gaining insights into learning and development in the areas of motor control, visual perception, and memory. Connectionism might form the psychological basis for an environmentalist theory of SLA, but environmentalist researchers have been primarily interested in examining external influences on learning, and they often have little to say about what goes on inside learners' heads. On the other hand, these theories have a good deal to say about social and cultural factors that influence acquisition.

Schumann's Acculturation Model

The principal environmentalist theory of SLA is Schumann's (1978) acculturation model. Schumann's model is classified as environmentalist because he claims that acquisition is the result of external factors acting on the learner. He does not discuss any internal cognitive processing that might take place. He bases his theory on studies of individuals learning a second language. Much of the theory can be understood by examining Schumann's analysis of one learner, Alberto.

Alberto, an adult from Costa Rica, acquired English without formal instruction. Alberto's English proficiency was much lower than might be expected, and it improved little over the ten months Schumann studied him. Even though he was intelligent and interacted regularly with native speakers of English, Alberto's own English remained limited. Schumann claimed that Alberto's social and psychological distance from speakers of the target language accounted for his lack of proficiency.

According to Schumann, social distance refers to the relationships between two social groups. He identifies eight factors that influence social distance: social dominance, integration pattern, enclosure, cohesiveness, size, cultural congruence, attitude, and intended length of residence. In almost every case, Alberto fell into a category that predicted limited acquisition. For example, in the area of social dominance, Alberto, who worked in a factory, was in a subordinate social group to those English speakers with whom he was in contact. His group had what Schumann refers to as "high enclosure." They had their own churches and publications, including newspapers, and this kept them apart from the mainstream culture. He was part of a fairly large, cohesive group of Latin American immigrants, and this limited his contact with English speakers as well. His culture differed from that of the target culture, and attitudes between the groups were either neutral or negative. In addition, Alberto only intended to stay in the United States a short time, so he had little interest in becoming proficient.

In addition to social distance, which describes relationships among social groups, Schumann identifies psychological distance, a characteristic of individuals. In situations where social distance neither strongly promotes nor inhibits language acquisition, psychological distance may play a crucial role. A person undergoing culture shock, for example, would experience psychological distance, whereas someone with high motivation to learn the target language would not be so likely to suffer from it. These affective psychological and social factors, according to Schumann, determine the progress of a learner's second language acquisition. As Brown (1980) explains, "Schumann's hypothesis is that the greater the social distance between two cultures, the greater the difficulty the learner will have in learning the second language, and conversely, the smaller the social distance (the greater the social solidarity between the two cultures), the better will be the language learning situation" (p. 133).

Matt and Francesca, two members of an adult ESL class, represent both extremes of Schumann's hypothesis. Matt emigrated to the United States from Yugoslavia as a boy. His parents came to live in a coastal village in northern California. Matt became a fisherman like his father, married, and had a family. Though he maintained his native language, he also was surrounded by English speakers and participated in social events in the fishing community. After he retired, his wife died and his children moved away. He was lonely, so he arranged to marry a woman from Yugoslavia who wanted to come to the United States.

When the couple began attending adult ESL classes, Matt was nearly eighty years old and his wife, Francesca, was seventy-two. They had been married for five years. Matt spoke perfect English, but he felt Francesca needed to learn some English so that she could get around the community. Francesca was a strong and demanding woman who was constantly frustrated by her new country and culture. She liked to cook and sew but did not like to do things outside of the home unless it was to attend church or visit the few other women in the community who could speak her language. The couple came to class almost daily, but Francesca resisted even listening most of the time unless the class discussions centered around shopping, cooking, gardening, or finding bargains. Finally, the couple stopped coming to class. Matt felt he was too old to insist, and Francesca decided she didn't need to learn any more English since she was able to do her shopping and meet her basic needs. Among other factors, such as their different ages when they came to the United States, Matt and Francesca represent two extremes in social distance. Matt felt close to the mainstream culture. Francesca remained distant from it, and one result was her limited proficiency in English.

Schumann also noted the similarities between early stages of SLA and pidginization. Pidgins are languages formed when groups with different languages come into contact, usually for business purposes. Pidgins are quite simple linguistically. For example, plurals are indicated by numbers without inflectional morphology being added to the noun (three boy). Schumann's hypothesis is that social and psychological distance can prevent a second language learner, like Alberto, from moving beyond an interlanguage that resembles a pidgin. Again, Francesca seems to fit the description. Her English was similar to a pidgin. She used English primarily for business transactions.

Some of the second language learners we described in Chapter 1 seem to fit Schumann's analysis quite well. For example, Eugenia, who was the daughter of migrant workers who had been assimilated into their small farming community, would be classified as having little social or psychological distance from the mainstream culture, and she succeeded at school. Juan, on the other hand, was part of a migrant family that was socially distant from the mainstream, and that distance seemed to prevent him from developing English proficiency. Tou, the Hmong boy who became involved with gangs, was alienated from mainstream culture, and this social distance may have contributed to his lack of academic success.

On the other hand, some students are able to maintain their first language and culture and still learn English and succeed academically. For these students the social distance from the mainstream does not seem to inhibit learning. Sharma, the Punjabi girl, for example, maintained many of her Indian customs but did well in school. José Luis, Guillermo, and Patricia were successful even though their goal was to return to El Salvador as soon as possible. Because they had had high social status in El Salvador, the three did not see themselves in a subordinate social position to native English speakers as Alberto did. Also they did not isolate themselves from the mainstream English speakers, but they willingly attended a church where they were the only second language speakers. They also spent time with our American family. They did not feel part of the cohesive Mexican-American group, so they were more likely to be part of the Anglo activities at school. Finally, they believed they could and would succeed and saw United States culture and society as congruent with their needs and desires.

In the final chapters we will explore in more detail the social factors that promote or inhibit language learning by examining different types of minority groups. Students from some groups that remain socially and psychologically distant from the mainstream culture still are able to learn English and succeed academically, and this suggests that social distance is only one factor involved in acquiring a second language. Schumann claims that for a learner to acquire full proficiency in a second language, he or she must be acculturated because SLA is just one aspect of the larger process of acculturation. A learner who is socially distant from members of the target language group might develop referential functions of language (basic communication) but not develop expressive or integrative functions.

Schumann's theory has been attacked on several fronts. For one thing, there are significant differences between pidgins and interlanguages. Larsen-Freeman and Long (1991) conclude their review of Schumann's theory by commenting that

> both group and individual social and psychological factors must surely have some role in a comprehensive theory of SLA, perhaps most obviously as variables conditioning the amount and type of target-language exposure the learner experiences. Equally clearly, on the other hand, it should come as no surprise if a mental process, (second language learning), is not successfully explicable by any theory which ignores linguistic and cognitive variables (p. 266).

Despite these limitations, Schumann's theory provides useful ideas about the effects of external factors on learning. Concepts such as social and psychological distance are useful in helping us understand why certain people succeed or fail in learning a new language, but the help is limited because Schumann says so little about language and cognitive processing.

Environmentalist theories of SLA, like Schumann's, are consistent with an image of the learner as a plant. According to these theories, it is the effect of the environment on the learner that determines whether or not development will occur. If the learner is a plant, then the teacher must be a gardener. The teacher's role is to create an atmosphere in which students can bloom. The teacher (or other students) must also provide the language. Learning takes place, then, in response to the effects of these external stimuli. What the learner brings to the situation is not so important as the social environment.

What are the implications of Schumann's theory for teachers? An environmentalist view would suggest the importance of focusing on social factors in learning and on creating a classroom atmosphere in which students could develop positive attitudes toward speakers of the target language. Beyond that, the theory has little to say about how teachers can plan instruction that would promote language acquisition. Perhaps for this reason, environmentalist approaches to SLA have not led to specific language teaching methods.

Nativist Theories

Nativist theories of SLA assume that humans have a kind of built-in language ability, what Chomsky has called a Language Acquisition Device (LAD). It is this ability that enables children to learn their first language(s) with little apparent effort. As Larsen-Freeman and Long state, "Nativist theories are those which purport to explain acquisition by positing an innate biological endowment that makes learning possible" (p. 227). Although the role of social interaction is prominent in environmentalist theories of SLA, it is minimized in nativist theories.

Krashen's Monitor Model

Krashen's (1982) Monitor Model, based on Chomsky's linguistic theories, is the principal nativist theory of SLA and has probably had the greatest impact on classroom practice. Even though Krashen's ideas have been debated and sometimes discounted by researchers, they have been widely accepted by practitioners because they are understandable and because teachers can see positive results in the classroom.

Krashen suggests that in the early stages of learning a new language, students need messages they can understand, but they do not need to produce the language immediately. They may go through a silent period. When teachers use pictures, gestures, and other means to make the new language comprehensible, and at the same time reduce expectations for student production, students seem to grasp the new language much more quickly without resorting to translation.

The value of the application of this part of Krashen's theory became clear to us as we worked with student teachers in Venezuela. Because of their own experiences as students in English classes, the new teachers at first asked their students to say everything in complete sentences and even asked them to stand and recite what they were learning. Use of visuals was minimal, and chalkboards were filled with vocabulary lists and language structures. Although the topics of the lessons were personally interesting ones to the students—explaining likes and dislikes, or discussing similarities and differences among classmates—the beginning-level English students spent so much energy trying to pronounce words, learn vocabulary, get verb endings right, and put sentences together that little real language acquisition took place.

The student teachers began to use a variety of visuals and to allow students to show comprehension through gestures and one-word answers. In addition, their discussion strategies included more comprehensible input from the teacher. The emphasis in the classroom moved from control of vocabulary and structure to comprehension and interaction. What was most exciting was that the teachers saw how much more the students were remembering and how much more interested they were.

Krashen's Monitor Model consists of five interrelated hypotheses. We explain each and then provide examples and analysis.

The Acquisition-Learning Hypothesis

Krashen begins by making an important distinction between two ways of getting a new language. The first of these is acquisition. According to Krashen we acquire a new language subconsciously as we use the language for various purposes. For example, if we are living in a foreign country and go to the store to buy some food, we may acquire new vocabulary or syntactic structures in the process of negotiating the purchase. We are not focused on the language. Rather, we are using the language for real purposes, and acquisition occurs naturally as we attempt to conduct our business. Krashen (1985) also suggests we can acquire language as we read. In fact, since we can read more rapidly than people speak, written language is a better source for acquisition than oral language.

Acquisition is contrasted with learning in Krashen's theory. Learning is a conscious process in which we focus on various aspects of the language itself. It is what generally occurs in classrooms when teachers divide language up into chunks, present one chunk at a time, and provide students with feedback to indicate how well they have mastered the various aspects of language that have been taught. A teacher might present a lesson on regular verbs in the present tense, for example, giving attention to the "s" that is added to third-person forms in sentences such as "He walks." It is this structure that students are expected to learn, so learning is associated with explicit instruction.

A good example of the acquisition-learning distinction comes from the experiences of José Luis, Guillermo, and Patricia. The teens studied English in El Salvador. This was a case of learning the rules and structures of the language. When they came to Tucson, they did know some English, but it was very limited. In Tucson they were immersed in English and began to acquire the language as they used it daily.

Krashen argues that children acquire (they don't learn) their first language(s) as they use language to communicate and to make sense of the world. Krashen claims that both children and adults have the capacity to acquire language because they possess a Language Acquisition Device. He claims that acquisition accounts for almost all of our language development and that learning plays a minimal role. Second language classrooms can be places for acquisition, but more often they are arenas for learning.

Yvonne was constantly struggling with the difference between acquisition and learning, though she had not studied Krashen's theory and did not even know about it until graduate school. She was worried that students needed to learn the grammar because that is how she had been taught language. However, she saw that students were more involved and more successful when they talked and read about things that were related to their lives. Discussions of taxes, unemployment, nutrition, cultural conflicts, and television programs got students involved in using language, and they acquired language as they used it. Yet, the textbooks available for teaching all seemed to emphasize direct or indirect teaching of grammar and vocabulary. Yvonne had to depart from traditional approaches to change her classroom from a place for learning to a setting for acquisition.

Acquisition/Learning—Fred   Fred Jones studied three years of German in high school and two more years in college. After college he joined the Army and was sent to Germany. He found that he could read signs and some newspaper articles, but he had a great deal of trouble in trying to communicate with native Germans. After he was discharged, he went to work for a company that assigned him to head a branch in Mexico City. On arrival, he took a crash course in Spanish. At the same time he had to try to communicate with his fellow workers, entertain important Mexican businessmen, and use Spanish for daily life such as shopping. After only six months, Fred's spoken Spanish was much better than his German had ever been. What might account for this?

Analysis   Fred learned German in school, but this learned knowledge was not very helpful to him in Germany. On the other hand, he both learned and acquired Spanish in the course of his studies and his daily interactions in Mexico. As a result, his ability to understand and speak Spanish is much better than his German proficiency.

Acquisition/Learning—John John studied four years of high school Spanish. Despite lots of drill and practice with dialogs and exercises with grammar, he could not really understand the Spanish of Hispanics in his community. In college he met María and fell in love. Her family, who felt that maintaining their native language was very important, spoke only Spanish at home. John found that within a short period of time, he was able to understand the conversations at family get-togethers and even contribute at times in Spanish. What would account for his rapid increase in Spanish proficiency?

Analysis This is another contrast between acquisition and learning. John had learned some Spanish in school, but with María and her family he was in an ideal situation for acquisition in a natural setting. Family discussions were on topics of interest to John, or conversations were rich in context. For example, María and her mother would discuss a recipe while cooking, or John and his in-laws would watch a sports event on the Spanish television station. The Spanish input from María's family was comprehensible. As a result, his proficiency improved rapidly.

The Natural Order Hypothesis

Language, according to Krashen, is acquired in a natural order. Linguists have some general ideas about the order of acquisition, but they do not have complete knowledge of the sequence for any language. As a result, the order in which grammatical structures are presented in textbooks is not the same as the natural order of acquisition. Not surprisingly, a study of different second language textbooks reveals different orders of presentation of grammar points.

The Natural Order Hypothesis holds that some aspects of a language are picked up earlier than others. For example, the plural "s" morpheme added to a word like *girl* to form *girls* comes earlier than the third person "s" added to *walk* in *He walks*. Most parents are aware that phonemes like /p/ or /m/ are acquired earlier than others like /r/. That's why English-speaking parents are called "papa" or "mama" by babies, not "rara." In the area of syntax, statements generally precede questions. Children do not acquire the structure of questions early, so they often use statement structures such as "I go store, too?" or "You like teddy?" to pose questions. Krashen points out that all learners of a particular language, such as English, seem to acquire the language in the same order no matter what their first language may be.

The Natural Order applies to language that is acquired, not language that is learned. In fact, students may be asked to learn aspects of language before they are ready to acquire them. The result may be good performance of the items on a test but inability to use the same items in a natural setting. In these cases, students' performance may exceed their competence.

In teaching Spanish, Yvonne found that the expression for "like" was a late acquired item. In Spanish "I like" is "Me gusta" ("It is pleasing to me"). If the things I like are plural, I say, "Me gustan" ("They are pleasing to me"). This structure caused no end of confusion for Yvonne's beginning students. She worked with them diligently explaining how the structure worked and giving examples. Even those who did well on the department test that covered the structure, however, had not acquired it. When Yvonne asked her students to evaluate the course in their daily diary at the end of the semester, almost all the students incorrectly wrote "Yo gusto" for "I like." They had learned that "yo" meant "I" and knew the verb "gustar" was "to like." So they simply conjugated the verb as a regular verb despite all the emphasis on learning the expression "Me gusta."

Teachers who are effective kid watchers and who understand language development do know generally the expected order of acquisition, and they find ways to support students' development. At the same time, they recognize that in a class of thirty students, learners will be at different stages, and a particular lesson would be appropriate for some of the students (because it would fall into their Zone of Proximal Development), but not for others. These teachers recognize that a preset curriculum designed to meet the needs of all the students will probably only meet the needs of a few at any given time.

Natural Order—Mrs. Gomez   Mrs. Gomez is a bilingual fourth-grade teacher. She does lots of reading and writing with her students in Spanish. During ESL time, she believes that students need large doses of drill and practice to master English. She teaches her students how to make plurals and how to form the third-person singular by adding "s" to verbs. What she cannot understand is that when her students speak English with their peers, they use the plural form correctly but consistently leave the "s" off their third-person verbs. What might be the reason for this?

Analysis   Several different factors are at work here. Mrs. Gonzalez seems to feel that while first languages are acquired, second languages must be learned. As a result, she drills her students on parts of the language during ESL time. Mrs. Gonzalez doesn't recognize the difference between learning and acquisition and may not be aware of the natural order of acquisition. She drills her students on the third-person "s," but since they haven't acquired it yet (the third-person "s" is acquired late), they don't use it in natural situations. The third-person "s" is different from the plural "s," which is acquired much earlier.

The Monitor Hypothesis

Krashen explains that learned rules can be used to monitor output as we speak or write, while acquisition provides us with the language we need. Learning can be used to help us check what we produce. The monitor can operate when we have time, when we focus on form, and when we know the rules.

Yvonne applied her monitor during her oral exams for her doctorate. Her committee of five had asked her several questions in English about language acquisition and language learning that she had answered fairly comfortably. Then, one of her committee members asked a question in Spanish, a clear suggestion that Yvonne should also answer in Spanish. Her most vivid memory of the incident was how much she was checking to be sure her Spanish was correct, how much she was applying her monitor. In particular, she was careful to watch for the correct use of the subjunctive mood, verb endings, and adjective agreement, all aspects of Spanish that she had learned rather than acquired. In this situation, Yvonne was focusing on form. She did not want members of her doctoral committee to judge her Spanish as substandard. It seemed especially important in this setting to speak "proper" Spanish. Of course, what she actually said was secondary and to this day she cannot even remember what the question was.

The problem with using the monitor during speaking is that one must sacrifice meaning for accuracy. A person can't concentrate on the form and the meaning at the same time. On the other hand, the monitor is useful in the editing stage of writing. At that point, a writer has time to think about correct form, and the focus on form, rather than meaning, is appropriate. In contrast, at the rough-draft stage, writers who slow down and think about correct form may forget what they were going to write. Monitoring is helpful if the monitor is not over- or underused, but even then the monitor can only check the output.

The teens from El Salvador differed in their use of the monitor. Guillermo in particular focused on communication. He seldom monitored his output and was at times difficult to understand. Nevertheless, he was enthusiastic and personable and used a number of strategies (gestures, tone of voice, and so on) to be sure his listener understood. Guillermo underused his monitor even though he had studied English grammar and knew many of the rules.

His brother, José Luis, on the other hand, was quiet and shy. He did not like to speak English unless he could produce language that was grammatically correct. He too knew the rules, and he applied them carefully. His focus on form kept him from expressing his ideas freely. He overused the monitor.

Patricia seemed less self-conscious than José Luis. She generally concentrated on what she wanted to say rather than how she would say it. At the same time, she did check her output to be sure she was producing understandable English. She also knew the rules and seemed to have found an optimal use of the monitor.

Krashen (1985) claims that error correction in learning situations allows students to modify their knowledge of learned rules, but it has no effect on their acquired language: "According to the theory, the practice of error correction affects learning, not acquisition. When our errors are corrected, we rethink and adjust our conscious rules" (p. 8). Since the monitor can only be accessed under certain conditions, error correction has limited value. Learning, according to Krashen, has no effect on basic language competence.

Monitor—Miss Smith   Miss Smith studied Spanish extensively in high school and college and spent a summer in Guadalajara, Mexico, where she lived with a Mexican family and spoke Spanish every day. After graduation, her company sent her to work in Spain. During her first meeting with local Spanish company representatives, she was conversing fluently in Spanish until she began to use an irregular verb in the subjunctive and couldn't remember the correct verb form. As she tried to decide what form to use, she paused and lost her train of thought. For the rest of the meeting her Spanish was halting and stilted. What could account for her performance?

Analysis   Miss Smith has acquired a good deal of Spanish. However, in a formal setting she begins to overuse her monitor. She tries to remember and apply the rules for the subjunctive and carry on a conversation at the same time. As a result, her rate of speech slows down. She can't focus on what she is saying and how to say it at the same time. She is overusing her monitor to the point that she can no longer communicate effectively.

Monitor—Mary   When Mary was in the first and second grade, she lived in Mexico City and attended a bilingual school where she and her sister were the only *gringas*. While there, she learned to speak Spanish fluently. After returning to the United States, she attended a bilingual school. She also made friends with some children recently arrived from El Salvador. When Mary conversed with her Salvadoran friends, her Spanish was fluent, but when she had to take a Spanish course in high school several years later, she was frustrated at times by the rules of grammar and accents. What might be causing Mary's frustration?

Analysis   Mary has acquired Spanish, but the school puts an emphasis on rules that must be learned. Even though Mary can understand and speak Spanish, she has not studied the rules needed for formal written Spanish, so she does not have the rules to monitor her speech and writing.

Monitor—Yvonne   Yvonne studied Spanish in college, lived in Mexico and South America, and taught Spanish courses. After completing graduate studies, she got a position at a college as Director of Bilingual Education. Because of her ability to speak Spanish and her interest in language arts, local school districts began to ask her to address parents in Spanish. Despite the fact she feels comfortable speaking Spanish with Spanish-speaking friends, she gets nervous when addressing large groups in Spanish. Why might this be?

Analysis   Yvonne has learned Spanish and also been in a number of situations where she acquired Spanish. Normally, she can converse without overusing her monitor. However, when speaking in formal situations, she becomes nervous so she begins to overuse her monitor.

The Input Hypothesis

People acquire language when they receive oral or written messages they understand. Krashen says these messages provide comprehensible input. In order for acquisition to take place, learners must receive input that is slightly beyond their current ability level. Krashen calls this input $i + 1$ (input plus one). If the input contains no structures beyond current competence ($i + 0$), no acquisition takes place. There is nothing new to pick up. On the other hand, if the input is too far beyond the person's current competence ($i + 10$), it becomes incomprehensible noise, and again no acquisition can take place.

Robert, the Hmong boy that Sharon studied, is a good example of a second language learner who did not receive the comprehensible input he needed to acquire English. At home the family spoke Hmong, and many of his friends were also Hmong speakers. In his first two years at school, Robert's teachers did not make extra efforts to be sure that the instruction was understandable. Both teachers used a part-to-whole approach that fragmented the curriculum. As a result, Robert concentrated on math, art, and physical activities. Sharon is now trying a variety of techniques to provide Robert with the input he needs to develop English, but his earlier school experiences delayed his acquisition.

According to Krashen, comprehensible input is the source of all acquired language. He believes that only input leads to acquisition and so output—speaking or writing—is not important. Students do not have to produce language in order to acquire it. However, Krashen (1990) also notes that output can help people learn content, or as he puts it, output can make you smarter.

Input—Mr. Roberts   The students in Mr. Roberts' first-year Spanish class do well in his structured program, although they seem bored at times. Mr. Roberts is careful to introduce only one new structure at a time and drill that structure until the students have mastered it. Although the students are making satisfactory progress, the class seems to lack animation, so to liven things up Mr. Roberts decides to bring in a guest speaker to talk about dating customs among Mexican teenagers. Despite the fact that Mr. Roberts warned the speaker to limit his vocabulary and grammatical structures, the speaker gets carried away with his subject and uses the full range of Spanish. Surprisingly, although the students don't understand everything, they seem to be following most of the lecture. In addition, for the first time all year, they seem interested. What is going on here?

Analysis   The speaker is using structures slightly beyond the students' current level of comprehension. The input is comprehensible because of the students' background knowledge, so it will contribute to their acquisition of Spanish. In addition, the students are interested in the topic and make an effort to understand it. For that reason, the input becomes intake and contributes to acquisition. (See also The Affective Filter Hypothesis section below.)

Input—José   José is in the fifth grade and doing very well this year despite the fact that his fourth-grade teacher, Mrs. George, recommended him for special education. Mrs. George contended that José was in the lowest reading group, had done poorly on standardized tests, and could not do the worksheets assigned to him. José's parents asked that he be given another chance. In fifth grade his teacher had students do lots of reading and writing and work on projects in groups. The children did not use the basal readers or worksheets but did work with literature using drama, art, and music. In only two months, José's English has improved noticeably, and he is reading and writing in English enthusiastically. When Mrs. George insisted that he be tested with the basal reader, José proved that he had jumped two grade levels despite the fact that he had not been working with worksheets or basal readers. What might be the reason for this dramatic progress?

Analysis   Mrs. George emphasized the need for learning. Compared to native speakers of English, José did not do well with formal rules of the new language. José is now in a classroom where activities are designed to increase his acquisition and less emphasis is placed on learning of formal rules. In addition, the kinds of activities his new teacher uses make the English input comprehensible for José. Because of this, José has acquired a great deal of English in a short time, and this acquired language has increased his overall proficiency, as shown on the reading tests.

The Affective Filter Hypothesis

Even if a teacher provides comprehensible input, acquisition may not take place. Affective factors such as anxiety or boredom may serve as a filter that blocks input. When the filter is up, input can't reach those parts of the brain (the LAD) where acquisition occurs. Many language learners realize that the reason they have trouble is because they are nervous or embarrassed and simply "can't concentrate." Lack of desire to learn can also "clog" the affective filter.

Juan Medina, the migrant student, was in a very good school situation. He received academic support in his first language, and he also had two hours a day of English with extra help from tutors and migrant aides. During this time, he received the input needed for acquisition. However, a number of factors served to raise Juan's affective filter and to block the input from becoming intake. Other students at the school and their parents looked down on Juan and referred to him as a "wetback." He was preoccupied with everyday living arrangements, and the possibility that his home would be torn down. He felt the pressures to work and earn money rather than going to school. All of these factors kept Juan from acquiring English even though his classes provided the comprehensible input he needed.

Yvonne's first high school Spanish class included twenty-three boys, who were all on the junior varsity football team, and three girls. Most of the students had signed up for the "new" teacher mainly because they had failed Spanish One the year before. Positive affective factors such as high interest or motivation can help keep the filter down, but those students had neither. Yvonne's major job was to try to lower the students' filter by getting them interested and convincing them they wanted to learn some Spanish!

Since Krashen's theory of language acquisition is based on input, in his discussion of the affective filter he only refers to language that is coming in, not to language the person is attempting to produce. There may also be an output filter. Factors such as nervousness may limit a student's performance. This was the case for Francisco, the Mexican student we described in Chapter 4. Because he was confused and nervous, Francisco's performance did not reflect his competence. We could say that an output filter was blocking his ability to use English. However, when Krashen refers to an affective filter, he is only referring to factors that block input.

Affective Filter—David   David accepts a teaching job in Colombia, South America, even though he doesn't speak any Spanish. Fortunately, his wife speaks good Spanish. David and his wife agree that she will translate for the two of them and also teach him the language when they get there. For the first few months of their stay, the couple lives with a Colombian family in which no one speaks any English. During meals David is frustrated because he can understand little and say nothing. He starts to resent being in his new culture. Besides, he is embarrassed by his inability to speak. After a few weeks he even refuses to try to speak Spanish and discontinues the lessons with his wife. Despite being immersed in Spanish, he doesn't seem to be learning anything. What might be the reason for this?

Analysis   Although David is receiving comprehensible input, the input doesn't become intake that contributes to acquisition because David's affective filter is high. The filter blocks the input from activating the LAD. Factors such as culture shock and being dependent on his wife raised his filter.

Summary

As these scenarios show, Krashen's theory helps explain a number of common situations in which second language learners find themselves. The five interrelated hypotheses constitute Krashen's Monitor Model of SLA. Krashen (1985) sums up his claims by stating, "We acquire when we obtain comprehensible input in a low-anxiety situation, when we are presented with interesting messages, and when we understand these messages" (p. 10).

Kristene, a graduate student and a bilingual teacher, wrote a reflection on her own acquisition of Spanish as a second language after studying Krashen's theory:

> Perhaps my success in Spanish language classes (audiolingual in junior high and grammar-translation in high school) came about because my first exposure to Spanish was through communicative practice in real situations as Krashen suggests. I lived in Spain at the age of ten for six months. My parents hired a tutor who spoke only Spanish. She took us to the beach, to town on the bus, shopping at "la plaza," to church, to the movies, to the park, to buy bread at the bread shop. (I can still remember the fabulous aroma and taste of freshly baked Spanish bread some thirty years later!) The input was comprehensible!

Krashen would take this example from Kristene to support his theory. He views acquisition as a process that depends primarily on the workings of an innate "mental organ," the Language Acquisition Device. The LAD will operate, given comprehensible input and a low affective filter, without the conscious awareness of the person acquiring the new language. Returning to our earlier discussion of images of the learner, Krashen's view seems to be that of the builder. Language learners have an innate ability to gather information from the raw material of the language all around them. They use this information to make hypotheses about language and to build their linguistic competence. As long as they receive the necessary input, humans have the biological endowment that enables them to develop language without conscious attention to the process.

Environmentalist theories, such as Schumann's, seem to complement nativist theories like Krashen's. One accounts for external, social factors while the other focuses on the internal, psychological forces. One might, for example, take Schumann's theory as an expansion of Krashen's notion of the affective filter. That is, one could say that the filter is raised by increased social or psychological distance, but that the cognitive processes of SLA are essentially those outlined by Krashen. In this way, one would have a theory that includes the linguistic and cognitive variables as well as the social factors.

While environmentalist and nativist theories of SLA focus on different factors, in some respects the two types of theories are similar. Schumann pays little attention to internal mental processes. He is more interested in factors like social and psychological distance between learners and native speakers of the language. Krashen also is interested in external factors. He says that under the right affective conditions, learners will acquire a new language if they get enough comprehensible input, but he assumes that an innate language learning ability accounts for the process of turning the input into language proficiency.

Krashen's insistence on the importance of providing learners with comprehensible input in a risk-free environment sends an important message to teachers. As a result, Krashen's theory of SLA has had a strong influence on teaching methods. Krashen claims that older students can acquire a second language in the same way they acquired their first language, going through the same developmental stages, and that a classroom can be an optimal source of comprehensible input. In fact, the classroom may provide more comprehensible input than a trip to a foreign country where no attempt is made to ensure that input is comprehensible.

Krashen teamed with Tracy Terrell to develop The Natural Approach (Krashen and Terrell 1983), a method that turns the second or foreign language classroom into a source of comprehensible input. Krashen and Terrell identify four stages of language acquisition for second language learners: preproduction, early production, speech emergence, and intermediate fluency, and suggest appropriate instruction and expected student responses at each stage (see Freeman and Freeman 1992a for a critique of The Natural Approach from a whole language perspective). For example, a typical series of The Natural Approach lessons in an elementary classroom would be based on the development of vocabulary centered around a theme. Students would interact with their teacher and peers according to their proficiency. Figures 5-1 and 5-2, taken from promotional materials for *The Rainbow Collection,* depict how a unit developed for The Natural Approach would look at the preproduction and speech emergence stages. Students' growing acquisition of English is evident in Figure 5-2.

Krashen has also promoted the concept of sheltered content teaching based on Canadian immersion models. As in The Natural Approach, teachers make an effort in sheltered content instruction to make the content of their classes comprehensible using visuals, realia, gestures, role play, and other context-enriching strategies. Teachers focus on the content rather than the structure of the language. In general, teaching consistent with Krashen's theory emphasizes meaning instead of linguistic form, avoids error correction, and attempts to create a positive affective climate.

Elementary and secondary teachers have been especially receptive to Krashen's theory. An understanding of the theory does not require detailed linguistic knowledge, and teachers are encouraged to teach their normal content, making the language understandable, instead of having to teach the language itself. At the same time, researchers and some ESL teachers have been critical of the theory, perhaps because it seems so accessible. As Larsen-Freeman and Long (1991) put it, the theory has been attacked precisely because it did not require any special expertise in linguistics or psychology. "It was easily understood, even by the nonspecialist" (p. 245).

Researchers have pointed out that the claims of Krashen's theory would be difficult to test or falsify. The five hypotheses are so interrelated that it would be nearly impossible to separate them out for empirical analysis. In addition, there have been few carefully controlled studies that show that methods based on the Monitor Model are clearly superior to methods based on other theories of SLA. Larsen-Freeman and Long conclude their critique of the Monitor Model by noting, "While some of the original claims no longer excite much interest among researchers and/or have been superseded by other developments, they served a valuable purpose by identifying some of the relevant issues, and, where apparently wrong, by obliging critics to seek out and substantiate alternatives" (p. 249).

Despite the fact that researchers have moved on to other issues, classroom teachers are continuing to use methods based on Krashen's theories. Until other theories, no matter how well regarded they are by researchers, are made accessible to teachers, and until methods based on those new theories are clearly shown to be more effective in promoting SLA than methods based on Krashen's Monitor Model, they will be unlikely to have much effect on students learning a second or foreign language.

Figure 5-1   Rainbow collection

Figure 5-2   Rainbow collection

Beyond Comprehensible Input

Krashen argues that acquisition occurs when learners receive comprehensible input, messages that they understand. Krashen's notion of comprehensible input builds on the earlier concept of simplified input developed by Hatch (1983). Other researchers, in turn, have suggested extensions of the concept of comprehensible input. These researchers have looked at the process of interaction and the role of output in language acquisition.

Simplified Input

Studies by Hatch and others suggest that the kind of input that leads to language development is simplified input. According to these researchers, simplified input includes caregiver talk, teacher talk, and talk to nonnative speakers. Hatch identified some characteristics of simplified talk. The phonology includes fewer reduced vowels and contractions, and the rate of speech is slower with longer pauses. The vocabulary is characterized by more high-frequency items, fewer idioms, and less slang. There are fewer pronouns, and speakers often use gestures and pictures. At the level of syntax, sentences are shorter with more repetitions and restatements. Discourse includes more requests for clarification and fewer interruptions.

The problem with claiming that simplified input leads to acquisition is that simplified input may not contain new language structures or items. Krashen claims that we acquire language when we receive input that contains language slightly beyond our current level of competence. We could say that simplified input is necessary but not sufficient for acquisition.

During our year in Venezuela, one thing we noticed in early interactions with colleagues was that they often tried to provide us with simplified input. When speaking directly to us in a meeting, for example, they obviously slowed their speech. In fact, if someone in the meeting would use slang, the meeting would usually stop and everyone would try to explain the expression. Our landlord spoke no English at all and was nervous about talking to us. In our first meeting, she used very slow speech and lots of gestures and pointing. She used all the techniques of an excellent language teacher even though she is a lawyer by profession!

Interaction

One criticism of theories of SLA based on input alone is that they are one-way theories to describe a two-way process. We use a new language to talk as well as to listen. Long (1983) hypothesized that we learn language as we interact with speakers of the language. Learners' comprehension is increased as they learn to negotiate meaning during conversational interactions. Long's focus is on developing discourse competence. His theory, however, is seen as limited. Conversational features are just one type of assistance a learner needs.

Comprehensible Output

Swain (1985) also argues that language learners need the opportunity for output. She noted that students in French immersion classes did not reach native-like proficiency in French. These students were in classes where teachers did most of the talking. Peer interaction was limited, and when interaction occurred, students spoke only with others learning French rather than with native speakers of French. Based on her observations of these students, Swain proposed that second language acquisition depends on output as well as input. According to Scarcella (1990), Swain's comprehensible output hypothesis:

> Suggests that students need tasks which elicit . . . talk at the student's i + 1, that is, a level of second language proficiency which is just a bit beyond the current second language proficiency level. She claims that such output provides opportunities for meaningful context-embedded use for the second language which allows students to test out their hypotheses about the language and "move the learner from a purely semantic analysis of the language to a syntactic analysis of it" (p. 70).

When we receive input that we understand, we focus on meaning—or the semantic level. However, in talking, we need to string sentences together, and that requires attention to syntax. Our syntactic analysis is probably not conscious, but producing output requires us to access different parts of the language system than we use to comprehend input. Output plays an important role in most communicative methods of second language teaching. Enright and McCloskey (1988), for example, describe how to organize curriculum and arrange the classroom to promote the kind of social interaction that encourages student output. They critique traditional classes where students are silent, listening to teachers do all the talking.

Van Lier's Model of SLA

One model of SLA that includes both input and output has been developed by Van Lier (1988) and is shown in Figure 5-3. Van Lier claims that certain conditions are necessary for certain outcomes. According to this model, if learners are receptive

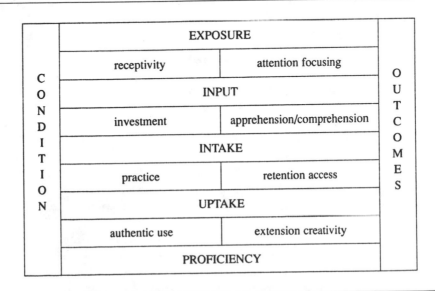

Figure 5-3   Van Lier's model of SLA

during exposure to a new language, their attention will be focused. If attention is focused, the language becomes input. If learners invest some mental energy in the input, they will begin to comprehend it. Language that is comprehended changes from input to intake. If learners practice with intake, they can retain the language and access it later. Language that can be accessed is considered uptake. Finally, with authentic use, learners can extend their language and use it creatively. It is the ability to use language creatively that is a measure of proficiency.

Van Lier's model traces the process of language acquisition from input to controlled output (practice) to authentic use in social interaction. This model is consistent with the model of learning presented in Chapter 3. For example, exposure is similar to a demonstration. If attention is focused, exposure becomes input. This parallels step two of the learning model: forming an intent. Investing mental energy turns input into intake, and this is similar to deciding to take the risk to learn. Intake becomes uptake if learners practice, and this is an instance of learning by doing. Uptake leads to proficiency during authentic use. In this stage, learners receive feedback and also integrate their new knowledge into their previous understanding.

Additional Views of Acquisition and Learning

Krashen uses the term "acquisition" to refer to an individual psychological process of developing a language. If acquiring a language involves much more than developing grammatical competence, as we suggested in Chapter 4, then the notion of acquisition needs to be extended. Gee (1990; 1992) does this by regarding acquisition as a part of a larger process of enculturation into a discourse: "Discourses are always ways of displaying (through words, actions, values, and beliefs) membership in a particular social group" (1992, p. 107). Since they are complex, "Discourses are mastered through acquisition, not learning" (p. 114).

Gee's definition of acquisition differs from Krashen's in that it includes a social component:

> Acquisition is a process of acquiring something subconsciously by exposure to models, a process of trial and error, and practice within social groups, without formal teaching. It happens in natural settings that are meaningful and functional in the sense that acquirers know that they need to acquire the thing they are exposed to in order to function and that they in fact want to so function (p. 113).

While Krashen focuses on the individual receiving comprehensible input to develop grammatical competence, Gee speaks of people in social groups who acquire grammatical, pragmatic, and communicative competence as well as a new way of viewing the world. When we acquire a new language, we move into new discourse communities, and we have to learn how to use language appropriately in those different contexts.

An example of this process comes from Yvonne's adult ESL class. Yvonne recalls one very respectful Hispanic man in her class. He worked in a lumber mill and learned a great deal of vocabulary from fellow workers. However, the teacher and several other students were a bit taken aback when he expressed his enthusiasm one day with "God damn right!" and his disappointment at his own stumbling with "Shit!" These terms were appropriate at work and even indicated camaraderie. In the classroom, they were not socially acceptable. The student in Yvonne's class had figured out how important it was to use certain profanities at work to be part of that discourse. He had to learn, however, that the classroom was a different discourse, and he had to acquire the ways of speaking that were proper there.

For Gee, output, as well as input, plays an important role in developing communicative competence within a discourse. Gee comments, "Discourses are not mastered by overt instruction . . . but by enculturation . . . into social practices through scaffolded and supported interaction with people who have already mastered the Discourse" (p. 114).

Gee also suggests that learning plays a more important role in language development than merely monitoring output. He modifies Krashen's definition to include learning through reflection on experience: "Learning is a process that involves conscious knowledge gained through teaching . . . or through certain life experiences that trigger conscious reflection. The teaching or reflection involves explanation and analysis, that is, breaking down the thing to be learned into its analytic parts. It inherently involves attaining, along with the matter being taught, some degree of metaknowledge about the matter" (p. 115).

For Krashen, who is concerned primarily with the development of grammatical competence, learning only refers to the knowledge of grammatical rules that can be applied to monitor output. Gee suggests that learning also occurs as we reflect on and analyze our experience including, presumably, our use of language. By analyzing our linguistic performance, we can make changes and improve our pragmatic and communicative competence. Thus, Gee suggests that learning plays an expanded role in developing language proficiency.

The Roles of Learning and Acquisition in Education

Gee makes two other points about the learning-acquisition distinction. First, he notes that cultures differ in how they instruct their young. Some cultures value acquisition. They assume that children will learn by being around adults who are performing certain activities. That is, they acquire knowledge in apprentice situations. Phillips (1972) in her Warm Springs Reservation study found that Native Americans value this type of learning and performed poorly in classroom contexts that emphasized learning through direct instruction, competition, and individualized performance.

Second, Gee argues that acquisition and learning lead to different kinds of abilities: "We are better at performing what we acquire, but we consciously know more about what we have learned" (p. 114). In the case of second languages, acquisition allows us to speak and understand, read and write the language, and learning allows us to talk about (or pass exams on) the language. Many adults who have studied a foreign language in high school and/or college and received high grades never learned to speak or understand the languages they studied. Their performance on grammar and translation tests determined their grades.

Schools, in fact, often reward knowledge about subjects more than the ability to actually use the knowledge. Freire (1970) says that students in classes where teachers transmit knowledge (where students are treated like plants) only gain the ability to describe the content of the knowledge. "Mechanically memorizing the description of an object does not constitute knowing the object" (p. 33). In other words, knowledge (learning) without experience (acquisition) puts us in a position where we possess only a hollow sort of understanding.

In some classrooms, reading is taught as a process of sounding out and pronouncing words. Some students can do this even if they don't understand the words at all. Other students do understand the words at a certain level, but they lack the experiences needed to fully comprehend what they are reading. Still others have rich background experiences that allow a different kind of knowledge to emerge from their reading. Freire (Freire and Macedo 1987) recalls his own introduction to reading: "My parents introduced me to reading the word at a certain moment in this rich experience of understanding my immediate world. Deciphering the word flowed naturally from reading my particular world; it was not something superimposed on it" (p. 32). In Freire's terms, we must learn to read the world before we read the words.

While in Venezuela, Yvonne read children's literature in Spanish weekly with a second grader and a third grader. These children had been exposed to a system of teaching reading that emphasized "word calling." Students are rewarded for reading the words out loud without making an error. However, they never had been asked to talk about or encouraged to evaluate what they read and had seldom read anything of real interest to them. When the children first began reading the beautifully illustrated children's literature, they glanced briefly at the pictures and then dutifully read quickly and accurately. They were amazed when Yvonne encouraged them to talk about the stories, look at the pictures, and predict what might happen next. For these children, reading was reading the word only. The idea of reading their world in the words took some time for them to develop. It had never occurred to them that their world could have a connection to what they read.

Piaget also believed that learning should be based on students' real-life experiences. If students have only learning without the concrete experiences, their knowledge is of a kind they can't really put to productive use. Unfortunately, for many foreign language students, this is exactly what happens to them. They study language (usually language structure only) in a classroom but never use it for real purposes. Therefore, they quickly forget what little they once knew.

The difference between the effects of acquisition (performance) and learning (metaknowledge) is most evident in the case of language learning. As Gee (1988) comments, "It appears that some substantive degree of incidental learning [acquisition] must take place before intentional learning [learning] is very efficacious" (p. 217). Otherwise, students learn about language, but they do not learn language. If acquisition precedes learning, and students can actually speak a language, it may be valuable for them to be able to talk, read, and write about what they can do and how they do it.

Mary and Ann provide a real-life example of Gee's incidental [acquisition] and intentional learning [learning]. The two girls went to Mexico to live when they were in kindergarten, first, and second grades. While there, they attended a Spanish/English bilingual school where they were the only nonnative speakers of Spanish. Through social interaction with their peers and the study of content in Spanish, the two girls acquired enough Spanish (incidental learning) to pass Mexican government exams at the end of their two-year stay in Mexico.

When they returned to the United States, they attended a Spanish/English bilingual school in Tucson, Arizona, and made friends with a family of El Salvadoran refugees. These experiences gave the girls enough Spanish input to continue their acquisition of Spanish in a natural setting (more incidental learning). However, when they moved to Fresno, California, their only exposure to Spanish was in structured Spanish (as a foreign language) classes where worksheets and drills (intentional learning) drove Mary to drop Spanish altogether. Ann continued to study Spanish and soon joined a Spanish for Spanish speakers class where there was more natural conversation and discussion in Spanish (incidental and intentional learning). In addition, Ann spent part of her senior year of high school as an exchange student studying content subjects in a Mexican school (incidental learning).

Both girls are now in college. Mary is taking up Spanish again, though she was reluctant at first. However, she is now seeing that her acquisition supports her intentional learning of Spanish grammar as Gee suggests. She recently explained that she feels sorry for students "who don't already know Spanish" and are trying to understand the classroom conversation and also learn the grammar and structure. Ann is in advanced grammar classes where she is analyzing details of the language and also is coming to understand how her previous incidental learning is supporting the intentional learning she is now doing.

The concepts of Krashen's Monitor Model have been extended and refined by other theorists. Even though we may question some of Krashen's claims, the theoretical constructs he has proposed have advanced the debate over the best way to help students develop a second language. We now look at a third theory of SLA.

Interactionist Theories

Interactionist theories recognize that both nature and nurture play important roles in SLA. "Interactionist theories . . . invoke both innate and environmental factors to explain language learning" (Larsen-Freeman and Long 1991, p. 266). It might appear that the image of the learner consistent with this type of theory is the explorer image. Although the explorer image, like interactionist theories, includes both innate learner factors and environmental factors, interactionist classrooms are not necessarily the same as explorer classrooms, as we will show below. To our knowledge, only one interactionist theory of SLA, the multidimensional model, has been developed in detail.

The Multidimensional Model

Research has been carried out in Germany for a number of years by members of the Zweitsprachenwerb Italienischer und Spanischer Arbeiter (ZISA) project. This research has examined how adults from a number of different language backgrounds acquire a second language in naturalistic and instructed settings. The researchers have also studied the learning of English as a second language in Australia. The model of SLA that ZISA has developed is called multidimensional because it takes into account both fixed developmental stages and variations in development among individual learners that result from psychological and social factors. The developmental stages reflect nature while the individual variations result from differences in nurture.

One finding of the ZISA group is that second language learners move through a series of developmental stages. According to Pienemann and Johnston (1987), English learners begin by producing single words or formulas like "I don't know." At a second stage they produce strings of words, but the order is based on meaning, not rules of syntax. Thus, if they want to express the idea "The dog chased the cat," they present the words in that order, not in some variation like "The cat was chased by the dog."

In the third stage, English learners can identify beginning and ending elements and move them. Thus, they can change "Yesterday, I sick" to "I sick yesterday." At the fourth stage, learners are able to identify different elements within the string of words and move them to do things like form questions. For example, they can change, "He can swim" to "Can he swim?" In the final stage, learners can make more complex moves. For example, they can produce sentences that combine two clauses, such as "He wanted her to go." In addition, at this stage some word endings, such as the "s" in "He works at the school" begin to appear. At earlier stages, learners might say, "Hes work at the school." Moving the "s" to the verb is a late development.

Learners in the different studies moved through all five of these stages in order. Movement to a new stage may be seen as the removal of a constraint that learners impose on what they process. They begin by assuming that all sentences follow a certain pattern, but as they move through developmental stages and adopt new strategies, they become aware that more possibilities exist. They begin with the most conservative hypothesis (for English, all sentences follow a noun-verb-noun pattern) and progressively realize that additional patterns are allowed in the language they are learning.

The theory has important implications for teaching. The strategies "constrain what is comprehensible, and so learnable at any time, and hence, what is teachable, implying that attempts to teach structures will be futile if they involve permutations and analysis beyond a learner's current processing level" (Larsen-Freeman and Long, 1991, p. 272). In other words, teachers can teach complex structures and students may be able to learn them to do well on a test. However, students will not acquire those structures for their everyday language use until they have had enough exposure to the language. This claim echoes Krashen's idea of acquisition following a natural order and occurring at i + 1 and Vygotsky's notion of the Zone of Proximal Development. In all cases, the idea is that learners can move forward one stage at a time. The ZISA group data is important because it specifies at least some elements of the natural order of acquisition and offers an explanation (in terms of psychological processing) for the order.

Another dimension of the Multidimensional Model is learner variation. The ZISA researchers claim that all learners go through the same developmental stages, but "individual learners nevertheless follow different paths, or routes, in SLA, principally in terms of the degree to which they display either a predominantly 'standard' orientation, favoring accuracy, or a predominantly 'simplifying' one, favoring communicative effectiveness" (Larsen-Freeman and Long, 1991, p. 280).

By looking at individual variation in this way, the ZISA researchers have been able to link psychological and social factors to the development of SLA. For example, learners who did not plan to stay in Germany long and who had less leisure-time contact with Germans tended to simplify their speech in a way that left out redundant endings and promoted basic communication over accuracy (more like certain pidgins), while learners who socialized more and intended to stay in Germany longer produced speech that contained extra redundant endings.

In other words, learners with a more positive orientation toward target-language speakers produced different kinds of speech errors than those with a neutral or negative attitude even though both groups used the same basic processing strategies. Although both groups of learners went through the same stages of development in their German, they differed in how they progressed through those stages and the kind of interlanguage they produced. Individual variations in their interlanguages could be traced to their attitudes toward native speakers of the target language. These findings would seem to support Schumann's arguments for the importance of social and psychological distance.

David's experiences in Colombia, Mexico, and Venezuela show that a learner's interlanguage can reflect an orientation toward either communication or accuracy, depending on the social context. When David lived and worked in both Colombia and Mexico, he developed enough Spanish to communicate basic needs and interact socially at a minimal level. In each of these cases, he was teaching English in his work and really did not need Spanish. His social contacts were primarily with English speakers or with people who wanted to learn English.

However, in Venezuela, he needed to use Spanish for his work, when he interacted with college professors at meetings, and during some workshops for teachers. Because the situation was different and his need for Spanish was greater, David was motivated to read daily in Spanish and to begin to analyze structures, vocabulary, and grammar rules on his own. His Spanish interlanguage in Venezuela showed a much stronger orientation toward accuracy.

The Multidimensional Model takes into account both the social factors that affect learning and the innate characteristics of the learner. Interactionist theories of SLA recognize that learning is constrained by both internal and external factors. Nevertheless, learners are seen as using the input provided by teachers or others to develop linguistic competence in much the same way as with nativist theories. The image of the learner that best fits this model is still the builder image. Teaching and learning that follows this model are not exploratory.

The ZISA group research is based on data gathered over time from learners of different language backgrounds in both naturalistic and instructed settings. The theory includes several different factors (linguistic, cognitive, and social) in its attempt to both describe and explain SLA. Both nature (the invariant developmental sequence) and nurture (individual variation as the result of social orientation) are held to be important. Further, the theory has some important implications for teaching. If learners are constrained in what they can learn at any given time by the processing strategies they are using, teaching that does not take those limits into account is not likely to be productive. Beyond this constraint, however, no clear implications for teaching and no ESL methods have emerged from the work of the ZISA group.

Images of the Learner and Theories of SLA

Earlier we suggested that a teacher's image of learners may strongly affect that teacher's practices. Both the theory of learning in general and the theory of second language acquisition that teachers operate on will help shape the image. Teachers who adopt an environmentalist theory of SLA often view learners as plants, capable of blooming if provided with the proper external stimuli. In contrast, teachers who favor nativist or interactionist theories of SLA are apt to see students as builders, active learners with an innate ability to use input to develop language proficiency.

Do these different images of the learner imply different kinds of teacher practice? In some ways, they do. Teachers who view students as plants may see their role as providing students with carefully structured and sequenced practice with the language so that students can develop good habits and avoid errors. Methods of teaching a second language based on this image, such as the audiolingual method, feature extremely active teachers and, frequently, passive learners.

Teachers who view students as builders may see their role as providing a rich context for acquisition. A teacher following a method consistent with interactionist theory must consider even more factors, promoting a positive social orientation and being sure to suit instruction to the learner's stage of development. However, the image of the learner is still a builder image because it is students who need to be learning actively.

It is important to note that, although the role of the teacher may seem to be different—depending on whether the teacher holds a plant or builder image—in both cases the teacher is in charge. Whether the teacher is directly providing the structured practice or creating the environment where comprehensible input is available, the learner is dependent. The teacher controls or holds the knowledge to be learned, and the class is teacher centered rather than learner centered.

Explorer classrooms, from our perspective, are places where learners are not entirely dependent on teachers. Instead, learners and teachers explore knowledge together. How does this work in the case of SLA? After all, if the teacher speaks the target language and the students don't, then the students must be dependent on the teacher.

The answer, we suggest, lies in the orientation toward language teaching that explorer teachers develop. Here the focus is not on the language itself. If the focus is on the language, learners may have little to contribute (at least at first) and may not be able to move beyond dependency. Instead, the focus is on some content area. All students can then contribute, even if their English proficiency is limited. As students and teachers inquire together, attempting to answer big questions by using content area knowledge, students learn a new language almost incidentally. They gain access to second language acquisition. The teacher is sensitive to the constraints put on learners by their level of proficiency in the new language, and the teacher takes opportunities (teachable moments) to point out things about the new language as they arise naturally, but class activity is always focused on content rather than language.

The view of SLA that we hold, then, is similar to Krashen's (1982) in that we believe that language is essentially acquired rather than learned. Like Gee (1988), we believe that acquisition is a social process of enculturation into the language club rather than an individual psychological process, and for that reason, social interaction is important. In addition, we believe that learning is not limited to a knowledge of grammatical rules. Learning also includes understanding that comes from reflection on our actions and experiences. Further, language development is a process of personal invention shaped by social conventions (Goodman and Goodman 1990) when language is used for a variety of authentic purposes. In explorer classrooms, students between worlds gain access to second language acquisition and learn language through content area study. In the next three chapters, we examine how teachers and students can work and learn together in explorer classrooms.

Applications

1. Fold a paper into three columns. Write at the top of the columns the words *environmentalist, nativist,* and *interactionist.* In small groups list characteristics of each view of SLA. In the large group, make a whole class list of each view together. Put these up on an overhead or butcher paper.

2. Whether we are learning a language or something else, we all have experienced the difference between learning and acquisition, what Gee calls incidental and intentional learning. Share a personal example.

3. Schumann's Acculturation Model suggests that the social and psychological distance a second language learner has from speakers of the target language affects language learning. Think of two second language learners you know who represent different social and psychological distances. Share with a partner.

4. Tape-record a young child who is acquiring his or her native language. Pick out examples where the child has overgeneralized language rules such as the example given in the chapter where the child added *ed* to *go* to form the past tense. Write down the examples and bring them to your group for discussion.

5. Share an experience you (or other people learning a second language) had when you applied your monitor (your learning) to your output.

6. Krashen claims that only input results in language acquisition. Swain disagrees, citing examples of the importance of "comprehensible output." Do you agree with Krashen or Swain? Can you find any evidence to support your position? Discuss with a group.

7. We have discussed three images of the learner: the plant, the builder, and the explorer. Watch a class with second language learners or think about second language learners in your own classroom. Which of the images do class activities reflect?

CHAPTER SIX

How Do Explorer Teachers Provide Access to Second Language Acquisition?

This is the cover of a survival kit Ramón created for incoming seventh graders at King's Canyon Middle School, an inner-city junior high school. Seventh-grade students like Ramón make a survival kit each year. Kathy, the teacher of the Hmong student, Tou, described in Chapter 1, is the language arts teacher who supervises this survival kit project. She works with a team of three other content area teachers to help the diverse students in their school achieve success.

Figure 6-1 Ramón's survival kit cover

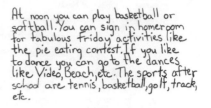

Welcome to Kings Canyon. Our schedule is from 8:05 to 2:35.

Homeroom 8:05-8:17
2   8:21-9:13
3   9:17-10:09
4   10:19-11:11
           11:15-12:07
Lunch   12:07-12:42
5   12:47-1:39
6   1:43-2:35

The classes are 52 minutes long. They are Geography, Math, Language, Physical Education, and Life Skills. There are electives like Exploratory Wheel, Chorus, Spanish, etc.

There is breakfast. You can also eat lunch, buy things at the snack bar. You can buy food in room 20, 47, or 13.

There are many activities you can do.

At noon you can play basketball or softball. You can sign in homeroom for fabulous friday activities like the pie eating contest. If you like to dance you can go to the dances like Video, Beach, etc. The sports after school are tennis, basketball, golf, track, etc.

Have a good Year!

Figure 6-2   Ramón's school schedule

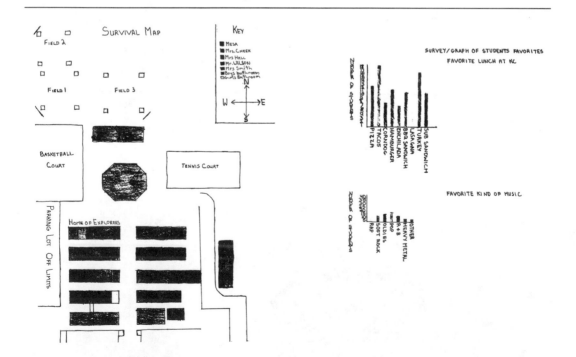

Figure 6-3   Color-keyed map

Figure 6-4   Survey results

FAVORITE SHOES ARE

NIKE

FAVORITE NOONTIME ACTIVITY

SOFTBALL

ARE THERE "FINE" BOYS AT K.C.? 69% VOTED YES 31% VOTED NO
ARE THERE "FINE" GIRLS AT K.C.? 78% voted yes 22% VOTED NO.

RECIPE FOR HAPPY 7th GRADER

1 lb brains
1 cup student
1 pkg paper
½ tbs. pencils
1 tsp clothes
dash of love
Sprinkle a good year

Take 1 lb of brains add 1 cup student
blend 1 pkg paper with ½ tbs pencils stir in
1 tsp clothes add a dash of love sprinkle
good year. Bake at 100° for 6periods serve
at K.C.

Figure 6-5   Survey results   **Figure 6-6**   Ramón's recipe for a happy seventh grader

Interview

Ed Corea

He is married for 27 years. He was
married when he was 20. He has
been working at K.C. for 5 years,
He likes working here. He has been
working in FUSD for 11 years. He
likes the 49ers, Lakers, Giants, Oldies,
and the color blue. He has 3
children. Veronica is 26, Cathy is 23,
and Andrew is 20. He was born in
Phoenix, Arizona. His race is Hispanic.
He was a cleanup boy. He used to
work in the fields. He vacations
4 weeks anytime, and he drives a
Chevy pickup. He works from 5:30
to 2:30. He regrets not going to
college. He likes to work out K.C. because
of the kids. He is plant coordinator.
He likes California teams. This
year there was a talent show in
his honor. He is 47 years old. He
used to work for Mrs. Smiths father
in law. He was fired for bruising the
grapes. That is the story of Ed Corea

Figure 6-7   Ed Corea

Kathy and her colleagues know that their students' needs are overwhelming. Pat, the history teacher; Cheryl, the math teacher; and Mike, the science teacher work together with Kathy to provide assignments that will engage the 140 students in their group, called the Explorer Team, in relevant academic work. In an attempt to provide all their students with access to second language acquisition and academic content, they decided to work together on themes and projects with the same group of students over a two-year period.

As the kit's cover shows, incoming students face many problems at King's Canyon. The population of approximately seventy-five percent Hispanic, ten percent Asian, eight percent African American, and seven percent non-Hispanic white students live in neighborhoods where violence, drugs, and poverty are a way of life. Many of the students have moved several times within the inner-city system since first entering school. Some, like Tou, are refugees of war or poverty in other countries. Others have never traveled outside the city itself.

The survival kit has proved to be one of many popular projects with Explorer Team students. In his kit, Ramón provides sixth graders with an overview of the school schedule with basic information and a color-keyed map (Figures 6-2 and 6-3). He took surveys on topics such as dress, sports, food, and music and graphed the results as part of his math class (Figures 6-4 and 6-5). He made up a "Recipe For Happy 7th Grader" (Figure 6-6). He interviewed a favorite staff person and wrote a poignant summary of what he learned about him (Figure 6-7). Ramón created his survival kit with pride and care because the assignment had meaning and purpose for him.

Whole Language in Explorer Classrooms

We opened this chapter with Ramón's example because we believe it exemplifies a theoretically grounded orientation toward language, learning, teaching, and curriculum that benefits all students, especially second language students. In this and the following two chapters we outline how explorer teachers like Kathy provide access to the acquisition of English and academic content for students who are between worlds.

In *Whole Language for Second Language Learners* (Freeman and Freeman 1992a), we outlined the following seven principles of a whole language orientation:

1. Lessons should proceed from whole to part.
2. Lessons should be learner centered because learning is the active construction of knowledge by students.
3. Lessons should have meaning and purpose for the students now.
4. Lessons should engage groups of students in social interaction.
5. Lessons should develop both oral and written language.
6. Lessons should take place in the first language to build concepts and facilitate the acquisition of English.
7. Lessons should show faith in the learner in order to expand students' potential.

This orientation is consistent with the theory of learning and second language acquisition that we developed in the previous chapters. We believe that teachers who follow these principles provide teaching that is good for all students, and we are particularly interested in how this approach applies to English language learners. In whole language classes, students develop language as they investigate content area subjects (Freeman and Freeman 1992a). Teachers and students in whole language classes are explorers.

Jackie, who teaches music in the same city as Kathy, began to study whole language because she wanted to try to meet the needs of all her students in a school system that had up to eighty-nine different language groups at one time. She has recently completed graduate classes in language acquisition, reading and writing, cross-cultural communication, and methods of teaching a second language. Taking what she has learned from these classes, she reflected on why traditional approaches are not successful and why a whole language approach is:

> I think I am beginning to understand the rationale and philosophy of whole language teaching. Traditional approaches have not been successful, i.e., grammar-based, notional-functional, and vocabulary-based, because they are all aimed at future learning. Whole language means authentic, purposeful lessons in the here and now where a second language learner can learn the language while also broadening his/her knowledge about a certain subject area—one in which he/she has an interest. And this learning is most successful in group interaction where students and the teacher learn from each other. It's a whole new concept to me, but I feel like "Hey, I can do that!"

Jackie has read theories and research on literacy learning and second language acquisition and constructed her own understanding of what whole language is and how she can apply it. Because teachers must construct a personal concept of whole language and the best way to implement it, no two whole language classrooms look exactly alike.

As the students and conditions for education vary, so does the teaching and learning. However, while all whole language classrooms are not the same, many whole language teachers do agree on certain ideas about language, teaching, learning, and curriculum. They all attempt to create classrooms where teachers and students can explore the world of learning together.

Celebrating Learning

In classes like Kathy's, Ramón and the other students not only explore subjects, they also celebrate learning. During a discussion of whole language in a graduate seminar, Miriam, a Spanish/English bilingual math and adult ESL teacher, brought up a very important aspect of all learning: celebration. Teachers in explorer classes at all grade levels celebrate the learning they and their students share. Rather than seeing the diversity in their classrooms as a burden, they celebrate diversity, and this spirit of celebration is the first thing that strikes a visitor to their classes.

Respect for the Learner

Besides celebration, explorer classrooms are places where teachers show respect for the learner. Students learn when "they are respected for who they are and what they bring to the classroom as capable learners" (Fennacy and Manning 1993, p. 39). It is important for teachers to view students positively and plan meaningful instruction that enables all students to reach their potential.

Patty, one of our graduate students, recently shared with us a letter from one of her adult students, Kou, "not because I want to brag about my teaching, but to show you that what we have been studying works!" Kou's letter illustrates, from a student's point of view, the positive effects of an interactive classroom where teachers show respect for their students.

April 18, 93

Dear Patty Trask

I am very happy to come to study in your class, I hope you can improve my English better than the last classes. Since I have come to study in your class, I have had chance to talk to my classmates. You put everyone into group, you let us talk, you have a very good experience and gesture about teaching, you know what students want to do, you stimulate students, it makes the students to pay attention to what you say or teach.

Some of my teachers don't care about students, They just keep teaching and teaching They don't let the the students talk to each other, They don't let the students join in group to share ideas, it makes the students boring, sleepy and lazy.

Patty Trask, since I come to your class, you make me think of some of my vocabularies which I learned in the Refugee Camps, Thailand. I had studied a lot of vocabularies in the campos but now I forget them. I use some words once in a blue moon Then I never use again. I think when I was in Thailand, I was better in English than today, I don't know why? Do you know?

Thank you for accepting me to be your students, I will never forget what you have done for me forever. I have had a lot of teachers who taught me English, Lao, Thai, Braille, Sign Language and Hmong, but there are a few teachers who are friendly and care about students like you. I have a little bit experience about teaching, I know that most students like the friendly teachers, and the teachers who are for them, only.

Patty Trask, I know that I am still very poor in speaking, writing English but I am happy that I have you and my friendly classmates to help me improve it. I hope to speak better English in the future. Ok, I would like to stop writing like this.

Thank you for taking time to read this letter, may be it is difficult for you to read because my handwriting is not so good.

Thanks in advance

Kou Chang

*Please forgive me if you see the words and sentences that aren't correct in spelling and grammar!

Labels

Unfortunately, in many of our schools the first response to bilingual students is far from a respectful one. Instead, the first thing we do with our newcomers is test them for English proficiency. Many of these students are labeled LEP (limited English proficient) or NEP (non-English proficient) (Wink 1993). In addition, a disproportionate number of second language students are referred for special services (Cummins 1984). Once students are labeled, teachers may respond more to the label than to the student. Labels like LEP suggest that the student is limited in some way, and instruction may be planned with that restriction in mind. In fact, in one school district, the LEP students are further divided into "high" and "low" LEP, as if one label were not enough.

Maryann, a Spanish/English bilingual teacher, expressed her frustration at seeing second language learners at her school automatically labeled as having learning disabilities:

> I could never get over the amount of students being referred to Special Ed. or R.S.P. at our school when I first started teaching. It wasn't even suggested that they go to the ESL classes offered as a pull-out program at our school. Immediately teachers would assume that their class had learning problems. One teacher even went as far as to say (on a very serious note, mind you), that about 75% of his class must have some sort of learning disability and "Why didn't the school have some sort of program to work with these students?" I hardly need to tell you that 75%-85% of our school's population is ESL.

It is important for teachers to realize that students who are labeled often begin to see themselves as somehow limited, too. They develop low expectations, and those low expectations may confirm some teachers' beliefs that the students are deficient. In this way a cycle of failure is established.

Maryann shared how she was able to break that cycle by showing respect for her students' potential. She realized that one of her students did not have a learning problem but simply was a struggling second language learner:

> At the beginning of the year one student came to my class with the report (from the previous teacher) of not having the patience to learn anything, that he didn't even try, and that perhaps he should be referred to Special Ed. He was only here at the school from Mexico since the third grade, and I teach fifth grade.
>
> After a few weeks of knowing him, it was quite obvious that this young man was brilliant. He was eager to learn, but he just didn't know how to read and this was very humiliating to him. No one ever took the time to teach him to read in Spanish, and he had learned English too fast so he couldn't stay in our ESL program. Whenever we did written assignments, he left the room mentally and started disrupting others. I began giving assignments orally in Spanish and English and giving this student some extra positive attention. This has changed his attitude. He has begun to read in Spanish and accepts help from his classmates willingly.

When teachers look at students instead of labels, they begin to view their bilingual students as a source of enrichment for their classrooms and treat them as assets rather than as liabilities. The students, in turn, develop positive feelings and set high goals for themselves. Many teachers who view their bilingual students with respect have replaced the negative labels and refer to them as PEP (potentially English proficient) (Hamayan 1989) rather than LEP (limited English proficient) as a first step toward appreciating their assets. Another new positive label is LG (linguistically gifted) students. Many teachers like this term for the validation of the special talents bilingual students have.

Explorer teachers have respect for all their students and see the diversity in their classrooms as an opportunity to expand all students' experiences with both language and academic content. Instead of subscribing to the "melting pot" image, these teachers see their students as part of a great patchwork quilt. Each piece of the quilt is unique and adds beauty to the entire effect. The diverse languages and cultures bilingual students bring to the classroom can provide that beauty in classes where teachers celebrate diversity.

In *Embracing Diversity* (Olsen and Mullen 1990), a book about thirty-six teachers successfully "embracing the diversity" of California classrooms, Moyra Contreras describes her approach to bilingual students: "My role is to respect the kids as they come into the classroom as opposed to trying to change them into something they are not" (p. 28). When educators have this alternative view, bilingual students are seen as valuable, important, contributing members of every classroom community.

We believe that respect for the learner is the most important characteristic of an explorer classroom. When explorer teachers have respect for their students, they organize their classroom in ways that show that respect and also help students respect one another. They involve them in curriculum that helps students become bilingual and biliterate. Explorer teachers provide opportunities for all their students in all their diversity to reach their potential.

Respect for the Learner and Discipline

Sometimes even when teachers recognize that their students have academic potential, they have difficulty in believing that all their students really want to learn. Their past teaching experiences may have convinced them that some students are just in school to cause trouble. As a result, teachers may spend a great deal of time on classroom discipline. In fact, many teachers find that maintaining discipline is the most discouraging aspect of teaching. It is frustrating to spend time planning exciting learning experiences and then have some students disrupt the entire class.

In most schools discipline is a major concern. Some schools have adopted discipline programs that seem to work quite well. One of these systems is "assertive discipline." King Elementary School in Fresno, California, uses assertive discipline, and school officials are pleased with the results. A newspaper article (Silver 1992) describes how assertive discipline works at King, a school situated between two housing projects that serve as gang headquarters. Despite being located in a violent neighborhood, King is a peaceful school.

Assertive discipline, as practiced at King and other schools, consists of establishing a set of rules and then punishing violations consistently while, at the same time, rewarding good behavior. According to Silver, "Each teacher has the rules posted in his or her classroom: Follow all directions the first time given; no running on blacktop; use equipment properly; no play fighting; no seeds, candy, or gum allowed; stop moving when the bell rings" (p. B3). The first time students break a rule, they are warned; the second offense leads to counseling; the third violation results in parent contact; and students can be suspended after four or five offenses.

The system of punishments is balanced by a system of rewards. Students receive gold slips for good behavior. They can redeem the slips for candy or other prizes. Teachers can also reward whole classes for being good, and good classes get extra rewards. "In December, classes that earned 70 gold slips won a visit from Santa Claus, who brought a sack full of goodies" (p. B3). In addition, at monthly ceremonies students and classes who have shown exceptional behavior receive prizes such as bicycles or pizza parties.

It has taken about three years for assertive discipline to become firmly established at King. The result is an orderly school with respectful students. As one administrator commented, "Very few schools have the kind of atmosphere and polite behavior of students that King does" (p. B3). Teachers report that they spend less time on discipline and more time actually teaching. The program has also resulted in a sharp reduction in student suspensions from ninety-two students to just five in two years.

Assertive discipline seems to work well when everyone at a school understands the rules for conduct and when enforcement of those rules is consistent. As practiced at King, punishments are balanced by rewards, so students who behave well earn various kinds of prizes. Assertive discipline has had positive results at King and a number of other schools. Nevertheless, some aspects of it seem to run counter to our beliefs about teaching and learning. Respect for the students is replaced by respect for the efficacy of a system to control students.

How do explorer teachers who have respect for their students deal with discipline? Clearly, none of the exciting curriculum ideas that teachers and learners have will work if there is no control in the classroom. However, we believe that one goal of education is the development of self-control. The problem with assertive discipline and other similar programs is that the control is external rather than internal.

When curriculum centers on learners, and when learning is meaningful, many discipline problems seem to disappear. Instead of punishing students for misbehaving, explorer teachers try to understand why students are not engaging in the learning process or are keeping others from learning. This may lead teachers to try changes in their lessons instead of devising a system of rewards and punishments that coerce students into doing things they find meaningless. This was the approach Maryann took with her bilingual student.

Fennacy and Manning (1993) write about how literature helped solve a conflict in Manning's second-grade classroom. Greg was a student who tended to lash out at others when he did not get his way. One day, Keisha, an African-American student, wrote her teacher a note:

> Dear Mrs. Manning,
> I do not want to stay at this table because Jay and Greg be talking about my color (p. 32).

Though his teacher tried everything to change his attitude, it wasn't until Greg chose to read *The Story of Jackie Robinson, Bravest Man in Baseball* (Davidson 1988) that he began to change. He wrote about the book's influence on him in his literature log:

> I feel horrible for Jackie Robinson because a little white girl across the street said, "Nigger, nigger, nigger boy." I think if I was that girl I would have made friends with Jackie Robinson. He was a nice boy. Now I know why Jackie was a brave boy because he doesn't run away from his names. That is being brave and strong . . . I wonder where Jackie Robinson is right now because I don't want his life to end like this or anybody else's. Because it's not nice or funny at all (p. 33).

Fennacy and Manning describe how Greg's attitude changed even further through the effect of the reading:

> In a later journal entry, Greg wrote that he would never again call anyone nigger. It took a story about a baseball hero to touch Greg in a way no one else could. By respecting the language of quality literature in the classroom, we acknowledge the potential that language has to touch our students' lives (p. 33).

In even the best explorer classes, however, some students misbehave at times. These students are often responding to what is going on outside the classroom. If they are having trouble at home or with their peers in other contexts, they may have difficulty working with classmates in productive ways. Tou, described in Chapter 1, is a good example. Even though Kathy had organized effective curriculum, the problems Tou had at home, and the influence of gang membership on his behavior, outweighed the good classroom atmosphere. The community or home context strongly influences the school context.

As a result, it is important for explorer teachers to develop a discipline plan that fits with their general orientation toward teaching and learning. Such a plan would have as its goal the development of positive (or prosocial) behavior for all students. Sumara (1993) explains how Michelle, the whole language teacher described in Chapter 2, was able to create a classroom environment where students worked as a cohesive community:

> Michelle's classroom was governed by specific rules, values and expectations that she, as the teacher, established at the very beginning of the school year. In the classroom, in large, colored letters, were the words, *Responsibility, Cooperation,* and *Independence.* These three "rules" had been narrowed down from a long list of rules that Michelle had used in her early years of teaching.

Michelle's classroom did not automatically work because those words were up in the room. First of all, Michelle was in charge of her classroom. Sumara explains, "Michelle felt (like most good teachers) that the students needed to learn immediately that she was the instructional leader of this classroom, and that they must respect her both as a teacher and as a person" (p. 139).

In addition to the central role of the teacher, Sumara points out that it is important to understand that the motive for the rules that Michelle had for her classroom was different from the motives for rules in many other classrooms: "For Michelle, the purpose for rules was not so much to *control* or be *controlling* as to foster a sense of *self-control* and *self-discipline* in her students" (p. 139). Of course, self-control did not just happen in Michelle's classroom. At first Michelle "needed to adopt an authoritative stance," and "cooperation and collaboration among students" was at first mandated and then learned (p. 139).

Sumara summarizes the expectations and principles in Michelle's classroom that he believes helped her create a positive learning environment:

1. Cooperating and collaborating with other students and other adults in the room was valued and promoted.
2. Experimenting with learning (venturing guesses) was valued as a way to negotiate meaning. "I think that" was valued over "I don't know."
3. Knowledge, experience, and expertise were meant to be shared. Sharing work was not considered cheating in this room.
4. Taking risks was valued over "feeling safe." Learning was seen as an empowering and challenging activity in which everyone could be successful (p. 139).

Michelle established a classroom community where students collaborated and took risks. She did this through her own understanding of teaching and learning and years of experience. For teachers who are beginning to set up an explorer classroom, it is helpful to have some sort of plan as a guide. One such plan has been developed by Ron Claassen and associates at the Center for Conflict Studies and Peacemaking at Fresno Pacific College.

Claassen describes three possible ways to reduce conflict: coercive power, outside authority, and cooperative resolution. In some situations, one party in the conflict has power to coerce the other party. The other party must go along, even if he would prefer not to. When individual teachers use assertive discipline, they employ coercive power. Assertive discipline works best, though, when the whole school adopts the system. Teachers are then supported by an outside authority (the office) and do not have to wield their coercive power alone. In fact, teachers in schools with established discipline policies may have no choice but to follow the procedure. When conflicts are resolved by outside authorities, the parties involved are not part of the decision-making process. No respect is shown for either party.

Claassen notes several possible responses to a discipline system that relies on coercive power or outside authority. The group who is coerced may feel resentment, may take revenge, may rebel, or may retreat and be more careful not to get caught the next time. Retreat may also lead to reduced self-value. The threat of punishment, even coupled with a reward system, does not seem to help students develop the kind of self-control and positive self-image that should be the goal of any discipline system.

The best approach, according to Claassen, is cooperative resolution. With cooperative resolution there is respect shown to all involved. The parties in conflict come to their own agreement about how to resolve the problem. They may need assistance from an outside party, but no solution is imposed. Instead, the people involved make the final decision. Claassen notes that three factors may keep teachers from using cooperative resolution: Those involved may lack the skills, format, and structure to use it; they may have no one to encourage or help them; or they may believe that their job requires that they should punish anyone who violates a rule.

Cooperative resolution is not easy. Teachers need support to develop this approach to discipline. Further, students may interpret a new approach as a sign of weakness. However, some teachers have had considerable success in working through resolution of conflicts with their students. They do this with class meetings and with individual conferences. In fact, some teachers have made conflict and peacemaking an area of content that students can investigate. Certainly, many students experience conflict at home and in social situations outside school, and they are interested in ways to resolve conflicts and establish peaceful relationships with others.

Roxanne Claassen (1993) reports on using "discipline that restores" with her fourth- and fifth-grade students by following the peacemaking model developed by her husband at the Center for Conflict Studies. She explains, "Working with the children in my classroom is a joy that I look forward to each day. Part of that joy, believe it or not, is working at issues of discipline together with them" (p. 17). Roxanne worked with her students from the first day of school to build community and to decide together how they would solve problems. She wanted the classroom to be a place where "all of us could feel safe and valued for our unique gifts and personalities" (p. 17). Roxanne describes what she and her students did:

> We talked about solving the problems between us in ways that would restore relationships rather than in ways that would separate persons from each other. We set up a plan that included rules with consequences that would be related to the problem, that

would be restorative rather than punitive, that would be reasonable rather than unreasonable, and that would be respectful of the people involved (reasonable, related, and respectful consequences come from Jane Nelson's book, *Cooperative Discipline*). Our plan also includes peer mediator training and class meetings (p. 17).

In Roxanne's class the day always begins with each person signing up for a job of their choice for that day, something that was decided at a class meeting. However, from the start this caused problems since students were soon waiting at the door before school, arguing, shoving, and name calling to get their first choice. The conflict-resolution process was put into practice at a class meeting. This included a time for reviewing and recognizing injustices, a time for making restitution (apologies given and accepted), and a time for deciding how to solve the problem to avoid future difficulties. Students worked together toward a resolution:

> All suggestions were recorded on the chalkboard. When we ran out of ideas, we went back and checked each suggestion to see if they were respectful, related, restorative, and reasonable. We eliminated any that did not meet our criteria. Using consensus, we decided on a solution that seemed like it would really work well for us. Our solution was one that called for a random drawing of numbers each morning to decide your place in line and a rule that you could only do a particular job once a week unless no one else wanted to do it (p. 18).

A trial period and follow-up meeting were then set up to decide how the plan was working. In fact, with a few modifications, the plan resolved the problem. The conflict-resolution process proved to be efficient because it took about thirty minutes and solved the problem so well that more time was not spent on the issue.

Roxanne describes an incident with John and Nasario who began to chase one another in the classroom. When Nasario hit John with a book, it was clear the problem had to be resolved: "We were in the middle of a project that they also needed to be involved in so I asked them if they would be willing to discuss the problem after lunch with peer mediators" (p. 18). The peer mediators began the process by having the boys describe the incident from their perspective and being sure that both listened to one another. Each boy then related what he heard the other one say:

> The injustices both had experienced had begun at recess during a football game. Nasario felt John was not including him in the game enough. . . . They exchanged angry words. John was very surprised. . . . He had not deliberately left Nasario out of the game. . . . He told Nasario right away he was sorry . . . and Nasario apologized for getting so angry. The discussion turned to what they could both do to keep this from happening again. They decided to "check things out better" before getting mad. A follow-up meeting was scheduled for two days later to see how things were going and whether or not they were keeping their agreement (p. 19).

Perhaps the most important part of cooperative conflict resolution is the pride that both the mediators and those solving their conflict feel in settling the differences without a coercive outside power. Roxanne has seen students follow the demonstrations of others and find solutions without the formal conflict-resolution process.

Cooperative resolution does not happen by itself. Teachers need support to develop this approach to discipline. Roxanne, for example, has been able to share this process in her school so that teachers and students at different grade levels, including junior high students, could use the process.

Other teachers have tried a similar approach to discipline. Charlene worked toward conflict resolution by engaging her students in a literature study on the theme of peace. The students read a number of different books on the topic and discussed them in small groups. They wrote about their books and linked their study to discussions of violence in their community. When two boys in her class from different ethnic groups got into a fight at recess and called each other racially charged names, Charlene asked them to discuss their differences in front of the whole class and to explain their actions in light of what they had been reading and talking about during their literature study.

Explorer teachers attempt cooperative resolution to conflict because they see the development of self-discipline and prosocial skills as an important part of the curriculum. These teachers have respect for their students and show them that they believe they can learn anything, including learning to get along with one another.

Respect is one important characteristic of explorer classrooms. In addition, teachers in these classrooms provide their students with comprehensible input by teaching whole to part and by teaching language through content.

Learning Whole to Part

Kathy, Maryann, Jackie, and Debbie Manning realize that the instruction that many bilingual learners have received in schools has been, for the most part, fragmented and disempowering (Crawford 1989; Cummins 1989; Fitzgerald 1993; Flores 1982). This instruction has often been based on a set of assumptions that show a lack of respect for bilingual learners and serve to limit their potential (Freeman and Freeman 1989). The term "whole" in whole language reflects an understanding that curriculum should not be fragmented and language should not be broken up into parts because language development begins with meaningful wholes and progresses toward the differentiation of parts out of those wholes.

Implicit in this orientation toward teaching and learning is the belief that learners are capable of making sense of the whole when their experiences are mediated by teachers and their peers. As we explained in Chapter 3, language development is a creative process of personal invention shaped by social conventions (Goodman and Goodman 1990). English learners, for example, hear and see language around them, they form hypotheses about language, and they refine these hypotheses as they receive feedback from others. In this way, their personal inventions are shaped by the social conventions operating in the community. Research in both oral and written first and second language acquisition supports the idea that acquiring a language involves moving from whole to part—even though it sometimes doesn't look that way—through the processes of invention and convention.

Oral and Written Language Development

In oral language, for example, both young children and second language learners often use one-word sentences at first. These single words give the impression of part-to-whole learning, but in fact they express whole ideas. Yvonne remembers her first experience in Mexico. On the train down to Guadalajara, she needed to find the bathroom. Though she had studied Spanish in high school and the first two years of college, she felt tongue-tied when she tried to speak the language. Finally, she found a porter who understood that her one-word utterance, "baño," meant "Where is the bathroom?" Upon arriving in Guadalajara she was given a hotel room with no toilet paper. By telling the maid "baño" and "papel" ("paper"), she was able to convey the need for "papel higiénico" ("toilet paper"). As the summer wore on and she gained confidence, she found she used more words to express the whole ideas she had earlier expressed with one-word sentences.

Later when Yvonne moved to Mexico to live and teach, she reflected upon how amazing it was that she had been able to communicate with so little language in her early experiences, especially when she now had long discussions in Spanish with the plumber who often came to work on the toilets or when she bargained with vendors over the prices of their produce. Language learners always begin with whole ideas, and as their language proficiency develops, they learn to express their ideas by using more parts—more words and more complex syntactic constructions.

In addition, Yvonne reflected on how much Spanish she had learned because of the influence of social convention. Each time she was in a different situation where she needed Spanish, she learned better how to express her needs. When she tried to explain things for which she did not have the vocabulary or syntax, she would paraphrase with what she did know. Then the plumber or the vendor, for example, would say, "Oh, you mean . . ." or "Do you want me to . . ." The next time, Yvonne would know how to explain what she needed.

Written language also develops from whole to part through invention. Beginning writers often represent a whole word with a single letter. As students continue to write, they add more letters, and move toward conventional spelling because they see print around them and revise their original hypotheses. Kristen, a kindergartener, showed both her invention and how she used a part (a letter) to express a whole in a letter to her friend Derrick. The class was working on the theme of "Who are we?" and had been talking about how people are the same and how they are different. Kristen showed the important understanding of the concept that boys and girls are different, but they are both people when she wrote in invented spelling starting at the bottom of the page and working up: "Derrick, we are the same except for what we are." (See Figure 6-8.)

Eugenia, the case study student in Cándida's class, learned naturally from whole to part. Cándida explained that when Eugenia entered school she already knew the letters of her name. With her teacher's encouragement, Eugenia started with these letters and invented messages for her teacher and her classmates. In this supportive community, her inventions moved toward conventional spelling as she wrote daily.

Cándida reads complete stories to her students. These predictable books provide models of conventional spelling and also introduce students to reading with a whole-to-part approach. Over time, students like Eugenia become aware of the individual words, but at first they focus on the whole story. Eugenia and her classmates are learning to read and write because Cándida uses a whole-to-part approach to literacy that encourages personal invention in a supportive classroom community where students become aware of the social conventions.

Research shows how reading develops naturally from whole concepts to parts. Goodman, Altwerger, and Marek (1989) have developed a series of tasks to determine children's hypotheses—concepts about print—by asking very young children to read environmental print on various products. They found that children use the logos on

Figure 6-8   Melissa's drawing and letter

the products to help them read and make sense of the words. At first children identify "Cheerios," for example, as cereal. When asked where it says "cereal," young children point to the word "Cheerios" and carefully read "cer-e-al." They have formed hypotheses about what the print must mean, and as they are exposed to more print, they begin to pay attention to the parts and distinguish between words. Eventually, when they focus on the words more and interact with others around them, they come to realize that the word "cereal" appears elsewhere on the package in much smaller letters than "Cheerios."

When reading books, children also begin with their own inventions. Often people notice a three- or four-year-old sitting on a chair pointing to pictures and "reading" a favorite book and say, "Isn't that cute? She thinks she's reading." In reality, that child *is* reading. She is in an early stage of reading. She knows that books hold meaning and that pictures are related to the story. She is telling the story she has heard someone read to her, and she knows that the meaning is contained in those pages.

Goodman et al. (1989) also developed book-handling tasks based on those of Clay (1973) that help teachers see what hypotheses children have made about reading. For example, during a reading of *Goldilocks and the Three Bears*, if asked where it says, "The three bears went out for a walk," a young reader might at first point to the picture of the three bears leaving their house. This child believes that the meaning must be in the picture. Later the same child will reform the original hypothesis because of more experience with reading and will point generally to where the words are on the page. The child now understands the social convention that readers rely on the print to construct meaning. Soon the child begins to distinguish individual words. In this way, children move from whole, general concepts about reading to being able to make sense by attending to the parts of whole texts. Their original hypotheses (personal inventions) are rethought because of the influence of readers around them (social convention).

Romero (1983) did research with Spanish-speaking children using a translation of the Concepts About Print Task (Letreros en el ambiente—Signs in the Environment) and the Book-Handling Task (Conocimiento pre-escolar del manejo de libros—Preschool Knowledge of Book Handling). This research shows that young children learning to read in Spanish develop similarly to those learning to read in English. Romero found that native Spanish-speaking children also were aware of print in the environment and that they also developed hypotheses about reading that moved from the whole to part.

In her bilingual first grade, Kristene drew upon the importance of supporting children's hypotheses about print by having a "Podemos Leer" ("We Can Read") bulletin board right by the door of the classroom so that everyone could see it. Students brought in products they used with their families such as Cheerios boxes, Sprite cans, Mi Rancho tortilla bags, and VIVA paper towel wrappers to put up on the board. The colorful, familiar product labels in Spanish and English provided the rich context Kristene's students needed to move into reading. Kristene found this real-world bilingual bulletin board often was the center of lively discussion in Spanish and English for her first graders as they formed hypotheses and began to distinguish the parts within the wholes provided by the labels.

Part-to-Whole Curriculum

Robert, Sharon's case study student, had not acquired very much English by the time he reached her class. To a great extent this was because of the part-to-whole curriculum his kindergarten and first-grade teachers used. Part-to-whole teaching inhibits invention because students do not receive the comprehensible input they need.

Pat, an experienced teacher who has taken classes in both reading and language development, has had the opportunity to visit many different classrooms with second language learners. Too often she has seen classrooms like Robert's where part-to-whole teaching hampers bilingual students. In her responses for a graduate class, she wrote about two separate incidents that disturbed her. In the first classroom, students were working on a very controlled phonics program. Pat described the scene:

> I saw twenty-nine second graders respond to flash cards by reciting the sounds, key words, and the rule it exemplified. Two Hmong girls, three very limited English-speaking Hispanics, ten ESL Hispanics, and almost fourteen "at-risk" children knew

the rules forward and backward but could not apply them when they were given any text to read. The frustration level of this class was very high, and this instruction is not empowering them to become creative or resourceful.

The teacher undoubtedly had good intentions. She may have thought that giving these students whole books to read was too overwhelming especially because many of the children were second language learners. It may have seemed logical to the teacher to start with smaller parts and build up to complete stories. However, the students did not understand how the isolated practice of parts was related to anything else. Even though the students appeared to be actively involved in the lesson, this activity was not helping them become more proficient readers. The students were responding to the visual cues, but the focus on phonics exercises kept them from seeing that whole texts make sense. The approach the teacher was taking inhibited the natural process of the formation of hypotheses that readers develop when exposed to whole stories.

In another classroom that Pat observed, the teacher was using basal readers with traditional ability groups. Pat described the scene in one reading group that she had been asked to lead:

> The students read in a round-robin fashion. The students aggressively monitored each other, allowing no slips to pass unreported. One girl read very well, and I proceeded to ask her what she thought would happen next. When she did not respond, another child in the group said, "She doesn't know. She only understands Spanish." She had apparently become quite adept at word calling, but since discussion does not seem to be encouraged she had no idea what she was reading.

In this classroom, students corrected each other when words were misread. Reading was presented as identifying and correctly pronouncing words. Students, such as the girl Pat describes, focused on this external aspect of reading and failed to build up an internal representation of the story. It did not seem to matter if the students had absolutely no idea what they were reading as long as they could "word call" correctly! This "reading" activity did not empower these students because there was such a strong emphasis on the parts, students did not even realize that reading is supposed to make sense. In fact, as mentioned earlier, we need to respect the ability of our learners to be able to take the wholes and hypothesize about language instead of assuming that they need the parts first. Of course, in reality, the parts are harder because they do not make sense and do not allow for invention.

In contrast to what Pat saw in the two reading lessons, Fitzgerald (1993) believes that it is critical to "promote attention to 'big things' in initial reading and writing acquisition" (p. 645) for second language learners. She gives specific suggestions:

> Teachers who help ESL learners get the big things first while reading and writing will highlight getting and giving main ideas or gists; making important inferences; seeing and making structures for texts; and developing metacognitive strategies such as rereading to search for needed information (p. 645).

Fitzgerald does not believe that "small things" should be ignored but "initially de-emphasized" (p. 645). She lists the kinds of "small things" she means, "getting and making details, using correct grammar, standard punctuation and spelling, pronouncing words correctly, and using word recognition techniques such as phonics" (p. 645). In other words, learners first need to understand the whole before they can pay attention to the parts.

Joyce, a teacher of adult ESL, reflected on the idea of teaching language from whole to part in a response for a graduate class. In the first part of the response, she recounts an experience she had where her views of part-to-whole language learning were first challenged:

> About a year ago I was being interviewed by a member of the UC Davis Education Department regarding my general beliefs about teaching English. Among other things I indicated that basic grammar skills had their place in the English curriculum. My interviewer doubted that, and to prove her point, she asked me if I'd ever studied a foreign language. I indicated that I had studied French, and at her request described the method I learned by, a method which mainly consisted of memorizing vocabulary and learning grammar rules. Then she asked me if I can speak French, and of course, the answer is no.

As Joyce contemplated this revelation further, she compared her French classes with the German classes that a friend of hers took:

> I took four years of French in high school. The bulk of the curriculum consisted of memorizing vocabulary lists, verb conjugations, and grammar rules. The teacher explained the complex theories of tenses and structure on the blackboard. We did practice of sentences out of the text, and we memorized masses of information for tests and quizzes. I was good at all these things. On paper I was one of the top students, in fact, although I never spoke unless called upon.
>
> My teacher also made a point to supplement the skills with other, more authentic language activities. We wrote and performed plays one year. We did oral and written reports. We even read a different novel each year. At the end of four years, I was not comfortable speaking French, and though I could read and write it, I couldn't understand it very well if it was spoken to me.
>
> My friend Susan's experience with German was somewhat different. While she too memorized some vocabulary and read and talked about grammar rules, the emphasis was placed on acquiring knowledge and fluency by being surrounded by and using the language. The teacher immersed the students in visual and auditory context by showing slides of things and accompanying them with the spoken German. The students themselves spoke, read, wrote, and interacted in German right from the beginning.
>
> Susan did go to Germany where she became fluent, but when I asked her how she feels about the way she was first introduced to the language, she has no doubt that the basic comfort and ease she has in speaking German now stems from the nature of her first exposure. She went on to say that she feels like she is still filling in the gaps of vocabulary and structure as she continues to use the language, but that she has always had a natural feel for German which she attributes to the way she first learned it.

Joyce goes on to make a final conclusion that summarizes well why whole-to-part learning is so important:

> I think the conclusion I can draw from this comparison is that trying to learn a language by mastering its parts is not likely to result in any significant proficiency. Learning it by experiencing it in its whole and natural state, on the other hand, is more likely to produce a basic competency which can be built on to increase sophistication over time. There were both skill and whole language elements in the methods of each of our teachers. I think the difference was that my teacher supplemented skills with authentic text, whereas Susan's teacher started with the language in a more intact

state and reinforced the natural learning with rules and vocabulary. In short, one went from part to whole, and the other went from whole to part.

Organizing Around Themes

Explorer teachers of second language students teach whole to part by organizing curriculum around themes and teaching language through content. As second language learners study content, they make hypotheses about both the content and their new language (personal inventions) that are refined as they interact with their teacher and classmates who help them develop awareness of social conventions.

Edelsky, Altwerger, and Flores (1991) describe this approach as using theme cycles. In a theme cycle, students often focus on central questions and use information from different content areas to answer their questions. Organizing curriculum with theme cycles helps bilingual students because when they know the overall theme (the whole), they come to recognize related vocabulary (the parts), and they can predict content. This organization contrasts with traditional practices where the day is divided into time periods, and math, science, social studies, reading, and language arts are taught separately without any connections being made among the subjects.

Rhoda, who wrote her case study on the Punjabi student, Sharma, commented on the importance of theme study to her for developing vocabulary:

> An element I've focused on has been helping language minority students develop academic language/vocabulary. . . . I have often found there is so much academic language in content areas that meaning often is lost in a maze of technical words. It struck me that the real backbone of meaningful academic language development has to come through integrated study. When students are given more than one slant on a topic, they have a greater chance to form deeper meaning and come away with a firmer grasp of a concept. It maintains students' dignity and self-esteem without forcing them to do meaningless vocabulary drills that have no context base and make them feel they are in the low/inept group.

Sharma along with Rhoda's other second language students benefitted from her whole-to-part approach to teaching language through content.

Theme Study Through Literature

The topics for theme cycles can be drawn from state or district guidelines and should be related to students' experiences. María, a bilingual second-grade teacher in a central California farming community, for example, worked with her students on the long-term theme of growth, which eventually dealt not only with plant and human growth and development, but also population growth and the growth of industries. These topics led to a study of the effects of growth on our world. A list of the readings used in this unit and others on this topic is in Appendix C.

María's class is similar to many in farming communities in California. Some of her students are Spanish speakers who speak very little English. Others are monolingual English speakers. María wants all her students to develop literacy and academic concepts in their primary language, but she avoids isolating and teaching vocabulary directly in English or Spanish. In order to ensure that her Spanish-speaking students develop strong reading and writing skills in their first language, she has them read and discuss books in Spanish, write journals in Spanish (to which she responds), publish books in Spanish for author's chair and the classroom library, and keep content journals in Spanish as they learn science, math, and social studies concepts. In these ways, María provides the same rich experiences for her Spanish speakers as she does for the monolingual English-speaking children. In addition, she promotes bilingualism and provides demonstrations of the value of knowing two languages. For that reason, when the whole class begins a theme study, María sometimes introduces the unit with readings and discussions in both Spanish and English to give equal status to both languages.

María and her students began their study of the growth unit with the question "How do plants grow?" She began by reading *Growing Radishes and Carrots* (Bolton 1986), a small, pop-up content book that first describes how to plant and grow radishes and carrots and then discusses differences in their growth time. After María read the book, her students talked in small groups about the ideas presented and their own experiences with the farms in their community, using English and Spanish in their discussion groups.

Each student then planted both radish and carrot seeds. Class members made journals and recorded watering and growth patterns. Both Spanish and English speakers kept their journals in their first languages. A week later when the radish seeds had sprouted but no growth was seen in the carrots, María decided it was time to reinforce the differences in growth time that the students had discussed earlier after reading *Growing Radishes and Carrots.* To do this, she read a book her students knew from earlier grades, *The Carrot Seed* (Krauss 1945) in English as well as *La semilla de zanahoria* (Krauss 1945, 1978 trans.), the Spanish translation. The class talked about how the boy in the story had to be very patient and how he trusted that his carrot would grow if he took good care of it. María encouraged the Spanish-speaking students to summarize in Spanish and the English speakers to speak in English. Soon children were working together, looking at both books and studying and comparing the Spanish and English texts.

Next, María read *Una semilla nada más* and the English version, *Just One Seed* (Ada 1990). These pop-up big books tell about a plant that grows and grows and seems to be just an ordinary plant until one day a huge sunflower opens (the pop-up page). The book is predictable and is very similar to *The Carrot Seed.* The boy in each story has faith in the plant and cares for it while others in his family keep telling him it's just an ordinary plant. The vocabulary of the two books and the concepts developed are similar.

Choosing this theme allowed María to help all her students understand the importance of the work many of her migrant students' parents were doing. To further develop the theme, María read several big books (which also come in small-book size) about agriculture. The book *Granjas* (Madrigal 1992) and its translation into English, *Farms,* were especially key because they describe agriculture as "la actividad más importante del mundo" ("the most important activity in the world") and through colorful pictures show what is involved in modern farming, including the growing and harvesting of grains, vegetables, and citrus fruits. In addition, one section describes and illustrates a modern dairy farm.

An Ecuadorian folktale, *Ton-ton el gigantón* (Cumpiano 1992) (*Hugo Hogget* in English), was another of the books María read to the students as they discussed farms and how farms are run. This story deals with a wise woman, who, through riddles and a plant-rotation plan, tricks the giant, Ton-ton, who claims she stole his land.

The students and teacher finished this first section of the growth unit by looking at different products that are made from plants. The book they had read earlier, *Una semilla nada más,* ends by showing all the uses of sunflower seeds. This led the class into discussions about how we use plants in many ways every day. *Las cosas cambian* and the English version, *Things Change* (Montenegro-Bourne 1992), extended this discussion. In these books colorful photographs illustrate the many steps necessary to convert cotton balls into jeans. These books all helped students to see the importance of farming in everyone's life.

Throughout the unit, María encouraged students to use different resources published in Spanish and English (see Appendix C) as well as an issue of *Scholastic News* that featured plants (March 1993, Week 4). These publications allowed both her English and her Spanish speakers to develop primary language literacy and academic concepts. Since these resources were available in the classroom, students used them during individual and small-group investigations. At times students worked in groups with others who shared their primary language, and sometimes groups were mixed for discussion and sharing of ideas.

In addition to the science content study, the students did a literature study. English speakers read *The Corn Grows Ripe* (Rhodes 1993). In this short novel a Mayan Indian boy learns how to plant, care for, and harvest the corn his family needs to survive. This book served to help English-speaking Hispanic students learn about their roots and also provided a contrast to the modern farming methods the students experience in the Central Valley of California.

At the same time, Spanish speakers read "El prado del tío Pedro" (Puncel 1993), the story of three brothers who inherit a meadow and keep adding more sheep until the land is overgrazed. This tale raises important questions about proper land use. This story is interesting because the author provides three different possible endings. The first two endings are sad, and the third is happy. Then the author asks, "Este parece un buen final . . . ¿ Podría encontrarse otro mejor? A mí me gustaría conocerlo" ("This one seems like a good ending . . . Can you think up a better one? I'd like to know about it"), an invitation that led to student writing.

Through the different readings and discussions, the students in María's class developed concepts about how plants are the same and different, how to care for and grow plants, the stages of plant growth, the importance of seeds, the structure of different plants, plant rotation, and products that come from plants. In addition, they learned specialized vocabulary about plants in both Spanish and English.

María was able to teach whole to part by beginning with a general question, "How do plants grow?" and then moving to the parts, specific information about plants and growth. Throughout the unit, María involved her students in reading whole stories that introduced general concepts. She helped students learn through hands-on experiences and lots of reading, writing, and discussion. As the students and their teacher studied growth, they learned academic content and developed language in a natural way.

Explorer Teachers Use Relevant Themes

Teachers like María start with the whole by considering big questions that arise naturally from experiences and concerns that their students have. Basing themes on topics relevant to the learners is one way teachers show their respect for students and helps build students' self-respect. Kathy, the teacher whose unit on survival we described at the beginning of this chapter, explained the rationale for a unit, "One World/One Family," that she and her colleagues use (Freeman and Freeman, in Weaver 1994):

> Adolescence is an emotionally vulnerable time. Middle school students are beginning to see themselves as individuals separate from a family unit but unsure about where they really belong. We strive for them to see themselves as part of one human family with cultural, language, and ethnic diversity as positive and beneficial to the well-being and fulfillment of all people.

At Kathy's school the interdisciplinary team of teachers organize their curriculum around a theme cycle to provide continuity. In one theme cycle, Kathy's team explored questions of how people feel about differences. Kathy began the unit in language arts by showing the students the twelve-minute film "A Day in the Life of Bonnie Consolo"[*] (Barr Films 1975), which goes through the day of a woman born without arms. Students in Kathy's class did quickwrites (uninterrupted writing for one or two minutes) in their journals and then discussed their responses to the difficulties Bonnie faced.

After discussing the film and the main character's struggles, the class read *The Acorn People* by Ron Jones (1976). This book tells the true story of the author's work as a counselor with severely handicapped children at a summer camp. The teens in Kathy's class were initially repulsed by the handicaps of the children, especially Spider, who has stumps for arms and legs, and Arid, who must carry his waste in a plastic bag because he has no bladder. But soon the students began to realize that these children with physical deformities are people with feelings like every other kid.

In the process of reading, discussing, and writing about the book, Kathy's students carried out activities and discussed topics that were relevant to their own lives. In pairs they made labels that represented different characters in the book. They guessed which characters the labels of other pairs referred to and then discussed how people get labeled and how they can have positive or negative connotations. The students explained why they chose the symbols they invented to represent the characters: A carrot represented the "vegetable" label given the severely disabled kids in the book who were considered worthless and incapable of human feelings; a light bulb represented Martin, who, though blind, had brightness and ideas about the world and life; a crown represented Arid, who is crowned king at the dance in the story and is, in fact, as noble as a king; and an envelope represented the envelope given Ron Jones, the counselor and book's author, at the funeral of one of the campers. In the envelope was a note from the boy's mother explaining that the child had never forgotten the camp experience.

During the time that students discussed the labels, Kathy asked them to write in their literature logs about a time that they had experienced something similar to what happened to the characters in the book. These journal entries served as the beginnings of individual "autobiographical incidents," papers that are required by the district curriculum guides.

In the students' final project, done with their partner, they designed and presented a graphic that represented setting, plot, character, and theme. In Figure 6-9 a pair of students show the camp in the foreground on the right for the setting, the symbolic

---

[*]Note: Teachers may find this at local school libraries, but we have no address for purchase.

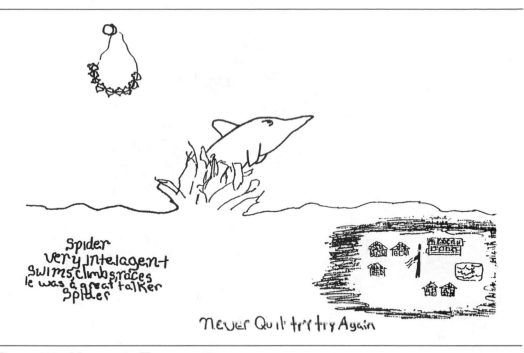

Spider
very intelagent
swims climbs races
le was a great talker
spider

never Quit try try Again

Figure 6-9   Never quit, Try, try again

acorn necklaces in the upper left for plot, and, for character, a dolphin in the middle to represent Spider, the boy with no arms or legs who, once in the water, was able to do anything. They titled their work "Never Quit, Try Try Again," which was their choice of theme.

Another pair of students chose the theme "Don't Judge a Book by Its Cover." Figure 6-10 shows their representation of the camp. The acorn necklace has a crown as a symbol of victory. The character Martin, the blind boy, is described in an acrostic.

At the end of the unit, students reflected in writing on what they had learned. Several explained that they had discovered that all people are the same inside, and you should not judge people by the way they look. Other students told Kathy that reading about how these boys overcame their disabilities to live and enjoy life the best way they could gave them hope to keep trying always and never give up on the goals they set for themselves. The students in Kathy's class began with the whole, the idea of being different, of suffering prejudice, of struggling. There were no lists of vocabulary to study before reading, no worksheets of questions to fill out to check comprehension, no written tests on setting, plot, character, or theme. Kathy's students read, wrote, discussed, and completed their graphics, and as they did this, the second language students in her class learned the parts including vocabulary and important literary elements.

Since Kathy is the team's English teacher, she engaged her students in a number of literacy activities. Other teachers in the team addressed the same questions but focused on other content areas, science, math, and social studies. In this way, the students received a unified curriculum presented whole to part. This continuity was

Figure 6-10   Don't judge a book by its cover

especially important for the second language students because the same concepts and vocabulary came up in their different classes. A fragmented curriculum disempowers second language students, but a unified curriculum allows all students to develop their full potential.

Conclusion

We opened this chapter with Ramón's survival kit for incoming seventh-grade students at King's Canyon Middle School, and we have described the theme study on differences those students carried out. We will close the chapter with the story of the eighth-grade graduation for Ramón and his 139 other Explorer Team members. The graduation was a true celebration not only for the students, but also for Pat, Cheryl, Mike, and Kathy, the teachers who worked so hard with them over a two-year period. The celebration, like so many special occasions, was both happy and sad. Tears flowed as proud students and teachers hugged and promised to stay in touch. Something very special had happened with this group. They had bonded as they learned. They had formed a group that cared about one another.

During the last month of school before graduation, several very special events took place that the teachers and students will not forget. The first was a carefully planned Career Day to which sixteen different community speakers were invited. All 140 eighth graders prepared for the day by reading about a variety of careers in the language arts class, by studying the economic aspects of careers, including reading graphs and charts in math class, and reviewing different career options in science class. The history teacher worked on a computer with all 140 students to access a database about career interests each had. When the Career Day arrived, the students had all thought about, read about, and talked about possible career options.

The speakers for the Career Day represented the diversity of the students of the Explorer Team. A Hispanic described how he had given up a $60,000-a-year job to earn $40,000 as a high school counselor. When the kids asked him why, he said, "Because you kids are dropping out! That's why!" He then repeated his message in Spanish for emphasis! The students got the message. A retired African-American principal told the kids, "I know it's hard. But it's not as hard for you to get to college as it was for me forty years ago!" A Hispanic female professor of sociology echoed his message telling the students about how she grew up in a migrant family. She described moving from school to school and how she had had to work in the fields after school and then do her homework after that. A Hmong woman who had recently been the commencement speaker at her college graduation explained how she had made it through high school and college essentially on her own. In her culture it was extremely unusual for a Hmong to go to college, but for a Hmong woman to go to college was almost unheard of! The students in the Explorer Team listened intently to the speakers, took notes eagerly, and wrote summaries of what they had learned. Several of the students chose a goal during Career Day, including a Hmong boy who had listened to a policeman explain how important he believed his job was to the community.

As a follow-up to Career Day all 140 students were hosted by a local junior college for a day of tours and a free lunch. The guides for the many small groups were all junior college students who at one time had dropped out of school and were now studying again. Part of the time the guides spent with the Kings Canyon students involved sharing the struggles they had endured and the decisions they had made to return to college. The guides wanted to impress upon the junior high school students how important school right now was for their futures.

Three days before graduation all 140 students from the Explorer Team met in the school library with the teachers for a special good-bye ceremony. The session began with Pat, the history teacher, showing an hour-long videotape he had made. The tape captured many of the activities the students had participated in during their two years together. Students laughed as they saw themselves as seventh graders and were surprised at how much they had changed. After the video, awards—some serious and some humorous—were presented to the students. Every student received *something* and the positive vibrations could be felt throughout the room. Kathy recalled one girl in particular. She had been difficult at times, as all the Explorer Team teachers would admit, but when she heard her name called for most improved in history class, she was visibly moved. It was obvious that she did not expect to get anything, and it is possible that this may have been the only academic award she had ever received.

The bonding of students and faculty on the Explorer Team was celebrated that day. The principal, who had passed through several times during the four-hour session, told the teachers later that he would not have believed that 140 eighth graders could sit together so totally involved for so long for any reason. This time was special for every student there. Self-esteem was built and friendships were cemented. Perhaps

June 9, 1993

Dear Explorers Teachers,

It's been two years since I know you guys. All of the teachers have been very helpful and just being a teacher when I needed you. You guys have been very encouraging about what is right for me and wrong for me. Thank you all for your support.

Mrs. Sereda, I want to thank you for being a helpful teacher. You've helped me on homework and just there when I need something. Also, thank you for letting me be in your homeroom again.

Mr. Wilson, thank you for being a teacher. I'm sorry for being a pain. You've been a great teacher and wish you the bestest luck in your marriage. What are you going to name your children?

Mrs. Smith, thank you for encouraging me in doing what is right for me. You've helped me a lot these two years. I wish you could be my english teacher in the ninth grade. I'll never forget you for what you have done for me. Thank you for these lovely two years.

Figure 6-11   Kia's journal

most important of all was that everyone felt a sense of "Yes, it was hard work, but it was worth it!" Because the teachers respected their students and organized a unified curriculum that provided whole-to-part instruction, the students had developed a respect for their own abilities.

This sense of accomplishment and support for the Explorer Team concept was expressed by the students in their last journal entries for Kathy's class. Jessica wrote, "These have been the greatest 2 years of my life! I don't like saying Good bye so I'll say, 'See ya Later!'" Excerpts from Kia's journal (Figure 6-11) tell how much she appreciated the support and encouragement from her team of teachers. She even apologizes for "being a pain." Juanita (Figure 6-12) summarized what the Explorer Team was all about when she said it "feels like one great big Family" and "I could tell that all of you must (be) great teachers to care so much on how we grow up & live are lives."

Graduation was the ultimate validation for students and especially for Pat, Cheryl, Mike, and Kathy. Although they comprised less than a third of all the graduates, the students from the Explorer Team received ninety percent of all the awards given out

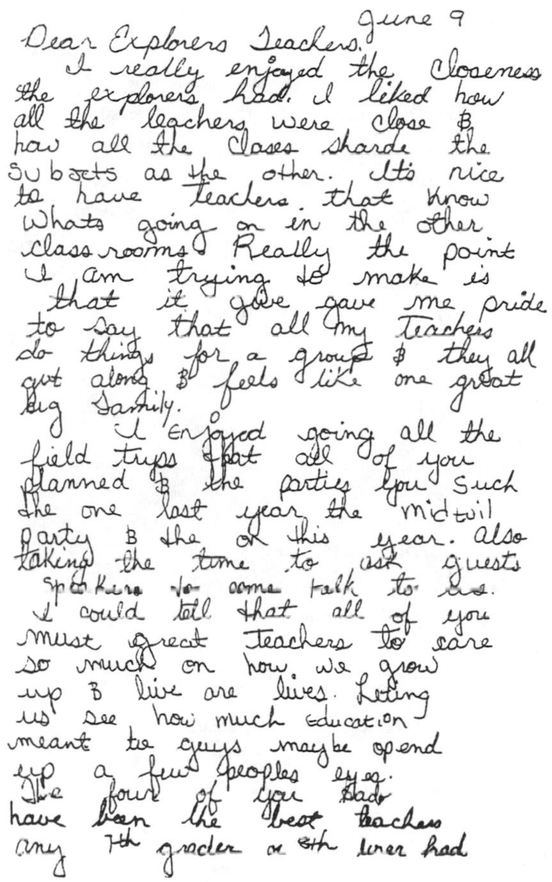

Dear Explorers Teachers,

June 9

I really enjoyed the closeness the explorers had. I liked how all the teachers were close & how all the classes sharde the subjets as the other. It's nice to have teachers that know whats going on in the other class rooms. Really the point I am trying to make is that it give gave me pride to say that all my teachers do things for a group & they all got along & feels like one great big family.

I enjoyed going all the field trips that all of you planned & the parties you. Such the one last year the mid-twil party & the one this year. Also taking the time to ask guest spekers to come talk to us. I could tell that all of you must great teachers to care so much on how we grow up & live are lives. Letting us see how much education meant to you guys maybe opend up a few peoples eyes. The four of you had have been the best teachers any 7th grader or 8th liver had

Figure 6-12   Juanita's journal

at the ceremony, including academic, athletic, and good citizenship awards. When the Spanish teacher described the all-around outstanding student in Spanish, it was an Explorer Team student; when the computer instructor named the top student in computers, it was an Explorer Team student; the highest honor in woodshop went to an Explorer Team student; when the home economics teacher announced the all-around outstanding student, it was an Explorer Team student; and when the principal and vice principal gave out the outstanding citizenship awards, they went to Explorer Team students.

At the end of the ceremony everyone—teachers, administrators, parents, and the students themselves—marveled together. The students had begun as a diverse group of inner-city, average to below-average students from many different backgrounds. Few thought much about their futures and, if they did, they did not consider college. When they graduated, they were students with expectations, students with determination, students with hope, and especially students with a future. All of them now felt that they had access to further education.

What happened at Kings Canyon Middle School with the Explorer Team can happen anywhere when teachers show respect for their students and make sure that all students have access to learning. Explorer teachers give all students, and especially bilingual students, a greater chance to succeed. These teachers carefully observe their students' learning, and they celebrate their successes. When explorer teachers see young readers making sense out of text by looking at pictures, they know they are at the beginning stages of reading. As students watch plant growth and record what they see, explorer teachers share their excitement. When students raise questions about differences and prejudice, teachers and students read, write, and talk together and share their new understandings with others. Explorer teachers celebrate their students' work because they know that each of these efforts signals progress as students gain respect for both themselves and learning. Access to acquisition of language and concepts is open to students between worlds in explorer classrooms.

Applications

1. Second language learners are usually given either official school labels or other labels. What kinds of labels have second language learners you have worked with been given? How might those students have been affected by those labels? Discuss in groups.

2. What kind of discipline system have you used or experienced in school? Read the description of the assertive discipline system in King Elementary School and the cooperative conflict resolution system in Roxanne Claassen's classroom. Compare and contrast the two systems with a partner or a small group. Which system do you prefer? Why?

3. Read over Joyce's description of her French language learning and Susan's learning of German. Compare those experiences with a language-learning experience you have had. Discuss.

4. In small groups list some part-to-whole activities you have used or seen used with second language learners. Discuss.

5. In small groups discuss how organizing teaching around themes helps second language learners. Share ideas about themes that could be used with your students.

6. Bring to class a list of books and other support materials that could be used for a theme with your students. Share and discuss.

7. Think of a personal example from your own life or teaching of personal invention in learning. Did social convention alter the hypothesis? Share with a partner.

CHAPTER SEVEN

How Do Explorer Teachers Focus on Learners and Their Strengths?

E xplorer teachers show respect for their students and organize curriculum around themes so students can investigate topics from whole to part. In explorer classrooms students' personal inventions are refined as they move toward conventional ways of using language and of understanding content area concepts. A third important characteristic of explorer classes is that teachers focus on their learners and build on their strengths. They do this by providing them with choices, by helping them ask important questions, by making curriculum meaningful for them, by helping them work together collaboratively, and by encouraging them to employ a variety of modes for learning and expressing understandings.

Focus on the Learner

Parents know that young (and older) children pay attention if discussion is focused on them, their needs, or their interests. A crying baby is distracted when a parent plays a favorite game, waves a familiar toy, or simply directs the conversation to the child: "Oh! Is that Bobbie crying? Look, he's stopped! You're a good boy, aren't you! You just wanted some attention, didn't you?" Noisy and cranky ten-year-olds can turn into engrossed and eager children when a new game (or an old favorite) is pulled out, especially if adults will play, too.

However, not all classrooms reflect this basic understanding of the importance of focusing on the learner. In many traditional classrooms, the teacher or the content take center stage. With second language learners, the temptation is even greater to create a teacher-centered classroom. Because the teacher has the English proficiency the students need, it seems natural that the teacher should model the language and direct the lessons. However, teachers can't directly transmit knowledge of the English language any more than any other set of concepts.

Lindfors (1987) provides an example of the pitfalls of a teacher-centered orientation with an excerpt from a textbook written for second language elementary school students. (*Note: T* = teacher, *C* = class, *P* = individual pupil)

T: Class, ask [Juan/María], "How do you feel?"
C: How do you feel?
P: I feel [fine/good/well].
T: Class, ask [him/her], "Are you happy?"
C: Are you happy?
P: Yes, I am.
T: Ask [him/her], "Do you need to lie down?"
C: Do you need to lie down?
P: No, I don't need to lie down. (p. 438)

This lesson at first glance seems to focus on the learner. Students are asking each other how they feel and whether they need to rest. A closer look, though, makes it clear that this is a teacher-directed lesson. Some students are told what to ask, and their classmate has only limited choices in answering. The student can be "fine," "well," or "good," but not sick. In fact, the sequence of sentences makes little sense. If the student is happy, why should classmates ask if he or she wants to lie down? Even though students may be actively involved in the lesson, it doesn't focus on them, their needs, or their interests.

Henrietta, a German ancestry South American studying for her master's degree in TESOL (Teachers of English to Speakers of Other Languages), described a lesson she taught that stands in sharp contrast to the traditional lesson described above. She wrote about discovering the power of focusing on the learner when she was tutoring some college-aged international students:

> I always wondered, "How do I find out what is of interest to the students?" Last week I had a wonderful experience with two of the adult ESL students I am working with for my practicum. I met with an Armenian student in a small room that had a world map attached to its wall. To start our meeting casually, I walked over to the map and asked her about the location of her home country and if she could tell me something about it. This initial question triggered an hour of her telling me about her country, the economic situation, the Moslem/Christian conflict, her family, her journey to America and many details about her personal life. . . . I asked her if she would be willing to write an essay about her country, her story, and some of the struggles she went through. She is now working on that essay.
>
> The other student I met with comes from Thailand. I do not remember how we got to talk about his job, but suddenly I found him talking about what mattered to him. He is a pastor of the Khmu people here in Fresno. He shared about his concern with the church and the young Christians in Thailand. His eyes glowed with excitement. Again, I asked him if he would be willing to share his story in an essay. This was exciting. This would give me the opportunity to learn more about him, about his concerns and interests, and about his literacy. It really happened—students had talked to me about what mattered to them!

A focus on the learner can allow a teacher to discover students' strengths and build on them as Henrietta did. Even students with limited English proficiency can communicate information about themselves, and in the process of authentic language use, they develop English.

Explorer teachers like Henrietta focus on the learner to help students who are between worlds gain access to English, but more importantly, this focus allows teachers to gain important insights into the real needs of students. This knowledge helps teachers decide what is important. Lurette gives an example that shows how important this focus on the learner can be. She writes about an early high school teaching experience:

> Very early in my teaching career I learned, incredibly painfully, how meaningless, how useless, and how absurd the nonstudent-centered classroom really is.
>
> I am an English teacher, a teacher of communication skills, a liberator of the human spirit. From the beginning, I glowed with desire to share the light-giving, door-opening knowledge of reading and writing, of words.
>
> I remember standing before the eleventh-grade class I inherited from a seriously ill teacher. Upgraded from substitute to emergency credential-holding English teacher, I dreamed of essay structures at night. My lesson plan book swarmed with grammar exercise notation; each morning I appeared in class erupting worksheets.
>
> My low socioeconomic students responded to the new, young, enthusiastic teacher who obviously wanted to adopt every one of them. Attentive, quiet María was typical: every worksheet came in; her excellent grades danced across the gradebook.
>
> When María's schoolwide English Proficiency Test came back with a 90%, I remember floating down the hall one morning in early April to congratulate her. She always waited for me at the classroom door before school. But she wasn't there. And when class began, her desk was still vacant.

I was diligently teaching Comma Rule 3, Drill 1–7 when the uniformed police arrived. A cardboard face listened to my protest that María was "never" absent, that she was an excellent student. The policeman dropped his card on my desk. "If you see her, contact us."

At break in the faculty room, I found out that my A— student, my quiet little worker, my top scorer on the English Proficiency Test had stabbed her father to death that morning.

Stunned, I had to see María. She was in juvenile hall. She was embarrassed when she saw her English teacher. She apologized for "everything." I muttered something about, "María, my God, are you okay? What happened?"

She didn't say anything. She just pulled up her blouse enough to reveal dime-sized burns on her stomach. "I'm not going to be nobody's ashtray no more," she said simply. "I couldn't tell nobody. I'm not good at words. But I'm not nobody's ashtray no more."

I will never forget those words. I will never forget the words my A— María, my 90% Proficiency Test Pride and Joy who couldn't find the words, who couldn't tell anyone, so silently stabbed her father to death.

And I was her teacher of communication skills, the purveyor of the power of words, the liberator of the human spirit.

In her reflection Lurette is really a bit hard on herself, but her powerful response shows us how important it is for teachers to focus first on the needs of the learners. Even though teachers like Lurette do have a responsibility to engage students in academic content, the greater responsibility is to meet human needs. When teachers begin by having their students write about what is important to them instead of starting with comma rules, they might provide students like María the chance to communicate their real-life dilemmas. In the next section we discuss how teachers can meet the demands of the academic curriculum and still keep a focus on the personal needs of learners.

Providing Students with Choice

Barnes (1990) and others have argued that learning involves the active construction of concepts by the learner. That does not mean, however, that the teacher does not have an important role. Vygotsky (1978) pointed out that we form concepts when adults or more capable peers help us solve problems that are slightly beyond our current ability level. The teacher's role is to assist students as they engage in problem-solving activities that allow them to develop new concepts and the language that is used to express those concepts. Teachers mediate students' learning by asking questions and pointing out aspects of problems to help focus students' perceptions. Teachers provide demonstrations, they model, and they build scaffolds that help students learn.

Teachers, then, can and should have a clear idea of what learning goals they have for their students. In addition, they should understand that they are the professionals in charge of their classrooms. At the same time, explorer teachers want to focus on learners and build curriculum around their students' needs and interests. How can teachers be in charge (the expedition leaders) and still focus on the learner? One way is by providing choice. Through choice teachers can focus on their learners and help them become true explorers. Sumara (1993) describes how Michelle, the teacher we saw in Chapters 2 and 5, provides choice. We would call Michelle an explorer teacher as well:

There would appear to be a contradiction between suggesting that a teacher who was quite directive and one who planned specific activities thoughtfully and carefully would be empowering students with *choice,* yet this is precisely what seemed to be occurring in Michelle's classroom. Although students did not have much choice with *what* kinds of activities they would engage in, or even with *when* they would engage with them, they had considerable freedom and choice with *how* they would complete specific tasks (p. 140).

One example of choice in Michelle's classroom was during library time. This was scheduled for all students by Michelle, but students were not forced to check out books or even read at that time. During those periods Sumara observed students reading quietly, reading to each other, looking through picture or photo books, doing other homework, or talking quietly to one another. While not all the students were doing what one might expect during a library period, they "were engaged in some kind of 'reading' activity, whether it was with written text or with oral or graphic text; there was always an exchange of information" (p. 141).

Sumara goes on to explain how Michelle's expectations were clear (students did not disturb others or overtly "goof off" in the library), but she did want students to take responsibility for their learning. "Although Michelle was clear about what was to be accomplished, she appeared to be intentionally ambiguous about how this learning would occur" (p. 140). She also allowed the students to chose the *who.* There was choice for students in deciding with whom to sit during library time or with whom to explore the themes they were studying. With clear expectations and choice, Michelle and her students explored learning together.

Onore (1990) makes a similar point. She explains that teachers who organize curriculum around students' interests and questions still help to set the educational agenda. She describes a unit on Thanksgiving involving second graders. The teacher chose the topic because "every class in her school will be studying Thanksgiving as well as celebrating the holiday in some way" (p. 62). Onore comments, "The topic of their inquiry is nonnegotiable. What the children choose to learn, how they will go about learning, and how they will share their learning is, however, open to negotiation" (p. 62).

Kari, a seventh-grade teacher, provides a specific example of what Sumara and Onore discuss. Kari had her students, many of whom were second language learners, write and edit a magazine as a final evaluation of what they had learned:

> Our culminating writing project was for each student to create their own magazine. The students chose their own topics of interest to write on. Included in the magazine they created were cartoons, advertisements, coupons, and whatever else their imaginations could come up with. I received some wonderful magazines on a wide variety of topics including animals, cars, sports, rock music and Hollywood stars. The students were enthusiastic about their work, and we were able to read one another's magazines when finished.

Choice, then, is one key to help explorer teachers focus on the learner.

Starting with Students' Questions

Explorer teachers also focus on the learner by starting with questions and concerns that relate directly to their students' lives. They follow Dewey's (1929) advice that "the child is the starting point, the center, and the end" (p. 14) of all curriculum decisions. While the curriculum in all classrooms should begin with the learner, it is especially important for teachers with second language students to do this. Often, the life experiences of English language learners differ from those of mainstream students, around which traditional curriculum was structured. Explorer teachers concentrate on topics that connect to students' lives, realizing that as the students develop concepts, they will also develop the English needed to discuss them.

Roxie described how much drawing on her students' lives and backgrounds encouraged both student and parent involvement:

> Last month my first-grade class did a presentation on Mexico for multicultural day. It really built on my students' self-esteem and had an overwhelming response from the parents, too. One mother and her daughter volunteered to teach the students the real version of the "Mexican Hat Dance," two other parents volunteered to help teach the students the song "De Colores," and another went out and got all the material we needed for our presentation. I had never seen such student and parent involvement.

Cultural events can be very enriching, but it is also important to draw students into the curriculum content at different grade levels. Clark (1988) has pointed out that curriculum should involve students "in some of the significant issues in life" and therefore encourages teachers to design their curriculum around "questions worth arguing about" (p. 29). He suggests questions for different age groups including several that would be especially for immigrant students: "How am I a member of many families?" (K–1); "What are the patterns that make communities work?" (2–3); "How do humans and culture evolve and change?" (4–5); "How does one live responsibly as a member of the global village?" (6, 7, 8).

Sizer (1990) draws on the same idea by suggesting that organizing around "Essential Questions" leads to "engaging and effective curricula." In social studies, teachers responsible for teaching U.S. history might begin with broad questions such as "Who is American?" "Who should stay?" "Who should stay out?" "Whose country is it anyway?" (p. 49). Sizer suggests larger questions for long-term planning and smaller, engaging questions to fit within the broader ones. For example, an essential question in botany might be "What is life, growth, 'natural' development and what factors most influence healthy development?" A small engaging question might be "Do stems of germinating seedlings always grow upwards and the roots downwards?" (p. 50).

Kay, a bilingual resource teacher in a rural school with a high Hispanic population, focused on her third-grade pull-out students by raising an engaging question from their own experiences (Freeman and Goodman 1993). Since many of her students had come to this country as refugees, she decided she could start with questions related to immigration. Kay read her students a portion of a newspaper article entitled "America as Seen through Daddy's Eyes" (Blum 1991). The article ended with the line "When we stop taking in immigrants, that's when we stop being great" (p. H4).

Kay talked to her students about the many immigrants who have come to America and asked them what they thought "When we stop taking in immigrants, that's when we stop being great" might mean. The children discussed this in both Spanish and English and decided to talk with their families about why they came to America. Then Kay read the students the book *Mira, cómo salen las estrellas* (*Watch How the Stars Come Out*) (Levinson 1987). The children brainstormed in Spanish what they remembered about this story of two immigrant children coming alone to the United States in the early 1900s on a large ship full of other immigrants. Kay wrote what they said on a large piece of butcher paper.

The next day the students read *How Many Days to America?* (Bunting 1988) another story about refugees. The students then compared and contrasted the two stories. After the students had read and discussed the newspaper article, taken their surveys, and compared and contrasted the two stories, they decided to write and illustrate a Spanish book that summarized *Mira, cómo salen las estrellas* in their own words. They then chose to read their summaries in Spanish to the rest of their third-grade class. They first read their classmates *How Many Days to America?* (Bunting 1988) in English "so they would have an idea about the other story in Spanish," and then they read their own stories in Spanish. Far from being insecure because they were less fluent in English than their peers, they showed pride in what they had been learning in Spanish and English. By starting with questions directly related to her students' own experiences, Kay was able to focus on the learner and engage her students in meaningful literacy activities.

One way that teachers in explorer classrooms organize curriculum around questions worth asking is by following Don Howard's Wonderfilled Way of Learning questions (Y. Freeman and D. Freeman 1992a).

1. What do you know about . . . ?
2. What do you wonder about . . . ?
3. How will you find out about . . . ?
4. What kind of action plan will you make?
5. How will you celebrate learning?

Cheryl is a fifth-grade teacher in a farming community. She has recently begun to view her Hispanic students as explorers. Cheryl decided to try organizing her teaching of the required curriculum content by using the wonderfilled questions. She reflected on her attempts at focusing her curriculum on her students:

> Today in class I used the "What do you know?," "What would you like to know?" method to learn about Abraham Lincoln. First, I asked the students to raise their hands to tell me what they knew about Lincoln. No response. Then I told them to talk about it in their groups and write down any ideas about the man that they might have. It was wonderful! I put his picture on the wall and wrote the students' ideas on a transparency. Three students came to me afterwards and asked if they could do a special project about him.

This lesson was quite different from a traditional lesson on Lincoln. Cheryl focused on her students and found ways for them to connect with this content area study. She succeeded in involving her students in answering questions that they helped to raise, and the result was that they were eager to investigate the topic. It is important to point out that in an explorer class like Cheryl's, the questions come primarily from the students; however, as a member of the learning community, the teacher can also raise questions that focus on the learner.

In addition to Howard's Wonderfilled Way of Learning to organize curriculum, we have also suggested a way of using questions for the day by day as well as the week by week lesson plans that all teachers must do (Y. Freeman and D. Freeman 1992a, 1992b). Our method uses theme cycles and is organized around big questions. Both student teachers and experienced teachers have reported success in using our format.

Questioning Lesson Plan

1. What is the question worth talking about? Can the topic for this lesson be formulated in a question? What is the engaging smaller question that fits into your broader question for your overall theme?

2. How does the question fit into your overall plan? What is the broad question/theme that you and your students are exploring over time? How does the smaller, engaging question support the concepts you are working on with this broad question?

3. How will you find out what the students already know about the question? What are different ways your students might show what they already know about answering the question? You might brainstorm, do an experiment, interview someone, etc.

4. What strategies will you use together to explore the question? What are ways the question might be answered? You and your students might read, do an experiment, brainstorm, ask an expert, work out a problem together, etc. Ask the students if they have ideas about how to answer the question.

5. What materials will you use together to explore the question? List the resources, including people, that students might use to answer the question. Again, ask the students if they have ideas about this.

6. What steps will you and the students take to explore the question? In order to be sure that you are keeping in mind principles about learning, consult the Whole Language Checklist (see Applications). Do the activities you suggest incorporate whole language principles?

7. How will you observe the students' learning? What are some different ways to evaluate the process of your students' learning? Be sure to consider alternatives to traditional tests including group presentations, a group-produced book or newspaper, the results of an experiment, a drawing or schemata, etc. (1992a, p. 50)

This lesson plan format is designed to help teachers reconceptualize curriculum as a series of questions generated by the students and the teacher as they explore topics together. The questions encourage teachers to keep in focus the broad concepts being studied.

Dennette, an elementary school teacher with experience in Arizona and California, has organized curriculum around theme cycles. She, like other teachers, must submit lesson plans to administrators. She has experimented with the Questioning Lesson Plan in an effort to make preplanned lessons learner centered. Below we present one of Denette's plans based on the question "How do things work?"

Denette's "How Things Work" Questioning Lesson Plan
1. What is the question worth talking about?
    "How does something work at your house?"

2. How does this question fit into your overall plan? The overall theme question is "How do things work?" This possible year-long theme is important because it helps us use things more efficiently, helps us understand malfunctions, could help avoid accidents, could help save money, and raises self-esteem as students understand better how things around them work. The question also meets curriculum needs in science, math, social studies, reading, and writing.

3. How will you find out what the students know? Before students explore the question of how something works in their home, have them brainstorm what they are curious about. This may include, but is certainly not limited to, the sewer system, water system, electrical appliances, gas system, automobile, recycling, or garbage disposal systems.

4. What strategies will you use to explore the question? Students will identify interests and form groups. They might invite in community professional experts to interview. They might prepare demonstrations and set up learning centers for the rest of the class. They might choose to write a directions manual or create a filmstrip, video, or slide show. They might choose to go on field trips to the power company, telephone company, or other relevant businesses.

5. What materials can be used? Books, experts, videos, films, appliance manuals, assembly directions, broken things such as appliances and motors.

6. What steps will the students use to explore? Read material available. Formulate interview questions and interview experts. Organize and take field trips. Dismantle, reassemble, or repair available "things."

7. How will you observe learning? Observe student presentations. Evaluate projects students create that show learning including posters, directions, kits, films, slide shows, learning centers. A student-generated checksheet of expectations will be used, and peers as well as the teacher will evaluate.

Planning lessons with the Questioning Lesson Plan is one way teachers can start with their learners as they organize. In explorer classes, teachers work so that students' interest is not based simply on the desire to do well on a test or get some other kind of extrinsic reward. Instead, explorer students "buy into" the curriculum because they honestly are interested in answering the questions that they have helped raise.

Making Curriculum Meaningful for Students

Research has shown that children learn their first language because it serves a purpose for them (Halliday 1984; Smith 1983). Babies' first words are ones that identify primary caregivers—"mamá," "dada," "bapa"—or immediate needs that they have—"wawa," "agua" (Spanish for "water"). These needs are similar in different cultures. For Hmong children, for example, common early words are "mov" ("food/rice") and "mis" ("milk"). As children grow older, they continue to learn the language that is necessary for them to get what they need.

In the same way, when students find school activities meaningful, they engage more fully and develop both language and concepts more quickly. This is what happened in Katie's prefirst class. Katie helped the students plan a trip to a pizza parlor. Later, they wrote about their experience. Khmer-speaking Sophal contributed to brainstorming for the class newsletter with his first spoken word in English: "pizza." Later in the year, after Valentine's day, Pa, a bilingual Hmong-English speaker, writing in her journal to Katie, requested another party (see Figure 7-1). The activities, going to the pizza parlor and having a Valentine's Day party, helped Katie's students begin to use English because her curriculum was meaningful to these young second language learners.

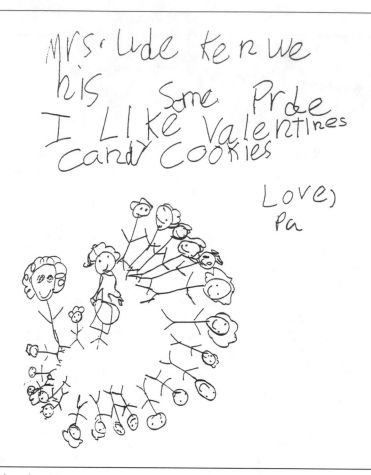

Figure 7-1   Pa's valentine request

Another teacher, Joan, reported on one of her first graders who spoke no English: "Roberta wasn't too interested in reading from the books we had, but being the people person she was, she soon learned to read the names of all the kids on our sign-in sheet!" By having her students sign in, Joan developed a meaningful activity that helped Roberta move into reading.

Teachers and researchers (Cummins 1981) have found that bilingual students often learn the English expressions used in playground games or other social situations before developing more formal classroom English. It is not surprising that social language generally develops first; it serves students' immediate needs. However, besides learning the language for interpersonal communication, students must also develop academic language. Unfortunately, in many classrooms academic language develops slowly because the curriculum is future oriented. Students are told to study a subject because "someday you are going to need to know what is being taught today." Kindergarten gets children "ready" for first grade, first grade prepares children for second, and this future orientation continues through high school or even college. The problem with this process is that human beings usually don't learn things until they see a need for them. Explorer teachers like Joan and Katie have found activities that are meaningful, and their students have begun to use English for both social and academic purposes.

Culture and Family History

Many teachers of bilingual students have discovered that students learn both language and content when lessons are centered on students' culture and family history. These topics are naturally meaningful to all students. Student authors in Wayland's middle school ESL class, for example, are encouraged to share their experiences and culture through a book the class publishes each year. The book is bound by a local library bindery and sold to students, parents, and community members. Students choose their own theme for the book and write about things that are important to them.

In the 1990 book *New Americans*, Chao Vang showed the changes that his family had experienced across three generations (Figure 7-2). He illustrated and labeled items that represented his culture, his parents' culture, and his grandparents' culture, showing differences in homes, schools, food, games, and celebrations. In the process of researching his topic, drawing and labeling his pictures, and discussing the project with his teacher and his classmates, Chao developed both his academic English proficiency and important social studies concepts (Y. Freeman and D. Freeman 1993).

Obviously, Chao invested a great deal of time and energy in his contribution for the book because it was personally meaningful to him. In explorer classrooms like Wayland's, student diversity becomes a celebrated resource for learning.

In another middle school classroom, Shelly developed a long-term unit for her seventh- and eighth-grade social studies ESL students whose first languages include Spanish, Hmong, and Khmer. Since the seventh-grade social studies curriculum at her school begins with material about ways people research the past, Shelly decided to make the curriculum meaningful to the students by having them research their own past and then helping them connect their past to the present. Under the broad theme of "Culture: A Pattern of Civilization," Shelly and her students explored the question "What's my part in my family and my culture?"

To begin the unit the students and teacher chose several questions to explore:

Where do I come from?

What is my culture?

How does culture fit into society?

What are the cultural aspects of my family?

What is my role in my family and culture?

Why is culture important?

Shelly's rationale for her unit showed that she understood the idea of making learning meaningful for her students. "By creating a unit that validates the student's culture and personal views, the student will learn to appreciate his/her own culture as well as other cultures. If the student can appreciate other cultures, then the social studies material will have meaning and the students will enjoy studying it."

Figure 7-2   Chao Vang's generation chart

Making a Time Line

Goal: For students to understand how to construct a time line and the uses and importance of using time lines.

Purpose: Students must often keep events and ideas ordered and prioritized. By understanding how to use a time line students will have a skill to help them with their studies as well as understand time lines in their history classes.

Objective: Each student created a time line of the important events in his/her life.

Materials:
1. pencil and crayons
2. long strip of paper
3. ruler

Procedure:
1. Reviewed concept of time line using example we have in class.
2. Discussed purpose of time line and what is on a time line.
3. Each child made a list of important events in his/her life.
4. Each student marked the years of his/her life on the strip of paper and wrote the important events of each year.
5. Students decorated their time lines.

Summary/Evaluation: Students shared their time lines with each other and put them up on the wall for display. I asked the students to share their most important events and why they chose to put them on their times lines.

Extension: We constructed and put up time lines around the room so that as the year progresses we will continue to add to the time line of historical events. This will help reinforce the ideas of chronological time and also help the students put "time" into perspective. This helps the students learn to put events into perspective chronologically.

Figure 7-3 Making a time line

A description of one activity Shelly did with her students, "Making a Time Line" (see Figure 7-3), shows how Shelly was able to make content learning meaningful to her second language learners. In her written evaluation of the time line activity for a teacher education class, Shelly explained how engagement in that activity helped her students develop important concepts.

> This assignment took the place of having the students simply look at time lines in a text. The students were excited since the subject was their life. This supports the idea that if the subject matter is relevant, a student will be interested and motivated to complete an assignment. My students practiced thinking about order of events as they prepared their time lines. It is important for the students to be able to order events

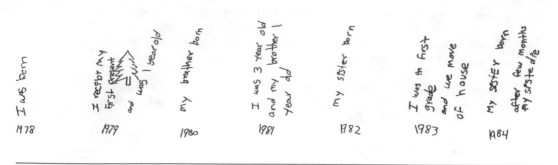

Figure 7-4   Juan's time line

in time. Students need to order events when they are reading, thinking about plots, or predicting events. They also need to order their thoughts before writing.

When her students did not know dates, Shelly suggested that they ask their families. This additional family involvement was so successful that she has decided to include families in the time line the next time she does the activity. Shelly also found that the time lines served as a nonthreatening way for some students to share things about their past, including tragic deaths in the family. Juan, a Mexican student, recorded the birth and death of a sister, his separation from his parents when they came to the United States to work, and his arrival in this country (see Figure 7-4).

After the students had completed their time lines, they displayed them around the room and shared what they considered to be significant events. They also created a large whole-class time line with dates of historical events they were studying. Students helped fill in that time line and enjoyed adding to it each time they studied a new event. Shelly explained how the personal time lines helped the students understand how one works: "They have been able to compare their short lives with centuries of events, to put history in perspective, and to develop the concept that all things are connected through time."

By drawing on the diversity of experiences in the lives of their students, explorer teachers like Shelly create rich learning environments in their classrooms. They create situations in which all their students develop academic content and both academic and social language as they engage in activities that are meaningful to them.

A Word of Caution

Our orientation toward curriculum in an explorer classroom is consistent with whole language. However, some educators have critiqued the way whole language has been implemented with certain student populations. Harman and Edelsky (1989) have questioned the cultural integrity of whole language approaches to literacy because some English language learners have become alienated from their roots in the process of becoming empowered through reading and writing. Harman and Edelsky argue that this empowerment can be seen by families and communities as a force that moves children away from parents as they seek success in the Anglo culture.

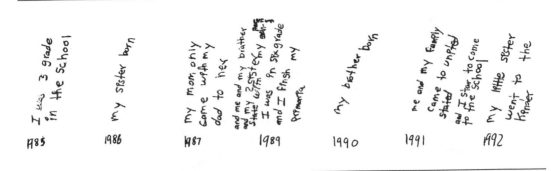

Figure 7-4 Juan's time line *(continued)*

In addition, empowered learners themselves may feel estranged from their families or communities once their learning introduces them to different views. Rodríguez (1982) has written about his own alienation in *Hunger of Memory: The Education of Richard Rodríguez*. Even though there are cases such as Rodríguez', educators like Shelly are teaching their diverse students literacy through a focus on culture and helping them to actually understand and become closer to their roots. Far from being alienated, they develop new pride in who they are and deeper understandings of their cultural heritage.

Another criticism of whole language comes from Delpit (1988), who argues that whole language teachers do not teach African-American children the skills that the system requires of them. In addition, she claims that these teachers do not listen to the voices of African-American parents when they try to explain what they want for their children. Delpit's view of whole language is different from what we are presenting here. The whole language teachers we have worked with move from the whole to the parts. They don't ignore skills. However, their goal is not to teach the skills but to help students become skilled language users (Edelsky, Altwerger, and Flores 1991). In addition, these teachers focus on the needs and interests of their students and the concerns of parents, so if students lack skills in certain aspects of literacy, explorer teachers find ways to engage them in activities during which they can develop those skills.

Explorer teachers focus on their students. They provide choice and build curriculum around students' questions. They engage students in meaningful learning, and they are sensitive to students' backgrounds. In some cases, however, teachers wish to involve their students with certain topics on which the students have little background. In these instances, it may be difficult to provide choice and tap into students' questions because the students simply don't have enough experience with the topic to raise meaningful questions. If the teacher feels that the topic is an important one, he or she may need to move beyond simply nudging students. There are times in explorer classrooms when the teacher becomes the expedition's leader.

Sumara (1993) provides an example of a teacher who took charge of the curriculum to build the background her students needed. Michelle, the teacher mentioned earlier, began a unit on dinosaurs with a brainstorming session. The recent immigrants in her culturally diverse classroom who had no past experience with dinosaurs were not able to participate. As Sumara notes, they "became isolated and marginalized." However, Michelle kept the focus on the learners:

> Michelle sensed this difficulty immediately and modified her teaching plan. Rather than assuming prior knowledge, she came to understand that it was essential to give these culturally different students access to experiences which would allow them success with the remainder of the unit. . . . Michelle decided to assign a "dinosaur anthology" assignment. Very simply, it consisted of assigning a different species of dinosaur to each student, asking them to use the classroom and library books to research that species, and to compose a one-page summary of the research (p. 143).

Sumara explains that he was disturbed by the assignment because it was not authentic or meaningful, and students had little choice. In addition, several students complained about it, and others found it difficult and tedious. However, as the week progressed Sumara noted that students worked together and this, with the aid of adults in the room, helped all the students produce a "polished piece of expository writing." These individual pieces were bound into *Dinosaur Field Guides*. All students were then given a copy to use as a resource during the rest of the unit. Michelle had kept the focus on the learner to ensure that all her students could participate in the dinosaur unit, even though that meant being directive at the beginning.

Learning Through Collaboration

Michelle provided all her students access to the acquisition of English and content knowledge by having them work collaboratively with both peers and adults. Explorer teachers like Michelle focus on their students and build on their strengths by providing them with opportunities to work together. Students build both communicative and academic competence as they negotiate meaning with others. In this process, students' personal inventions are tested against social conventions. Social interaction is especially important for students learning a second language.

McGroarty (1993) points out that cooperative activities promote second language acquisition. Students need to learn to use language that is appropriate to a variety of situations in order to develop sociolinguistic competence, and cooperative learning provides those situations. "Attainment of a complete communicative repertoire comes about through multiple experiences of different contexts for communication, each of which may have its own conventions for appropriate linguistic forms and usage patterns" (p. 25). Cooperative groups provide the "multiple social contexts" (p. 25) needed for language acquisition.

When a second language learner is using language for real communication, language is acquired because conventional forms are needed in order to get messages across. During our time in Venezuela, we often received puzzled looks from our maid or in the marketplace. These were clues that our Spanish inventions were not close enough to conventional Spanish. As we negotiated meaning, we picked up more conventional structures and vocabulary needed to communicate successfully. We learned through social interactions.

Scotty, a graduate student studying to teach ESL to adult learners, recently shared a personal experience that supported his understanding of the importance of social interaction in his learning a second language:

> When I was in college, I continued my study of Spanish and did well in the classes, but I was very aware that my speaking and comprehension were much worse than my reading and writing. Then, one day at an outdoor school party I struck up a conversation with an attractive female student who was from Colombia. We began speaking in Spanish and continued for so long that I ceased to be aware that I was not speaking English. This was the only time that I ever made the leap into thinking in Spanish. Obviously, this was social interaction. Perhaps it is not precisely the kind of interaction that can be set up in a classroom, but it was such a significant experience for me that I have a visceral understanding of the way that learning can take place in social interaction.

The difference between Scotty's school experience and his social experience highlights the importance of teachers finding ways to promote social interaction. However, Scotty, in reflecting on this encounter, is quite right when he points out that he is unlikely to have such an experience in the classroom. In part, this is because classrooms are not purely social arenas. In some classes students socialize at the expense of learning the academic content they are in school to learn. In explorer classrooms like Michelle's, students interact socially as they work collaboratively to solve problems, and they draw on different content areas to answer their questions. In this process they develop both interpersonal and academic language.

Research by McGroarty (1993) shows that group work benefits second language learners in three ways: input, interaction, and contextualization of knowledge. First, during whole-class instruction, it is difficult for teachers to provide comprehensible input at the appropriate level for each student. On the other hand, when students work in small groups, they are more apt to receive input that is only slightly beyond their current level of competence. Further, in whole-class instruction, learners get little opportunity to interact in the language. In small groups, interaction is much greater. All students have more opportunities to participate. They ask more real questions. And they produce "comprehensible output" (Swain 1985). Finally, group tasks allow students to develop academic language and content knowledge together as they solve problems. The problem-solving situation helps contextualize the language, making it more comprehensible. Students develop language as they negotiate meaning. According to McGroarty (1993), "While there are many types of cooperative activities useful in a variety of subject areas, those requiring some negotiation among students who must solve a problem or come to a consensus are optimal for second language development" (p. 37).

Explorer teachers with second language learners work to organize for social interaction (Enright and McCloskey 1985, 1988; D. Holt 1993). They know that language develops in contexts of functional use. For that reason they create situations in which all their students use language for a variety of purposes and with a variety of people. In these classrooms students frequently work collaboratively rather than individually. Research on collaborative learning highlights the importance of heterogeneous grouping (Kagan 1986), so explorer teachers with bilingual students capitalize on the diversity their students provide. In their classrooms diversity provides an enriched social context for learning.

Classroom Characteristics and Social Interaction

Restricts Social Interaction	*Facilitates Social Interaction*
Straight rows	Desks together in groups or tables and chairs.
Students do not move from seats.	Students move freely around the room.
Materials are controlled only by the teacher.	Students have ownership of the room and use and care for materials.
Teacher works with reading groups while others work individually on worksheets.	Students do shared reading, literature studies, and writers workshop.
Work is completed by individuals for individual grades.	Students work together on group projects for group grades.
Silence is the golden rule.	Students are encouraged to talk together to share ideas.

Figure 7-5   Classroom social interaction

A number of factors can promote collaboration. Both the physical setup of the classroom and the kinds of activities that are planned can inhibit or facilitate social interaction (see Figure 7-5). When teachers control the structure and materials used in the classrooms, students have no reason to interact, negotiate, and take responsibility themselves. If students are asked to complete worksheets or read chapters and answer questions individually, there is little opportunity for collaboration. On the other hand, if students explore questions and solve problems together in math, social studies, and science, they have opportunities for social interaction. In classes with traditional reading groups, two groups do individual seat work while students in the third group read one by one for the teacher. In contrast, when students do shared readings, read with a peer or cross-age tutors, write in a writers workshop, and discuss their books during literature studies, they teach each other as they interact.

In classes where students work individually, student diversity may be regarded as a problem. After all, management is easier when all the students can be given the same worksheet with the expectation that all can successfully work on it by themselves and all will finish in about the same amount of time. When students work collaboratively, diversity is an asset to be celebrated since the varied experiences, knowledge, and interests students in each group bring to the task at hand add to the potential for learning. This exchange is particularly important for students who are developing English proficiency because as students talk, they learn both language and content.

Collaborative versus Cooperative Learning

Cooperative learning has often been suggested as being important for second language learners because social interaction reduces competition and provides encouragement. In addition, research has shown that when students work together, the positive interdependence that develops fosters prosocial behavior and improves ethnic relations (Kagan 1986). Certainly, working together helps language development as well because students have the opportunity to use language for a variety of purposes.

However, it is important to think about how groups are formed and what students are doing when they work in cooperative groups. In explorer classes, students often form groups to study questions of common interest. Or a group of students might all choose to read the same book. These groupings serve real purposes because all the students in a particular group have made a choice to read a certain book or to investigate a particular topic. Students with different language proficiency levels may be grouped together because of their common interests. They work in groups since that is the most efficient and effective social structure for accomplishing their task.

In contrast, in some classes that have adopted cooperative learning, groups may be formed based on other criteria. For example, each group might have a "high," "middle," and "low" student. This kind of grouping creates heterogeneity but may ignore student interests and purposes. In addition, the groups in these classes may be given spelling lists to memorize or math facts to learn. These activities are based on a part-to-whole approach to learning, and they do not reflect a focus on the learner's needs and interests. Often, the work could be done just as well alone (at least by some of the students). For that reason, some students resist this kind of cooperative learning.

Explorer teachers prefer to use the term "collaboration" rather than "cooperative learning" to describe what goes on in their classes. Pat, the teacher whose experience in a classroom with traditional reading groups was described earlier, wrote about trying cooperative learning with second graders when she was substitute teaching. Pat observed that students corrected each other frequently during reading. Their classroom was characterized by competition, and the curriculum was based on structured worksheets. Pat noticed the following cooperative learning chart posted in the classroom:

1. Choose a partner.
2. Decide together how to find the answers to the problems on the worksheet.
3. Work problems individually.
4. Compare answers.
5. Write answers.

She decided she would try to do an activity using those steps. However, when students were given the activity, Pat found a disabled group that could not work together even to find the answers in a textbook. Pat described the scene:

> The usual procedures outlined for this class allow the children little choice, no opportunity to help each other discover or think critically, no opportunity to develop language skills and no change in class structure. . . . When I tried the cooperative learning steps for an activity and encouraged students to use Spanish to discuss and write if they wished, some used inappropriate language in Spanish, then half returned to working independently while the others wandered repeatedly, asking direction. Cooperative learning is so much more than checking your answers with a neighbor.

Pat understood that working together involves more than doing an exercise to get a correct answer and that students who usually work individually do not automatically begin to work together in meaningful ways.

Cooperative learning activities are generally organized so that each person in the group has a responsibility for the assigned task. Roles might include recorder, checker, praiser, taskmaster, gatekeeper, gofer, and reporter (Kagan 1988, p. 88). Students practice how to do each of these tasks and are even given sample phrases to say. However, assigning roles doesn't necessarily guarantee meaningful learning either. Gayleen, a first-grade teacher in a multilingual inner-city classroom, expressed her concerns about cooperative learning and her beliefs about necessary conditions for positive social interaction:

> While I agree with the principles of cooperative learning, I find myself questioning the sometimes highly structured practice. I think too often our field takes a good idea and structures it to a degree where some things are lost. I am referring to the idea of having a recorder, time keeper, etc., which in my experience can make it artificial. Interaction can occur within an environment where everyone is a teacher and learner, or where the roles are interchangeable.

Gayleen's points are important. For social interaction to be meaningful, all participants must have a real investment in what they are doing.

Students learn together in explorer classrooms doing many different kinds of things. They may read with a buddy or a cross-age tutor. Then, they discuss what they have read during a literature study. They confer with classmates and the teacher about their writing and then share the finished product by reading it to the class. They write letters for pen pals in other classes or other schools. They form teams to investigate topics and answer questions, and in this process of inquiry they explore all the different content areas. Together, they decide on ways they can take the information they have gathered and actually apply it to their lives. They consider how they can use what they have learned to solve real-world problems. In these classes students collaborate because the social group structures serve real purposes.

Collaboration and Second Language Learners

When students study a new language, they expect to be able to communicate in it. Rigg and Allen (1989) comment, "Learning a language means learning to do the things you want to do with people who speak that language." When students share their ideas and their knowledge in social settings, individual concepts are developed within a social context. Explorer classrooms buzz with a kind of controlled noise. Students, both those who speak English as a first language and those learning English as another language, are constantly talking with their classmates and their teachers, using the language or languages they possess to learn.

In some cases, teachers arrange for social interaction that involves students from beyond their own classrooms. Yolanda, a sixth-grade Spanish/English teacher, has found that cross-age tutoring has many positive effects for her bilingual students:

> Cross-age tutoring has worked well for me. I have buddied up with a second-grade bilingual class. We match our students, and they keep the same child all year long (Spanish readers with Spanish readers). They meet once a week for thirty minutes. My sixth-graders have learned so much from this experience. Once in a while I would worry about the noise level, but as I would walk around or sit and watch, I knew language was blossoming, self-esteem was rising, and relationships were building.

Denise, a third-grade teacher with many second language students, has begun to encourage more social interaction in her classroom. She reflects on her experiences:

> We as teachers try everything to get second language students to talk, then structure our classes to discourage everyone from talking! I now allow my students choice, and they can "pass" in oral activities. I have begun to do "show and tell" again in my

classroom, only now everyone shares with a partner first, to be able to think of vocabulary and try the English out first. Then a few share with the whole group. Instead of saying, "Do your own work," I now say, "Ask someone in your group for help." I am hoping that bit by bit I will be able to tailor my classroom activities to benefit all my students, not just the Anglos.

Yolanda and Denise are creating collaborative classrooms. Teachers like these two build on the synergy that results from authentic social interaction among students who come from diverse backgrounds and have a variety of interests. These teachers help their students value one another as they learn from one another.

A final example makes the important point that social interaction actually improves students' academic work (Freeman and Freeman 1994). Darrin, a high school teacher who was discouraged by the lack of interest his Hispanic students had shown in class activities, came back to graduate school to tool himself for a different type of teaching job. After he read about the importance of social interaction, he decided to encourage it in his classroom. The results were positive:

> Today I had students pair up and talk about the 4th of July weekend, about what they usually do on the 4th, and a 4th of July weekend they'll never forget. I went around to every single student and asked what he or she had done. I learned the Spanish word for "fireworks," heard a hilarious story about a student who got run over by a boy on a bike, and found out that one student and her family had spent the night on the floor because their house was shot up last night and the night before. I felt uneasy taking a half hour of class, but when it was time to write, I couldn't believe the volume of stories that seemed to gush out of the students. Each student had two other students read and sign his paper. I've realized that for my students' language acquisition, and my own sanity, that I must begin to initiate and foster social interaction in the classroom.

Darrin's lesson succeeded, and his students produced much better writing than ever before. Collaboration encourages second language learners to use language, raises their self-esteem, and helps them succeed academically.

Learning Through Different Modes

Some traditional teachers, especially those working with students who are considered at risk, feel that students' oral language must be fully developed before the introduction of literacy. In the same way traditional methods of teaching ESL follow a sequence of listening, speaking, reading, and writing. Many ESL materials provide separate lessons or even separate books for each modality. Often, for older students, there are even separate classes for each of the four areas.

The idea that oral language should precede the development of literacy for bilingual students comes from the observation that children acquiring their first language first listen, then speak, and only later do they read and write. While it is true that babies develop oral language first, what they are really doing is developing the kind of language that most immediately meets their needs. Written language allows people to communicate across time and space, but a two-year-old communicates about the here and now, so reading and writing do not serve a meaningful function. Though research shows that young children notice environmental print and make hypotheses about written language (Goodman, Goodman, and Flores 1979; Ferreiro and Teberosky 1982), they do not usually read or write before they speak.

In contrast, school-age students are already old enough to use all modes of language. All students need to use written language in school to succeed academically. If second language students have to wait until their oral English is well developed before beginning to read and write, they fall behind their native English-speaking classmates in academic content areas. For this reason, explorer teachers who focus on the learner provide choice and make learning meaningful by encouraging students to use a variety of ways to learn and express their understandings of both language and content.

Second language acquisition researchers have shown that students learning a second language often read or write their new language before they speak (Fitzgerald 1993; Hudelson 1984, 1986; Lindfors 1989; Rigg and Allen 1989; Rigg and Enright 1986; Rigg and Hudelson 1986; Urzúa 1987). In fact, many adult second language learners write and read their second language but never speak it! Students may learn to write first because they recognize the importance schools place on written language. Further, oral language passes by quickly, but written language is available for reexamination. The speaker sets the pace for oral language, but the reader or writer sets the pace for written language. Many second language students do better on written assignments than oral exercises because they can (and are willing to) take more time to process the written language (except for timed written tests).

One argument for developing all four modes simultaneously is that each supports the others. For example, what students hear can be the basis for what they later write or talk about. What students read can later be the basis for what they understand and talk or write about. Certainly, it is easier to understand something we are learning if we can read about it, talk about it, and write about it.

In fact, this idea of developing language and concepts by using both oral and written language together can and should be extended to include other ways of knowing. Educators have begun to move beyond the traditional four modes of learning. They are encouraging learning through other modes including art, music, and movement (Gardner 1984).

Denise, the third-grade teacher mentioned earlier, developed a unit that exemplifies the importance of focusing on the learner and building on their strengths by the use of different modalities. Denise's class includes many Southeast Asian refugee children. She felt strongly that her students should not only learn about the traditional American Thanksgiving with pilgrims and Indians. She decided to center her curriculum around the question "What or who is a pilgrim?" She began with a literature book identified by the district for her grade level, *Molly's Pilgrim* (Cohen 1983). This book tells the story of a Russian refugee girl who teaches others in her class that recent immigrants are today's pilgrims. Denise believed that it was important for all the students in her class to really consider what a pilgrim was and the ways they themselves were pilgrims. The class then read and discussed *Sara Morton's Day: A Day in the Life of a Pilgrim* (Waters 1989) to get an idea of the typical daily life of a pilgrim in colonial times. The class also read and discussed a book about two immigrant children sailing to America, *Watch the Stars Come Out* (Levinson 1985), the English version of the book Kay had used in her immigrant theme discussed earlier.

Figure 7-6   Pilgrim dolls

Next, Denise read *How Many Days to America?* (Bunting 1988). Denise knew that most of her Hmong and Laotian students, like the family in that book, were in this country because they had had to flee their own. The students and teacher discussed the difference between immigrants and refugees. Using a Venn diagram to organize their ideas, they decided that immigrants come to a new country because they want a better way of life and refugees more often come because their lives are being threatened. As a homework assignment, the children interviewed their families, asking three questions: "Where did our ancestors come from?," "Where did they settle?," and "When did they come to the United States and why?"

Denise was well aware that many of her Hmong students' parents were very sensitive about this type of interview. Public sentiment is sometimes negative toward Hmong refugees because of a lack of understanding about why they came to the United States. Many people do not realize that the lives of most of the Hmong were in danger once the United States troops left Southeast Asia at the end of the Vietnam War. Because of the terrible memories of the war and the persecutions they have suffered, many of the Hmong parents will not discuss their past with their children. However, usually older siblings know what happened and believe it is important for the younger generation to understand their history. Denise found that these brothers and sisters or older cousins were usually glad to answer the interview questions. After conducting the interviews, the children then shared in small groups what they learned about their past rather than having to report to a large group. After the reading, the discussions, and the interviews, the whole class watched the video of *Molly's Pilgrim*.

As a final part of the unit, Denise had the students do an art project. Just as Molly's mother made and dressed a pilgrim doll in *Molly's Pilgrim,* Denise invited her

```
                    The Pilgrims


        The pilgrim came from Laos to Fresno.And his name is
John he really come for freedom he come to American over
there.They have lots of people kill lots of people. So he come
they Country to are Country. He wear short and t-surt and pants
he like to play restling.




                    My Doll


        My doll came from Thailand because she came to have
freedom. She came to have her own church and have her own place
to live and get freedom. The soldiers were killing them. She did
not want to be hurt so she came to have freedom in America.
```

Figure 7-7   Youa and Joe's pilgrim stories

students to dress and make a paper doll as their ancestors must have dressed (see Figure 7-6). Denise explained how she organized this:

> Many mothers sew and the children bring in fabulous pieces of fabric from Thailand and other countries. I put out all the scraps, give students a template of a doll run off on tagboard, and with scissors and glue they make a pilgrim.

After the pilgrim dolls were made, Denise invited her students to write a story about each doll. The children typed their stories on a word processor. Figure 7-7 shows the stories two of Denise's students wrote. The students' pilgrims and pilgrim stories were put on a bulletin board which Denise said "truly reflected the diverse cultures in my classroom."

Denise focused on her students' interests, helped them ask important questions on a meaningful, personal topic, provided them with choice, encouraged collaboration, and allowed them to show their learning through the use of several different modalities. Students and teacher read together, talked together, wrote together, and watched the video, which was comprehensible to them after all their reading and discussion. In addition, Denise allowed her students to design a doll costume that reflected their own cultural background. She explained how exciting it was to do these activities with her students:

> I wanted to move away from the basal reader so I decided to try to extend a piece of quality literature that was relevant to my students. I had no idea this would be so successful. The bulletin board display attracted a lot of attention, and this was a positive, learning experience not only for my students but for many others at the school.

Moving beyond the traditional ways of teaching helps in the development of concepts, especially for students for whom English is another language. Teri, a new teacher taking graduate classes because she wanted to be more effective with her English language learners, found that using visuals and encouraging movement not only is enjoyable for middle-grade students, but also helps them understand concepts and learn their new language. She wrote about how she involved her students in part of a lesson on the food chain:

> While standing in a semi-circle, each student was given a color-coded card with the name and picture of a carnivore (red), an omnivore (blue), an herbivore (green), or a plant (yellow). The students were instructed, one group at a time to link the strings attached to their cards to one or more cards of animals or plants which they could eat. Cards were eliminated as they were "eaten." The remaining cards were those at the top of the food chain. Much discussion occurred as students worked together to find their place in the food chain and all students were highly motivated.

Teri and Denise have found that their students succeed in English and learn academic content when they give them lots of rich exposure to language and to concepts through listening, speaking, reading, writing, art, and movement.

Certainly, music is another important mode that encourages language development, concept development, and the building of self-esteem. Two teachers in a graduate bilingual methods and materials class shared numerous songs that they have used with the diverse students they teach in inner-city schools in Fresno, California. One of the teachers, Gayleen, the first-grade teacher mentioned earlier, is of Japanese descent. The other, also named Gaylene (with a different spelling), is a music teacher of Chinese ancestry. Because of their ethnic backgrounds, both feel strongly that diversity should be celebrated in our schools and that music is an especially powerful way to do this.

In their presentation to the other teachers in their graduate class, Gaylene and Gayleen began by reading *We Are All Alike: We Are All Different* (Scholastic 1991), a book written and illustrated by the Cheltenham Elementary School kindergarten class. The book includes pictures and photographs of the children in the class and discusses the students' diverse backgrounds and interests. They then shared *People* (Spier 1980), a book about how people are alike and different all over the world. After reading both books, they led the teachers in the class as they sang together the traditional song "Good Morning," which has the words "Good morning, good morning, good morning to you. Good morning, good morning, and how do you do?" (Birkenshow 1989). Then they put a huge rainbow up on the wall and asked class members to teach "good morning" to us in other languages. Their classmates came up and put the words in

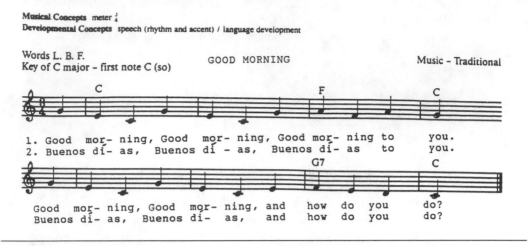

Figure 7-8   Good morning song

different languages onto the colors of the rainbow and taught the others how to pronounce the words for "good morning" in French, Italian, Portuguese, Russian, German, Dutch, Greek, Tagalog, Lao, Vietnamese, Japanese, Mandarin, Cantonese, and Hmong. Each time the class learned the words in a new language, they sang the song again, substituting the new words for "good morning" in the song. The following week the two music teachers handed out the words and music to the song in English and Spanish and encouraged the teachers to have their own second language students add the words in their languages (see Figure 7-8).

Gaylene and Gayleen believe that songs can be used to celebrate cultural and language diversity in all classrooms, and they encourage their students to learn about other cultures and to sing in languages that they don't normally speak. When teachers like these share with others what they are doing to help their students celebrate diversity, they are also helping many second language students learn language and celebrate themselves. Music is one of many modes that allows bilingual learners to develop both language proficiency and the academic concepts they need to succeed in school.

Conclusion

"Good morning" and the other songs were not merely frills. Instead, they were an integral part of a unit developed around the question of how people are alike and how they are different. This unit exemplifies how explorer teachers focus on their students' needs and interests. Gaylene and Gayleen made the unit learner centered by beginning with songs that were familiar to their students. Students could see a purpose in exploring the question of how they were like others and how they were different, so the unit was meaningful. In the process of discussing similarities and differences, the class worked together collaboratively. The students developed both concepts and language while using several modalities.

During this unit, the two music teachers were also able to draw on students' knowledge of their primary languages and cultures. In the next chapter we discuss the importance of supporting students' first languages. Since explorer teachers celebrate diversity and focus on their learners, they draw on all the experiences and languages that students bring to the class including their students' first languages.

Applications

1. Consider a unit you are planning to teach this year. How can you focus on your learners? List some ways you could begin the unit by building on the experiences and interests of the students. Share your list with others.

2. We have suggested that teachers use the Whole Language Checklist (Y. Freeman and D. Freeman 1992a) to review the lessons they plan. The checklist is a series of questions based on whole language principles, which focus on the needs of learners. Choose one of the units described in this chapter, or you might prefer to share a unit of study you have developed with your students and evaluate it using the Whole Language Checklist. Share your conclusions with others.

> **Whole Language Checklist**
> 1. Does the teacher demonstrate faith that students will succeed?
> 2. Does the lesson move from the whole to the parts? Are details presented within a general conceptual framework?
> 3. Is there an attempt to draw on student background knowledge and interests? Are students given choices?
> 4. Is the content meaningful? Does it serve a purpose for the learners?
> 5. Do students work together collaboratively? Do students interact with one another or do they only react to the teacher?
> 6. Do students have an opportunity to read and write as well as speak and listen during the lesson? Do students use other modalities?
> 7. Is there support for the students' first languages and cultures?

3. Students often find meaning in assignments when they are given some choice. Think of an assignment you plan to make. Is there a way that you could build choice into the assignment. Choice could involve allowing students input in the questions they investigate or in allowing students different ways of showing what they have learned.

4. Figure 7-5 lists some characteristics of classrooms that either inhibit or promote social interaction. Use that chart as a checklist and evaluate your own classroom. Then list some changes you could make that would promote interaction.

5. Explorer teachers recognize the importance of helping students develop both oral and written language. In addition, students and teachers can use other modalities to promote or show evidence of learning. In a small group, brainstorm some different modalities (besides or in addition to oral and written language) you have used to present ideas and that you have suggested that your students use to show their understanding.

6. Bob Wortman, a principal in Tucson, Arizona, has developed a checklist of factors that show evidence of a positive language-learning environment. We have reproduced his questions here. Use this chart to evaluate your classroom and then list some things you could change to make the environment for learning even more positive.

Evidences of a Positive Language-Learning Environment
Bob Wortman
1. What is present in the room that encourages/invites/promotes/facilitates oral language development?
2. What is present in the room that encourages/invites/promotes/facilitates reading?
3. What is present in the room that encourages/invites/promotes/facilitates writing?
4. What utensils/resources are easily accessible to students for literacy activities?
5. What is present in the room that illustrates the relationships among talking, writing, and reading?
6. What is present in the room that reflects/promotes languages or dialects other than standard English that may be spoken by all or some of the students?
7. What is present in the room that fosters understanding of and respect for the cultural diversity of your community?

CHAPTER EIGHT

How Do Explorer Teachers Celebrate Students' First Languages and Cultures?

*L*ian, a graduate student from mainland China recently read a children's story in Chinese to her fellow teachers in Yvonne's bilingual methods course. After she finished, she told the class with an obvious show of emotion, "I just want to tell you all that it must be very important for children to have their first language spoken in school. I am a graduate student, and you don't know how much it means to me to have been asked to read this book to you in my native language, in Chinese!" Lian's experience helped the other teachers in the class understand how important first language support is in building self-esteem for the students in their classrooms who live between worlds.

Lian's reading was just one way that these teachers, most of whom are monolingual English speakers, were sensitized to their own second language students. Many of the teachers in this class experienced for themselves what learning in a second language is like because the course content, including the rationale, theory, and research support for bilingual education, was taught bilingually in Spanish and English. For teachers who speak little or no Spanish, being presented content in a language other than English provides a new perspective on their second language learners. After only one class meeting, Paulette wrote the following:

> I noticed I felt kinder after last Tuesday's class toward my migrant and ESL pull-out students. As you lectured in Spanish, it surprised me to find how short my attention span was. And when I was no longer willing to listen or make an effort to interpret, how easy it was to talk or think of something else. It was good to see you cope with all of us good naturedly and patiently. There are many similarities between my 7- to 8-year-olds and your 30+-year-olds!

The teachers' final self-evaluations for the graduate class have been revealing: "I have learned what it feels like to be in a classroom where the teacher speaks in a language other than mine." "Having a class that was conducted in part in a language that I didn't know was refreshing, but I got more than that out of it because I resensitized myself to the needs of my students." These responses show that the teachers not only learned theory, but also internalized their understanding of the need for first language support for their own students.

Genaro, a Spanish/English bilingual fourth-grade teacher, had not really understood the importance of first language support until he began graduate coursework:

> Prior to undertaking classes in bilingual education, my understanding of bilingual education was limited, and even though learning was taking place in my classroom, I feel it was more extrinsically motivated than intrinsically motivated. Allowing the children to utilize anything that can help them express themselves has really opened them up. They feel comfortable to use Spanish and English concurrently to communicate with the teacher and fellow classmates. Even the ones in my class that claimed that they were Anglophones. I found to my surprise that they were very bilingual!

Genaro has discovered that by allowing his students to use their first language, he has helped them become better learners in both languages.

Explorer teachers respect their students and teach whole to part to provide all their students with access to English and academic content. These teachers focus on the learners and build on their strengths—one of the most important being their first language and culture. Explorer teachers recognize the need to support and develop this strength, but this may seem a difficult task, especially when teachers do not speak the first languages of all their students and when they lack materials for primary-language instruction.

Only a small percentage of second language learners have bilingual teachers. The number of students in public schools who speak English as another language has grown steadily over the past few years. Olsen (1991) reports that during the 1989–1990 school year, five percent of all students K–12 in the United States were classified as limited or non-English proficient (LEP or NEP). In 1990 California identified 742,000 second language learners, but there were only 8,033 credentialed bilingual teachers. This resulted in a shortage of 22,365 bilingual teachers. The numbers of bilingual learners in the state has continued to grow at a rate of about fifteen percent each year, rising to 1,078,705 in 1992. The projected need for bilingual teachers by the year 2000 is much greater, but the anticipated supply is only 16,600 (California 1991b). Even in cases where schools are able to provide bilingual teachers, they may not have books, magazines, and other resources needed for primary-language literacy development.

Schools face the challenge of educating a growing number of second language learners without enough bilingual teachers or primary-language materials. Some schools and some teachers, however, are meeting this challenge successfully. After looking at current research and theory that form the rationale for primary-language instruction for second language learners, we describe the ways some teachers provide their bilingual students with first language support even if they do not speak the first languages of all their students.

Theoretical and Research Base for Bilingual Education

Teachers working with second language students recognize the importance of helping them develop competence in English. It seems logical that the best way to help students develop English proficiency is to immerse them in an environment where they hear, speak, read, and write English all day. Although the idea that "more English leads to more English" is logical, it is contrary to research that shows that the most effective way for bilingual students to develop both academic concepts and English language proficiency is through their first language (Collier 1989; Crawford 1989; Cummins 1989; Hudelson 1987; Krashen 1985; Krashen and Biber 1988; Olsen and Mullen 1990; Ramírez 1991).

Bilingual education may take on different forms, but it must include sufficient primary-language instruction. In bilingual classes students learn English, and at the same time, they continue to develop academic content through first language instruction. Krashen (1982) argues that we acquire language when we receive comprehensible input, messages that we understand. To learn a second language, students need to have an understanding of what they hear or read. If students enter our schools speaking languages other than English, and if English is the only language of instruction, then the students may simply not understand enough English to acquire English or to learn any subjects taught in English.

As we discussed in Chapter 2, we cannot learn what we do not understand. Smith (1983) tells us that learning involves demonstrations (we see people doing things), engagement (we decide we want to do those things), and sensitivity (nothing is done or said that convinces us we can't do those things). When the demonstrations are in English, nonnative speakers may not understand what they are seeing or hearing and won't choose to engage in the activity. And if they don't participate in classroom activities, they may become convinced that they can't learn. At all three stages, instruction in English simply may not be comprehensible enough for learning to take place. Students who don't understand quickly lose interest and are either directly or indirectly isolated from the classroom community. Smith (1988) argues that students who do not learn to read and write fluently do not feel they are members of the "literacy club." Similarly, second language learners who do not participate in classroom activities may never see themselves as members of the "English-users' club."

Skutnabb-Kangas (1983) provides further reasons that instruction in a second language may not result in learning. She begins by asking what happens when "the child sits in a submersion classroom (where many of the students have L2, the language of instruction, as their mother tongue), listening to the teacher explaining something that the child is then supposed to use for problem solving." In this situation "the child gets less information than a child listening to her mother tongue" (p. 116). If a child fails to understand even a few words, he or she may lose the meaning of an explanation. In addition, listening to a second language is more tiring than listening to one's native language. Second language learners may appear to have shorter attention spans than native speakers, but in reality, those students may be suffering from the fatigue of trying to make sense out of their new language. An observer in Yvonne's bilingual methods class might have concluded that Paulette had a short attention span, but as Paulette wrote, it is very tiring to try to listen to something you don't understand.

First language instruction provides the comprehensible input students need to develop academic concepts. And concepts learned in one language transfer to a second language. Language and thinking are interrelated. We can learn in one language and discuss what we've learned in another because the concepts themselves form the basis for our underlying proficiency. Cummins (1981) calls this knowledge a "common underlying proficiency." If a student understands the law of supply and demand, for example, it doesn't matter what language he or she learned it in, or in what language the student demonstrates comprehension. The concept still forms part of the student's underlying academic proficiency.

Students also build up an underlying language proficiency. This is why it is so important for students to fully develop their first languages. If students stop using their first languages when they enter school and begin using English, it may be more difficult for them to develop their general linguistic proficiency. On the other hand, in classes that encourage use of first languages as well as English, all students can continue to develop their common underlying proficiency in both language and academic content.

Cummins (1981) contrasts the idea of a common underlying proficiency with that of a separate underlying proficiency. If what I learn in English is only available when I use English, and what I learn in Spanish is only accessible when I use Spanish, then ideas must be stored in language-specific locations in the brain. Research by Cummins and others finds support for a common, rather than a separate, proficiency, and if that is the case, then concepts learned in one language can transfer to another. By supporting the use of primary languages, teachers facilitate the development of all students' common underlying linguistic and academic proficiencies.

One rainy night Yvonne was able to bring home the idea of a common underlying proficiency clearly to teachers in the graduate bilingual methodology class with two

Figure 8-1   Spanish poster

different demonstrations. In one she showed the class a large poster of different cloud formations with Spanish labels (*Scholastic News* 1992—see Figure 8-1). Pointing to the poster, using gestures, and drawing attention to the rain and clouds outside the classroom, Yvonne explained the different types of formations in Spanish. Afterwards, teachers discussed what made the discussion comprehensible. A major point several made was that they had taught about those same cloud formations in science in English. Therefore, their background knowledge helped them predict the Spanish and make sense of it.

In a second demonstration, Yvonne gave the teachers individual copies of the *Scholastic News* issue on newly elected President Clinton, "¡Nuestro nuevo presidente!" (January 1993). Because the topic was one the teachers knew about, because there were many names and pictures of people and places they recognized, because Yvonne encouraged the teachers to discuss the reading and help one another, all the teachers, even those who had never before tried to read anything in Spanish, were able to get most of the information that the newsletter provided.

Cummins' (1981) idea of a common underlying proficiency helps to explain why students with previous education in their own country often do better academically than students who have been in English-speaking schools longer but never received any schooling in their native language. Students who have had instruction from the beginning in a language they can understand develop concepts, negotiate meaning, and learn to read and write. When they begin studying in an English-speaking country,

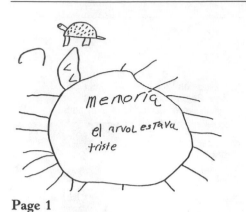

Page 1

Page 2

el arvol estava triste
por que   no tenia
amigos y una vez

Page 3

llego una flor y
          dijo cieres aser
mi   amigo y el arvol
le dijo si ciero aser tv

Page 4

amigo y el arvol dijo
vamos a jugar y la
flor dijo si vamos a
jugar y el arvol

Page 5

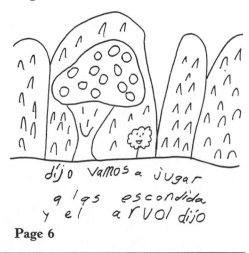

dijo vamos a jugar
     a las escondida
y el   arvol dijo

Page 6

Figure 8-2   María's story

*tv vas a contar y
la Flor dijo sí
veinte volla contarasta*

Page 7

Page 1
Memoria
El árbol estaba triste
Memory.
The tree was sad.

Page 2
El árbol que no tiene amigos
The tree that does not have friends

Page 3
El árbol estaba triste
por que no tenía
amigos y una vez
The tree was sad
because it didn't have
friends and one time

Page 4
llegó una flor y
dijo, "Quieres hacer
mi amigo?" Y el árbol
le dijo, "Sí, quiero hacer tu
a flower arrived
and said, "Do you want to be
my friend?" /and the tree
said to him/her (the flower), "Yes, I want to be your

Page 5
amigo" y el árbol dijo,
"Vamos a jugar," y la
flor dijo, "Sí vamos a
jugar," y el árbol
friend" and the tree said,
"Let's play" and the
flower said, "Yes, let's
play." and the tree

Page 6
dijo, "Vamos a jugar
a las escondida."
"Y el árbol dijo
said, "Let's play
hide-and-seek"
and the tree said,

Page 7
"Tú vas a contar y
la Flor dijo. "Sí.
voy a contar hasta
veinte."
you count and
the flower said, "Yes
I am going to count up to
twenty."

Figure 8-2 María's story *(continued)*. In conventional spelling Spanish. Accents and punctuation added. English translation.

they transfer those abilities to the new setting. On the other hand, second language learners with no schooling in their first language may have difficulty making sense of English instruction because they lack the background knowledge that the students who were educated in their own countries had already received.

In Kerman, California, the school district has developed a Spanish-immersion program that strongly supports Hispanic children's development of early literacy in their first language. Many of the children in their schools are from migrant families and because of the families' high transiency rate, students may enter school with little, if any, previous education in their first or second language. Carolina, who has kept the same group of students for first and second grade, tries to provide a Spanish-speaking explorer classroom for them. Students in Carolina's classroom write in journals, publish books, share during author's chair, keep science logs, and read with buddies using their first language, Spanish. Their spelling in their mother tongue has moved naturally toward conventionality because these children read from a large variety of quality children's literature in Spanish (Freeman and Cervantes 1991a, 1991b) and write several times daily.

The most exciting part of the program for Carolina has been watching her students' growing self-confidence. Children who were reluctant even to talk, children whose parents did not believe they would succeed in school, are now at the end of second grade discussing trade books, publishing books of their own, describing experiences with detail and creativity, and sharing confidently.

María, one of Carolina's students, caught Yvonne's eye during a visit to the classroom. María smiled shyly but did not push herself on the visitor. During author's chair, she listened quietly as other students shared their books. Then María volunteered to read her story. She answered the questions of her peers quietly but confidently. Later, during free-choice time, María joined a group of three others who were continuing author's chair on their own. Although she had not asked questions in the large group setting when other students read their stories, María's questions in the more intimate setting proved that she understood how to interact with the texts that her peers had written. Later, when María was working on a new story, Yvonne asked if María would read a classroom-published story she had authored. María chose her story about "El arvol que no tiene amigas" ("The Tree that Doesn't Have Any Friends"). See Figure 8-2.

When Yvonne talked to Carolina later about María, Carolina explained that early in the school year, María's parents had wanted to have her tested for learning disabilities because María's writing was still not legible. Carolina had insisted that María was enjoying books, and she was progressing daily. When María published this book, it became clear to everyone that she was both capable and creative. With this strong base in her first language, she has something to draw upon as she begins to learn English.

Strategies to Support Primary Languages

When students in bilingual classes receive support in their native language, they can develop both academic concepts and English language proficiency. In many schools, though, bilingual education is not feasible because a school may lack bilingual teachers, or classes may include students with a variety of primary languages. Even in these circumstances teachers can find ways to use their bilingual students' first languages and promote academic success. Several researchers and teachers (Auerbach 1993; Brisk and Bou-Zeineddine 1993; D. Freeman and Y. Freeman 1993; Kitagawa 1989; Moll 1989) have reported ways teachers have successfully supported students' first languages when the teachers themselves did not speak all those languages. These are some of the creative ways that teachers have successfully supported students' primary languages. The strategies include the following:

1. Ensure that environmental print reflects students' first languages.
2. Supply school and classroom libraries with books, magazines, and other resources in languages in addition to English.
3. Encourage bilingual students to publish books and share their stories in languages other than English.
4. Allow bilingual students to respond in their primary languages to demonstrate comprehension of content taught in English.
5. Have bilingual students read and write with aides, parents, or other students who speak their first language.
6. Use videotapes produced professionally or by the students to support academic learning and raise self-esteem.

Below we have provided examples of how teachers have implemented these strategies to promote their students' first languages.

Environmental Print

One of the first things many teachers do is to enrich the print environment in their classrooms. Research supports the importance of environmental print in children's development of literacy (Ferreiro and Teberosky 1982; Freeman and Whitesel 1985; Goodman, Goodman, and Flores 1979). Students notice environmental print, and Carolina discovered that students transfer this knowledge to school tasks. One of the second graders in the Spanish-immersion program we described, René, was asked to write about substance abuse and poisons for a portfolio entry. He handed Carolina the entry shown in Figure 8-3 (Freeman and Freeman 1994).

René's portfolio writing and drawing demonstrated to Carolina that he not only understood how important it was to keep poisons out of reach, but also that he realized that labels and signs are often used to warn people. In this case, René showed he had noticed how signs use arrows and drawings to indicate where people should not place poisons.

Kathy, a kindergarten teacher who has students from Mexico, Laos, and Cambodia, has made it a point to have the number and color words on her bulletin board written in English, Spanish, Hmong, and Khmer. She enlisted the aid of district bilingual tutors and parents to help her with this project. In the process of collecting this information, she discovered that in Cambodia, Khmer numerals are different from the Arabic numerals we use, so she put both the numerals and the number words up in Khmer (see Figure 8-4).

Lonna, who works with older students, had both students and bilingual aides write proverbs in their first languages and then translate them into English. These were then typed or printed neatly on colored construction paper, laminated, and cut to make bilingual bookmarks for students and classroom visitors. On one side of each bookmark the proverb is written in the native language, and on the other it is translated into

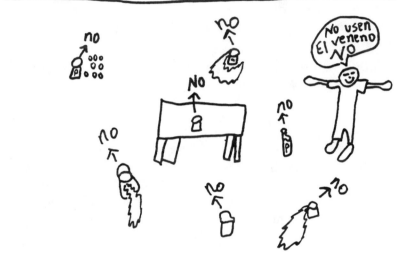

SOCIAL STUDIES WRITING SAMPLE   TOPIC _Poison_

Name _René_   Date _5-12-92_ Teacher _Cervantes_ Grade _2nd_

El veneno no Tenemos
que dejarlo en lo bajito
sola mente en el lo al-
to y No Tenemos que
Tomar El veneno Porque es
malo

El veneno no tenemos
que dejarlo en lo bajito
solamente en lo alto y no
tenemos que tomar el
veneno porque es malo

*Poison we should not leave
down low only (put it) up
high and we should not
take poison because it is
bad (for us).*

Figure 8-3   René's poison poster

English. Figure 8-5 shows the messages on both sides of two bookmarks, one in Laotian and English and one in Hmong and English.

Kathy, a third-grade teacher, works at a school with many Southeast Asian students. To encourage students in their first languages, Kathy uses bilingual stamps to mark student work. Stamps should not replace teachers' comments, but if the papers are being sent home, bilingual stamps send a message to parents that their first languages are valued and that their children are making good progress. Figure 8-6 shows stamps in Hmong, Lao, Cambodian, and English that Kathy and other teachers at her school use.

Sam, a bilingual resource teacher in a farming community with a high Hispanic population, encourages teachers to have students write signs to announce school events in Spanish as well as English. Sam was working with a group of Spanish-speaking children who were planning a sing-along. The group wanted to invite the principal, so

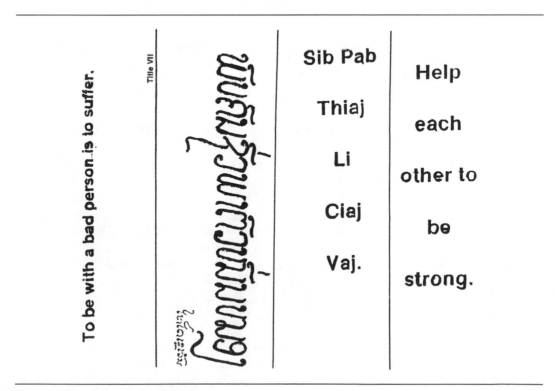

English twelve

Spanish doce

Hmong kaum-ob

Khmer (Cambodian) Numeral

Khmer (Cambodian) Number Word

black

negro

dub

white

blanco

dawb

green

verde

ntsuab

Figure 8-4 Kathy's color and number words

To be with a bad person is to suffer.

Title VII

Sib Pab

Thiaj

Li

Ciaj

Vaj.

Help

each

other to

be

strong.

Figure 8-5 Lonna's bookmarks

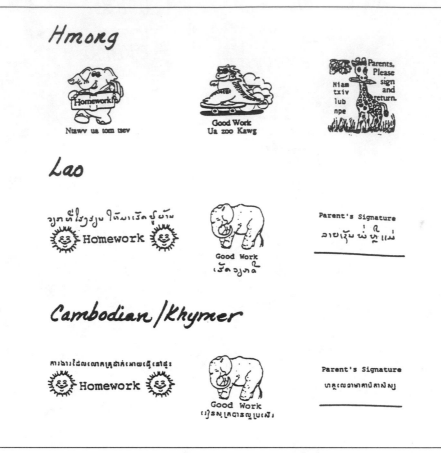

Figure 8-6   Kathy's stamps

Sam suggested that they make a sign. The principal was delighted with the large butcher paper sign the first graders wrote in Spanish. Despite a few invented spellings, the message was clear: "QueRemos envitrLa a cantar con nosotros el miércoles al Las 1:30 P.M., en el cuarto de La musica" ("We want to invite you to sing with us on Wednesday at 1:30 P.M. in the music room"). The first graders showed a sophisticated understanding of writing conventions by adding the accent over *miércoles* correctly and by experimenting with comma usage. The principal put the sign up in her office so visitors could see it. She also made a point of coming to the sing-along.

Another teacher had a student arrive from Ethiopia. He spoke no English and no one spoke his native language, Amharic. The teacher decided to begin a unit on Africa so that everyone in the class could learn from their new classmate. The room was filled with pictures of Africa, books about Africa, a map of Africa, and artifacts from Africa, some of which the new student brought to school. He even became a teacher and taught the whole class a few words in Amharic!

Teachers have also posted inspirational messages in their students' first languages. One group of English-speaking teachers who was studying Spanish used familiar slogans from commercial ads in Spanish as the basis for signs for their rooms. For example, "¡Viajemos juntos por el mundo de la literatura y conocerás GRANDES RIQUEZAS!" ("Let's travel through the world of literature and you'll get to know great riches!"). Figure 8-7 shows some other signs in Spanish that the teachers used to enrich the environmental print in their classrooms.

Each semester teachers in Yvonne's bilingual methodology class look for signs and publications in their communities that are printed in languages other than English. During one class period, teachers share what they have found. They draw some of the signs on butcher paper. The teachers with limited Spanish proficiency, using their background knowledge of advertisements, make their best predictions about what the signs might mean. Other teachers bring in photographs they have taken of signs along with samples of menus, information booklets, and pamphlets in other languages. Discussion centers on the kinds of signs that are in languages other than English. The teachers also notice the location of the signs. They always report a high number of signs in Spanish advertising alcohol and tobacco. Some students also comment on the fact that areas of town where people with higher incomes live have almost no signs in other languages while low-income areas have many. As teachers become more aware of the environmental print in other languages, they also become more aware of the politics of advertising.

Resources in Languages Other than English

Environmental print in students' primary languages sends a strong message that the school values diversity in language, literacy, and culture. For students to develop into proficient readers, however, they also need books, magazines, and other resources in their primary languages (Collier 1989; Hudelson 1987). Teachers who make the extra effort to support literacy in languages other than English have seen the difference this makes.

After sharing the signs they found around their communities, the teachers in Yvonne's bilingual methodology class spent part of a class period looking at a variety of materials in other languages, including newspapers, magazines, and books. In small groups they then brainstormed various ways they could use these materials in their classrooms. Figure 8-8 is a list of ideas one class collected after their brainstorming session.

Materials in other languages can also be used very specifically to support the class curriculum. For example, Melissa teaches fourth grade in a school with a high Latino population. The district encourages instruction in Spanish and has given teachers at each grade level money to buy Spanish books. The teachers in the fourth grade pooled their allotted money and bought books in Spanish that provided resources for the various themes they were studying, including studies of the ancient world. Melissa has found that her second language students, even those who appear to be very proficient in their conversational English, first go to books in Spanish when they select materials for research on the thematic units. As the students learn more about the content, they switch between books in Spanish and English.

Sue, another monolingual teacher in the same school district, was concerned that many of her Hispanic students seldom took part in literature study discussions. Even though she could not read Spanish well, she decided to encourage the quietest of her bilingual students to organize a literature study group using a chapter book in Spanish. She immediately noticed the difference in the way these third graders responded.

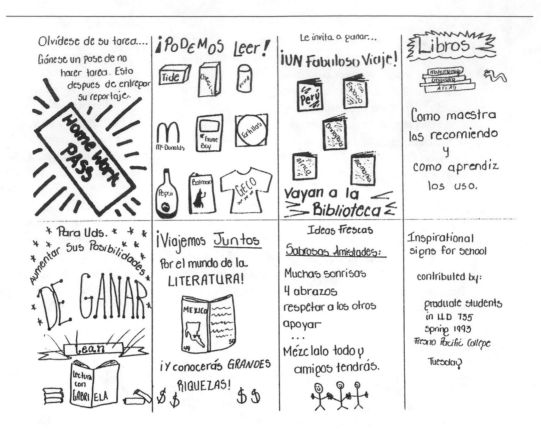

Olvídese de su tarea . . . Gánese un pase de no hacer tarea. Esto después de entregar su reportaje.
Forget your homework. Earn a pass for not doing your homework. This (you'll get) after turning in your report.

¡Podemos leer! *We can read!* (Followed by enironmental print signs)

Le invita a ganar . . . ¡Un fabuloso viaje¡ Vayan a la biblioteca.
You are invited to win . . . A fabulous trip! Go to your library.

Libros . . . Como maestra los recomiendo y como aprendiz los uso.
Books . . . As a teacher I recommend them and as a learner I use them.

Para Uds. Aumentar Sus Posibilidades DE GANA . . . Lean
For all of you . . . Increase you possibilities OF WINNING . . . Read

¡Viajemos Juntos por el mundo de la LITERATURA! ¡Y conocerás GRANDES RIQUEZAS!
Let's travel together through the world of LITERATURE! And you will get to know (discover) great riches!

Ideas Frescas	*Fresh Ideas*
Sabrosas Amistades:	*Delicious Friendships*
Muchas sonrisas	*Many smiles*
4 abrazos	*four hugs*
respetar a los otros	*respect others*
apoyar	*support*
Mézcalo todo y amigos tendrás	*Mix it all and you'll have friends*

Figure 8-7 Teacher made signs

Ideas for the Use of Materials in Other Languages
LLD 735 Sp. 93

1. Make them easily accessible around classroom.
2. Follow format of newspapers to create students' own newsletter.
3. Use recipes and publications about food to publish a class cookbook.
4. Include publication choices from different cultures.
5. Compare advertisements. Look at positive and negative messages.
6. Create comic strips in students' first language.
7. Write a letter to the editor or publisher.
8. Make your own ads using slogans.
9. Explain a graph or chart found in a magazine or newspaper. Write about it in your journal.
10. Dramatize folktales or use puppets to tell the story of a book in another language.
11. Interview each other. Take pictures for a celebrity column.
12. Do classification excerises.
13. Use materials for a research report.
14. Read articles for discussion and writing for point of view.
15. Read stories to younger or other-language students.
16. Develop a set of questions/answers for a game.
17. Find health information.
18. Use newletters, magazines, and newspapers for science.
19. Do a treasure hunt finding certain kinds of things in the books, magazines, or newspapers.
20. Make collages.
21. Make alphabet books using ads and pictures.
22. Include these materials in your classroom library.
23. Do partner reading.
24. Read articles about Hispanics and Southeast Asian successes to raise self-esteem.
25. Set up a checkout for hands-on home reading for parents.
26. Look for culturally rich magazines.
27. Study components or elements of a story or article. Compare kinds of writing found in newspapers and magazines.
28. Translate main ideas from one language to another.
29. Make sports predictions.
30. Look through classified ads for jobs and lost and found.

Figure 8-8   Ideas for using materials in other languages

Although they had been quiet and reluctant to participate in literature study groups when the books and discussion were in English, they were animated in their response to books in Spanish. When the literature studies had been all in English, these students had not entirely understood the texts and/or they had not felt confident enough to participate. They had watched as others had engaged in literature studies in English, so they knew what a literature study was and were able to lead themselves through the book. They summarized in English for Sue what they were discussing and learning. Because of this positive experience, Sue has already begun the search for a wider selection of interesting chapter books in Spanish for the next literature study.

Sometimes it is difficult to gather a variety of resources. When Kay, a bilingual resource teacher, found there were not enough books in Spanish for her school, she applied to the local reading association for a minigrant for books in Spanish. Her school now has a very exciting selection of literature books in Spanish for teachers to share. Sharon, another teacher at Kay's school, wrote a grant proposal to provide the school with quality children's encyclopedias and dictionaries in Spanish so that Spanish-speaking children could engage in the same type of research as their English-speaking peers.

Administrators have also discovered ways to provide first language books for classrooms. In a school with a high Latino population, the principal bought library book carts with wheels for each classroom. He filled the carts with a variety of children's literature, including books in Spanish and put one cart in each class. The carts were then moved periodically to different classrooms. In this way, every classroom had an interesting new supply of books every few weeks.

Finding resources is often the greatest obstacle to having books in languages other than English. The largest and richest supply of children's books in other languages is in Spanish. Various listings of Spanish children's literature can be obtained through publishers and distributors. Appendix D contains the addresses for many of them.

Educators have also compiled specialized bibliographies of Spanish language books. Freeman and Cervantes (1991a) have annotated over three hundred children's books in Spanish that they consider quality literature. This bibliography has been translated into Spanish (Freeman and Cervantes 1993). At the University of San Marcos, Schon (1992) has organized the Centro para el estudio de libros infantiles y juveniles en español (Center for the Study of Books in Spanish for Children and Adolescents), which has a wide variety of resources including bibliographies. The State Department of California has also published a listing of *Recommended Readings in Spanish Literature* (California 1991a).

Magazines, newsletters, informational booklets, and pamphlets in other languages can also be made available in the classroom for all students to read and use as resources. Government agencies and medical groups often publish legal and health information in different languages. Several high-quality and colorful popular magazines are now published in Spanish and English about Hispanics. In addition, there are comic books and student newspapers reporting in Spanish on current events that can be purchased for classroom use (see Appendix D).

In the last five years, more and more distributors have tried to make children's books available in languages other than English or Spanish. In California, for example, a great need exists for children's books in Southeast Asian languages. Though this market is still very small, some distributors are specializing in this area (see Appendix D).

Student-Authored Literature

While it is important to have professionally published books and magazines in students' primary languages, students are often equally interested in reading stories or articles their classmates write. Many teachers have students publish quite professional-looking books in English for their classroom libraries. In addition, schools often publish newspapers or newsletters. Second language learners should not be left out of these important experiences. Instead, they should be encouraged to write and publish in their first languages to enrich the second language resources in the classroom (Freeman and Freeman 1992b).

Sam and Yvonne discovered the importance of encouraging reading and publishing in the first language when they worked with Juanita. Before Sam took his bilingual resource position, Yvonne worked with him in his first/second combination bilingual classroom in a large inner-city school (Freeman and Nofziger 1991). At that time, Sam was not as fluent in Spanish as he would have liked to have been. Despite this, Sam and Yvonne worked to incorporate as much first language support for the students as possible. They read books in Spanish to the whole class, brainstormed with students, welcoming both Spanish and English contributions, did literature studies with books in Spanish and English, and encouraged the children to write in Spanish during writers workshop.

When Juanita entered Sam's class as a second grader, Sam was told that the school was considering testing her for learning disabilities because she was so quiet and seldom participated in class activities. Indeed, for the first several months, Juanita seldom wrote during writers workshop, did not participate voluntarily in class activities, and did very little talking. Sam learned that Juanita had not been in a bilingual classroom in kindergarten or first grade. Both Sam and Yvonne noticed how closely she paid attention, especially when activities were in Spanish.

When the class began a unit on living things and how things grow, Juanita really began to respond. The class had read *The Carrot Seed* (Krauss 1989) and other books in English and Spanish about plant growth and had discussed how plants grow and had also grown plants of their own. Everyone celebrated when Juanita published her first book, which showed her understanding of written language, story, sequence, and plant growth (see Figure 8-9) (Freeman and Nofziger 1991).

Dan, a sixth-grade bilingual teacher, wanted his students to make bilingual books for his classroom by drawing on their family traditions (Freeman and Freeman 1992a). He asked students to write rhymes and songs they remembered from their native Mexico. Some students used parents and grandparents as resources when they were not sure of the words. The finished book contained not only traditional popular poetry, but also humorous rhymes, including jump rope jingles, typical of students their age around the world (see Figure 8-10).

Juanita's story and Dan's book became part of their class libraries. Some student writing has an even wider audience. Jefferson School is a fourth-, fifth-, and sixth-grade school in the farming community of Hanford, California. Each month one grade level is responsible for publishing the school newsletter, *The Jefferson Connection*. Except for a one-column message written by the principal, the entire paper is planned, written, laid out, and illustrated by the students. Each classroom has a computer, and students learn to use different software programs to produce a professional-looking paper. Articles feature people and events related to the school. Each newsletter begins with the following affirmation:

Un dia Palnte una cemiya

La flor

La flor *(The flower)*   **1**

Un día planté una flor. *(One day I planted a flower.)*   **2**

Y desPues ceso Porito

ycorso mas

Y después creció un poquito
(And afterwards it grew a little bit.)   **3**

Y creció más. *(And it grew more.)*   **4**

Y mas

y mas

Y más. *(and more.)*   **5**

Y más. *(and more.)*   **6**

Y mas

Y ceyso bien gane.

Y más. *(and more.)*   **7**

Y creció bien grande. *(And it grew really big.)*   **8**

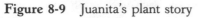

Figure 8-9 Juanita's plant story

Mi Madre Y Mi Padre

Mi Madre es una rosa.
Mi padre es un clavel.
Y yo soy un botorcito
que acaba de nacer.

My Mother is a rose
My father is a carnation
and I'm a little button
that has just bloomed

Me adoran mis Padres

Me adora mi madre querida.
Me adora mi padre también.
Nadien me quiere en la vida
como ellos me saben querer.

My loveable mother loves me,
My father loves me too.
Nobody loves in the life like
they know how to love me too.

Me gusta la coca me
gusta la pepsi pero
mas me gusta el
sabor de tu boca

I like coconut
I like Pepsi but
I like most
the taste of your mouth

Uvas y fresas frescas
si no me quieres para
que me besas.

Fresh grapes and strawberries
if you don't love me
why do you kiss me

Mexico, Texco

Mexico, Texeco all cover Mexico
do the Splits. Splits have a kick
turn around, and touch the ground
get out of town, come back to town
pay your taxes 1, 2, 3, 4, 5.

Mexico, Texeco

Mexico Texeco por todo Mexico
Abrete de patas I tira una
patada depacio balteate alrededor
I tocka el suelo Saltede el poublo
I boulbe para el poublo I page los
taxes 1, 2, 3, 4, 5.

Mexico, Texco
Mexico, Texco all cover Mexico
do the splits, splits have a kick
turn around and touch the ground
get out of town, come back to town
pay your taxes 1, 2, 3, 4, 5

México, Texeco
México, Texeco por todo México
Abrete de patas y tira una
patada despacio, voltecito alrededor
Y toca el suelo, salte del pueblo
Y vuelve para el pueblo y paga los
taxes 1, 2, 3, 4, 5,

Figure 8-10   Dan's class book

JEFFERSON CONNECTION   MARCH 1992   PAGE 8

Las Misiones

Nuestra clase esta estudiando de las misiones. Nosotros les vamos a mandar una carta para que nos den información. Les pedimos para que nos manden una foto de las misiones para saber como se miran. La información debería ayudarnos con nuestro reporte. Estamos escribiendo para recibir una idea de como se peliaban en las misiones. Nosotros pensamos que todos deben estudiar de las misiones.

Enrique Bello
Mario Puga
Salón 62

EL NIÑO PERDIDO

Un día un niño dijo hace mucho frio. dijo. "no tengo casa." Despues hallo periodicos y discos. Ahi se durmio y cuando. despertó se encontro una casa. Alli estaba una señora y le pregunto. "Ya despertastes." El niño dijo. "¿Quien es usted?" La señora dijo. "soy tu mama." El niño dijo. "ya me acorde." y vivio feliz con su mama en su casa.

Rogelio Arnaga

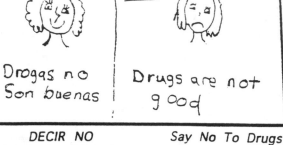

DECIR NO A LAS DROGAS

Les anuncio este mensaje para que sepan que a las personas que toman drogas se pueden enfermar de los pulmones.   Porque sus pulmones se ponen negros y los dientes amarillos. Si alguien dice que si te da un poco de droga mejor di. si a la vida y no a las drogas. y por favor sigue estas reglas que te dice el papel.

¿Qué es una familia?

Es cuando agarro regalos todos los dias porque me quiere mi familia.
Es compartir mi carta de reporte con mi familia.
Es cuando nos compran ropa.
Es las mamas que nos quieren.
Es la que nos hace de comer.
Es la que nos da dinero.
¡Eso es una familia!

Enrique Bello

Say No To Drugs

I tell you this message so you could know the persons that take drugs. They get sick from their lungs. Their lungs get black and their teeth turn yellow.   If somebody says take drugs say no and walk away. Say yes to life and please follow these rules. for your own happiness.

Blanca De Lira
Room 12

EL DÍA DEL AMOR

Durante el día del amor toda mi familia y yo hicimos una fiesta porque era el dia de San Valentin. Mi mama hizo carne de pollo y otras cosas. Lo último que comimos era un pastel de fresas. Mi papá nos dio dinero a todos. Ese día era el primer dia que celebramos juntos aquí en Hanford.

Figure 8-11   Jefferson newsletter

At Jefferson School we are committed to developing productive citizens by providing equal opportunity for each child to attain his/her maximum potential, academically, socially, emotionally, and physically. We strongly believe that this goal can only be accomplished by the combined efforts of a united staff, students, parents, and community.

In an effort to ensure equal opportunity for all students to write and for all parents to read, pages of each newsletter, called "Comunicación Escolar al Hogar" ("School Communication to the Home") are written in Spanish (see Figure 8-11).

All of the classes in the school have a writers workshop time daily. When their grade level is responsible for the paper, classes brainstorm possible topics for informational articles, editorials, creative writing pieces, and even comics. This school is a magnet school for both gifted and newcomer students. The two groups work together on many projects. Often, the students in the gifted program help second language learners as they edit their pieces in English. The native Spanish speakers, in turn, teach the non-Spanish speakers some Spanish as they help them translate what they have written for pages in Spanish. The students in the school feel very proud of their publication. Participation is great as 250 to 300 students, including non-English-speaking students, see their writing in print each year. The total school population is around 600, so almost all students have an opportunity to publish something during the three years they attend Jefferson School.

Another example of a student publication with a wide audience comes from Ripperdan, a small K–8 school in Central California. About eighty-five percent of the students are Hispanic, many of them from families of migrant workers. Pam, who teaches seventh- and eighth-grade language arts at Ripperdan, shared an all-school project, which is an example of how schools can publish student work. For the past six years the entire school has been involved in process writing, an area of the curriculum strongly supported by the school administration. For the last two years, the teachers and the principal have worked together to collect poetry for an anthology. All the students in the school are invited to participate. Nobody's piece is rejected. Since the students all have writing folders, they pick their favorite poem to submit for the book.

Poetry is published in both Spanish and English and students' pictures often are included. Figure 8-12 shows one page of poems that students wrote to their mothers.

When the book is completed, an ice cream social is held. Parents and other relatives are invited. The student authors read their poetry in Spanish and English. Each family receives a copy of the book. The dedication pages for the 1993 book, written in both Spanish and English, show how the entire community is valued at Ripperdan School (see Figure 8-13). The poetry anthology is now on sale at a local children's book store, and the students are excited and pleased that people are actually buying their book.

Allowing Students to Respond in Their Primary Languages

Many times non-English-speaking students sit silently in classrooms where the content is taught only in English. It is easy for teachers who do not speak their students' first languages to assume that their second language students are not understanding or learning anything. It is important to give students some way of demonstrating that they have understood the course content and that they have learned something from what has gone on in class.

Padres - Divino Tesoro

Mi Mamá

La primavera
Me gusta ver con el sol -
Brillando.
Pero mas me gusta
Mirar mi mamá -
Sonriendo.

Catalina Hernandez
Cuatro grado

Madre

Madre. cuando yo sea
Grande te voy a comprar
Un carro para que te
Deleites manejando.

Te dare muchisimas
Joyas y te comprare
Un vestuario.
Una mansión te obsequiaré.

Los mares navegarás
En el barco que tendrás.
Mascotas y regalos
Mil, en las navidades.
    ¡Abundaran!

Kenia Rivera
Tercer Grado

Cuando Sea Grande

Madre, cuando sea grande
Te compraré un carro,
O un tren, o tal vez un
    ¡Avion!

O quizas te compre una mansión.
O simplemente flores de colores.
    ¡Muchos colores!

Rocio Zuniga
Tercer grado

Figure 8-12   Ripperdan poetry

Dedication

We, at Ripperdan School, dedicate this book, our <u>Poet Tree</u>, to our students and their families. Our children have rooted themselves in life, in love and their wonderful country surroundings. They have allowed their families and nature to touch their hearts and to make them strong within. And, like a tree, they are reaching to the sky and allowing their thoughts and ideals to soar to new heights in marvelous poetic expressions.

Dedicación

Nosotros en la escuela de Ripperdan, dedicamos esta antologia de pocmas a nuestros alumnos, quienes raíces han brotado de la bella naturaleza y alrededores donde han crecido fuertes con el amor de sus familias. Ellos han alcanzado grandes alturas y tocado el cielo con sus pensamientos e ideales.

Figure 8-13   Dedication pages

Jane, a monolingual teacher who serves as the language arts mentor in a school district where ninety-eight percent of the students are Hispanic, worked with fifth graders on a unit on Martin Luther King, Jr. The students saw a film about Martin Luther King, Jr., they read a book about his life, and they read and talked about his "I Have a Dream" speech. A few students did not really participate much in the class activities because they spoke little or no English. At the end of the unit, Jane asked all her students to write a summary of what they had learned. She encouraged the students who were not confident enough to write in English to summarize in Spanish. Lucinda, who had recently arrived from Mexico and spoke little or no English, showed in her summary (Figure 8-14) that she had understood a great deal (Y. Freeman and D. Freeman 1992a).

Lucinda's summary shows that she not only understood what was happening as the class was studying Martin Luther King, Jr., but also that she had some background in schooling in Spanish. Though her Spanish is not completely standard, she writes clearly and uses fairly sophisticated vocabulary and structures.

Martin Luther King Jr

Martin Luther King Jr nacio el dia 25de Enero del 29. el era negro y defendio alos de su raza porque en ese tiempo obia mucha descriminacion en los autobuces los negros tenian que sentarce atras de los autobuses porque entrenter era solo para los blancos. el los defendio asta que los mataron el queria que todos tuvieran liverdad. murio el 4 de abril del 68.

Martin Luther King Jr was born on the 25th of January in [19]29. He was a black man and defended those of his race because in that time there was much discrimination on the buses the black people had to sit down in the back of the buses because in front was only for the white people he defended them until they killed him he wanted everyone to have freedom He died the fourth of April of [19]68.

Figure 8-14   Lucinda's summary

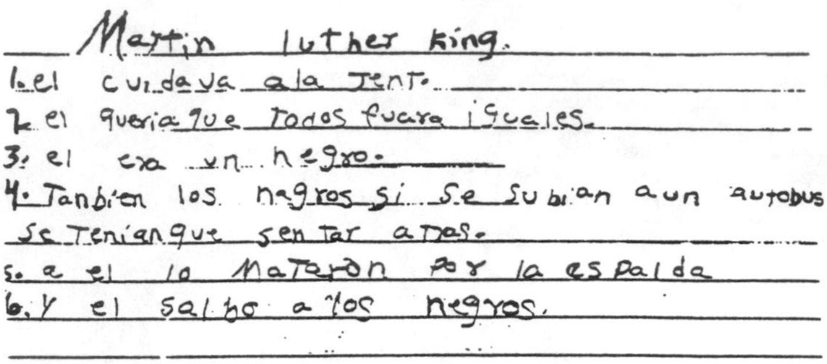

Martin luther King.

1. el cuidava ala Jent.
2. el queria que Todos fuara iguales.
3. el era un negro.
4. Tanbien los negros si se subian a un autobus se Tenian que sentar atras.
5. a el lo Mataron por la espalda
6. y el salvo a los negros.

Martin luther King

1. he took care of the people.
2. he wanted everyone to be equal.
3. he was a black man.
4. Also if the black people got on a bus they had to sit in the back.
5. they killed him from the back.
6. he saved the black people.

Figure 8-15   Roberto's Martin Luther King Jr. example

Another summary shows us a very different kind of second language learner. Roberto had had very limited previous schooling in Mexico where he had lived in a remote village. Like Lucinda, he remained silent during the class activities centered on Martin Luther King, Jr. However, when asked to summarize, he hesitated and indicated to Jane that he really didn't write well. Jane encouraged Roberto to do the best he could. His writing revealed his limited previous schooling, but it also showed Jane that he had, in fact, understood and learned from the unit (see Figure 8-15).

Too often students who come to school with little educational background are left out of the academic studies in which other students participate. It is important to include all students, even those who do not read and write fluently in their first languages. In fact, when students are not literate in their first languages, they can be encouraged to draw to show what they have understood of the content that has been taught in English.

Janet teaches middle school science. She was unsure of what to do with the new students who came into her class from Mexico. They spoke no English, but they were eager to participate in whatever way they could. Because the class was studying the parts and functions of the body, Janet was able to use different methods to enrich the context for all her students, but especially for those non-English speakers. She showed a film that discussed and illustrated parts of the body and their functions. She also had a model of a body that students could disassemble. In groups, students discussed the body parts and functions. They were allowed to use their first language as they did this. After the group discussion, Janet answered questions using lots of gestures and drawing on the board.

As a culminating activity all the students drew bodies on large pieces of paper, showing the organs inside. They then labeled the parts and explained the functions as they understood them. Janet's Spanish-speaking students pleased and surprised her with their depth of understanding as they labeled the bodies they drew and described the functions (see Figures 8-16 and 8-17). In fact, class time was spent sharing the vocabulary of the body in Spanish so that all the English-speaking students could learn some Spanish.

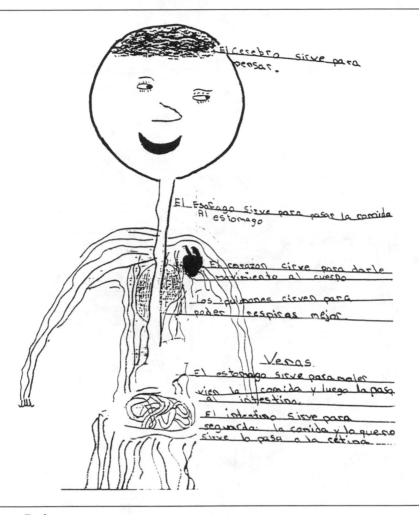

El cerebro sirve para pensar.

El Esofago sirve para pasar la comida al estomago

El corazon sirve para darle movimiento al cuerpo

Los pulmones sirven para poder respirar mejor.

Venas.

El estomago sirve para moler vien la comida y luego la pasa al intestino.

El intestino sirve para seguarda la comida y lo queso sirve lo pasa a la cetina

Figure 8-16   Body parts

Help from Aides, Parents, and Other Students

Once primary-language books and magazines are available, students need help in using these materials. If teachers do not read and write all the languages of their students, they can find others who will work with them. These "others" may include bilingual aides, parents, and bilingual students.

Bilingual paraprofessionals can help in a number of ways. For example, they can read to and with students in the students' primary languages. If students engage in literature studies using primary-language literature, aides can meet with groups to join in their discussions. They can also respond to students' writing. During writers workshop, they can confer with students writing in other languages. Aides can also assist in content area instruction by providing previews in the first language for concepts the class will investigate in English. After students have conducted content area study, aides can review the concepts in students' first languages.

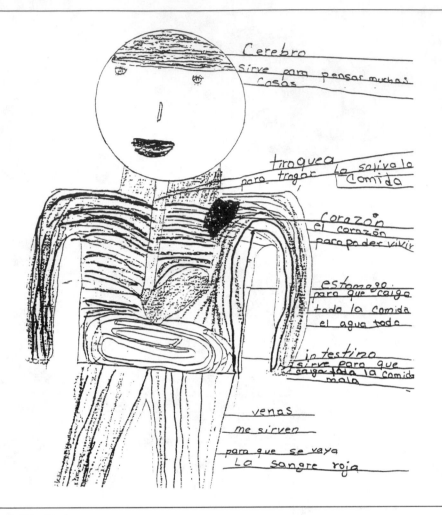

Figure 8-17   Body parts

In some classes, unfortunately, the bilingual aides are assigned the job of teaching English to the second language students. We say that this is unfortunate because these aides are hired for their proficiency in another language, not their proficiency in English. In many cases, they may be the only adults in the classroom who can provide primary-language support. For that reason, teachers should enlist their help when necessary, such as having them preview in the students' first language a story the teacher plans to read in English later.

Bilingual parents are excellent resources of primary-language support. Several teachers we have worked with have invited parents of their bilingual students to participate in classroom events by reading to the whole class in their first language, by teaching the class songs in the first language, and by leading context-rich activities such as crafts and cooking in the first language. The teachers have found that all the students have enjoyed these activities even if they have not understood everything. These bilingual experiences have led English-speaking students to ask interesting questions and encouraged class discussions about the positive benefits of bilingualism. In addition, the bilingual parents and their children feel a sense of pride in their heritage language and culture.

Older students can also provide first language support. Kay, the bilingual resource specialist mentioned earlier, established a cross-age tutoring program at her school to support Spanish speakers. She organized the program so that students in grades seven through high school read and wrote with elementary students during an elective period. Kay matched these "Teachers of Tomorrow" with younger students who had the same first language. Kay insisted that her tutors *only* read and write in Spanish or Punjabi, the two second languages represented in the school district. She told them, "English is all around. You are the experts for the younger kids who need primary-language instruction." Not only did the younger students benefit from the academic support provided by their tutors, but they also had positive role models.

Kay prepared the older students well for working with the younger students. She provided demonstrations of how to support reading and writing and how to encourage the younger students to talk about what they were learning. The "Teachers of Tomorrow" actually made their own plans for their time with their younger charges. During two classes each week they discussed with Kay and others how their teaching time had gone. An exciting result for the older students was their changing perception of themselves and their future. With Kay's enthusiastic support, several have begun to investigate college programs to prepare themselves to become teachers.

Bilingual peers can also provide first language support. Rhoda, a fifth-grade teacher who speaks very little Spanish, has found that having one bilingual student help another benefits both students. Orlando, a fluent English speaker, had been reluctant to use his first language, Spanish, since he had been transferred out of the bilingual program in first grade. He did not want anyone to think he could not speak English. However, when Javier came to the fourth-grade classroom from Mexico, he needed help in Spanish. At first Javier struggled along without any first language support, but Rhoda was not satisfied with his work. She decided to ask Orlando to help her by reading with Javier and editing his pieces in writers workshop. She explained to Orlando that she could not read Spanish, and Javier needed someone who could work with him. Soon the boys were reading books together and having animated discussions. Javier's writing changed dramatically from only two to three lines to full-page stories in Spanish because he now had a real audience for what he wrote.

Orlando, in turn, took a new pride and interest in his native language. During a minilesson on English capitalization rules, Orlando pulled out a book in Spanish that he had been reading with Javier to explain to the whole class "In Spanish, it's different! You don't capitalize days of the week or the months." Both Orlando and Javier benefitted from working together in their first language.

Videotapes

Teachers of bilingual students can use both print and nonprint resources to involve their students in literacy activities. Increasingly, professional videotapes are available in students' primary languages. Some teachers have discovered videotapes in Spanish that support different theme studies. (Madera Cinevideo, 525 East Yosemite Avenue, Madera, CA 93638). For example, a video of a museum display on dinosaurs is available in Spanish and English for children of elementary school age. Several teachers who have large numbers of Hispanic students use the video in Spanish as a preview for a class field trip and then as a review for discussion after the trip. These same teachers show the video in English as well because the preview in Spanish and the real experience at the museum help provide the context their Spanish-speaking students need to understand the video in English. Teachers who have English language learners who speak languages other than Spanish recognize that the dinosaur video in English can be a useful tool. It provides important background when shown before a museum visit and can also be used during follow-up discussions.

Mary, a Spanish/English bilingual first-grade teacher, discovered some bilingual videos about history, science, social studies, art, and folklore. One day in class, she showed the video *The Glass Blowers of Tonolá* (Madera Cinevideo) in Spanish to her students. When the narrator explained where this factory was located, Feliciana exclaimed, "That's the town where my dad was born!" After the video the students brainstormed in Spanish and English what they had seen. The following day the students enjoyed watching the video with English narration and then did their daily journal writing. Mary wrote about Jorge's response:

> We wrote in our journals after watching *The Glass Blowers*. Jorge asked me which encyclopedia would tell about glass blowing. I helped him find "glass," and he drew a picture like one he had seen in the video in his journal. It was exciting to see how he had been moved to seek something in our room to "stay in touch with" this new ' information.

Perhaps even more important than the content the students learned is that they knew this video took place in their native country. The video begins with a shot of the Mexican flag blowing in the wind. As Mary began the video, Felipe, a boy who seldom spoke up in class, showed that he immediately connected with the video by proudly announcing, "México, eso es mi país" ("Mexico, that is my country").

In an effort to give some needed first language support in languages other than Spanish, school districts have produced videos in various languages. One school district has produced five videos in Hmong centered on five big book stories, such as *The Little Red Hen* and *The Three Billy Goats Gruff*. In each video a Hmong-speaking narrator first provides background on the story. For example, *The Little Red Hen* video shows wheat growing and discusses in Hmong how the grain is separated and ground to make flour. Then the scene shifts to a bakery to show the steps in making bread. *The Three Billy Goats Gruff* video begins at the zoo with a close-up look at goats. The film then moves to different kinds of bridges with a discussion of what one normally sees under them. Each tape ends with a reading of the story in Hmong as the pages of the big book are shown. These videos help prepare Hmong-speaking students to participate when the teacher later reads the books in English.

Eva, who has a large number of Hmong-speaking students in her classroom, used *The Three Billy Goats Gruff* video and was very excited about how her first graders responded. In a journal entry she wrote for a graduate class, she described the experience in some detail:

> The day we viewed it, I began by reading the story in English to my entire class. One of my children, Yee, who has very little English had trouble paying attention while I read. She played with paper scraps on the floor, tried to braid a classmate's hair, etc. Then I put on the video. This time Yee watched attentively. She grinned from ear to

ear as she listened to the story. You could see the English-only students were getting a little bored with the video, but generally they were trying to follow along.

At the end of the video, I asked the class how it felt to not be able to understand. They acknowledged that it was hard. I told them that was how Yee must often feel. We decided that maybe now if we read it again in English, Yee might find it easier to pay attention. The students decided that it might be fun to change the "Clip, Clop, Clip, Clop" to the "Tee, Tah, Tee, Tah" that we heard on the video. It worked! Yee not only paid attention to this second reading, but read along with us. You couldn't help but see how happy it made her.

Elaine drew upon Eva's experience and extended it. She decided to use *The Little Red Hen* with her fourth-grade class of Hmong-, Spanish-, Laotian-, and Khmer-speaking students. She first read the story to the whole class in English, and the class discussed it in English. She described in a journal entry how she drew on her students not only to help one another, but also to analyze effective strategies for understanding what is being said in another language:

> I then told the students we were going to watch a video in a language that only some of us could speak and asked them how we could understand. They immediately said that we could ask the people who spoke that language or we could look at the pictures. I turned on the video and the fun started!
>
> My students are encouraged to speak their own language in the classroom, but I have never seen so much enthusiasm to speak someone else's language. All of the students were leaning on the Hmong students to explain what was being said, and the Hmong students just glowed in happiness. My Hmong students became the experts that the other students relied on.
>
> It was interesting how the students were asking questions when there weren't pictures, but when there were pictures, the questions seemed to lessen.

Elaine was most excited about how well all of her students responded to the experience of watching the Hmong video. She was so impressed with how intent all the students were that when it was over, she asked them which words of the story were repeated. The students responded with "Not I," "hen," "cat," "dog," and "mouse." She described what she did next.

> I asked the Hmong students to teach us how to say each of these words in their language. The Hmong students were so patient to teach us, and they loved to hear me speak their language, even though I made many errors. We then read the story over in English. However, this time we substituted the Hmong words for the ones we had just been taught doing a diglot weave as suggested by Celce-Murcia (1991). All the students were speaking some Hmong and they loved it!!!
>
> The video has triggered my students to ask each other how to say words in their language. It has also encouraged them to make videos of different students reading stories in *all* of the languages of our class. It proves that we not only need to allow and encourage our students' native language in the classroom, we also need to try to learn it to show that it *is* beneficial to know more than one language.

Elaine asked her students to write about how they felt watching the video in Hmong, a language that had not been used for school instruction before. Juan, a native Spanish speaker, told how he felt and how he solved his problem. Being a second language learner himself, he knew that his classmates could be a helpful resource (see Figure 8-18).

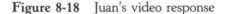

Where I was listening and speacing Hmong I was all confused. So I sat betwing Zong, Long to tell me what ther soing so they did it was funney.

When I was listening and speaking Hmong I was all confused. So I sat between Zong, Long to tell me what they are saying so they did it was funny.

Figure 8-18   Juan's video response

Hmong students seldom have the opportunity for instruction in their first language because there are almost no Hmong-speaking teachers and not enough aides to meet the needs. The response to the video from Mai, a Hmong girl in Elaine's class, showed Elaine why it is so very important to use students' first languages when there is the opportunity (see Figure 8-19). As Mai points out in her journal response, "I am a Hmong person and I am going to speak Hmong almost my whole life." In fact, we hope she will never lose her first language and that teachers understand how important it is for second language learners not only to learn English but also to maintain their first languages.

In many cases, professionally made videos are not available. However, students and teachers can work together to create their own resources. Paulina, a Spanish/ English bilingual second-grade teacher, used a student-made video for a Halloween celebration. She and her students love the predictable book *It Didn't Frighten Me* (Goss and Harste 1985), which is also available in Spanish, *No me asustó a mí*. In this predictable, patterned book, a young boy talks about all the different creatures he sees outside his window after his mother turns out the light at night. These creatures, including an orange alligator, a pink dinosaur, a blue bear, and a spotted snake, do not frighten him.

Paulina and her students decided they could reenact the story, choosing their own characters and adding their own adjectives. They made a picture-frame stage for the children to stand in. Each child chose a creature or character and dressed up like that character. In addition, they made themselves name cards with descriptive adjectives. Children chose costumes and labels to fit descriptions such as "a big, black witch" or "a great green Ninja turtle." Then the entire class recited the book's pattern in both Spanish and English, filling in the names of the creatures in the frame. Other classes were invited to watch this bilingual presentation as part of the Halloween celebration. In addition, the presentation was videotaped for parents to see on Back to School Night. Paulina and the parents especially noticed how proud the children felt as they played their parts and later watched themselves on video. This video is now available for Paulina to use with future classes.

Encouraging students to make videos in their first languages not only gives students a sense of pride, but it can also help monolingual English-speaking teachers view their students in new ways. Linda, a pull-out ESL teacher, discovered how

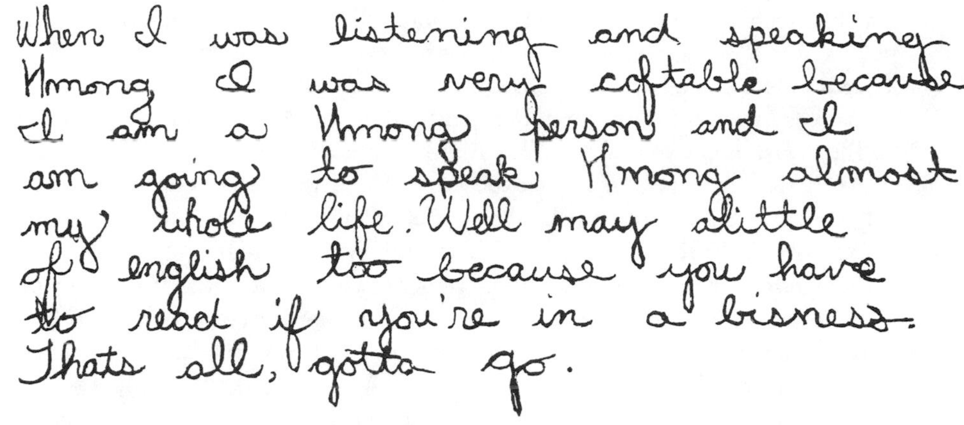

> When I was listening and speaking Hmong I was very cftable because I am a Hmong person and I am going to speak Hmong almost my whole life. Well may alittle of english too because you have to read if you're in a bisness. Thats all, I gotta go.

Figure 8-19 Mai's video response

important it is, both for the students and for their teachers, to allow students to use their first languages. Several of her second language learners came from a fourth-grade classroom that was reading *Stone Soup*. When the whole class decided to dramatize the story in English and videotape the results for an open house, Linda's students produced a second version in Spanish. She wrote about her experience watching her ESL students perform the play in Spanish:

> It was so exciting to see the video of the Spanish-speaking play. The students were confident, they spoke fluently, and their performance was superb. They were not the same students that I hear trying to speak and read haltingly in English. As I watched those students, I couldn't help but wonder how many of our very own second language learners have been labeled as learning disabled or even handicapped, or at the best, have succeeded only to an academic level of mediocrity when in their own language they would have been at the top of the class!

Professionally made videos in other languages can enrich the context for bilingual students by providing important background support that allows students to better understand academic content. Perhaps even more important, however, are bilingual videos made by the students themselves because these videos help students value their first languages and themselves.

Promoting Bilingualism

Teachers like Eva, Elaine, Mary, Paulina, and Linda have found how well students respond to the extra efforts that they make to support their students' first languages. In particular, Linda discovered that her ESL students were capable of much more than she had expected. That lesson is an extremely important one.

In fact, as teachers, we sometimes forget to emphasize the value of bilingualism in our students. Evelyn decided to try an experiment with her second graders to see how her classroom of mainly native English-speaking students would respond to an experience in another language. In an effort to help her students understand that a story can be told in many ways, and there are no right and wrong ways of writing or telling a story, Evelyn had her class read several versions of *Jack and the Beanstalk* together over a period of two weeks. Some of the versions were from the classroom, some came from the library, and still others were brought from home by the students. One boy wrote his own version on his home computer, and this was also read. Another child brought in a film version of the story starring Abbott and Costello for the class to enjoy!

After the students had been exposed to these different versions of the story, Evelyn invited her vice principal, who speaks Spanish fluently, into the classroom to tell the story to the class in Spanish. She and the vice principal agreed they would not tell the children ahead of time what was going to happen and that the story would be told expressively, but no props or pictures would be used. Evelyn also asked her three Spanish-speaking children privately ahead of time not to translate even if their class-mates asked them to.

The vice principal came in, greeted the students, and began the story without any preface. When she began speaking in Spanish, the students did turn to their Spanish-speaking peers, but after finding they were not going to translate, the students settled down to follow what was being said. When they heard their storyteller say "Jack," the whole class exclaimed excitedly, "Jack and the Beanstalk!" In response to "frijoles," several students shouted, "beans." The vice principal held out five fingers as she said "cinco," and the students responded, "five." "It's the giant," the students exclaimed when they heard "Fee, fi, fo, fum." And when the vice principal rubbed her stomach, the class responded with "eat." Because of their familiarity with the story, the class followed along and knew exactly what part was being told.

After the storytelling, the vice principal left and Evelyn asked the second graders what they thought about hearing the story in Spanish. The students were excited as they discussed how they had known what was happening when the story was being told. One child indicated one of the Spanish-speaking students in the class and said, "I bet Andrea knew all those words!" Evelyn took this opportunity to tell her Hispanic students how lucky they were because they were bilingual and how their skills would be sought after in the future. In addition, she encouraged her native English speakers to become bilingual, to study other languages.

Brigeen, a high school French teacher, would applaud Evelyn's efforts. She is concerned with how reluctant her students are to try to learn a new language. By the time they reach high school, many students develop a fear of foreign languages. They think they won't be able to learn a new language, and they are very apprehensive about even trying. More positive experiences with other languages at an early age would help prepare students for foreign language classes later.

A final example of how teachers can help others value bilingualism comes from Roxie. Like Evelyn, Roxie teaches in a school with very few bilingual children. How-ever, last year she had a Portuguese-speaking child, Melissa, in her first-grade class-room. Roxie made sure that Melissa got help from the classroom aide and that Melissa's older brothers often read with her at home. Melissa's parents showed great interest in her work and were always ready to do whatever was needed to help their daughter succeed. Though Melissa struggled with English, she also participated and made good progress, so it was decided she could go on to second grade.

This year as Roxie was sitting in the teacher's lounge one day, she was surprised when one of her fellow teachers, who had never had Melissa in a class, commented, "Melissa is behind her classmates because she doesn't speak English at home." Roxie felt it was important to respond to the teacher's comment. She told her, "I really do not feel that Melissa is behind her classmates because if you look at the whole picture, she is the only one in her class who speaks two languages fluently, and she's only seven! I think that's an accomplishment." Later Roxie felt especially good to see Melissa on the playground and have her announce proudly that on her last report card, she had received four A's.

The teachers whose classroom activities we have described provide us with examples of how bilingual students' first languages can be supported. As the number of second language students continues to increase, our challenge is to continue to search out materials and experiment with methods that allow bilingual students to become fully proficient in both their languages so they do not have to choose between two worlds but can live successfully in both their worlds.

We have spent several chapters exploring the world of the school and developing ideas about language, learning, teaching, and curriculum because those are the areas over which teachers have the most immediate control. However, we recognize that students' school success or failure often depends as much on what goes on outside the classroom as inside it. Many of the students we presented in the case studies in the first chapter were in classrooms with excellent teachers. It was factors in the societal context beyond the school that affected these students more than what happened in their classrooms. In the next section of this book, we step back to look at the broader social context and the factors in that context that affect the school performance of students between worlds.

Applications

1. Think of a second language learner that you know. Does that student speak, read, and write his/her first language fluently? How do you know? How might the students' first language proficiency be affecting the learning of a second language? Discuss this in a group.

2. Did any of the six strategies discussed remind you of something you have done or seen done with second language students? Discuss this with a small group. Can you think of additional strategies?

3. In Yvonne's class, students observed signs in their towns in languages other than English. They took pictures of the signs or wrote down what the signs said and where they were located. Then they discussed their findings with other teachers. Try this in your community. Are there signs in languages other than English? What kinds of things are advertised and where are the signs located? Share your results with others.

4. Yvonne's teachers also collected menus, newspapers, and other resources in languages other than English. Try this in your community. What non-English print resources are available that could be brought in to your class?

5. In a small group brainstorm additional possibilities for implementing each of the six strategies suggested. Compile one list with the large group.

6. Take one of the strategies that you would like to try with second language learners. Use the strategy, or your variation of the strategy, and come back and share your experience with others.

OUTSIDE
THE
CLASSROOM

CHAPTER NINE

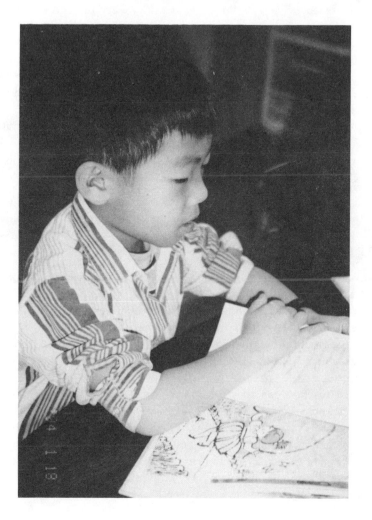

How Do Community Attitudes and the Politics of English Only Affect Bilingual Students?

When we consider our case study students from Chapter 1, we realize that a great number of different factors affected their chances for success. Their teachers' view of language, learning, teaching, and curriculum all make a difference, but factors from the societal context outside the school play an important role as well. Teachers may not have control of all the forces, in or out of school, that affect student learning. Nevertheless, it is important for teachers to be aware of these factors. We have been focusing on the world of the school. Now, we consider factors from the world outside school, and examine the connections between external factors and teaching practices.

We recognize that whether a particular student succeeds or fails may have little to do with curriculum itself. Success or failure may be more related to what goes on *outside* the classroom. Sue and Padilla (1986) say the following about this:

> There is no question that English proficiency is essential to educational success, occupational achievement, and socio-economic mobility, but these occur in a socio-cultural context. Understanding this context can help to explain educational attainments of ethnic minority students and to provide alternatives that can lead to improved educational outcomes for these students (p. 35).

An understanding of the various elements that influence student school performance can help teachers in several ways. First, it can keep teachers from blaming themselves, the curriculum, or student ability if students are not doing well. Second, when teachers understand the role of external factors, they can begin to work for changes that would benefit their students in areas beyond the classroom. In particular, parents play an important role in student achievement, and teachers can help initiate effective programs for parents (we will discuss this more in Chapter 13).

Finally, teachers can resist acceptance of negative stereotypes about minorities, and they can help their students develop positive attitudes toward diversity. They can do this by discussing with students the various factors that contribute to their academic success or failure, including the negative attitudes others may hold toward them because they are members of minority groups. They can then enlist the support of students and community members in creating positive environments for learning for all students.

Cortés' Contextual Interaction Model

We base our analysis of the factors that affect student success on Cortés' (1986) Contextual Interaction Model. Schools are charged with educating all students. If some students or groups of students fail consistently, an explanation must be found. Cortés warns against single-cause explanations, "This model rejects single-cause explanations and instead seeks to corporate a multiplicity of factors that may influence educational achievement" (p. 23). According to Cortés, any one factor—such as intelligence, language proficiency, or socioeconomic status—cannot be expected to account for varying degrees of success among different groups. He points out that we have often attributed success or failure to single causes because we have confused cause and correlation. Just because two things occur together, we cannot conclude that one causes the other. For example, students who speak English as another language may do poorly in school, but speaking a second language does not necessarily cause school

CONTEXTUAL INTERACTION MODEL

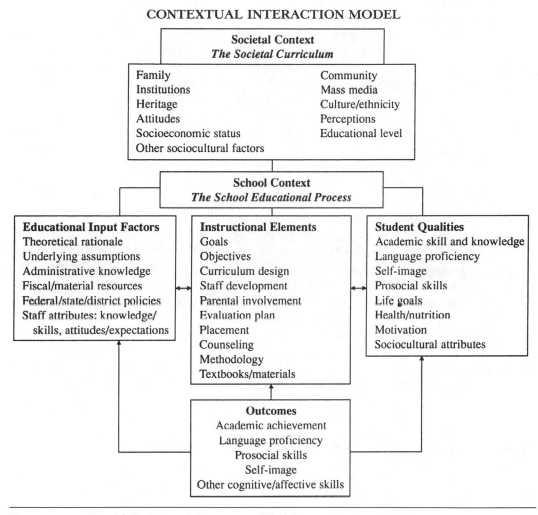

Figure 9-1   Cortés' Contextual Interaction Model

failure. Finally, "there has been a tendency to decontextualize explanations" (p. 16). Often, specific factors such as race, language, or socioeconomic status may contribute to school success or failure, but looking at any one of these factors, or even some combination of them, out of context may lead to false conclusions. According to Cortés, the question we need to ask is "Under what conditions do students with similar sociocultural characteristics succeed educationally and under what conditions do they perform poorly in school? In other words, within what contexts—educational and societal—do students of similar backgrounds succeed and within what contexts do they do less well?" (p. 17).

Cortés' Contextual Interaction Model provides a framework for answering this question. Figure 9-1 illustrates the ways that the societal context influences the school context. The societal context includes family; community; nonschool institutions, such as clubs and churches; the mass media; ethnic and cultural heritage; attitudes; perceptions; socioeconomic status; and educational level of community members. These societal factors create the context in which schools function and influence three areas of education: educational input factors, student qualities, and instructional elements.

Educational input factors include the knowledge, skills, and attitudes of teachers, counselors, and administrators, as well as school resources and policies. Student qualities include their knowledge and language proficiency, their motivation, and their social skills. Instructional elements include teaching styles and materials along with counseling, placement, and evaluation. Each of these three areas is in turn influenced by one another as well as by the societal context in which they operate. For example, teacher attitudes may be shaped in part by perceived student qualities and attitudes, and those qualities and attitudes may be determined in part by their family backgrounds.

This Contextual Interaction Model is dynamic. Societal and educational contexts constantly change as new families enter the community and the school. It is also a two-way model. The school context is influenced by the larger social context, but the social context is also impacted by attitudes, knowledge, and skills of the students who leave schools and return to the community.

Students' success or failure results from complex interactions of dynamic contexts. Recognizing this, it is still useful to consider in more detail some of the elements that are involved. By making changes in one or more areas, educators may be able to create environments in which certain groups of students are more likely to succeed. No one factor can explain success or failure by itself, but change in any one area may alter the dynamics of the whole system in such a way that success is more likely.

The Societal Context: National and Community Attitudes

One dominant societal context is the wider national political environment. This forms the attitudes and perceptions of community members, which in turn help shape school programs and policies.

On December 27, 1992, an article entitled "Why Hmong Came to America" was published in *The Fresno Bee*. The author, Lypao Yang, is the publisher of the *California Hmong Times* where the article first appeared. In the first part of his story Yang tells about people who have called his office since he began publishing the Hmong newspaper:

> Some of the people who called me at my office were terrifying, telling me that "American people don't need the Hmong; Hmong people came to America to collect American tax dollars; Hmong people are lazy, just like the Hispanic and African-American people. Hmong people just want to produce babies after babies and they don't want to work (p. B9)."

In the article Yang explains that within fifteen years of coming here "Hmong-speaking people have become successful businessmen, lawyers, doctors, engineers, dentists, and pharmacists." He describes the Hmong as working hard to do well in school, having strong family values, and as being friendly and helpful. He goes on to make the following points:

American people have forgotten what they have done to our country. In the early 1960s the American people came to Laos and used the Hmong people to work for them during the Vietnam War. . . . We fought the American war—there were more than 30,000 Hmong dead. When it was over, American people left the Hmong people behind for the communist Pathet Lao to do whatever they wanted. . . . In the 17 years since Laos fell to communists, some 72,000 Laotians, most of them Hmong, have died in the forgotten war that was created by the United States (p. B9).

Yang ends his article on a positive note, stating, "We are learning how to become productive Hmong-Americans. We, like many other refugee and immigrant groups before us, bring skills, talents, and values to this society to share" (p. B9). However, the article was not the end of the misconceptions and misunderstanding.

Shortly thereafter, a local doctor wrote a letter to the editor in response to Yang's article. In this letter the doctor criticizes the Hmong for wanting to maintain their own culture and language. He was frustrated, for example, that the Hmong often relied on tribal healers and only came to him when their condition was life threatening. Even when he provided the necessary medical services, Hmong people showed little appreciation. This lack of gratitude was also reflected in their attitude toward welfare payments. The doctor points out that people receiving a government handout have no right to complain if they think the amount of payment is too small. The doctor asserts that what happened in the past has little bearing on the present and concludes that Americans don't need to learn more about the Hmong; instead, the Hmong need to learn more about Americans.

This letter rejecting Yang's premises prompted a series of other letters to the editor, some agreeing completely with the doctor, while others appealed to him to be more reasonable in his stance; still others were sharply critical of his comments (see Figure 9-2).

We present these letters because we believe that the ideas expressed in them represent the variety of beliefs and attitudes about immigrants in the communities our schools serve. Such feelings are a powerful force that shapes the educational context for language-minority students. In a community such as Fresno, which has a large Hmong school-age population, attitudes such as the ones expressed in these letters resulted in concrete educational consequences. For example, the influx of immigrants has caused overcrowding in schools, but citizens have voted down school bonds that would have provided money to build new schools. Many people who vote against the bonds state plainly that they have no intention of paying for the education of the immigrants in our schools.

New groups of immigrants, such as the Hmong, raise the kinds of fears and prejudices reflected in some of the letters to the editor. Negative emotions toward other minority groups may cause less public furor, but these attitudes are equally important in forming the societal context for schools. In many communities, Hispanics have constituted a large percentage of the population for years. However, recently the number of Hispanics in the United States has increased sharply. According to the 1990 census, twenty-five percent of California's population was Hispanic.

This group contains people with very different backgrounds and needs. Illegal immigrants coming to work from across the Mexican border are resented by migrant workers such as Juan and his family, described earlier. Juan's family is here legally and has been here for many years. José Luis, Patricia, and Guillermo, the refugee teens from El Salvador, do not fit in with other Hispanic teenagers. Unlike Chicano youths,

Widening the gap

[The doctor's] letter regarding Hmong refugees and their need to know more about us stood in sharp contrast to Peggy Mullen's statements the same day regarding the need to eradicate prejudice in our society against all people. Her letter clearly represents the type of attitude that all of us have a responsibility to strive for in our culturally diverse society.

Tears came to my eyes when I read [the doctor's] criticisms against the Hmong people because he as an educated professional, more than anyone else, should realize that education is often a long and enduring process. It is also a two-way street. His remarks exemplify an attitude which make it more difficult for the Hmong people to integrate into mainstream society —that is, the more we distance ourselves from understanding the Hmong point of view, the wider the cultural gap becomes.

My own educational experience illustrates that without the kind support and understanding of the many Americans sensitive to my cultural background, the achievement of my higher education would not have been possible. Fortunately, I know of many individuals, professionals, agencies, and churches that are dedicated, and I am grateful to them. If an individual is in a position to help, as [the doctor] is, it is important to do so with an open mind, heart, and soul.

Tony Vang
Fresno

The writer is an instructor of Asian-American Studies at Fresno City College.

Figure 9-2   Letters to the editor

they do not feel alienated. Unlike illegal Mexicans or other new Mexican immigrants with little educational background, the three from El Salvador are educated and see Americans as supportive and the United States as a place full of opportunities. However, the support José Luis, Guillermo, and Patricia experience is not felt by many other refugees. In general, a negative attitude exists in many communities toward Hispanics, who are seen as a homogeneous group.

In August of 1993 the governor of California began an active campaign to reduce services to undocumented immigrants and their children. Through a private, noncampaign organization of supporters, the Governor Wilson Forum, Wilson sent a full-page open letter to President Clinton in *The New York Times, USA Today,* and the *Washington Post* calling for wholesale reform and urging congressional repeal of federal laws requiring states to pay for education, incarceration, and health services for illegal immigrants. In addition, he proposed that the children of illegal immigrants born in this country not be given citizenship, a proposal that would call for a change in the Fourteenth Amendment of the U.S. Constitution.

More on Hmong, assimilation

We in America do not need to know more about the Hmong people, or any others who migrate here.

That is what is wrong with our great country. Many people who come here want us to become the country they left. It ain't going to happen. The faster these people become Americans, the better for all of us.

We can't and shouldn't try to make a hundred different countries out of one as good as ours.

Juanita Paxton
Visalia

•

I sympathize with some of the frustration evidenced by [the doctor's] recent letter, regarding providing medical care to Hmong people in Fresno. His observations are undoubtedly based on his own experiences.

I would like to offer some observations based on my experience providing medical care to Hmong people. My practice includes a cultural and ethnic cross section of Fresno.

The Hmong I have met are intelligent and hard-working. Over the last several years I have observed a number of my patients and members of their families move off welfare and into productive jobs. Just like other ethnic groups, they don't want to be on welfare.

Although the Vietnam War took place a "generation ago," the Hmong people in Fresno would not be here if they had not laid their lives on the line alongside our own troops in that war. We do owe this group some obligation of loyalty as former allies in time of war.

I have received many expressions of gratitude from Hmong patients, verbal thanks and gifts of food or handwork. They are like most people. When treated with respect, dignity and kindness, they respond favorably.

Much rapport may be generated by a doctor going to the trouble of learning two or three words of the Hmong language. This sometimes results in greater communication and understanding about why they don't want to accept a certain treatment. Friendly, respectful attention occasionally even results in them accepting a medical procedure which they might not have otherwise.

As far as who should learn whose culture, of course we both should learn each other's culture. Personally, I am constantly enriched by sharing in the cultural heritage of the numerous ethnic groups in Fresno. But the economic success of Hmong people, like other immigrant groups, will be severely hampered until more of them learn English and learn how to get along in "American" culture. Many volunteers working in church groups and other organizations are performing an invaluable service by providing classes in English language and American customs. These classes are well attended by many Hmong people who wish to succeed and become part of the American dream.

David V. Young, M.D.
Fresno

The writer is immediate past medical staff president, Community Hospitals of Central California.

Figure 9-2   Letters to the editor *(continued)*

'Being American is also being Hmong'

[The doctor's] letter is as naive as it is dangerous. The concept of original sin is a Western one. The Hmong don't believe that America has to pay for the war that LBJ started. Nevertheless, the war in Vietnam may have been a generation ago, but the people from there, no matter where they are now living, are still trying to recover from it. The Hmong would not be here if it were not because of the war. They are civilized enough to appreciate the help they get to start out in their new country but [the doctor's] self-proclaimed "generosity" is quite inflated.

[The doctor] should not feel so frustrated because his patients do not immediately listen to his opinions. The writer of this letter happens to be a physician also [the doctor] refuse to heed my advice almost daily. It may be their physicians. Patients, who may be Yang, Lee, Lopez and also Brogan, refuse to heed my advice almost daily. It may be our professional opinion, but it's their body and their life. As a physician, I try the best I can to communicate and to advise, but I also respect patients' final decisions. After all, I am their physician, not their master. They make their decision about their own treatment.

This may come as a surprise to [the doctor], but being American is also being Hmong. America is not just British, German or Italian. Hmong culture is now part of America's. This richly mixed heritage and the acceptance of it makes our American culture unique and great. The Hmong should learn to live in this country as [the doctor] and/or his ancestors did, but America is also trying to understand in order to integrate the Hmong just as she did for [the doctor] in the past.

Instead of being disappointed, [the doctor] could be a contented physician who thinks that taking care of the Hmong is rewarding — if he would just spend his time learning more about his patients who happen to be Hmong instead of counting his fee, his taxes and his "generosity."

Robert Nguyen, M.D.
Fresno

Figure 9-2   Letters to the editor *(continued)*

Political opponents claimed that this stance was in opposition to his actions as a U.S. senator. In 1986 Wilson supported a federal law to allow one million migrants to come into the country to work as inexpensive farm laborers for the agricultural industry. Democratic opponents accused him of timing his more recent proposal to reduce services for immigrants to gain popularity for the 1994 election. They believed Wilson was blaming the depressed state economy and debt on immigrants to provide a scapegoat (McCormick 1993; Chavez 1993).

Navarrette (1993) points out that Wilson's proposal came when the *Los Angeles Times* reported that his approval rating was only fifteen percent. As Navarrette commented, "Wilson is apparently willing to solidify an entire underclass of people in return for an issue that California voters will lash out against in place of him. He chose the right one" (p. B6). Indeed, this type of proposal did draw support in economically depressed times. The same day news of his letter to Clinton was released, a letter to the editor appeared in the local paper entitled "Cost of Illegals" in which the author responds angrily to a letter that appeared earlier in support of the plight of immigrants:

> "All they want is to work," etc. Wrong! Many of them come here because they know they get on the "dole." . . . They are "people willing to take jobs that Americans will not deign to do at wages they will not accept." Many of us have worked at jobs we didn't want to, but why should we work and pay taxes to support someone who doesn't like the job? . . . America takes in more legal immigrants than the rest of the world because we are the biggest suckers!

Wilson's letter presented at the national level helped create an atmosphere in which others at the community level felt free to express negative attitudes toward immigrants. Only a few days after Wilson's letter to Clinton was published, the following letter to the editor appeared:

> This city has seen an unprecedented boom in both legal and illegal immigration in recent years, and now we have high crime rates, housing developments, and neighbor-hoods being turned into squalid, rat-infested havens of crime and crowded with wrecked cars. In general, cities and towns . . . are rapidly decaying because of unedu-cated and uncaring residents from other countries who are not used to running water or basic sanitary conditions.

Immigrant students entering school, whether they are in the United States legally or illegally, are affected by community attitudes reflected in letters like this and supported by politicians like Wilson. These attitudes form an important part of the societal context within which the educational context operates.

Negative attitudes toward immigrants are by no means limited to states like California. In his article, Navarrette refers to a poll conducted by *Newsweek* that found that sixty percent of Americans consider immigration to be bad for the country. Further, when asked whether immigration should be made easier or harder, those polled were evenly divided in their opinions about immigrants from Eastern Europe, with thirty-nine percent in favor of easing restrictions and thirty-nine percent in favor of making immigration more difficult. When asked whether immigration should be easier or harder for Latinos, thirty percent thought it should be easier, while forty-seven percent wished for tighter controls. Asked about Haitians, only twenty percent wanted to ease immigration policies, while fifty-five percent wanted immigration to be made more difficult. Generally, a negative attitude toward immigrants now exists—particularly against certain groups.

Community Attitudes and School Programs: Bilingual Education

In some parts of the Central Valley of California, the adverse feelings of the general public toward services for immigrant children are so strong that David, one of our graduate students, wrote a letter in defense of the group, pleading for support and understanding (see Figure 9-3).

LETTERS TO THE EDITOR

Immigrants, schools

The "burden on schools" that Valerie Reeves spoke of in her April 11 letter is not the burden of educating immigrant children, but of producing caring, productive citizens who think beyond the racial borders so firmly entrenched in America's psyche.

The children of illegal taxpaying immigrants are poor and brown of skin. Their culture is different from that of the average white, middle-class American. Whenever publicity blesses this group, it is usually of a negative nature. It seems only natural to turn against this group, particularly when the state is in a financial crisis. It appears that California could be following Hitler's footsteps in "dealing" with the "problem" of immigration.

As an educator who works primarily with immigrant children, I know that almost all of them stay in this country for the rest of their lives. If we choose to hide our heads in the sand and deny an education to these children, their future and our future will be no better, only worse.

To deny these children an education because of immigration status seems cruel and mean-spirited. These children have no control over their parents' decisions. They do, however, hold the keys to their future through the power of education.

I became a teacher because I felt children deserved a fair chance at life. I wonder why Ms. Reeves became a teacher.

J. David East
Squaw Valley

Figure 9-3 David's letter

In schools, public sentiment against immigrants is felt by administrators, teachers, and students alike. Programs like bilingual education, which are perceived as being only for illegal immigrants, are criticized at the very least and often eliminated because of misunderstanding and the desire of those in power to maintain the status quo even in the face of a growing non-English-speaking population. David's letter to the editor in support of bilingual education is an attempt to help people think through the needs of migrant children.

Cheryl, the bilingual fifth-grade teacher described in Chapter 7, writes about her experiences in the same small farming community where David works before she became a teacher and before she was bilingual:

In 1973, I was a young housewife with two small children. My daughter was entering kindergarten in the fall, and our family needed extra income. As it turned out, I wasn't qualified to be an aide because I wasn't bilingual. Instead, I was hired as a community aide for the Follow-Through program. The district had a bilingual program that had a parent-involvement component. I was one of seven women who were hired to be a liaison between the school and the community.

I was the only non-Hispanic community aide in a community that was composed of approximately 80% Hispanics. I was assigned the "north side" of town because most of these community members were fluent in English. In fact, most were Anglo property owners who saw the Follow-Through program as a threat to the community. I couldn't understand it then, and I have a difficult time understanding now how educating and empowering your community is considered a negative thing.

The community (the ones with the power) fought this program with a hateful vengeance. The school board fired administrators who implemented and favored the program. They even fired the district superintendent. They also made it unbearable for many young, idealistic teachers who came to the district with ideas of making exciting changes in the system. Most of them left by 1974. The board finally refused enormous amounts of federal dollars and phased things back to the way they were.

Cheryl's letter shows the link between community attitudes and school practices. In her district, school programs were abandoned because of community sentiment, not because of any educational deficiencies.

The controversy surrounding bilingual education provides a good example of how national and community attitudes impact school policies and practices. In Chapter 8 we reviewed the theoretical base for bilingual education. This base is sufficiently strong to warrant implementation of bilingual programs. In addition, strong research evidence exists to support the use of primary-language instruction. We will review this research and look at the effect of national campaigns against bilingual education that have resulted in the research being suppressed or ignored.

Research Support for Bilingual Education

Bilingual education has come to symbolize both the waves of immigration and the social and economic problems that communities perceive as resulting from that immigration. Unfortunately, little positive publicity has been offered as to how bilingual education could help remedy some of the problems. In fact, a general attitude of "English only" has definitely been a part of the educational philosophy at many schools. Toni, a bilingual kindergarten teacher, wrote of her experience growing up in a small farming community:

> It was my deepest desire (as I was growing up) to become completely assimilated into the American culture as quickly as possible. I did not care to use the language of my parents except when I absolutely had to. Of course, the school I attended had a lot to do with developing this attitude especially when there were signs in the hallway that read "Speak English for Your Own Benefit" and you were punished for speaking Spanish. I was not proud to be Mexican American, and, in fact, I always had an inferiority complex especially being the darker-skinned version.

The pedagogical benefits of bilingual education were largely ignored in the days Toni went to school and, unfortunately, are not understood well today. Nevertheless, educators and researchers have known for some time the benefits of bilingual education for academic success. Appendix E lists some of the key research on bilingual education.

Studies continue to support bilingual education, calling for more first language instruction rather than less (Berman 1992; Collier 1992; Ramírez 1991). A summary of the 1991 Aguirre International Study (Ramírez 1991) and a synthesis of studies on language minority students (Collier 1992) provides some of the strongest support for bilingual education as well as an idea of what types of programs are the most effective.

The United States Department of Education contracted with Aguirre International in San Mateo, California, to do a longitudinal study of over two thousand native Spanish-speaking elementary school children for over four years. The study looked at the effectiveness of three instructional strategies used with language-minority students: structured English immersion, early-exit transitional bilingual education, and late-exit bilingual education (Ramírez 1991).

Each of the three strategies are commonly used with bilingual students. In the structured immersion programs, all instruction was given in English with first language support provided on a one-to-one basis to clarify English instruction. The structured programs were modeled after the Canadian Immersion programs. Teachers were given specialized training to teach content, and all teachers had credentials in bilingual education or ESL. In addition, teachers had strong receptive skills in Spanish. The goal was to mainstream students out of the structured immersion classes within two or three years.

Students in the early-exit programs had thirty to sixty minutes a day of instruction in Spanish initially. Usually, primary-language support was for the teaching of reading only. Other instruction was given in English with the first language being used only for clarification. If a student entered in kindergarten, most first language instruction would be phased out by second grade since the goal was to mainstream students within three years.

The late-exit programs had considerably more first language support. Students in the late-exit programs received a minimum of forty percent of their total instructional time in Spanish including Spanish language arts, reading, and other content areas. Students remained in the late-exit programs even when they were reclassified from non-English proficient to fluent English proficient (East 1993; Ramírez 1991).

The conclusions of this study have significant implications for education. In the first place, it was found that "LEP students can be provided with substantial amounts of primary-language instruction without impeding their acquisition of English language and reading skills" (Ramírez 1991, p. 43). That is, students in the late-exit programs, even though they received less instruction in English than students in the other two types of programs, acquired English just as fast. This is significant when one reflects on the sign in Toni's school that gave students the impression that the use of Spanish would hurt their chances for school success.

A second and even more important conclusion of the study was that those students in the late-exit programs who continued to receive first language support increased their academic achievement while they were learning English, thus keeping up with English-speaking students. Since they received academic instruction in a language they could understand, they did not fall behind. In contrast, students in the structured immersion and early-exit programs did not keep up with the other students. Over time, they fell further behind in academic subjects. There were, of course, other important conclusions of the study, but those two are very important for the support of bilingual education: Students who receive instruction in their primary language develop both English and academic skills more effectively than students who receive little or no primary-language instruction.

Collier (1992) has reviewed the literature on some of the long-term studies of academic achievement of language-minority students carried out in the 1980s. Each study compared bilingually schooled language-minority students to comparable monolingually schooled language-minority students. In addition to the Ramírez study discussed above, Collier reviewed standardized test score results for students in two-way bilingual programs, late-exit (maintenance) bilingual programs, early-exit (transitional) bilingual programs, and programs with no first language support. The late-exit and early-exit programs are defined above. "Two-way bilingual education is an integrated program in which language-majority students work together academically with language-minority students, learning language and content through both L1 and L2"

(p. 196). In these programs, all students learn through two languages. Collier's findings were similar to those of the Aguirre study:

> The greater the amount of L1 instructional support for language-minority students, combined with balanced L2 support, the higher they are able to achieve academically in L2 in each succeeding academic year, in comparison to matched groups being schooled monolingually in L2 (p. 205).

What all these studies have found is that students who receive sustained first language support develop both English proficiency and academic competence. The research results seem quite clear, but negative attitudes toward bilinguals and bilingual education have prevented many schools from adopting the most effective practices.

Bilingual education in many parts of the United States is perceived as a remedial program designed solely for minorities (as opposed to the enrichment view of bilingualism held in most of the rest of the world). As a result, decisions about implementing this educational program are strongly influenced by national and community attitudes toward minorities. For this reason, bilingual education provides a good example of how factors in the societal context affect the educational context for schooling.

Bilingual Education or English Only?

At the national level, the opposition to bilingual education has taken the form of a movement known as English Only. The call for instruction in only the English language is heard in every state. The controversy is heated despite the overwhelming amount of research that shows that bilingual support for second language students promotes academic success in English. Crawford (1992), in his introduction to *Language Loyalties: A Source Book on the Official English Controversy*, gives some history of the English Only movement, explaining that the present movement for Official English legislation, begun by Senator S. I. Hayakawa in 1981, had a thrust "not only *for* English but *against* bilingualism" (p. 1). Crawford summarizes the "polarizing issues" and the "enormous gap in perceptions" centered around Official English:

> For supporters, the case is obvious: English has always been our common language, a means of resolving conflicts in a nation of diverse racial, ethnic, and religious groups. Reaffirming the preeminence of English means reaffirming a unifying force in American life. Moreover, English is an essential tool of social mobility and economic advancement. The English Language Amendment would "send a message" to immigrants, encouraging them to join in rather than remain apart, and to government, cautioning against policies that might retard English acquisition.
>
> For opponents, Official English is synonymous with English Only: a mean-spirited attempt to coerce Anglo-conformity by terminating essential services in other languages. The amendment poses a threat to civil rights, educational opportunities, and free speech, even in the private sector. It is an insult to the heritage of cultural minorities, including groups whose roots in this country go deeper than English speakers: Mexican Americans, Puerto Ricans, and American Indians. Worst of all, the English Only movement serves to justify racist and nativist biases under the cover of American patriotism (pp. 2–3).

Crawford's own interest in bilingual education began when he was an investigative reporter newly assigned to education. The then secretary of education, Bennett had recently delivered a speech calling the Bilingual Education Act a "failed path, a bankrupt course," and a waste of taxpayers' money (Bennett 1985). When the education community reacted, Bennett's office claimed they were receiving hundreds of letters and those letters were five-to-one in favor of Bennett's view.

Crawford read the letters and what he found disturbed him:

> Most of the "supporting" letters had less to do with schooling for non-English-speaking students than with illegal aliens on welfare, communities being "overrun" by Asians and Hispanics, "macho-oriented" foreigners trying to impose their culture on Americans, and—a special concern—the out-of-control birthrates of linguistic minorities (p. 4).

Crawford explained that many of the letters ended with calls for Official English, like "WHOSE AMERICA IS THIS? ONE FLAG. ONE LANGUAGE" (p. 4).

What was and still is disturbing about this kind of response is that bilingual education has "become a lightning rod for tensions about demographic and cultural change, increased immigration from the Third World, reforms in civil rights, and the political empowerment of minorities" (p. 4).

For example, newspaper headlines that feature demographic growth seem to encourage this tension. Even in the state of Maine, where the number of people speaking languages other than English actually declined by 6.6 percent in the last decade, a recent headline read "Some 32 million Americans speak other languages at home" (Bovee, T., *Sun-Journal,* Lewiston, Maine, April 28, 1993, p. A3).

Opponents of bilingual education encourage this feeling of overwhelming numbers and claim that teaching in languages other than English will (1) cause division and dissension, and (2) keep immigrants from learning English. In addition, they make it clear that speaking English is American and speaking other languages is un-American. Holmes (1993) in an article entitled "Are politicians seized by linguistic panic?" summarizes the conclusions of Mitchell and other linguists at a world conference on nationalistic language policies. Mitchell believes that "America's upsurge of linguistic nationalism" can be seen "as a reaction to social and economic tensions" (p. 8).

Recognition of the research that shows how first language support leads to academic success is buried under the negative publicity. This publicity, fueled by organizations like English Only, creates a negative attitude toward bilinguals and toward bilingual education. In fact, proponents of bilingual education have labeled the information put out by these organizations "disinformation," a method of diverting people from facts. For further readings on the topic of English Only and the history of bilingual education in the United States, see the list in Appendix E.

Developing the Knowledge to Combat Disinformation

Stacey, a second-grade teacher in a farming community, found she agreed with Crawford's conclusions because she could relate them to personal experiences. When she read about the resentment toward the new immigrants, she thought of her own grandfather:

> For years I listened to my grandfather put down Hispanics in the Valley. He resented the fact that they were starting to take over the valley and how many job positions required Spanish-speaking skills. He had the typical old attitude, "You're in my

country, speak my language." The irony is my grandfather was born in Armenia and came to America when he was in the sixth grade only speaking Armenian. Like many first- and second-generation Armenians, he graduated from high school and then bought land and started farming. He lived a very affluent lifestyle until his death a couple of years ago.

Teachers in our graduate program studying language acquisition and bilingual education have read and talked about the rationale for bilingual education and studies like the Aguirre Report and the Collier synthesis. As they begin to learn about the history of English Only and the politics involved in the antibilingual education movements in the United States, they are surprised, dismayed, and angered by the way the research is ignored or dismissed. Rusty, a sixth-grade teacher, wrote of his feelings:

> Relatively speaking, I am appalled at how ignorant I am about the history of education in America, and specifically about bilingual education in the history of education in America. No wonder we (education as an institution) are in trouble.
>
> I have always assumed that everything in this country is tied to the political system, but I was not aware of the extent that education has been used to promote a certain sociopolitical philosophy. I guess the extent to which Bennett (Reagan) manipulated the system to promote what they thought was best for the country shouldn't be surprising, yet it was to me. Not so much that they would do it, but that they could be as effective as they were. I guess my ignorance and naiveté are what should be shocking. Am I the only one? I really don't think so.

Cummins (1989) argues that the problem is more than one of ignorance and naiveté as Rusty suggests. Cummins believes that academics "have collaborated in" a process of "disinformation" about bilingual education (p. 107). He suggests that the data that supports bilingual education has been deliberately denied or distorted in order to maintain the status quo. Understanding the theoretical base and research support for bilingual education as well as the history of movements such as English Only helps teachers become aware of the societal factors that affect their daily educational practices. Often, as teachers gain this knowledge, they have strong emotional reactions.

Perhaps one of the most poignant responses to English Only and the history of bilingual education came from Alicia, a bilingual teacher who herself has fought for an education and watches family and friends struggling still. She was especially upset to read that a Hispanic woman, Linda Chavez, was president of U.S. English for a time and that Chavez was quoted as saying the following:

> Unless we become serious about protecting our heritage as a unilingual society— bound by a common language—we may lose a precious resource that has helped us forge a national character and identity from so many diverse elements (Crawford 1989, p. 57).

Alicia learned that Chavez did not resign until a memorandum from the chairman for U.S. English, John Tanton, was published in which he "warned of a Hispanic political takeover in the United States through immigration and high birthrates" (p. 57). Tanton critiqued Hispanics for taking bribes, being Roman Catholics (which was a threat to separation of church and state), exhibiting low "educability" and high dropout rates, failure to use birth control, having limited concern for the environment, and dividing the country by speaking Spanish" (p. 57). In response to Chavez and Tanton's condemning memo, Alicia wrote a passionate response in Spanish. She commented on a number of things. She found it incredible that a Hispanic woman would support English Only and that she would believe that this organization would help immigrants. Alicia was also amazed that a Hispanic would think that immigrants would not want to better themselves. As she put it, "This is like saying we do not have aspirations or dreams and that we conform to the crumbs that are thrown to us" [author's translation].

She found it insulting that people feared Hispanics, with their high birth rate, would take over. "Perhaps they believe that by declaring English the official language, they are going to avoid the growth of the Hispanic family" [author's translation]. Alicia concluded that the response of English Only to the disintegrating social conditions in the country was an attempt to "blame somebody" and that the movement had nothing to do with improving educational opportunities for minorities.

When María, a graduate bilingual resource teacher, read about Tanton's memo, she argued, "I take it few Anglos have ever taken bribes or misappropriated funds. Limited concern for the environment? Who's producing the most devastating chemicals, products, and weapons? Hispanics?" Who indeed? Alicia and María, through their own education and reading, are becoming empowered educators who will speak out in favor of children and the pedagogy that supports them.

We end this section on a positive note. There are teachers who are informed and who, like the readers of this book, are giving up their time to study to better serve the diverse students in our schools. Toni, the bilingual kindergarten teacher, whose first language was discouraged by "Speak English for Your Own Benefit" signs around the school, recently wrote the following:

> As I attend class after class, I am so encouraged to see the number of Anglo teachers taking courses and learning how to empower minority students. I'm encouraged by their care and concern and by their putting all their learning into real practice. This change has been long overdue.

Toni's observation is important. Teachers have found ways to change what is happening with bilingual students at their schools. Their understanding of the history and politics that surround bilingual education have made them stronger advocates for their students and for educational practices that work for those students. Rusty, whose comments we related earlier, is an Anglo sixth-grade teacher who cares passionately about promoting a positive view of diversity:

> And there is some satisfaction in knowing that in spite of the fact that we have ignorant politicians making foolish decisions, organizations and researchers being used for the promotion of self-serving agendas, and fellow teachers impacting student lives based on erroneous assumptions, there are thirty-three kids in my classroom that are getting the best they could get anywhere in the world. Now how is that for self-confidence?

Teachers like Rusty can make a difference for language-minority students in schools, especially if they become advocates for their students and help to inform their communities about bilingual education issues. If bilingual education is really viewed from a pedagogical perspective rather than a political one, and if the public learns about bilingual education research, immigrant students may have hope for academic success.

Conclusion

National and community attitudes can directly impact educational programs. Despite strong research support for bilingual programs, negative political attitudes fostered by organizations like U.S. English have prevented widespread implementation. This is a clear case of how the attitudes of the society, the societal context, can influence school practices.

Teachers often attempt to change factors in the school context to improve education for all their students. They might, for example, adopt a new reading program or try new ways of teaching math. Although teachers need to continue to refine their practices, it may be that external, societal factors play a more influential role than they realize. By reading and discussing research and the history of movements like U.S. English, teachers can begin to develop the information base needed to combat widespread disinformation campaigns. Teachers can't change everything at once, and when changes within the school context are not effective, teachers must consider how they can change the societal context.

Applications

1. Read the letters to the editor in your local newspapers as well as the local and national editorials over several weeks. Clip any that have to do with changing population. What is the general attitude expressed? What are the problems that are brought up? Share the articles with the class or a small group for discussion. What are the group conclusions?

2. In a group make up a short series of interview questions about the immigrants in your community and/or beliefs about bilingual education. Interview seven to ten people, including people not in the field of education. Graph the group results. Discuss the findings.

3. María, a bilingual resource teacher for a district with a high Hispanic population, describes her struggles with the inconsistencies she sees as she studies the history of bilingual education and the politics involved:

> It seems the more I read, the more confused I become—English Only initiative, U.S. English movement, Bilingual Act repealed. So much conflicting information continues to be given, mostly by politicians with majority language constituencies that "squeak loudly" or have $ for lobbying. How can we teach English to children as quickly as possible? Seldom are the best interests or needs of children considered by policy makers.

Write a response to María. Do you see similar problems? Are there any solutions?

CHAPTER TEN

What Influences Student and Teacher Attitudes?

M ajority group attitudes toward schools and specific school programs, such as bilingual education, constitute an important component of the societal context for education. Equally important are the attitudes of minority group members toward school. Their feelings are shaped by the group's history and particularly its relationships with the majority culture. Language minority students' attitudes, which are reflected in their school performance, are influenced by their community's perceptions of school. Differences among minority groups' school performance result in part from the way different groups view school.

Types of Ethnic Minorities

Ogbu (1991, 1986) has identified differences in the backgrounds and experiences of minority groups in various countries. He believes that these differences account for the discrepancies in those groups' school success. Ogbu classifies minorities into three groups: immigrant minorities, involuntary minorities, and autonomous minorities. Autonomous minorities, such as the Amish, live apart from the majority culture and set their own criteria for success. They reject majority standards and live within their own cultural framework. Generally, these are small groups who may be isolated from the mainstream. Often the children of autonomous minorities attend their own schools. Therefore, students from autonomous minority groups have little impact on schooling in the majority culture.

On the other hand, immigrant and involuntary minorities now constitute the numerical majorities in many school systems, and both groups frequently experience discriminatory treatment at the hands of the dominant group. Ogbu notes, however, that the response of the two minority groups to this negative treatment is quite different, and as a result, immigrant minorities tend to succeed in schools while members of involuntary minority groups often fail.

When we review the performance of different minority groups in school, certain patterns do emerge. For example, Chinese and Cubans, who generally meet the criteria for immigrant minorities, have usually done quite well compared with involuntary minorities such as African Americans or Native Americans. However, it is important to note before further developing the differences between these two types of minorities that a number of factors determine whether any one person succeeds or fails in school. Further, it is not always possible to decide whether a particular individual falls into the immigrant or involuntary minority category. Therefore, as one considers the differences between these types, it is important not to make sweeping generalizations or to decide that certain students will fail or succeed if they belong to one group or the other. On the other hand, it is important to be aware of the differences between groups because an understanding may help us to make informed decisions about how best to work with our students.

Immigrant Minorities

Ogbu defines immigrant minorities as those who came from another country and retain their homeland as their reference point. Immigrants are not highly influenced by majority-group treatment even when they are given low-status jobs because they measure success by the standards of their homeland. As Ogbu writes, "The immigrants appear to interpret the economic, political, and social barriers against them as more or less temporary problems, as problems they will or can overcome with the passage of time, hard work, or more education" (1991, p. 11). Often they plan to return to their home, and they believe that they can return with new skills and degrees. They have what Ogbu calls a "positive dual frame of reference" (p. 11). They see themselves as outsiders in a new society and expect poor treatment and low status. They accept this treatment because they are still better off than they would be in their homeland.

The three teens from El Salvador, José Luis, Guillermo, and Patricia, are fairly clear examples of immigrant minorities. When they arrived, they were fleeing for their lives. They felt lucky to be alive and to be given the opportunity to get an education. Their aunt, in fact, constantly reminded them that education was their only opportunity to succeed. All three fully expected to return to El Salvador and were preparing themselves to be leaders in the rebuilding of their country. Both José Luis and Guillermo studied engineering with this in mind. Guillermo's interest in politics was also related to a hope that he would someday be involved in the politics of his own country. Patricia studied medicine because she knew there would be a need for medical workers when they returned to El Salvador.

All three suffered a great deal economically upon arrival. Their living conditions, their clothes, even their often meager diet reflected a big change from their lifestyle in El Salvador. Yet, they rarely complained. In school, they separated themselves from Hispanics who had been here for a long time and had different attitudes and interests. To this day, they never admit to having experienced any discrimination or prejudice though there were several incidents, especially at the beginning, when they were treated rudely or ignored because of their ethnicity and lack of English. Treatment by others really did not matter that much to them. They had pride in their heritage. They were part of an important family in El Salvador, and they had confidence that they could succeed if they worked hard. Their confidence and hard work paid off.

Teachers working with immigrant minorities often find them to be willing to work hard and to be very responsive to even small bits of encouragement. José Luis, Guillermo, and Patricia still speak fondly of their first ESL teacher and give that teacher and our family as their mentors the majority of the credit for their success. When one considers the actual help that was provided, it was slight in comparison with their effort. Yet their positive attitudes, along with that assistance, seemed to make an important difference to them and increased their chances for success.

Yvonne remembers the first Hmong teacher-education candidate she counseled. She was impressed with Xe from the first moment she walked into her office. Xe was enthusiastic and eager. She wanted not only to be a Hmong/English bilingual teacher, but also to learn Spanish "because there are so many Spanish-speaking people here." Though Xe was the only one of twelve children in a struggling Hmong immigrant family to attend college, she never felt sorry for herself. She resisted the pressure of her family to marry at a young age. She was, in fact, one of only a handful of Hmong women in the community to pursue a college education.

Yvonne counseled Xe through her college years, helped her apply for several different scholarships, arranged for her to teach and be paid for a Hmong culture course for teachers, and made herself available when Xe needed advice and encouragement. When Xe saw Hmong teenagers—including her own relatives—failing in school, she often talked to Yvonne of "helping the Hmong community appreciate our culture" by setting up a Hmong culture center. When Xe was elected to give the commencement speech at her college graduation, Yvonne helped her edit the speech. Xe, however, had done all the hard work herself. Despite the fact that she encountered negative responses on several fronts during her college career, she maintained a positive attitude and even now hopes not only to teach, but also to author children's books in Hmong and write her life story beginning with her escape from Laos as a young girl. Xe is a prime example of a successful immigrant minority.

Primary Cultural Differences

Ogbu identifies two kinds of cultural differences: primary and secondary. Immigrant minorities are characterized by primary cultural differences. These differences, such as language, food, and attire, are specific and easily recognizable. They existed before the dominant and immigrant groups came into contact.

Primary differences do not usually constitute barriers to students' educational success because immigrants are able to alternate their behavior between the home culture and the mainstream school culture. For example, they may speak one language at home, but they recognize the importance of speaking English at school. They may give low status to women in the home culture but still accept and respect female teachers at school. Alternation between two worlds is not threatening to immigrant minorities. They want to gain as much as possible from schools and the majority society generally, and they also want to retain their primary culture. They see no contradiction in pursuing both these goals simultaneously.

Xe is a clear example of a student with primary cultural differences. Her family speaks Hmong, eats traditional Hmong food, and takes part in Hmong religious and cultural ceremonies. Although she is unusual as a college-educated Hmong woman, just before college graduation she did marry a Hmong man who holds a technical job working with photographic equipment. The two are a modern "American" couple in many ways, but they have chosen to live with his family following the tradition of the culture. They are living in both worlds and working to succeed in both.

Another of our case studies, Sharma, is also an example of an immigrant minority with primary cultural differences. Her parents were educated in India, yet they were willing to come to the United States and take menial jobs in order to get a good education for their children. At home Sharma and her parents not only speak Punjabi and eat Punjabi food, they also practice the customs and religion of the people in their homeland. In fact, their school life and home life are kept very separate. While Sharma can dress in western clothes for school, she wears traditional clothing during the weekends and holidays. Sharma's family maintains their culture and language and is not really interested in becoming part of mainstream American culture.

Rhoda, Sharma's teacher, has found ways to support Sharma. Aware of Sharma's struggle to succeed in two cultures, Rhoda has taken the responsibility of finding support for her first language, Punjabi, and she is trying to respond sensitively to Sharma's attempt to live in both cultures. Rhoda has described the girl's struggles as Sharma's "self-conscious social episodes" (see Chapter 1). Because Rhoda is aware that Sharma and her family are immigrant minorities and knows about the effects of primary cultural differences, she can better respond to Sharma's needs.

Involuntary Minorities

Ogbu contrasts immigrant minorities with involuntary minorities. Examples of involuntary minorities include African Americans, Native Americans, Hispanics, and others who were born in the United States or arrived too young to identify with their heritage culture. They are often at least second- or third-generation Americans who have little connection with their ancestral homeland and lack a deep understanding of traditional cultural practices. Although immigrants have, to some degree, chosen to come to a country, members of involuntary minority groups have not. Immigrants may see their status as temporary, but involuntary minorities have become incorporated into a society quite permanently. The history of the relationships between involuntary minorities and mainstream society is often one of exploitation.

Tou, the Hmong junior high school student described in Chapter 1, seems to be a prime example of an involuntary minority struggling for identity. Unlike Xe, who remembers her childhood in Laos and her escape, Tou left the refugee camp as an infant. Xe's family strongly holds to traditional values and customs, but Tou's family seems to be unstable and certainly not the traditional Hmong family. In the Hmong culture, children live with their family even after marriage. Hmong families maintain close ties, but one of Tou's sisters has moved to Georgia, another lives in Sacramento with Tou's mother, and his brother, who is a known gang member, does not live with the family at all.

Tou, then, does not have strong support from his primary culture, and he struggles with his identity. Is he Hmong or American? As his teacher, Kathy, pointed out, he seemed to be doing a bit better after the visit with his father, and lots of nagging did get him through the seventh grade. However, his problems outside of school including the fights between classes with students from other cultural groups, and his eventual transfer to "opportunity" classes are discouraging. It is probable that Tou sees little hope, and he may try to find "family" through gang membership.

Juan, the twelve-year-old migrant boy living with his family in the temporary migrant camp, is also an involuntary minority. His family has been in this country for a number of years, and he has legal status. He sees himself as an American, not as a Mexican. However, he is aware that he is a member of a group being exploited by the mainstream culture.

Juan's case is both similar to and different from Tou's. Juan is devoted to his mother, stepfather, and younger brothers and sister, and he wants to do well, but the conditions for survival are overwhelming. Both Juan and Tou live in poverty with little hope of change. Tou lives in a tenement apartment in the inner city. Juan lives in temporary shelters with dirt floors without electricity or gas. Juan is polite in school and tries when he is able to attend, but it is clear that he has little hope that he will really succeed. Unlike Sharma, he lacks the support of any kind of church or community groups other than his family and those living in the migrant camps.

Understandably, Juan resents the rich Anglos who demand that the migrant camps be destroyed because they are an eyesore. He also feels anger at the label "wetback" since he and his family have legal papers to work. This country is their home. They will not go back to Mexico to live.

At the end of Brimmer's book, *A Migrant Family*, Juan says, "I've missed too much. Too much." Ogbu explains that new immigrants see economic, political, and social barriers against them as more or less temporary problems, as obstacles they will or can overcome with the passage of time, hard work, or more education. Involuntary minorities like Juan, however, see permanent problems and may have little hope of overcoming them. Although his father views education as the answer, Juan may not.

The major difference between immigrant and involuntary minorities lies in the ways they respond to discriminatory treatment and the folk theories for getting ahead that they develop. Immigrants are not highly influenced by majority-group treatment because they can alternate their behavior between home and school or workplace. In contrast, involuntary minorities are highly influenced by majority-group treatment. They strongly resent discriminatory practices such as tracking, exclusion from some social activities, or job ceilings. As a result, involuntary minorities develop a social identity in opposition to the dominant group. For example, members of involuntary minorities may adopt certain ways of talking or dressing to identify themselves with their cultural group in opposition to the majority culture. Many aspects of gang membership fall within this category. Involuntary minorities might also drive certain kinds of cars that they have decorated or changed to give their group a specific identity.

Secondary Cultural Differences

These differences between mainstream cultural groups and involuntary minorities are what Ogbu calls secondary cultural differences. They form after the two groups come into contact. In fact, according to Ogbu (1991), secondary cultural differences develop in opposition to the majority culture. As a result, members of involuntary minorities cannot alternate behaviors and be a "home boy" at home but a "school boy" at school. They do not picture themselves exporting their skills and knowledge to some home-land because *this* is their home. In addition, there may be considerable peer pressure for involuntary minorities to conform to group norms. "The secondary cultural system, on the whole, constitutes a new cultural frame of reference" (p. 15).

Attempts by school personnel to correct or change aspects of this cultural identity may be perceived as attacks on the minority group by the dominant group rather than as efforts to help group members succeed. They "distrust members of the dominant group and the societal institutions controlled by the latter" (p. 16). As a result, involuntary minorities develop a folk theory for success that places little value on education. Tou seems to fit into this category. He does not believe that his father and the school want the best for him. At this point, school just does not seem important to him. Juan does appear to value school, but he does not see school success as something attainable either.

Both immigrant and involuntary minorities often face unequal treatment by the dominant social group. However, the two minority groups respond differently to this treatment, and they develop different folk theories for getting ahead. Immigrant minorities, like the El Salvadorans, Xe, and Sharma, are generally able to alternate their behavior between home and school. As a result, they can maintain primary cultural differences while still getting ahead in mainstream society. They value school because education provides the skills and knowledge that increase their possibilities for financial success, and they use their accomplishments to improve their conditions.

Involuntary minorities are not able to alternate behavior because their secondary cultural differences such as manner of dress, their defiance of authority, or their way of talking were formed in opposition to the mainstream culture, and to give those up would be to abandon their primary social identity. Folk theories of success place limited value on schools or other social institutions controlled by the dominant culture. Members of involuntary minorities who do succeed in mainstream terms often move out of their original neighborhoods to areas where they can fit in with the dominant group. Thus, those members of the community that might challenge the theory that schools do not lead to success are not there to argue the case.

Yvette Meets the Challenge

How do schools begin to meet the challenges posed by minority students who do not seem to value school and gauge their success by other measures? Yvette, who was doing her final student teaching at an urban high school of over three thousand students, provides us with a powerful example of what is possible. The students in her sophomore English class came from many different ethnic backgrounds, and most were not considered college material. Many were members of different ethnically divided gangs and would be what Ogbu defines as involuntary minorities with secondary cultural differences.

Yvette herself was once in the category of an involuntary minority. She still refers to herself as a Chicana because she understands what it means to struggle in school. She grew up in a community controlled by Anglos who generally did not respect Hispanics. Her father had once been a gang member, but he managed to convince both his daughters that school would be a better route for them.

Even as a young student teacher, Yvette drew respect from her students because she showed respect for them, their lives, and their ideas. She centered her curriculum around topics the students found relevant and around the diversity of the students themselves. Because Yvette had faith in her students and showed them she believed they would succeed in her class, they responded positively.

Yvette's most successful unit began after the class had finished a required novel. The students and Yvette decided they were ready for a change. In an attempt to engage her students, Yvette had them read several articles on topics such as gangs, teenage pregnancy, and drug abuse. One that was especially popular came from the *Los Angeles Times,* "Cadillac Jim—Homage to an L.A. Homeboy" (Wilkinson and Chavez 1992). This article told of the funeral for a famous Los Angeles gang member and discussed both the rituals that have developed around the deaths of gang members and the concern over the growing numbers of such deaths.

One day as class began, Yvette heard the door open and close. When she heard soft laughter ripple through the room, she looked up, expecting that some student had walked out. Instead, she realized that a student had sneaked in! This student, a known gang member, had been expelled from school earlier, so he had not attended her class for some weeks. However, he had been talking with others in the class about what they were reading and was so interested that he wanted to take part even though he would not get any grades or credit. He begged Yvette to let him "read the stuff the other kids read" and even asked if he could do a response and send it in with a friend. Figure 10-1 shows his drawing. He drew a picture of the funeral of a homeboy and wrote two quotes from the *Los Angeles Times* article that impressed him. In addition, he carefully drew a "homeboy" (Figure 10-2). A short time later he even brought his brother as a visitor to show him how good the class was!

Figure 10-1   Homeboy funeral

During the last week of school, each student in Yvette's class turned in a project on a culture of his or her choice. The students could choose any culture represented in the school. The class agreed that gangs should be considered a culture along with the others chosen, including African American, Hispanic, Hmong, Vietnamese, and Khmer. The project required an oral presentation as well as a written report.

Robert, a Chicano gang member whose friends call him Bubba, decided to talk about his view of gang culture. Figure 10-3 is the written portion of Bubba's presentation, "My Opinion on Gangs," complete with his private gang signature. He shows his dislike for those in other gangs by putting crosses through words that refer to them. Bubba explains several things about gang culture. He comments "most people get into gangs because they don't have anywhere else to turn to." He makes it clear that the gang is a group he can depend on: "My homeboys to me are like another family there always there to back me up." For Bubba his gang's color gives him important membership in a group others do not belong to: "I would at this moment in my life be prepared to die for my color. You may think that's dumb to say, but it's more than a color to me it's my pride and vida (life)." Respect seems to be key and Bubba insists people "have to understand that this has a lot to do with respect. Some

Figure 10-2   Homeboy drawing

cholos or homeboy's that's all they ever ask for is some respect." Certainly, Bubba and his gang have set up a whole society based on what Ogbu calls secondary cultural differences.

Perhaps the clearest understanding of the importance of the gang and the loyalty of members to it comes from the poem Bubba wrote after his friend, Dreamer, died (Figure 10-4). Readers will notice the personal gang signs for Dreamer are drawn into the poem and in the epitaph that Bubba wrote for his friend (Figure 10-5).

Bubba and Dreamer are examples of what Ogbu would describe as involuntary minorities who have developed secondary characteristics to find identity. Yvette was able to draw on her students' strengths and interests to help them see some purpose in school. She had examined her own attitudes and beliefs and was able to develop practices that helped all her students begin to consider their attitudes. In fact, once Bubba experienced some academic success and was able to examine gang culture more objectively, he decided to reject it. By making issues from her students' lives central to her curriculum, Yvette was able to make school meaningful for all her students.

"MY OPINION ON GANGS"

As you know miss Vasquez me, my self are in a gang in this moment. Alot of people see a cholo walk down the street. They just see a thief, trouble-maker or hudlem. Alot of people think that if your in a gang that you have problems at home. That you don't have any respect for anyone and ect....

Well I am living evidence that that's not true. I love my mother very much. I also respect her and my elders as you know. It does bring me down that people put me down because of the way I dress. When you go some where they look at you different, but alot of home boys do have problems at home. I believe that most people get into gang's because they don't have anywhere else to turn to.

Sometimes when I have a problem sometimes I can't turn to my parents but I can depend on my home boys. Alot of people don't understand where I'm comeing from or d my prespective. My homeboys to me are like another family there always there to back me up. Plus and can relly on them in any moment I may need them. I can't actually put my life in there hands if some one had a gun on me and they had one I could really on them to take him out before he gets me and I would do the same.

I would be at this moment in my life be prepared to die for my color. You may think that's dumb to say but it's more than a color to me. It's my pride and vida. I will admit that sometimes people who aren't invo-lved get hurt. I really and truly do feel bad about that but acidents do happen. People have to realize that it's all a big game. there's the brown team and also black team. There's one thing thow that then splits up to the red rag and the blue rag.

It's sometimes hard to believe that were killing off our own race our people. When I see a chicano wear-ing blue I believe that he's disrespect-ing his own race. I would rather sit down with a black than sit with a sureno. The rest of the people I believe are just pawns in our game. Some people don't ask to get shoot, beat up or killed.

Sometimes the person that your aiming for aint the one that gets hit. That's sad but thats life rather they like it or not. Sometimes I think of alot of things like what it would be like to be able to walk down the street without having to keep look-ing back or every time you saw a

a car driveing slow thinking that you may be takeing the last few steps. If your takeing your last few breaths of air. I have to be ready to drop to the floor or even for the worst. Alot of people don't understand moste people don't live like that but a gangbanger does. It's either you pop them or you'll be the one in the ground. Plus you have to think think that if you do something they could hert your family of your girl-friend. People critize us but they don't know what it's like. If you live. They also have to under-stand that this has alot to do with respect. Some cholos or home-boy's thats all they ever ask for is some respect. If your resp-ected then you'll respect others as well. I hope that you under-stand where I'm comeing from. I'll admit that it's hard sometimes not being able to to walk around without knowing that your life could be taken away.

WRITEN BY:
BUBBA B.W.

Figure 10-3 Bubba's opinion of gangs

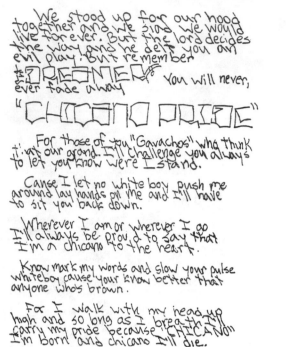

Chicano Pride Poem
We stood up for our hood
together and we siad we would
live forever. But the lord decides
the way and he delt you an
evil play. But remember
DREAMER You will never,
ever fade away
"CHICANO PRIDE"
For those of you "Gavachos" who think
that our grand. I'll challenge you always
to let you know were I stand.
Cause I let no white boy push me
around lay hands on me and I'll have
to sit you back down.
Wherever I am or wherever I go
I'll always be proud to say that
I'm a chicano to the heart.
Know mark my words and slow your pulse
whiteboy cause your know better that
anyone who's brown.
For I walk with my head up
high and so long as I breath I'll
carry my pride because "CHICANO"
I'm born and chicano I'll die.
(Words of poem typed as written)

Figure 10-4   Bubba's poem about Dreamer

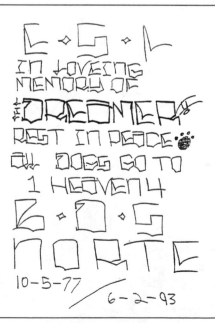

Figure 10-5   Epitaph

Ogbu's theory of different types of minorities helps explain differences in minority groups' school achievement. Again, however, it is important to note that not all Hispanics, for example, fall into the involuntary minority category and that within any group some students will succeed and some will fail. As Cortés points out, a great many different factors interact to create contexts for schooling and school success or failure, and any single-cause explanation is sure to prove invalid.

Community, Student, and Teacher Attitudes

Attitudes that teachers develop toward their students have a strong impact on educational practices. A dynamic exists here. When teachers work with immigrant minorities like Sharma or the teens from El Salvador they often develop positive outlooks because these students work hard and respond enthusiastically to teacher suggestions. On the other hand, working with involuntary minorities is difficult because students have developed secondary cultural differences in opposition to the mainstream, and they do not value school success. Over time, teachers may begin to develop negative attitudes toward these students, although some, like Yvette, have responded to the challenge admirably.

Lea, a young Latina teacher, was born in Mexico to an Irish-ancestry father and a Mexican mother. She has lived most of her life in the United States and is married to a man who was born in Mexico and came to this country with his family when he was in his teens. Lea considers herself to be a Mexican, but because of her light coloring, she often finds herself in the middle of conversations where Anglos make negative comments about minorities, believing that she is "one of them." She has both observed and experienced how teachers' attitudes can affect students' school success. She wrote about her feelings in response to readings about bilingual education:

> For some reason, in our culture, any language besides English is seen as inferior. Often, children whose native language is not English experience feelings of inferiority when they are in the American school system. Add to that their cultural history in the United States and their socioeconomic status, and you have a prescription for failure. To simply say students are failing because of "language deficiencies" takes away the focus from the real deficiencies in the U.S. educational system. Also, it leaves no explanation for African-American and Native American students' difficulties in school; therefore, they are seen as inherently retarded. I don't want to make learning English seem "irrelevant" to school success, but often people focus on that one issue. When Chinese-American students succeed in school and Mexican-American students don't, the blame automatically is placed upon those students and their parents. One woman with whom I work asked, "Do they (Mexicans) really want to succeed in school?" (No. . . . Mexican students *love to fail.*) No one, of course, would ever say that about an Anglo or Asian student.

The teachers who have made these comments to Lea would benefit from understanding Ogbu's distinctions between immigrant and involuntary minorities. In the next section we look more closely at teacher attitudes and how they can affect students' educational performance. As the school population changes, teachers need information that can help them work effectively with second language students.

Teachers' Prejudices and Perceptions

> During my student teaching experience, I had the opportunity to work with ESL classes in math, history, and English. In one of these classes the teacher was trying to give me some of her educational insight. She told me that the Asian students (Lao, Hmongs, etc.) were much better students than the Mexican students. She went on to say that these children wanted to learn and were not a behavioral problem like the others. I do not think she knew that I was Mexican. Needless to say, I was extremely bothered by her remarks, and I immediately went home and shared this experience with my parents. They were both angered by her false statements. They felt that this new wave of immigrants are being treated much better than they were when they were in school.

This quote from Loretta, a high school business teacher, demonstrates the kinds of attitudes that teachers working in schools with large numbers of immigrant students may develop. Communities form attitudes toward schools, and school personnel develop attitudes toward members of different community groups. Cortés states that a teacher's opinions on why students fail in schools have an important influence on the school context. We believe that some teachers may need to develop new attitudes for the new students in our schools (Freeman and Freeman 1990).

Throughout California and other states experiencing a flood of immigrant students, teachers are responding in various ways to the sudden changes in the student population. All teachers find these changes challenging, but some are coping better than others. Not all teachers are reluctant to work with language-minority students, but many are, at least initially. As we have worked with groups of teachers, we have seen five common responses in schools with high populations of bilingual learners. In describing these responses we will use hypothetical situations that represent what we have observed. The scenarios help illustrate Cortés' Contextual Interaction Model. In each, a number of factors come into play, and a single-cause explanation for success or failure is inadequate. And in each scenario, teacher attitudes and perceptions play an important role. Each case is then briefly analyzed, and some possible positive responses are offered.

Teaching just isn't like it used to be.

Mrs. Brown has taught kindergarten at Baker School in the south end of town for fifteen years. When she first began teaching there, the neighborhood was mostly middle-class whites, but over the years large numbers of minority families including African Americans, Hispanics, and Southeast Asians have moved into the area, causing a "white flight" to the north. The majority of her present students arrive with little or no English. She complains that they cannot do what her students in the past could. She remembers the past fondly. On the first day of school children arrived eager to learn, holding the hands of parents who offered support. Now, she complains, the students, especially the Southeast Asian children, enter the classroom reluctantly. They are either alone or with parents who don't speak English and seem anxious to escape as quickly as possible. Though she has an English-only rule for the classroom, she constantly has to remind students not to speak their native languages. Her biggest complaints are that the children just don't seem motivated and the parents don't care.

Analysis: There are several reasons that Mrs. Brown may be responding as she is. In the earlier days, most of her students spoke English and came from a background similar to their teacher's. She now finds herself trying to teach students who not only do not speak the same language literally, but also do not understand her customs and values any more than she does theirs. Mrs. Brown does not know how to change her teaching to help students, and she responds by blaming them and their families.

Positive Responses: Many teachers who suddenly find themselves with large numbers of English-language learners make it a point to inform themselves about their new students. They read and discuss books and articles about other teachers working with non-English speakers. They talk with their fellow teachers and share materials and ideas that have been successful. They attend workshops offered by school districts and local colleges. They join professional organizations for teachers of bilingual and second language learners.

Once they learn more about English language learners, they become advocates for them. They seek people and materials who can provide first language support, and they promote school events that highlight different cultural traditions. In addition, they make an effort to include the parents of their new students not only at special events, but in the regular classroom day. Even if parents do not speak English, they are invited to class to read a book in their first language, cook, or do crafts. Though all of these things require extra effort, they make their classrooms exciting places where all their students learn.

All these language-minority kids make me look like a failure!

Ms. Franklin is a second-year second-grade teacher. Like most nontenured teachers in the district, she has been assigned to a classroom of minority students, mostly Hispanic and Southeast Asian. Many of her students are classified as limited English proficient. Ms. Franklin's teacher-education program did not prepare her for teaching second language learners. However, as soon as she began to work with them last year, she fell in love with them. She attended a couple of inservices that encouraged her to read with the children, to let them write using invented spelling, and to develop activities that draw on their interests and knowledge. The children responded well to this type of program, and she could see lots of growth in their English.

Despite this success, Ms. Franklin has encountered problems. She teaches in a district where monthly skills-based tests in reading, writing, and math are mandated by the school and the results published. The test scores for her students have remained low, and the principal has talked about this with Ms. Franklin. Even though he did not threaten her directly, Ms. Franklin now feels her job is on the line. From the inservices she has attended and her own experiences, she realizes that standardized tests do not chart the progress of her bilingual students fairly. Still, she is tempted to try this year to "teach to the test," despite the fact that she does not feel that worksheets and drill are meaningful to her minority students. She is beginning to view her students as having deficits—deficits that could have direct consequences for her career. She is also beginning to wish that she could transfer to a school in the north part of town with fewer minority students.

Analysis: Ms. Franklin begins her teaching with enthusiasm and caring. She makes an extra effort to prepare herself to work with the diverse students she is teaching by attending inservices and then applying what she has learned. However, Ms. Franklin does not really understand why the things she has tried work or how long it takes to acquire a second language. So when her students' test scores are low, she cannot defend her curriculum. She is beginning to view the students she once was trying to help as the source of her problems. Her solution is to try to get away from her present teaching situation.

Positive Responses: Many of the teachers who take our graduate courses are like Ms. Franklin. They want to help their students and have learned a little bit about second language learning. However, they are concerned because they feel pressure from standardized testing and do not want to be judged by the poor performance of non-English speakers. Once these teachers understand how long it takes to really speak, read, and write a second language with near-native proficiency and how critical first language support is for content learning, they begin to view their teaching and the testing of their students differently. Many of these teachers keep portfolios of their students' work in both English and their students' first languages to show administrators and others the tremendous progress their students are making. In addition, in California at least, there is a strong movement to use alternative forms of assessment, such as portfolios, for all students so teachers can look for at least some support from the State Department of Education.

It's not fair to the rest of my class to give those students special attention.

Mr. Martin teaches in a farming community where he has lived since he was a child. At the beginning of the year his sixth-grade classroom consisted of a nice group of Anglo and Hispanic children who were all fairly proficient in English and all reasonably successful learners. At the end of the first month of school, the principal called Mr. Martin in to explain that five sixth-grade migrant children had just arrived from Mexico and that they would be placed in Mr. Martin's class.

Mr. Martin wasn't sure what to do with these new students whose English was extremely limited. The district paid for him to take training to learn new techniques, but he resented the idea that he had to attend extra classes and learn new ways to teach, especially when he had been successful for a number of years. Why should he be the one to change? If these students couldn't meet the expectations for his class, maybe they weren't ready for it.

Nevertheless, the students were in his class, and the principal was not about to transfer them out. Since he was a good teacher, Mr. Martin knew he should be doing something for them, and he felt guilty that they just sat quietly in the back of his classroom. On the other hand, it seemed to him that giving those students special attention wasn't fair to the rest of the class members, who were doing just fine with his traditional instruction. At the same time, the extra training he was receiving also made him feel guilty because it stressed that students should not simply be given busy work, but that they should be engaged in meaningful activities with other students in the classroom. However, Mr. Martin's teaching style did not include much student interaction. He became doubly frustrated as he felt he was not only being asked to deal with new students, but also to change his way of teaching.

Analysis: Mr. Martin, like Mrs. Brown, is a conscientious teacher in a school system that is changing. He has succeeded in the past and resents the fact that he has been designated to deal with the new students. It is probable that the principal chose Mr. Martin because she had confidence that he could do a good job. However, he feels picked on and resentful of the extra time and training necessary to work with second language students. In addition, he believes that giving them special instruction is actually going to be detrimental to his other students. At this point, Mr. Martin does not understand that what is good instruction for second language students is also good for first language students.

Positive Responses: Teachers we have worked with have come to realize that it is impossible to use a traditional transmission model of teaching to reach a very diverse student body. In addition, as they try interactive activities in which heterogeneous groups of students work on projects together, they see that all their students, including their excellent native English-speaking students, learn more. Several teachers who entered our graduate classes determined never to change their teaching styles, later give enthusiastic testimonials of how exciting teaching can be when it is organized around thematic units and includes literature studies, creative writing, and projects involving art, science, music, drama, and cooking.

Who wants to be the bilingual teacher?

Mr. González went into bilingual education because he himself had come to the United States as a non-English-speaking child, and he knew how difficult it was to succeed in school as a second language learner. His education classes had taught him that instruction in the first language helps children academically and actually speeds their success in English. During his first two years of teaching, he enthusiastically worked with his fourth graders, supporting their first language and helping them succeed in their second.

By the end of the third year when he was tenured, his enthusiasm began to wane. Mr. González was troubled by the subtle way his fellow teachers treated him. The bilingual program was considered remedial, and constant remarks in the teachers' lounge showed him that fellow teachers did not really believe bilingual kids were capable of the kind of success other students could achieve. On top of that, Mr. González soon discovered that Hispanic children who were discipline problems were transferred into his class throughout the year even though they were not second language learners. When he objected, the principal always explained that since he was Hispanic, he could understand those children better. Mr. González' attempts to explain that his program was geared to work with Spanish speakers to help them succeed academically, not with discipline problems, fell on deaf ears. He began to feel that his expertise was not respected and that his classroom was becoming a dumping ground. He put in a request to be taken out of the bilingual program.

Analysis: Mr. González' situation is one that has repeated itself many times in different school districts. When there is little understanding of what bilingual education really is and why it is important, bilingual teachers feel isolated and misunderstood. Often uninformed teachers have commonsense assumptions about bilingual learners and do not hesitate to express their opinions about the limited potential of that group of students. Administrators who have heard about the importance of ethnic and cultural role models but do not really know what the theory behind bilingual education is try to find quick and easy solutions to problems of minority students. In this case all

Hispanics are lumped together, and Mr. González is asked to solve all the "problems" of the Hispanics at the school. Bilingual teachers such as Mr. González find themselves, like their bilingual students, suffering prejudice and a lack of understanding. It is no wonder that many bilingual educators drop out of bilingual education.

Positive Responses: Bilingual teachers we have worked with have not found an easy answer to this situation. However, they are somewhat encouraged by recent publications from the state department of education that support first language learning. Often, a caring administrator will read a short article that explains the importance of bilingual education or attend a workshop on bilingual education when invited. Bilingual classrooms are beginning to be understood to be important for the success of bilingual learners rather than to be seen as a dumping ground for students with discipline problems. A few school districts around the country have even begun to offer financial incentives to bilingual teachers and to assure them they will have bilingual materials and administrative support if they come to work for the district. These changes are slow, however, and unfortunately, Mr. González' experience is still a common one.

Don't expect too much of these students.

Mrs. Williams is a pull-out ESL instructor who works with children grades K–8. Most of her students are either Hispanics whose parents are migrant workers or Southeast Asians whose parents were peasants before coming to this country. The Southeast Asian and Hispanic children whose parents are well-to-do are seldom in these pull-out programs. Mrs. Williams likes teaching small groups of children and, in fact, volunteered to become a district pull-out teacher because the idea of working with small groups of polite, respectful children appealed to her.

Mrs. Williams has had no special training in ESL teaching but because she has seen lots of second language learners over the years she feels she understands their problems. She firmly believes that many non-English speakers enter school with no language and that second language parents do not really value education. "After all," she explains, "their parents don't speak English nor do they read or write in their first language. What these children need is lots of oral-language development in English."

In the pull-out classes, the students get practice in pronouncing words, and they often do worksheets that focus on phonics. Since the students don't have control of the oral language, Mrs. Williams does not spend time having them do much reading or writing. "They simply aren't ready," she concludes. Mrs. Williams and her students appear to have reached a sort of truce. She won't push too hard or expect too much, and they will be orderly and complete the assignments she gives them. The regular teachers from whose classrooms the students are pulled out don't complain. They are happy to be relieved of the responsibility of teaching these students for a part of each day, so this arrangement seems satisfactory to all concerned.

The parents of Mrs. Williams' students don't pressure the school to do more either. They seem reluctant to talk to her and do not show up for the conferences she schedules, thus reinforcing Mrs. Williams' belief that parents do not care about their children's school success. Since the students, their parents, and the other teachers are satisfied with her program, Mrs. Williams sees no need to change and resents the assertion from a new district specialist for second language students that she isn't really teaching her ESL students anything.

Analysis: Mrs. Williams is a classic case of a teacher who loves her students and perceives herself as doing the best she can for them. However, it is important to realize that a limited view of students' potential leads to a limiting curriculum. Often people believe that simply knowing a language qualifies a person to teach it. Mrs. Williams does not see the need for any further education about second language learners or the teaching of a second language. If she had done some further study, she might have learned that students need lots of reading and writing as well as speaking and listening, and that worksheets and drills do not help with the natural acquisition of language. Mrs. Williams believes that the students' first language and culture are not really important for learning English. Stereotypes about the parents' lack of interest in the students' school success keep her from attempting to form links between the home and school. Perhaps most disturbing of all is the fact that the rest of the school is actually relieved that Mrs. Williams will take care of the "problem" of the second language children.

Positive Responses: In California and in other states, it is less and less possible for teachers like Mrs. Williams to choose to work with second language students without professional preparation. California, for example, requires teachers who have English language learners to have at least one of several possible kinds of certification. To be certified, teachers must at the very least have experience teaching English language learners and pass a state test about second language acquisition, second language teaching, culture, and linguistics. Many teachers take coursework or inservice that challenges attitudes and practices like those of Mrs. Williams.

Coping with Change

Despite the positive changes that are taking place, however, there is still much to be done to improve the education of English language learners. Each time we read and discuss these five scenarios with the teachers in our graduate programs, we are saddened to learn how many of them tell us these situations are entirely representative of what is still going on in many schools. Rusty, the sixth-grade teacher mentioned earlier, reflected what he has seen in his school by writing a poignant poem (Figure 10-6).

Although many teachers are learning about second language learners and are doing wonderful things in their schools, other teachers and schools still have a long way to go before they begin to meet their students' needs. With the growing number of second language students, the importance of developing new attitudes for the changing population becomes more critical daily.

For all teachers, though, coping with change is not easy. In their report on how California teachers are responding to an influx of immigrant students, researchers from the California Tomorrow group interviewed thirty-six teachers. Kate Duggan, a middle school teacher in a Los Angeles school district that has gone from ten percent language-minority students to sixty-three percent in just ten years, expresses the views of many teachers across the country:

> Change in itself is extremely stressful, and teaching now immerses you in change. Changes in the student population and cultures and races who enroll. New kids coming in and out all the time. And because traditional methods don't work, you

School Days, School Days

You can not see it,
So well it does hide,
Yet subtly it whittles,
Away all self-pride.

Through teeth straight and shiny,
You see the bright smile.
Yet no love is shown there,
Not even for a while.

The pros they can fake it,
They act like they care,
"No, Honey not here,
You sit over there."

"You don't speak our language,
I'm sure that will change."
She pokes little Susie,
"His home's on the range."

"Your mom calls you Carlos,
Now Charles is your name.
I'm sure that you realize
It all means the same."

"Oh, look at your free lunch,
Why, isn't that rice?
It's just like your home, dear,
Oh, isn't that nice?"

Yes, each day it happens
In room after room.
And kids really do wish
They'd stayed in the womb.

The talk, it is subtle,
It's impact so cruel,
Like slow-burning fire
when you've added some fuel.

It strikes at the heart
And pulls at the brain.
Like a strong locomotive,
That pulls the whole train.

We know what the law states,
and that is a start.
But can you really legislate,
Affairs of the heart?

We've had great examples,
In religions and creeds,
You'd think that would do it,
That's all we would need.

Yet man's basic nature,
His seeking of wealth,
Has caused him to stumble
All over himself

And so often the children
They stand in the way.
And push comes to shove,
And children, they pay.

Oh, teacher you must see,
You're the last hope
In helping that small child
With life just to cope.

His face may be dirty,
His clothes might have holes,
His stomach is growling,
He's had only stale rolls.

So reach out a hand please,
Bring a smile to his face.
Give each child a hug
Regardless of race.

No matter his language,
His color, his creeds,
As God is your witness
You must meet his needs.

And if you can't do it,
then please leave our ranks.
Go work in a factory
Or in one of the banks.

We're looking for teachers
With hearts big as stores
Who love *all* the children
And do a lot more.

So if you are willing
to look to the heart
Come quickly new teachers
We'll give you a part.

To show kids some justice
Some fairness and love,
With an abundant supply
That comes from above.

Challenges? Why yes,
Of course, that is true.
But no greater work
Can you ever do.
        Rusty DeRuiter, 1992

Figure 10-6   Rusty's poem

always have to be experimenting with different approaches so there are changes in what you're doing as a teacher. All this change affects the entire tone of the school (Olsen and Mullen 1990, p. 9).

Change is stressful, but a number of teachers are not only coping with change, but learning how to celebrate the diversity in their classrooms. These teachers find that the key to changing student and community attitudes toward schools is to develop a positive attitude themselves. They show faith in their diverse students as learners. We would like to end this chapter with the stories of two teachers, one an experienced teacher who organized curriculum to meet students' needs and the other a new teacher who succeeded with a new immigrant student. Their positive attitudes and willingness to take some risks helped their students develop a positive attitude as well.

Using Literature Studies to Promote Positive Attitudes

Charlene taught fourth grade in an inner-city school with many immigrants. She used literature in her classroom for an eight-week theme study on peace and conflict. (In Chapter 12 we go into more details on how to conduct literature studies and their importance for second language learners.) Earlier, we described how Charlene used this topic as a basis for establishing her discipline policy. For Charlene and her students the literature study was a way to (1) learn about literature itself, (2) learn about each other and the world, (3) explore content, and (4) understand social, political, and cultural concerns relevant to the students' lives (Short and Klassen, in press). This last goal was especially important to many of her students, whom Ogbu would classify as involuntary minorities. Most of Charlene's fourth graders were the children of Southeast Asian refugees. Their parents had fled for their lives, and now the children were trying to establish an identity in a country and culture very different from their parents'.

The peace and conflict theme arose from both student and parent concern with violence. A shooting at the neighborhood high school resulted in the death of a Southeast Asian boy who was known to several of Charlene's students. Students brought in newspaper clippings about the incident, and the resultant class discussions were emotional. Charlene wanted students to consider different aspects of peace and conflict, so she and the class discussed several books she had read to them which were related to this topic including *The Land I Lost* (Nhoung 1982), *People* (Spier 1980), *Faithful Elephants* (Tsuchiya 1988), *Nettie's Trip South* (Turner 1987), *A Chair for My Mother* (Williams 1982), and *We Came to America,* a book written by immigrants from a local elementary school.

Because many of her students were second language learners, Charlene allowed both whole-class and small-group opportunities to talk about the books. As Charlene explained, the full-class discussions were especially important:

> For some second language learners, whole-class discussions seemed less risky since there was more think-time available when they could consider their thoughts privately in their first language before sharing them in their second language (p. 8).

Besides the discussion of the books Charlene had read to the whole class, the students also selected one of four other historical or biographical books to read and discuss including *The Thousand Paper Cranes* (Coerr 1977), *In the Year of the*

Boar and Jackie Robinson (Lord 1984), *Marching to Freedom: The Story of Martin Luther King Jr.* (Milton 1987), and *Roll of Thunder, Hear My Cry* (Taylor 1976). Charlene met with each of these book groups to provide support to all her students but especially her second language learners. She explained her rationale: "I wanted to support these readers as they risked public dialogue in their second and third languages" and "I wanted to be available to pose questions and provide historical information when appropriate" (p. 10). (See Appendix G for literature study book references.)

The literature studies accomplished many different things for Charlene's students, but perhaps one of the most powerful was that they allowed her students to consider the social tensions in their lives. Lor, whose family came to America as Hmong refugees, read *In the Year of the Boar and Jackie Robinson.* She reflected upon her own life experiences as a result of the reading by writing in her literature log to Charlene:

> I lost my land because American they try to get our land. When they try they have to use their hands with weapons. America, when they first started they lie and (were traitors) to us. That killed our own tradition. . . . The American trick us. . . . Later they (Americans) lose and we was scared . . . we are against you Americans. . . . I don't like America land because in our land we don't have no robberies or murders. In America . . . they don't care. . . .

When Charlene read the log entry, she described her feelings: "I was stunned by Lor's anger. Her powerful reflection demanded action." The next morning Lor would not read her own words but gave Charlene permission to read them to the class for discussion. Charlene believed that it was necessary to talk about this. She wanted to recognize the conflicts in her students' lives so they could begin to deal with them (Freire and Macedo 1987). Charlene described how her other students responded to Lor's words:

> Other immigrant students voiced their frustrations about being labeled newcomers by some unfriendly American. I did not feel prepared to deal with the fears, anger, and hostility I heard from my students. Their feeling of being isolated as outsiders, their temporary state of mind about living in the United States, and their intense desire to return to their homeland shocked me. I clearly felt like a learner working to gain a more critical consciousness of my world.

As a result of this discussion and others, Charlene and her students listed social concerns they had about their community. They recorded the conflicts students dealt with daily including gangs, drugs, alcoholism, robbery, burglary, murder, and kidnapping. Then expert groups chose a topic for further study. The students decided to write reader's theater scripts from their information. These were enacted in a Kids' Court. This Kids' Court was videotaped and shown at the Peace Luncheon/Celebration the class had with parents at the end of the Peace and Conflict unit.

While no solutions were found, the "literature provided a way" for Charlene and her students "to know more about social and cultural tensions" and as Charlene admitted, "The complexities examined in our discussion created a greater awareness among students but especially for me. . . . These conversations emphasized . . . all I had to learn from my students" (p. 23). When teachers like Charlene recognize that they also have much to learn about their students and their students' needs, and when they can allow their students to explore social and cultural tensions, they provide a better chance for learners to understand their world and work effectively in it (Freire and Macedo 1987).

Creating Positive Contexts for New Students

Another example of a teacher who worked with student attitudes comes from Lori, who told of the experience she had in her second-third classroom:

> Julieta was placed in my class even though she did not speak or understand a word of English: I am the same with regards to Spanish. My first thought when she was delivered to my room that morning was "What on earth am I going to possibly be able to contribute to this child's education?"
>
> I greeted her warmly, introduced her to the class, seated her at a group table where several students spoke both Spanish and English, and tried to help her feel welcome and hide my nervousness at the same time. She was scared, and little did she realize, so was I!

Lori celebrated the arrival of a new student that first day by having everyone introduce themselves to her, having groups make books together, taking Julieta on a tour of the school, and inviting the principal to come to the classroom to officially welcome Julieta. However, Lori knew she couldn't do this every day. "I felt confident that we had helped Julieta to feel a part of our class or at least to view it as nonthreatening. But now I was faced with what to do next."

Lori teamed Julieta with others who could interpret for her, allowed her to write in Spanish, and gave her choices about what to read. She soon noticed that Julieta played with the other students at recess and that she was learning some English in that setting. Lori explained how the rest of the class took as much pride as Julieta in her learning English:

> We were all so proud when Julieta asked a neighbor for a red crayon—in English! Rarely did a day go by without someone from my class informing me of the latest English word Julieta had said. I firmly believe that my students helped Julieta with language far more than I did.

The positive results of this support showed themselves clearly in one memorable incident:

> During daily sharing time, Julieta would get up in front of the class and share in Spanish and then someone would translate whatever she had shared in English. I will never forget the day she shared that she didn't like white people at all when she first came to our school because they were mean to her. We were all sitting on the edge of our seats by the time the translator got to that point in her story! She then said that she liked white people now, especially her teacher, and she wanted to stay in this class at this school forever. Julieta then gave us all a big smile and said in English, "I finish my share" and sat down. It was the first time my class had ever applauded anyone during share time! After Julieta shared, we had a class discussion and came to the conclusion that prejudice and racism could be wiped out if we could all just understand where the other person is coming from and accept people that look or talk differently than us and try to help instead of making fun of them or simply ignoring them.

Even though she had not had experience working with children like Julieta before, Lori's positive attitude helped her create a context where Julieta could not only succeed, but develop a positive attitude as well.

Conclusion

In Cortés' Contextual Interaction Model, attitudes constitute part of both the societal context and the school context. Community members, students, and teachers all develop attitudes and perceptions about one another and about school. These attitudes often reflect the historical relationships between majority and minority group members. As teachers become more aware of the influence these different attitudes have on students' school performance, they can begin to work— as Yvette, Charlene, and Lori did—to develop positive contexts for schooling.

Teacher attitudes, which are formed by the values they hold, also play an important role in student performance. Frequently, without realizing it, teachers may have conflicting values in areas important to their educational beliefs and practices. In the next chapter we look more closely at value conflicts and consider ways of resolving such conflicts.

Applications

1. In Chapter 1 we suggested you might do a case study on a second language learner. Reflect back on that student or some other language learner you know and think about whether that person would fall under Ogbu's "immigrant" or "involuntary minority" category. Discuss with a partner.

2. Think about your case study or another second language learner you know. List the primary cultural differences you see in that person's life. Are there secondary cultural differences? What are they?

3. Yvette's student, Roberto, belonged to a gang. He displayed what Ogbu would call secondary cultural differences. Go back to his "My Opinion on Gangs," His "Chicano Pride" poem, and the epitaph he wrote. Discuss how secondary cultural differences have helped form Roberto's attitudes and perceptions. How might you respond to Roberto as a teacher?

4. How have schools in your community changed in the past ten years? How has the curriculum changed to meet new students' needs? Make a chart that reflects the relationship between the two.

5. Form five or ten different groups of about four or five people each. Each group takes one of the five scenarios described in this chapter. Each group can plan together a role play of one to two minutes to show how they would interpret the scenario happening. (If there are ten groups, this is even more interesting because there can be a comparison of how different groups choose to role-play the same scene.) After the role plays, discuss as a large group what impressed you. Finally, replay the scenarios applying a solution your group feels might work to resolve the conflict.

6. Read Rusty's poem, "School Days, School Days," with a partner. Discuss.

CHAPTER ELEVEN

How Can Teachers Recognize and Resolve Value Conflicts?

"*A*ll Asians are excellent students. Why aren't other minority groups as successful?"

"Juan started out the year way behind the other students. He's made great improvement, but I can't pass him because he only scored fifty-five percent on his final exam."

"At my school almost eighty percent of the students are Hispanics, but we have only two Hispanic teachers. We should hire more Hispanic teachers, but some of the applicants are not as well qualified as the Anglo candidates."

Statements such as these raise important questions. Are all Asians the same? Do all Asians do better in school than Hispanics? What do we do with a student who starts out way behind and makes great progress but still doesn't pass the final exam? Should we hire people because of their ethnicity? Often, the answers to these questions are based on underlying values.

The questions may not be easy to answer because, at times, the values we hold may be in conflict. We want to treat all students the same, but we recognize that they are not the same. We want to give everyone an equal chance, but we also want certain results. For example, we may want to hire minority teachers to serve as role models in a school with many minority students.

Teachers often come from a different social context than their students, and they bring to their teaching certain attitudes toward students and toward school. These attitudes were shaped by the values they developed in their home communities. By examining their personal convictions, teachers can more consistently adopt practices that promote success for their students who are between worlds.

Sue and Padilla (1986) believe that many educators hold conflicting values and "many of the values relevant to ethnic minority issues are in conflict" (p. 53). They examine five value conflicts that arise in schools with diverse populations. We have combined these five into two groups.

Alike or Different?

The first conflict involves two ways of looking at groups of people. One view focuses on similarities, while the other looks at differences. These two views are referred to as etic (focusing on similarities) and emic (focusing on differences). An *etic* view is based on the idea that humans are basically all alike and that it is reasonable to treat everyone the same. Teachers who take an etic view would feel justified in giving all students the same final exam. We might say that Mr. Martin, the teacher described in the previous chapter, takes an etic view because he expects to treat his migrant students who do not speak English the same way as he treats his fluent English speakers.

An *emic* view holds that humans differ according to culture. The statement that Asians are better students than Hispanics reflects an emic view. Mrs. Brown, the teacher who complained that students aren't like they used to be, also takes an emic view. She focuses on the differences between past and present students.

A related conflict involves looking at differences between groups or at differences within a group. When someone refers to Asians or Hispanics, that person is assuming that all members of the group are sufficiently similar to be grouped together. If we assume that members of a group share a significant number of characteristics, we can define a modal personality. For example, we might define Hispanics by saying they all share the characteristics of students we know from rural Mexico. Mrs. Williams, the ESL pull-out teacher described in the previous chapter, assumed that all her students were basically alike and could be treated similarly. Defining a modal personality allows us to study differences between groups. However, if we assume that considerable variability exists within any group, we would study differences within a particular group. In considering etic/emic or modal personality/individual differences value conflicts, the basic question is whether to focus on similarities or differences and whether we should treat people as the same or different.

The etic/emic value conflict does represent a paradox since both views can be justified. At a certain level, all students share certain characteristics. However, students from different cultures act and use language differently. Teachers who hold an etic view would focus on universal similarities and ignore cultural diversity. Such teachers might feel that any test is equally fair for all students and that norms of classroom behavior can be applied equally to all students. However, if students really are different, treating them the same does not result in equal treatment. Some students come to school already talking and acting in ways that fit school norms, while others come with different ways of using language. These two groups perform differently when measured by the same test.

Teachers who take an emic view would say that it is not possible to generalize or compare students across cultures. This practice could also lead to unequal treatment. If no comparisons are made, students might develop a false sense of success. They might be at the top of the class (or track) in their school, but good performance in one context might rank as only mediocre in another. Delpit (1988), for example, has argued that teachers who fail to teach students standard edited English do them a disservice in the long run because they will eventually be judged by that standard.

Sue and Padilla caution that "in the conflict between emic and etic positions, one must specify the exact standard, criteria, or issue being discussed" (p. 56). That would lead to a context-specific solution to the particular conflict in question. For example, if we say that all English speakers must learn to speak and write standard English, we may wish to consider the contexts where standard English is appropriate and the situations where students could be encouraged to use other varieties of English or other languages. In the debate between collaborative and competitive learning styles, we might want to specify situations in which students would benefit from either a more collaborative or a more competitive style.

An example of the importance of looking at individual differences and trying to avoid a strong etic view comes from a freshman at our college who is from Iran. This student had a great deal of trouble academically in large lecture classes with little personal interaction. These classes relied heavily on tests and papers. This student was perceived by some faculty (who took an etic view) as "not trying" and "not college material." Yet, it was discovered by one faculty member who worked closely with this student that he was very concerned about his grades and was unsure about how to approach other faculty. He realized he was perceived as a "poor student" with "little potential" even though he spoke seven different languages!

The conflict between modal personality and individual differences also presents a true paradox because both points of view are valid. It is possible to attribute certain characteristics to groups even while recognizing differences within a group. Stereotyping is a danger, but ignoring the language, values, and traditions of a particular culture may be equally harmful. It is helpful for teachers to reflect on their practice to

Figure 11-1   Chu's chopsticks

determine which point of view they take most often. In certain contexts it may be more useful to focus on group similarities, but in others, it is better to consider individual differences.

Sue and Padilla relate a story that illustrates the problems inherent in assuming a modal personality for a particular ethnic group. A teacher who had attended a workshop that stressed incorporation of students' ethnicity into the curriculum asked a Japanese-American fourth grader to demonstrate how she danced at home. When the child performed a typical American dance, the teacher was upset. She had expected that this student would perform a Japanese folk dance. She assumed that all Japanese background students would know about typical Japanese dances.

Katie, the prefirst teacher we mentioned earlier, provided a similar example. One of her students, Chu, speaks only Hmong at home although he speaks English at school. For a cooking activity, Katie's students steamed rice and then ate it using chopsticks. After this experience, Katie asked her students to write about what they had done. In his response (Figure 11-1), Chu shows that despite his background he doesn't fit the modal personality of an Asian, since he doesn't "no to uz chps."

As teachers are aware, many members of ethnic minority groups in the United States may not be familiar with the kinds of traditions (dances, clothes, foods) described in cultural handbooks or presented at cultural workshops. Many second- and third-generation Mexicans, for example, have no idea what "Las Posadas," the Christmas celebration replicating Joseph and Mary's trip to Bethlehem, is. Nevertheless, the handbooks and workshops can be valuable because it is necessary, at times, to make generalizations about different immigrant groups. Ogbu, for example, classifies minorities as either immigrant, involuntary, or autonomous. Yet, he cautions that there are great differences within each of these categories. As Sue and Padilla point out, "The challenge for educators is to identify critical differences between and within ethnic minority groups and to incorporate this information into classroom practice" (p. 62).

For example, in teaching writing, it is reasonable to assume that Southeast Asian students will leave off inflectional endings such as "ed" or "s" because of the differences between their languages and English. Knowing this, teachers may plan minilessons for a group of students on this feature. However, at the same time, it may not be necessary to include all or only the Southeast Asian students in the lesson, since within that group some students may not have difficulty with those inflectional endings. In this way, teachers can take both group similarities and the differences into consideration.

Value conflicts are always present for teachers working with immigrant students. One last example will perhaps make the etic/emic and the modal personality/individual differences distinctions a bit clearer. In Chapter 1 we discussed the case of Eugenia, who at the end of kindergarten seemed to be doing quite well. When one reviews her background, she has several challenges to meet in the years ahead as a low-income Hispanic in the school system. Her parents, struggling migrant workers, now work in a canning factory. They support her and care about her schooling. They have much hope for Eugenia despite the fact that a teenage son recently dropped out of school.

How can schools best help Eugenia succeed? From the etic perspective, Eugenia is like any other child in our schools and has an equal probability of success. However, this approach might ignore any special needs Eugenia might have including providing first language support. Even bilingual education might not be enough, since Eugenia's brother who dropped out had negative experiences in a bilingual classroom. It will be important that teachers take an emic view when they validate Eugenia's Hispanic roots and her first language. They should not, however, look at her as a modal personality and view her as a migrant child like all other migrant children and decide that because she is a migrant child, she has little hope of succeeding. Eugenia should also be viewed as an individual with individual potential.

We have spent some time discussing these distinctions because we believe that both positions have validity, and no easy single solution is available or morally justified. Instead, teachers need to examine carefully the values they are operating on in specific situations as they attempt to create optimal learning contexts for all their students.

Minority and Majority Conflicts

A second set of value conflicts centers on the relationships and interactions between minority and majority group members. If a society values homogeneity, it may force minority group members to assimilate. If, on the other hand, heterogeneity is seen as desirable, the society may promote diversity and become more pluralistic. If a society wishes minorities to assimilate, it may stress equal opportunity. In contrast, if it values diversity, it may promote equality of outcomes. Minority and majority group members may also differ in their view of whether or not equal opportunities exist depending on their perceptions of whether prejudice and discrimination are present or absent.

Assimilation or Pluralism?

A conflict exists between the goals of assimilation and pluralism. The assimilation view holds that minority groups should merge into the mainstream culture which becomes a melting pot. This was Mrs. Brown's position. Her new students should blend in and be like her old students. The effect of assimilation is a strengthening of the mainstream culture at the expense of ethnic cultures. Organizations like English Only raise fears of a fragmented society that would result from allowing a multiplicity of languages and cultures to have official status. People often point to Canada, where both French and English have official status, as an example of a country that would be stronger if all citizens were forced to assimilate.

A pluralistic stance allows for and appreciates cultural diversity. A good example of a pluralistic society is Switzerland. However, the result may be the coexistence of separate groups and a weakening of the mainstream. Minorities do need to assimilate to a new culture to some degree, but they risk losing their ethnic heritage. A society benefits from having a number of distinct ethnic groups represented but risks a loss of unity. We see this conflict between assimilation and pluralism being played out most clearly in countries such as the former Soviet Union or Yugoslavia.

In the assimilation/cultural pluralism conflict both sides may appear to be valid. However, at least in the educational context, assimilationist views do not seem productive and may be harmful. America has often been seen as a melting pot for immigrant groups. The melting pot metaphor suggests that different linguistic and ethnic groups succeed in the United States as they assimilate into the mainstream culture. Over time, these groups lose their distinctive ethnic characteristics, blend in, and achieve success. The melting pot metaphor has some validity—many minority students strive to blend in and avoid being different. Vince, a fourth-grade teacher in an inner-city school recalls the Southeast Asian girl who couldn't wait to be old enough to bleach blonde her beautiful long black hair and then to buy blue contact lenses! Roxie remembers a similar incident of denial of heritage that happened in a fifth-grade classroom when she was a student teacher:

> There were two bilingual Spanish-English-speaking girls in the class named María and Marta. I wrote to Marta daily in a journal. One day she wrote, "I was born in the United States, but María wasn't, she just tells everyone she was. She was really born in Mexico, but she doesn't want anyone to know." When I read that I felt sorry for María because it appeared to me that she was ashamed of her background.

A third example comes from Cándida, the bilingual teacher from Puerto Rico mentioned in Chapter 1. Cándida's story is both sad and also humorous:

> When I was very young, I assumed that being a Puerto Rican automatically meant that I would have to endure an accent. I prayed that I wouldn't sound like my parents or relatives that had come from Puerto Rico. Little did I know that being raised in the Bronx would endow me with an accent that was just as ridiculed, if not more, than a Spanish accent! As my mom would say, it's the "Castigo de Dios" ("God's punishment").

Although individuals such as these may wish to blend into the mainstream culture, a closer look at the history of schooling for ethnic minority groups suggests that the melting pot metaphor may not be appropriate. For one thing, not all groups have been assimilated. Native Americans, for example, have not done well in schools and have not generally been assimilated. For another, assimilation may not be desirable and may not be the only route to success. Cultural pluralism benefits both the nation and the various groups that contribute aspects of their heritage.

Cortés (1986) suggests that when we consider the history of schooling for language-minority students, a new metaphor is needed:

In short, rather than a melting pot a more cogent metaphor for the United States is that of a mosaic, a constantly-shifting mosaic in which the multihued pieces do not always fit together perfectly, as if an on-going historical earthquake has been challenging the society to attempt to resolve the unresolvable (p. 6).

In a mosaic, individual pieces maintain their shape, form, and color. They do not have to melt together. Yet, as Cortés suggests, these pieces may not always fit together neatly. His image is a dynamic one, reflecting the social upheaval caused by waves of immigration into the United States. It may well be that schools have been given the impossible task of resolving the unresolvable. And new pieces are being added to the puzzle all the time.

The Cambodians described in Chapter 1—Chham, Navy, and their family—are a good example of the struggle many immigrants face in the conflict between assimilation and pluralism. Chham realized that he and his wife needed to learn English and American customs, so they attended adult ESL classes faithfully. Despite the fact they had to take menial jobs in this country, they worked cheerfully and looked to the future rather than dwelling on the past.

The tragedy of the genocide in Cambodia, however, brought the conflict of assimilation versus pluralism to the surface for Chham and his family. With the realization that they needed to maintain the Khmer culture in this country, since it was being systematically eliminated in their own, Chham and Navy began to question whether their own children should attend public schools. They realized their children were losing their first language and adopting cultural values of their American peers. Chham and Navy's friends who had older children pressured these children to marry other Cambodians to preserve their culture. The adults feared that assimilation would lead to cultural extinction, but at the same time they recognized the need to fit in to survive economically.

At the classroom level the conflict between assimilation and pluralism often surfaces in decisions about bilingual programs. Teaching in English would be seen as promoting assimilation, and teaching in the primary language would foster pluralism. Within the school context, at least, it appears that both positions are not equally valid. Students can succeed academically without giving up their primary language and culture, as we saw in the description of immigrant minorities like Sharma. Bilingual programs that help students develop their first language as they learn English are additive programs. Assimilation models, on the other hand, lead to subtractive bilingualism.

When assimilation becomes the goal, bilingual bicultural students must give something up. Roberts (1993) asked students in his high school and junior college English classes to write about the pressure to assimilate. One of his students, Eric, explained his frustration at being forced to forget his first language and then later trying to regain it:

> I remember being fluent in Spanish, Italian, and English, but my teachers would always order me to speak in English because that was what everyone did. I had a hard time with this silly rule, and when I refused to obey this one-sided order, I was sent to the principal's office for disciplinary reasons.
>
> I was in second grade and my teacher Ms. Johnson was a very strict lady who did not see my Spanish as a necessity in her class. There were a few kids who did not speak English in our class so I used to try and explain to them what she was saying. It was not appreciated by her. I was constantly told to quiet down because she was the

teacher and I was not. I was suspended from extra activities for two weeks. My parents were told I was causing trouble, but they were not told of what the whole problem was. They were basically lied to and up to now still don't know the real truth.

As time went on I lost my ability to understand and speak my other languages. This did not bother me until I reached high school and took Spanish. I could not understand what was being taught and I was very confused because in grammar school I was not allowed to speak another language, but now my teachers were telling me I need to know a second language to make it in the world.

By this time I was not only confused, but I was angry that most of this was because of the ignorance of my teachers before not letting me speak and really understand my other languages. I lost some of the culture I had grown up with and I did not like it at all (pp. 51–52).

Eric's story points to serious problems with the assimilationist perspective. Sue and Padilla (1986) point out that "the assumption underlying assimilation, effective functioning can occur only if one assimilates, is not valid" (p. 58). Those cultural groups or individuals that can function effectively in two different frames of reference by alternating home and school behavior, for example, can succeed in both contexts, as Ogbu points out. They do not need to assimilate to do well in school. In fact, when they are forced to assimilate, students sometimes become alienated from both groups.

Loretta, the Hispanic high school business teacher we described earlier, has struggled with how she had to give up so much of her culture to get where she is now. In response to reading about how the denial of the first language at school confuses students about their identity, she wrote the following:

In the book we read about the idea of "language mismatch," the language at home is different from the language of the school. I understood this concept as what we, my family, called Spanglish. I feel that I fall under this category. My spoken and written English is not as good as I would like it to be, and my Spanish is even poorer. As a Mexican-American, I used to feel alienated from both groups of kids. I really did not fit in with the Anglo Americans because we did things differently at our home (ex. ate with a tortilla, instead of using a fork). Also I did not fit in with the Mexican-American students who spoke Spanish and were more traditional in their customs than my family. As a student, I was not proud of my culture because I felt I did not belong to any group. As an adult, I feel I was deprived of my language and of being proud of my culture. Presently, my goal is to become proficient in Spanish.

Two-way bilingual programs attempt to help students develop proficiency in two languages. In these programs English speakers learn in English and a second language and second language learners study in their first language and English. Both languages are equally valued and thus both cultures become valued. Second language learners in two-way programs can function in both their first language and in English. As Sue and Padilla note, "The continual challenge before us is to define what is meant by 'functional' and to explore ways in which individuals can develop educational competencies without losing the language, values, and identification with ethnic minority culture" (p. 58). Two-way bilingual programs seem to accomplish these goals.

Equal Opportunity or Equal Outcome?

A second, related value conflict is the conflict between equal opportunity and equality of outcomes. Proponents of equal opportunity would apply the same criteria for all. In hiring practices, for example, employers would consider job-related skills and not look at factors such as an applicant's ethnicity. In contrast, those favoring equality of outcomes would consider ethnicity in hiring because their goal would be to see that minority groups are represented proportionately. A school with large numbers of Hispanic students, for example, might feel that the ethnicity of a candidate for a teaching position is more important than other factors and hire a Hispanic to increase Hispanic representation on the staff. The goal would be to achieve a certain outcome: a balance in ethnicity between the percentage of teachers of certain ethnic groups and the percentage of students of those ethnic groups that the school serves.

Teachers are frequently faced with decisions that involve this value conflict, and they have to choose between providing equal opportunities and achieving equal outcomes. Some students come with more knowledge and better skills than others. Should the teacher treat all students equally by giving them the same assignments and the same tests? Often in schools the result of equal opportunities is that the rich get richer and the poor eventually drop out. Equal opportunities may result in unequal outcomes. However, in the process of achieving equal outcomes, people must engage in discrimination or differential treatment. Teachers may fear that if they try to ensure that all students succeed, the better students may be ignored or that they would be engaging in unfair practices.

In many cases, apparently equal opportunities are not really equal. Rather, they may serve as a mechanism for maintaining the status quo. The real question is at what point do equal opportunities begin? If students grow up in poor neighborhoods and attend inadequate schools, do they have equal chances when they apply for jobs? Books such as Kozol's *Savage Inequalities* (1991) suggest that opportunities for students from different backgrounds are not equal. Proponents of equality of outcomes argue that current practices in areas such as hiring must discriminate in favor of minorities now to overcome discrimination against minorities in the past. Of course, this raises a means-ends question. Are short-term discriminatory practices necessary to correct the results of long-term discrimination? Again, solutions to this conflict are not easy. Effective solutions must be specific to the situation. However, we agree with Sue and Padilla that "only after opportunities become truly equal can a color- or ethnic-blind system have any meaning" (p. 60).

Another example of the conflict between equal opportunities and equality of outcomes often occurs in discussions about bilingual education. Although there are some excellent bilingual programs other than English and Spanish, the vast majority of the bilingual programs that are fully implemented are in those two languages. We often have teachers ask us about equality: "Is it fair to give first language support to the Spanish-speaking students when we cannot provide it for Khmer, Vietnamese, Hmong, Punjabi, or Russian speakers?" This is an interesting application of the "equal opportunity" value. Our response is with another question: "If you know that many children in the world are hungry, but you only had food for some, do you withhold the food you can supply because it is not fair to the others that some children be fed?" In the same way, if we can provide first language support to some children, do we withhold it because we cannot give it to all the children?

Discrimination—Real or Imagined?

This leads us to the third conflict in this set, the presence or absence of discrimination. Here are two cases shared by Hispanic teachers studying in our graduate program. Paulina wrote of her experiences as a child in a small rural community in California:

As a migrant child in P., I was well aware of the town's prejudice. The Las Palmas Theatre had segregated seating along color lines. That was no cause for alarm, we accepted it. When I had my own experience, it was traumatic. In our third-grade class, we had seating arrangements in the traditional rows, and the five to six Hispanic students in that class sat in one row apart from the class. I didn't mind, I felt secure with my fellow brown-skinned peers. Our teacher was the traditional strict disciplinarian common in those days, and one day an active Anglo boy named Timmy was too much for her. In her desperate attempt to control him, she punished him by asking him to get a chair and to sit next to me. The class giggled as he obeyed her. When he sat next to me, I immediately got a stomach ache, and when he started sobbing, I felt that I must have been the worst person in the world. Why else was he sobbing so painfully? I can't recall much, but I do remember suffering stomach aches every time I walked into class. When I went home, I recall I took a bath and tried to wash my brown color off. I scraped so hard that when my mother asked what happened, I told her I scraped myself on the playground. I didn't have the courage or heart to tell her the truth. I wanted to spare her the pain I had felt. One of the many reasons I decided to teach was to put an end to the ignorance about different ethnic groups.

What is worth noting here is that when we speak of the presence or absence of prejudice, we are talking about the views individuals and groups hold. The question is not simply whether migrant workers in Arizona or Cambodians in Los Angeles face discrimination, but whether *they* think they face discrimination. What matters here is the perceptions of the groups involved more than any actual practices because cases of overt racism are relatively rare in U.S. society. However, discriminatory practices have often been institutionalized. Those who feel that overt or covert racism exists blame society and work toward eliminating racism. Those who feel that discrimination is not present may blame minority groups for their failure to succeed. They may feel that minority groups use discrimination as an excuse for poor performance.

Ogbu points out that immigrant and involuntary minorities respond differently to prejudicial treatment. Immigrants expect to face discrimination and find ways to circumvent unequal treatment. They develop a folk theory or cultural model for getting ahead that puts high value on education. As a result, members of immigrant groups often do succeed, and this reinforces their cultural model. Involuntary minorities, in contrast, resent prejudicial treatment and often respond by developing secondary cultural differences in opposition to the majority culture. The cultural model they develop places low importance on majority institutions such as schools. If group members fail at school, the folk theory that schools don't help you get ahead is reinforced.

Both groups face discrimination, but they respond to it differently. Their responses may reinforce attitudes of majority-group members toward the question of whether discrimination exists. If involuntary minorities fail in school, they may be blamed for not trying hard enough. If immigrants succeed, majority-group members may point to that as evidence that prejudice and discrimination do not exist and that all minorities have equal opportunities.

Teachers should be aware that even though they believe that discrimination has been eliminated in a particular school or class, what may really matter are the beliefs held by minority-group members. Their response to school may be more dependent on what they perceive than on the presence or absence of specific discriminatory acts. Their beliefs may be strongly influenced by the folk theory of school held by their community. Solutions to the conflict again need to be context specific. We have presented cases where one teacher engaged her students in a peace and conflict unit after two students got into a fight and called each other racially charged names, and another utilized the cooperative conflict resolution process. Later in this chapter we will see how Yvette worked with her high school students to help them appreciate one another's differences. Teachers may wish to use similar approaches and make discrimination a topic of class discussion.

Teacher Attitudes and Value Conflicts

Etic or emic? Modal personality or individual differences? Equal opportunities or equality of outcomes? These value conflicts are paradoxical because both sides have validity. Cultural groups do share certain characteristics, but individuals within any group still vary. We want to provide equal opportunities, but we also want to have certain outcomes. Solutions to these conflicts are not always simple. In the case of assimilation versus pluralism, it does seem possible for people to succeed and still maintain their cultural identities. But in the other cases it's harder to see how to resolve the conflicts. Our natural tendency to find a middle position may not always work if the conflict is a true paradox.

Sue and Padilla (1986, p. 54) list the possible effects of choosing between each of the value conflicts and also suggest possible responses (see Figure 11-2). When two values are in conflict, mediation may be possible. Sue and Padilla suggest that in the conflict between modal personality and individual differences a teacher could discuss cultural characteristics at an abstract level and then talk more specifically about differences within groups. In some cases alternation is a possible solution. For example, a school might use ethnicity as a criterion for hiring one time and not the next. In other cases, coexistence is feasible. In two-way bilingual programs, two languages and cultures coexist. Divergent thinking might also resolve a conflict. Sue and Padilla point out that educators often stress the need for assimilation in order to develop functional skills. A divergent approach might be to change the question and begin to consider what skills will truly be functional in the future. Assimilation might not be necessary to attain those skills. Some conflicts may be solved by moving to a higher level of abstraction. In the debate over equal opportunities or equal outcomes, we could imagine how our society should be in ten or twenty years and then make choices that would lead to that ideal state.

In the next section we present some real-life examples of the value conflicts we have described and suggest possible solutions. We hope that this discussion will lead teachers to reflect on their own situations, examine the values they are operating on, and consider possible courses of action they might take.

Solutions to Value Conflicts

Christina, a Hispanic girl, graduates from high school with high honors and receives a full scholarship to attend a university far from home. Christina and the school personnel are excited about this opportunity. However, Christina's parents do not want her to go far from home because the idea of a young girl living away from her loving

Conflicting elements	Effects	Possible solutions
Etic—Human beings are alike.	Ignores cultural diversity	Alternation
Emic—Human beings differ according to culture.	Can't generalize or compare cultures	Coexistence
Modal personality—study between-group differences	Ignores within-group variations	Divergent thinking Mediation
Individual differences—study within-group differences	Ignores between-group variations	Alternation
Assimilation—become American and merge into society	Loss of ethnic cultures	Coexistence Divergent thinking
Pluralism—allow for and appreciate cultural diversity	Coexistence of separate and distinct groups	
Equal opportunity—apply same color-blind criteria to all	Unequal outcomes	Mediation Alternation
Equality of outcomes—see that minorities are proportionately represented	Differential treatment (discrimination)	Higher level of abstraction
Presence of prejudice/ discrimination—Minorities are oppressed in society.	Blame society; must eliminate discrimination	Coexistence
Absence of prejudice/ discrimination— Opportunities are equal for all.	Blame minorities; up to minorities to achieve	

Figure 11-2   Value conflicts, effects, solutions

family is inappropriate culturally. These two perspectives create a paradox. Mainstream society would see Christina as lucky and on the road to success. However, her family and community might view leaving home for college as entirely unreasonable, something that is simply not done.

Possible solutions might include coexistence of the two positions or alternation between them. For Christina, a coexistence solution might be to have a sister or brother live with her when she goes far away to college, or she could live at home and attend a university nearby. There is coexistence because she lives with her family and is also getting a college education. An alternation solution does not work so well in this situation. However, Christina and her parents might agree that she should go to college, but that she would plan to spend all vacations at home and would visit frequently in between. That way she would alternate between being at home and being at college.

With other conflicts, different responses are possible. At times, using divergent thinking reveals new approaches. For example, high school minority students were doing poorly academically in a large inner-city school. They seemed uninterested in the curriculum, and few went to college. Personal counseling and the special classes, including ESL and summer school for courses required for graduation, did not seem

To facilitate this learning you will:

1. Keep a **Literature Log** with your response to the book you are reading. We will respond to your **Literature Log** entries in writing. The focus will be on your thinking about the story and not the punctuation and spelling although you need to make these as easy for us to read as possible. You will need to work on these outside of class time. The four required entries will be due Week 1-Wed. & Fri. Week 2-Tues. & Thurs.

2. Keep a **Learning Log** in which you reflect on what you are learning. It is helpful if you tell us what is making sense to you and where you are confused about any ideas that were presented. Again we will respond to these in writing. These logs will be done during class.

3. Keep a **Writing Folder** with all your writing work in it. There will be a section for in-process work and a section for the things completed for us to read. You will leave the **Writing Folder** in the classroom.

4. A **"ME" File** with four things that represent you as a learner as well as a reader and a writer. You may use any kind of folder/envelope/ box to put these things in. You must include in writing an explanation for each of your four choices.

We will be giving you several standardized tests the first/last day. These will be used only as confidence-builders so that you can begin to believe in your growth as a reader and a writer and see your potential for continued growth.

Schedule:

8:30-8:55	**Poetry and Philosophy**
9:00-11:30	**Literacy-Reading Strategies**
11:30-12:30	**Lunch/Fun and Games**
12:30-1:00	**Literature Study Groups**
1:00-4:30	**Literacy-Writing Strategies**

Composing on the Computer and Conferencing

Group 1	1:30-2:30	Smith/Medel
Group 2	2:30-3:30	Haggard/Baker
Group 3	3:30-4:30	Mason/Pankratz/Nicoletti

Figure 11-3   Learning Edge schedule

to be making any difference. Bobbi, a local college educator, decided to do something different for secondary "at risk" students. She got funding from the school district and then gathered together a small group of dedicated and innovative teachers who had been studying recent research and theory for language learning. They planned an intensive two-week session for "at risk" high school students on the college campus. Students and parents visited the campus and learned about the program that Bobbi and her colleagues called "The Learning Edge." During the two weeks, students read, wrote, and discussed topics including drugs, crime, and teenage pregnancy. They did literature studies using books about minority teenagers like themselves, wrote back and forth in learning logs with the teachers, and published their stories in an anthology that they all received at the end of the course. All the activities, including lunch together and planned outdoor games, led to the building of a strong community. Figure 11-3

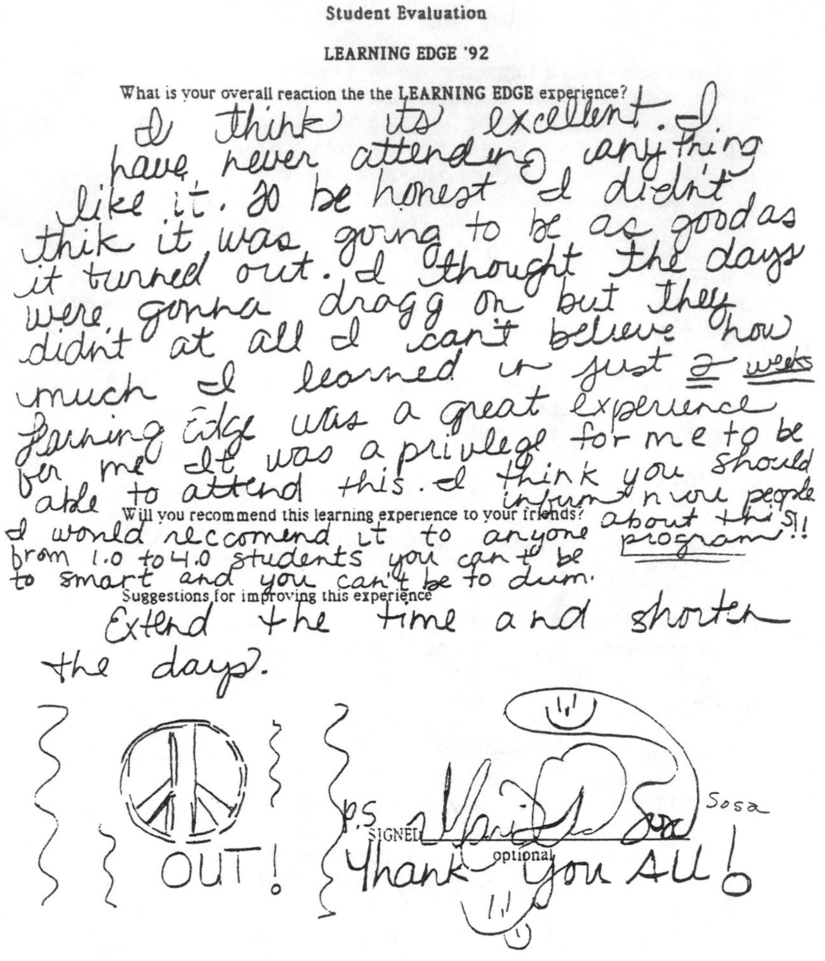

Figure 11-4   Leading Edge student evaluations

is a copy of the expectations for the students, the kinds of activities they did, and the daily schedule. Testimonials at the end of the sessions showed that students had learned much about reading, writing, and learning. Figure 11-4 shows what students wrote when they evaluated their two-week experience.

Bobbi certainly used divergent thinking to devise a curriculum for students who were considered "at risk." Instead of drills and discipline, she and the other teachers gave the students real reading and writing and caring responses. The results have been phenomenal. This year another group of students has returned to the campus for Learning Edge, but in addition the Learning Edge students from last year are back on campus for an intensive two weeks in math and science where topics of study include paleontology and AIDS. The group began their paleontology study with the reading of *Jurassic Park* by Michael Crichton just as the movie of the same name came out.

Student Evaluation

LEARNING EDGE '92

What is your overall reaction the the LEARNING EDGE experience?

I really enjoyed it. These two weeks were very intense and full of new experiences for me. I think the program has given me an edge over other people who did not take this course.

Will you recommend this learning experience to your friends?

Yes I would and will.

Suggestions for improving this experience

Make it 3 weeks.

Student Evaluation

LEARNING EDGE '92

What is your overall reaction the the LEARNING EDGE experience?

It's been a really fun experience And it's going to help me a lot in my future.

I learned a lot about the reading specially in how to find the big picture and also how to enjoy the reading piece.

In the writing this program really helped me, it made me organize my ideas better and express my feelings by showing, not telling. We were taught how to work smarter instead of harder! I also met a lot of people and had a great time.

Will you recommend this learning experience to your friends?

Of course, I encourage this program to everybody, because is great.

Suggestions for improving this experience

I think you got it all down!

Figure 11-4   Leading Edge student evaluations *(continued)*

Another solution to value conflicts that Sue and Padilla suggest is moving to a higher level of abstraction. For example, some teachers take a phonics approach to teaching reading, while others see reading as recognizing words. Many reading debates have centered on this issue. Should we teach sound-letter correspondences, or should we use flash cards and word lists to develop visual word identification skills?

A solution would be to move to a higher level of abstraction and begin to see reading as a process of constructing meaning rather than identifying words. Meaning construction includes using semantic and syntactic cues as well as visual and sound information. The phonics versus word recognition debate can be solved by moving to the bigger questions regarding the nature and purpose of reading.

Sue and Padilla warn against adopting quick answers to value conflicts. As they put it, "These solutions may require change over time since single, overall solutions may not always fit a changing context. Otherwise, today's solutions may well become tomorrow's problems" (p. 53). An example of a problem where a quick-fix solution hasn't worked may be seen in this case of phonics versus word identification. Moving toward a new view of reading has actually become a reality in some districts. However, school districts with instructional leaders who have the goal of creating lifelong readers have sometimes moved too quickly, insisting that all teachers throw out their phonics materials and flash cards and use only literature. Teachers with no literature materials or no idea how to use literature, rebel and believe they have been asked to do the impossible. In these situations, the quick and obvious solution creates new problems.

When both sides of a conflict are valid, solutions other than compromise are needed. Nevertheless, mediation is also a possible response if a middle ground can be found. Phillips (1972) provides a good example of the paradox presented by etic/emic and modal personality/individual differences positions. Her study of Native American Indians shows that outside school the students learn by working collaboratively in apprenticeship situations. They demonstrate their skill in an area when they feel prepared to do so, not when someone demands a performance. In addition, they generally prefer not to answer a question or present a project if doing so would make them look better than other students. This learning style conflicts in a number of ways with usual instructional practices in schools. If school instruction is suited to their preferred learning style, these students do better. Of course, this assumes that all Native Americans learn the same way, that there is a modal personality. Since there are individual differences, a possible solution is alternation between teaching styles.

However, Phillips explains that when they leave the reservation schools, these students become a minority in a large regional high school where more traditional, competitive practices are followed. The question, then, for teachers at the reservation school is whether to use cooperative approaches that allow the students more success immediately or to begin to prepare them for the kinds of classes they will encounter at the high school. In this case, teachers from the two schools might meet to discuss this conflict. The high school teachers could examine their competitive approach and experiment with incorporating more socially interactive activities into their curriculum, using both traditional teaching and cooperative groups. The possible solutions could be mediation (a compromise position where the two styles are blended), coexistence (where some teachers use one style and some another), or alternation (where teachers vary their style over time).

Conflict can also arise in perceptions of the presence or absence of prejudice. In this case, divergent thinking that produces new programs may be the solution. Dolson and Mayer (1992), in their discussion of effective programs for language-minority students, include a component that addresses prejudice. "Minority students, regardless of the efforts of the school to promote equal educational opportunities, will be faced with manifestations of discrimination and prejudice at school as well as within the larger community" (p. 143). Dolson and Mayer suggest that schools include a "survival" training component that would help all students deal with instances of discrimination and prejudice. "The training should consist of information on the presence of racism in the general society, how it affects minority and majority peoples, and schemes minority individuals can tap to counteract the negative influences it may have on their spirit and self-concept" (p. 142). Dolson and Mayer advocate involving students in studying attitudes toward minorities, their language, and culture as a part of the school curriculum. In the next section, we look at how one teacher succeeded in doing just this.

Helping Students Deal with Prejudice

Yvette, the teacher described earlier who developed a curriculum that was relevant to all her students, was disturbed by the lack of community within her classroom. She noticed that the different ethnic groups not only kept to themselves, but they lacked respect for one another. Drawing upon ideas for teaching about culture that others in her teacher education classes were trying with their students, Yvette suggested to her students that they might investigate the cultures represented in their class. The students' initial responses were less than enthusiastic. No one thought the idea would work. Yvette, however, persisted. She began by asking students to do a quickwrite on "What is a stereotype?" One of her students, who now laughs sheepishly at his ignorance, actually seriously wrote, "Typing while listening to a stereo!" (see Figure 11-5).

Yvette was somewhat shocked to learn how little her students knew about the whole idea of stereotyping and how close-minded they were. She had them read an article from the *Los Angeles Times,* "The stereotyping habit: Young people try to fight it" (Robinson-Flint, Manilton, Kirka, Rense, and White, November 30, 1992). In this article thirteen teenagers tell about their personal experiences with stereotyping.

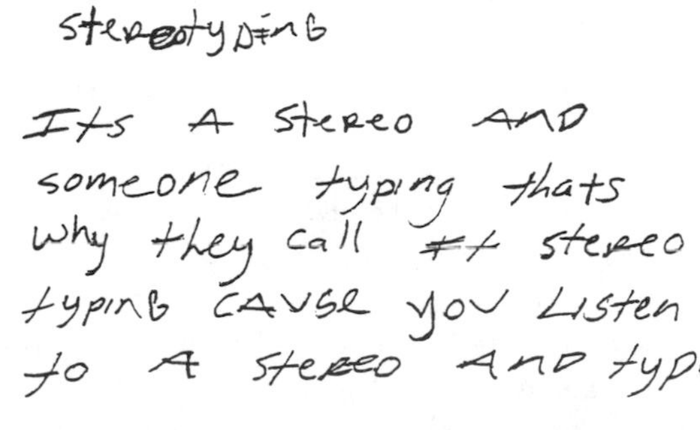
stereotyping

Its A stereo AND someone typing thats why they call it stereo typing cause you Listen to A stereo AND type

Figure 11-5 Stereotyping

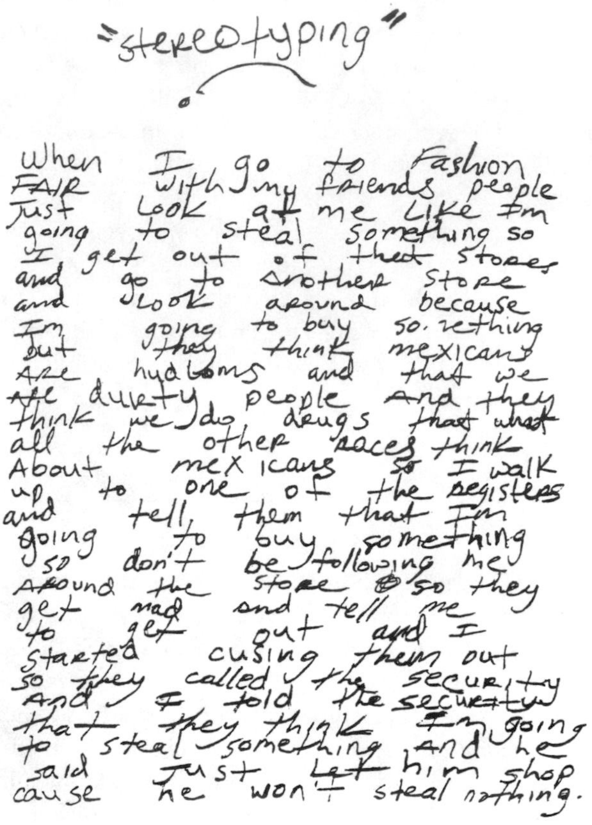

"stereotyping"

When I go to Fashion FAIR with my friends people just look at me like I'm going to steal something so I get out of that stores and go to another store and look around because I'm going to buy something but they think mexicans are hudloms and that we are durty people and they think we do drugs that what all the other races think About mexicans so I walk up to one of the registers and tell them that I'm going to buy something so don't be following me Around the store so they get mad and tell me to get out and I started cusing them out so they called the security And I told the security that they think I'm going to steal something and he said Just let him shop cause he won't steal nothing.

"Stereotyping"

When I go to Fashion Fair with my friends people just look at me like Im going to steal something so I get out of that store and go to another store and look around because Im going to buy something but they think Mexicans are hudloms and that we are durty people and they think we do drugs that what all the other races think about Mexicans so I walk up to one of the registers and tell them that Im going to buy something so don't be following me around the store so they get mad and tell me to get out and I started cusing them out so they called the security and I told the security that they think Im going to steal something and he said just let him shop cause he won't steal nothing.

Figure 11-6   Martin's response

Through class discussion and written responses, Yvette discovered that many of her students, like the teenagers in the article, suffered from being stereotyped. Youa, a Hmong girl, told how a clerk had treated her rudely in a store while she was looking at magazines. She was told, "You can't look at them!" Yet when another teenager came in, she was left alone. Vicki went on to describe how poorly she and other Asian students were always treated by office staff. Martín, a Hispanic, wrote about how he had been followed in stores in the past, so on one excursion he went to the register first to explain he wanted to buy something. The clerk's response was to call security guards! (See Figure 11-6.)

As the students discussed and wrote about stereotyping and beliefs about other cultural groups, it became clear that the Hispanics and African Americans in the class believed that all the Asians were alike, even though there were Vietnamese, Cambodian, and Hmong students in the class. The Asians were denigrated for being on welfare and "mooching off" the government. Though the students held stereotypes about all the groups represented, Yvette began the unit with readings about Asians. She brought in articles about how the U.S. government had used the Southeast Asians, especially the Hmong, during the Vietnam War. Students learned that Hmong boys as young as twelve were killed fighting for the U.S. cause. The students read how when

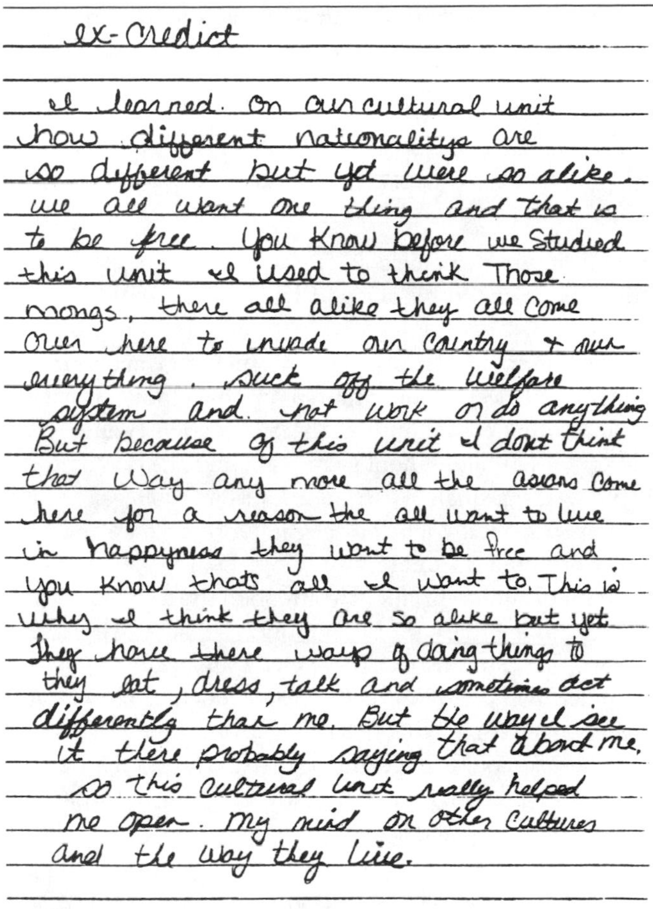

ex-Credict

el learned. On our cultural unit
how different nationalitys are
so different but yet were so alike.
we all want one thing and that is
to be free. You know before we Studied
this unit el used to think Those
mongs, there all alike they all Come
Over here to invade our Country + our
everything. suck off the welfare
system and not work or do anything
But because of this unit el dont think
that Way any more all the asians Come
here for a reason the all want to live
in happyness they want to be free and
you know thats all el want to. This is
why el think they are so alike but yet
They have there ways of doing things to
they eat, dress, talk and sometimes act
differently than me. But the way el see
it there probably saying that about me,
so this cultural unit really helped
me open. my mind on other cultures
and the way they live.

---

ex-credit

I learned on our cultural unit how different nationalitys are so different but yet were so alike. We all want one thing and that is to be free. You know before we studied this unit I used to think Those Mongs, there all alike they all come over here to invade our country and own everything. suck off the welfare system and not work or do anything But because of this unit I dont think that way any more all the Asians come here for a reason the all want to live in happyness they want to be free and you know thats all I want to. This is why I think they are so alike but yet They have there ways of doing things to they eat, dress, talk and sometimes act differently than me. But the way I see it there probably saying that about me, so this cultural unit really helped me open my mind on other cultures and the way they live.

Figure 11-7   Juana's cultural unit response

---

the United States left Laos, all Hmong were condemned to death by the Viet Cong if they were found in their own country.

Students read and discussed the other cultures represented in their class and school, including the different Hispanic cultures, African-American culture, and gang culture. The students were encouraged to write about what they had learned from doing the unit. Several wrote about how they learned that all groups were not alike and that there were two sides to all stories. Others mentioned how they would judge more carefully another time and how they were glad to have new friends now. Juana's poignant testimony demonstrates how the five-week unit changed her (Figure 11-7).

Yvette gave her students a voice. Through the reading, writing, and discussion in the class, students began to look at their beliefs and their values. Sometimes, as in the case of Juana, their values changed; other times students were simply given an opportunity to express what was important to them. Yvette believed in her students and showed them that what they had to offer was important. By using divergent thinking, she was able to develop innovative curriculum to get at the conflicts surrounding prejudice. An empowering curriculum is an essential component of an intercultural orientation. In the next chapter we show how explorer teachers like Yvette develop such an orientation.

Applications

1. Read the following descriptions of two Hispanic college students. In groups discuss the value conflicts and paradoxes as described by Sue and Padilla that might arise in each case.

Carmela is from a low-income Hispanic family. Her mother had six years of schooling and her father eight. There were four children in the family. Carmela attended school in a small, rural farming community in the San Joaquin Valley. The family is devoutly Catholic. Her grades in high school were high, and she qualified for grants and loans. She not only did well at a small Christian (Protestant) college, but she excelled. She presently is teaching successfully and has begun working on a master's degree. Eventually she plans to work on a doctorate.

A second student, Pedro, has a very similar profile. He attended the same Christian college as Carmela though he is from a Protestant background. Unlike Carmela, his high school work was only average. Despite this, Pedro received financial support for college studies. Pedro was a bit older than the traditional college student, married with children, and had health problems. He struggled constantly with his courses. Professors said he was intelligent, but he just couldn't "get it together." He graduated, but with a struggle and does not have a high enough grade point average to continue into the teacher education program as he had planned.

2. Read over the section "Minority and Majority Conflicts" and discuss in groups how the following quotes from the newspaper are related to these paradoxes. How might these paradoxes be resolved?

A. From "Immigration Contributing to California's Decline, Groups Say," *The Fresno Bee,* January 24, 1993, p. A3:

> Increasing activism on California immigration issues is a development that immigrant-rights advocates attribute to economic tensions and fear of foreigners in a state that in 1991 was the intended place of residence for 40% of all legal immigrants to the United States.
>
> Almost to a person, immigration-control activists say they are motivated by concerns over crime, unemployment or welfare costs, not racist, anti-immigrant attitudes. A spokesperson for one group says, "This is not a racial issue, it is an economic, ecologic and social survival issue. What we are faced with here is an out-and-out invasion of the United States of America. We've got to stop it. People don't want to admit it, but the numbers are there. We're essentially importing poverty."

B. From, "Woman Views New Immigrants as Takers, Not Contributors," *The Fresno Bee,* January 24, 1993, p. A3:

> Novato resident Bette Hammond is designing a logo for a new group she is forming to fight for more immigration control. It depicts the Statue of Liberty, her hands up to stop the tide of immigration, tears on her cheeks.

Hammond's mother was an Italian immigrant who came to the United States at age 12. But Hammond is convinced that today's immigrants are not as interested in assimilating as her mother was, a point she says is driven home when the automatic-teller machine asks her whether she wants to conduct business in English or Spanish.

"I'm offended that I even have to push a button before I can begin a transaction," she said. "It seems that today's immigrant is here to take what America has to offer, and they don't want to give anything back."

3. Issues such as diversity raise value conflicts, and we need to discuss our values and consider our responses. As we do this, it is important to keep before us the fact that we are discussing not abstractions, but persons. We provide an example of a real student at our college. This student may be seen to represent the conflicts we have described: etic-emic, assimilation-pluralism, and equal opportunity—equal outcome. Read this example, and think about your position in each of these three areas and which of the possible responses we have outlined you might apply. Discuss with a small group.

Ocatavio attended a community college while working as a bilingual teacher's aide in a school in his community. He represents not only Hispanics but Hispanic culture since he teaches Mexican folklore dance as well as working in the school. The administrators at the school have been extremely impressed with the way he handles his responsibility and have encouraged him to continue his education and get a teaching credential.

His grades at the junior college were good enough for him to transfer to a four year college. Because of the administration's recommendation and because he is a deeply religious person, he chose our Christian college over the state college. From the first time he counselled with his advisor, he talked about how important it was to him to be at this college though it was difficult working, commuting, and keeping up with the challenging academic work. Because he is so busy and so strapped for money and does not always understand how the system works, he has several times found himself on financial or academic probation.

This young man is not a complainer. He works hard, but is trying to overcome incredible odds. His counselor has had to explain to him his rights and inform him of resources such as free tutoring. Recently, he has admitted that a couple of his professors have been less than supportive and, though he did not want to admit it even to himself, he believes the fact he is Hispanic has not helped their opinion of him. His G.P.A. has suffered and because of the times that key classes are scheduled, next year he will not be able to do the teacher aide work while he attends college classes. We hope that Ocatavio will not drop out of college. The last time we saw him he promised he would not give up, but we worry about his finances and the other pressures on him. We are convinced that he has the potential to be an excellent teacher. The question is how can we help students like Ocatavio succeed?

CHAPTER TWELVE

How Can Teachers
Develop an
Intercultural Orientation?

W e have advocated an explorer orientation to language, teaching, learning, and curriculum. Teachers who adopt an explorer orientation show respect for their students and teach from whole to part. They focus on learners and build on their strengths, including their primary languages and cultures.

If school success for language-minority students depended entirely on interactions within classrooms—the school world—it would be enough for teachers to focus on developing an explorer orientation. However, schools operate within a societal context, and the orientation schools take toward the community strongly influences students' educational success.

Teachers' Orientation: Anglo Conformity or Intercultural?

Cummins (1989) defines two different orientations that schools can develop. The first, what Cummins calls an Anglo conformity orientation, would exclude students' native languages or bilingual education in favor of English-only programs. Teachers in a school with an Anglo conformity orientation generally follow a transmission model of instruction rather than an interactive model. "Transmission models exclude, and therefore, effectively suppress student experiences" (p. 65). The societal context influences the school context, but the orientation to curriculum determines to a great extent the degree to which school and community values can be shared. In many schools, the goal is to maintain the status quo, and as Cummins points out, "a genuine multicultural orientation is impossible within a transmission model of pedagogy" (p. 65). Testing from this orientation is often designed to separate the weaker students from the stronger instead of allowing all students to show their abilities. Not surprisingly, in schools where teachers take an Anglo conformity orientation parent involvement is limited.

In contrast, teachers can adopt an intercultural orientation. Cummins explains that teachers who take this approach incorporate minority students' languages and cultures into the school program, adopt pedagogical approaches that are interactive, and take an advocacy-oriented approach to assessment by replacing standardized test measures with other forms of evaluation, such as portfolios. In addition, these schools encourage community participation.

An intercultural orientation promotes positive relationships between school and community. As Cummins points out, "Minority students will succeed educationally to the extent that the patterns of interaction in school reverse those that prevail in the society at large" (p. 58). Generally, minority groups have received discriminatory treatment at the hands of majority group members. As discussed earlier, this treatment has led to the development of a folk theory for success that puts little value on schools for involuntary minorities.

Intercultural Orientation in Practice

A study of successful schools with high minority-student populations reveals that those schools had adopted an intercultural orientation. Lucas and her colleagues (1990) studied six high schools with high Latino populations. In these schools Latino students experienced considerable academic success as measured by low dropout rates, high standardized test scores, and a high level of college acceptance rates. Lucas found that educators at these schools had adopted an intercultural orientation and attributed their success to the following eight components:

1. In these schools the staff placed value on students' languages and cultures. Teachers learned students' languages and studied their culture. The schools offered advanced as well as basic courses in the students' first languages.

2. The staff held high expectations for language-minority students and made them concrete. The schools hired minority staff for leadership positions to act as role models. They provided counseling in the students' first language with information on college and scholarships. They worked with parents to get them to send students to college. They provided honors classes in the students' first language.

3. The school leaders made the education of language-minority students a priority. They hired teachers who were bilingual or trained to work with second language students. The school leaders themselves were knowledgeable about second language issues.

4. Staff development was explicitly designed to help teachers and other staff serve language-minority students more effectively. These schools provided incentives and compensation for staff development in the area of second language issues.

5. A variety of courses and programs for language-minority students was offered. These schools offered bilingual and sheltered courses at both basic and advanced levels.

6. Counseling programs at these schools gave special attention to second language students. They hired bilingual counselors and assigned students to counselors who spoke their first language and shared similar cultural backgrounds. They ensured that counselors knew about scholarships and college opportunities for second language students.

7. Parents of language minority students were encouraged to become involved in their children's education. The schools offered on-campus ESL classes for parents. The schools held monthly meetings for parents. These meetings were held in the parents' first language. They involved parents in planning students' schedules. They held early morning and neighborhood meetings for parents.

8. School staff members shared a strong commitment to empowering language-minority students through education. Staff members spent extra time working with second language students. They organized extracurricular programs for these students. They worked in community activities as advocates for minorities.

It is important to note that the eight factors do not simply deal with curriculum or course offerings. In fact, the major concentration of effort deals with creating positive attitudes and establishing high expectations. School teachers and staff were asked to "value students' languages and culture," to hold "high expectations," to "make language-minority students a priority," to have a counseling program that "gives special attention to language-minority students," to "encourage parents to be involved," and to "share a strong commitment to empower language-minority students." All these elements are consistent with Cummins' definition of an intercultural orientation.

Schools such as the ones Lucas and her colleagues studied have succeeded in educating language-minority students. In the process, these schools have involved parents and other community members, and in this way they have been able to create a supportive societal context that has positively impacted the school context. The general guidelines provided by Cummins and the features identified by Lucas et al. are extremely helpful when working with second language learners. However, it is not possible to simply transfer successful practices from one context to another. Instead, solutions to educational problems must always be context specific.

Working with parents and community members forms an important component of an intercultural orientation. Chapter 13 deals with successful parent programs and offers a number of resources for teachers who wish to work with parents and other community members. In this chapter we focus on teaching practices that are consistent with an intercultural orientation. We ask how teachers can incorporate students' languages and cultures into the classroom, and how teachers can use literature studies to help students develop cultural awareness. We conclude that Cummins' concept of an intercultural orientation is consistent with what we have called an exploratory orientation to language, learning, teaching, and curriculum.

Discourse Communities

In his Contextual Interaction Model Cortés identifies a number of elements that constitute the societal context of schools. Among these are family, community, and nonschool institutions, such as churches and clubs. In these social organizations, among other things, children learn to use language to serve a variety of functions. The language of the family, the community, and of community-based organizations may or may not be English. In each of these arenas children use the language or languages they have developed to serve various needs. They learn language as they use language for social purposes. In Gee's (1990) terms, each of these social groups is a discourse, and in any discourse language is used in particular ways.

Two of the success stories in Chapter 1 are examples of how important family, community, and nonschool organizations can be for immigrant students. Sharma, the fifth-grade Punjabi girl, receives strong parental support not only for her education, but also for her culture. Readers will recall that Sharma's parents were educated themselves and valued learning so much that they moved to the United States twice to be certain that their children were given a good education. Though Sharma's parents are willing to allow her enough flexibility to "fit in" socially with her peers at school, on the weekends they insist that she participate in church services and Punjabi community activities as well as study the Punjabi language.

Sharma is part of several discourse communities. Among these are the school, her family, and her church. In each of these, she uses language for different social purposes to fulfill different needs. Sharma has done well in school to this point. She may experience conflicts between the two cultures, but she is also being given a sense of her unique value through her family's belief in her and her church and cultural activities. Even if Sharma does reject some of these groups for a time in the future, it is probable that Sharma's family, community, and church will have helped her to succeed in the long run. She will probably be able to communicate and achieve her goals in different discourse situations.

José Luis, Guillermo, and Patricia have been part of many discourse communities both in El Salvador and in the United States. All of these communities have given them important experiences to help them succeed in the United States. In El Salvador they attended excellent private schools and were part of the upper-middle-class society. The discourse groups to which they belonged taught them the language functions necessary for school and social success. When the three siblings arrived in this country, they already understood how schools work, what teachers value, how to impress people in social situations, and what employers want. In fact, despite the fact that their spoken English was limited at first, they understood the importance of using different discourses in different settings, often much better than native English speakers. Wherever they went, people commented on their enthusiasm, their polite ways, their eagerness to learn, and their willingness to try.

José Luis, Guillermo, and Patricia had, of course, a strong sense of self and pride in their heritage. They were lucky, however, because once they arrived, they also had family and new friends from this country to rely on for advice about how things worked here. Our family, especially our young daughters, introduced them to the social discourse differences between this country and theirs. For example, the three teens soon learned that among peers they did not shake hands each time they greeted friends and that boys did not need to stand every time a girl or any adult walked into the room. It only took one day for them to realize that students in the United States do not stand when a teacher enters the room. They learned that "helping" with school work was considered cheating, and that teachers and other adults valued punctuality.

The church also was an important discourse group for them. The people in the church thought the three young people were wonderful, and the teens appreciated how they were accepted. Of course, in all the settings they learned lots of English. But they learned much more than the pronunciation, vocabulary, and grammar. They learned how people used different varieties of language in different settings, what people thought about a variety of topics, and what people valued. If José Luis, Guillermo, and Patricia had only spoken English and interacted with native English speakers at school, and had not come from a strong academic and social background, they might have taken longer to learn English, and they might not have been able to negotiate themselves through college, scholarships, invitations to Washington, D.C., and graduate school.

Juan Medina, the twelve-year-old migrant boy described in Chapter 1, provides an example of a student in our schools who has access to a limited range of discourse communities. Juan does have a supportive and caring family who believes that school is the way out of poverty. Juan's father says, "Here, I have hope—if not for me—then for my children" (Brimner 1992, p. 24). However, the family seems to be the only discourse community Juan has. In fact, members of his family rarely speak to anyone outside the migrant camp except for social service people or people who hire them to work. In both those cases, verbal interactions are limited, and, if anything, Juan has probably learned that it is safer to say as little as possible.

At school Juan seldom interacts with teachers though he does get some individual attention from tutors or migrant aides. Juan has few friends, and those he does have are other children from the migrant camps. For Juan there is no supportive church group or American who could help him find his way in the complex system of school. With limited opportunities to socialize with others, Juan does not have the experience he needs to predict what teachers and schools expect of him.

We wish to make it clear that we do not devalue Juan's strong family ties and the communication he has with others in the migrant community. Our point here is that Juan simply does not have the opportunities to use language for as many different purposes as those who are part of many different discourse communities. Teachers often assume that all students have had similar experiences. When students do not respond to them in expected ways, teachers may assume there is something wrong with the student.

Willet (1987) reported on the language acquisition of two non-English-speaking preschool girls over a year. Willet observed the two girls in school for five months and interviewed the girls' mothers, eliciting "opinions, attitudes, and value statements about child-rearing, language learning, and education" (p. 70). Both Jeni, a Korean child, and Alisia, a Brazilian child, acquired a great deal of English during the year in school. However, the interaction styles of the two children and the values of the mothers differed sharply.

Jeni rarely spoke to or played with any of the other children. She only participated in groups when teachers organized the activities, and she often sat alone. With adults, however, Jeni was quite talkative and often initiated conversations and worked hard to maintain contact. When interviewed about how children learn, Jeni's mother expressed the opinion that children learn by watching and imitating:

> If parents set a good example, the child will learn how to behave correctly. A wife shows respect to her mother and husband so the child will learn to respect her family and teachers. If a child has respect for her teachers, she will pay attention and work hard to learn what must be learned (p. 75).

When Willet asked Jeni's mother about the differences she saw between how Korean mothers and American mothers socialized their children, Jeni's mother felt American mothers "seemed to fuss over unimportant matters like insisting that the children say thank you for everything," but "that when it came to important matters, like learning, the children were left to their own devices with no guidelines" (p. 76). Though Jeni's mother thought the preschool was "quite nice and provided things for the children to do," she had hoped the teachers would give Jeni specific English lessons, and when they did not do this, she gave her daily lessons using a book she had brought from Korea.

Alisia responded very differently to preschool. She wanted to be included in all the social activities from the beginning. When the other children ignored her at first because she could not speak English, she was devastated. She constantly tried to be part of group activities and soon figured out ways that were not language dependent to play with the other children. After a few months, she participated fully and, though she did not have all the vocabulary of native English speakers, she spoke English without a noticeable Brazilian accent. When interviewed, Alisia's mother, in contrast to Jeni's, said she encouraged independence and independent thinking. She rarely disciplined Alisia and explained that she hoped her children would be "independent, sociable, and critical (not blindly accepting of others' views)" (p. 79). Alisia's mother saw her role as providing her children with opportunities and options in life rather than directing it.

From these examples, it is clear that the two children would come to school with different views about learning and different socialization expectations. Schools constitute a new community, and language minority students like Jeni and Alisia usually need to learn both a new language and new ways of using language to succeed in this new community.

Expanding Discourse in Schools

Teachers generally recognize that English learners need to develop a new language to function in school. What is frequently overlooked is that these students may also need to learn new ways to use language. As Heath says, "Not only is there the general expectation that all children will learn to speak English, but also the assumption that they have internalized *before* they start to school the norms of language used in academic life" (p. 148).

It is important, then, to think about the discourse opportunities students have outside school. Schools require children to use language in certain ways. If children's home discourses are different in significant ways from the discourse of school, children may experience school failure. Heath (1983, 1986) has written extensively about differences between uses of language, or ways with words, between homes and schools. She points out, "For all children, academic success depends less on the specific language they know than on the ways of using language they know" (p. 144). When children don't know the ways of using language that the school expects, they may fail. However, this does not necessarily imply that home language use must change. Heath also argues, "The school can promote academic and vocational success for all children, regardless of their first language background, by providing the greatest possible range of oral and written language uses" (p. 144).

In other words, schools can be places where students expand their repertoire of language use. Too often classroom discourse is limited to asking students questions, getting short answers, and affirming or rejecting those answers. Instead of a limited kind of discourse in schools, it would be beneficial to encompass the different ways with words that children bring to school rather than retaining a narrow range of uses that excludes much of the language of the home and the community. Children from some cultures, for example, do not see the model of competition as appropriate behavior but instead have always experienced cooperation. Therefore, when teachers value individual answers and no sharing, students who have not had experience with a competitive discourse may seem silent and uninterested. Phillips' (1972) classic study of Native American students discussed earlier found that these students succeeded in school when they were allowed to work together and share their knowledge. In fact, it was considered improper to show off knowledge or expertise. The culture strongly influenced how language should be used.

Like Gee, Heath views all language learning as cultural learning. As she puts it, "Children do not learn merely the building blocks of their mother tongue—its sounds, words, and order; they learn also how to use language to get what they want, protect themselves, express their wonderings and worries, and ask questions about the world" (p. 146).

Students enter school with an ability to use language to function effectively within the primary and secondary groups they have been part of. "Cultural learning includes all the learning that enables a member of a family and community to behave appropriately within that group" (p. 146). It is important for teachers to build on these language strengths that students bring to school.

However, teachers have been socialized into school language. For most teachers this kind of language seems natural, and as a result, many teachers are not aware of the special uses of language schools require. A conscious awareness of school discourse can help teachers work with students to develop the required language functions. Next we will examine some of the ways students are expected to be able to use language in schools.

Taking an Additive Approach

Teachers who take an intercultural orientation value the languages and ways of using words that students bring to school. Taking an additive approach, these teachers introduce additional language functions and language varieties. There are two issues here: *Language functions* refers to using language in certain ways. For example, in school teachers often expect students to answer questions that the teacher already knows the answer to. They may hold up an object and ask, "What color is this?" This way of using language may be unfamiliar to students who have only been around adults who ask questions when the adults don't know the answer. In addition, students may use a different language variety from the teacher when they speak. Language variety is a term we are using instead of *dialect,* which often has negative connotations. People often consider a dialect what somebody else (from a different region, socioeconomic class, or language background) speaks. In fact, we all speak one or more dialects of each language we know. The term "language variety" does not carry negative connotations, so we will use that term instead.

An additive approach affirms the importance of the functions of language students have developed and the varieties they speak while also recognizing that students may need to develop additional linguistic resources to succeed in arenas beyond their home communities.

Language Functions in the Classroom

Heath (1986) identifies six ways of using language that are common in schools: "The first two—label quests and meaning quests—are language activities that ground school learning; the latter four are genres in which these activities become integrated as the learner becomes fully skilled in a repertoire of genres" (p. 167).

Label quests are activities where children are asked to name items. Young children are expected to be able to label objects by their shapes and colors in response to questions from teachers like "What color is the apple?" or "What shape is the orange?" Teachers may also ask students the name of a character in a story or the date of a historical event. Label quests are activities where students answer who? what? or what kind of? It is common in many mainstream homes for parents to ask children to name things, such as "What does Bobbie have in his hands?" or "Who is that?" Schools continue this practice. Label quests are not common to all cultures, though, and in many cultures adults do not ask children to name things, particularly, as mentioned earlier, when the adult already knows the name of the object.

Meaning quests are language activities in which adults infer the meaning of a child's statement, provide the meaning of their own statements, or ask for explanations. Parents will often fill in what they think a child means. If a child says, "Down," the parent may respond, "Oh, you want to get down, don't you?" In addition, parents may provide explanations for their own actions. A father might say to a young child, "I'm going to get some gas. The car won't go if Daddy doesn't buy some gas" as he pulls the car into a service station. In school, children are frequently asked why certain things occur. They are asked to give interpretations. For example, they might be asked why the British taxed the colonists, or how cream turns to butter. To succeed in school, students not only need to tell what, they also need to explain why. Again, this function of language that many of us may assume to be universal is actually culture specific. Some children come to school from homes and communities where they are not asked to infer meanings for events.

Heath explains that these two language activities, label quests and meaning quests, are integrated into school discourse. Students use them as they use language in four ways, or genres. The four genres Heath describes are recounts, accounts, eventcasts, and stories. During a recount, a child is asked to retell an experience known to both the child and the adult. After a trip to the beach, for example, parents might ask their children to talk about what they did there. In the same way, after a field trip, a teacher may prompt students to recount the experience. Another familiar activity in which a student is asked to provide a recount is a report on a book the teacher has also read. Students are expected to summarize the main events of the story in a certain logical order. If students give recounts that do not follow school logic, they are generally corrected.

Accounts, on the other hand, provide the listener with new information. At home a child might be asked to tell his mother what happened at the birthday party he attended. At school, a student might be asked to write about what she did during summer vacation. Or a student might be asked to report on a book that her teacher and classmates have not read. The difference between the recount and the account is that in the former, both parties know the information, and in the latter, only the teller knows. In either case, the teacher may be more interested in having the student display knowledge (and the proper language) than in gaining new information. And in each case, students are expected to present the information in a certain logical order.

Eventcasts are a kind of running narrative describing what is going on or what will happen. Parents often provide these narratives as they go about feeding or changing a young child. "Mommy's going to give Mary her dinner. Look, Mommy's got some carrots. Yummy. Mommy's going to warm them and give them to Mary." Children will sometimes follow this demonstration and talk out loud while playing alone, giving a description of what they are doing. In school, teachers who explain the steps in a science experiment are performing an eventcast. An outline for an essay is a written eventcast because it gives the steps involved in accomplishing some goal.

Stories are a familiar genre. They are imaginative accounts of how a person (or other animate being) overcomes certain problems to achieve some goal. Parents read stories to children and expect children to be able to tell and write stories. While stories are common to all cultures, the organizational pattern of stories differs from one culture to another. In schools, though, generally only one type of story organization is considered logical.

Label quests and meaning quests are often part of accounts, recounts, eventcasts, and stories. Some children come to school with facility in using language in these ways. Teachers from mainstream cultures may find these ways with words to be "natural," and they may not realize that some children come to school with other ways of using language. For example, in schools, children are expected to be quiet and to answer teachers' questions (in certain ways), but in some communities, children are encouraged to jump in and gain the floor by telling clever stories. Children who upstage the teacher may not fare well in many school situations because teachers view them as rude or poorly disciplined.

School success depends to a great extent on a student's ability to use language in ways the school values. Heath suggests that schools can better serve all students by bringing to conscious attention the different functions of language students are expected to be able to use. For example, teachers can point out the different uses of language required by different school subjects. A good science report has a different form from a good English essay. Teachers can also ask students to observe language use in the school and contrast it with use in different institutions outside school. In the course of their investigations, students can record and transcribe conversations, analyze them, and write reports. This sociolinguistic study would make all students more aware of how language is used in different social contexts. Students can also examine how certain kinds of jokes, rhymes, and language games are specific to each culture. They can collect proverbs and try to find out if different cultures have similar sayings.

Through these linguistic studies, students would begin to understand how different kinds of language are used in different contexts to accomplish a variety of functions. As Heath says, "A major benefit of teachers' and children's attention to the wide variety of language uses outside the classroom is increased language awareness on the part of all" (p. 180). As students and teachers become more aware of the narrow range of language functions available in school, they can incorporate more of the community language uses in school activities. The result is a greater match between uses of language in home and school, and this benefits all students.

Language Varieties in the Classroom

Teachers who take an intercultural orientation find ways to incorporate students' languages and cultures into the curriculum. A conscious knowledge of both language functions and language varieties can help teachers do this.

Wolfram (1991) has written about how important it is for teachers to know about language varieties. He claims that teachers need to develop "an informed perspective on dialects." This involves an appreciation for "the complexity and naturalness of community language patterns" (p. 265). It is the attitude toward student language that is important here. Wolfram is concerned that teachers adopt positive attitudes toward the language varieties that students bring to the classroom. In addition, he encourages teachers to develop a more thorough understanding of different language varieties. "Knowledge of community language must, of course, extend beyond respect for the naturalness and complexity of community language systems. It should also involve knowledge of the structural details of the community language system" (p. 265). Wolfram's book provides the basic information necessary for teachers to conduct language study. That knowledge base helps prepare teachers to study the particular language varieties their students speak.

In a second useful book Wolfram and Christian (1989) state, "It is clear that teachers need to know about dialects in order to understand the oral and written language behavior of their students." They then ask, "Would any of this information be useful to students as well?" (p. 77). They describe ways teachers can involve students in the study of the language varieties of their own communities. As they note, "The study of community language and culture allows for the development of a full range of academic skills through meaningful content, lessening the gap between home and school. Students at all levels can conduct ethnographic and linguistic research, gathering information, testing hypotheses, and writing reports" (p. 78). Appendix F lists several resource books and articles that provide information about language varieties and language use in the classroom.

Delpit (1990) has argued that a failure to make students aware of the importance of certain language varieties limits their chances for success. She cautions against trying to correct students' ways of speaking, however. Correction raises the affective filter (Krashen 1982), leads to monitoring of speech, and may slow down acquisition of a new language or language variety. If teachers constantly criticize students' speech or writing, the students may also develop negative attitudes toward the teacher. Correction is not the answer to helping students acquire additional ways of using words. At the same time, "it is equally important to understand that students who do not have access to the politically popular dialect form in this country, i.e., standard English, are less likely to succeed economically than their peers who do" (Delpit 1990, p. 251).

Delpit points out that teachers can affirm students' primary discourse styles and still help them acquire other language forms by conducting lessons that contrast the two. She gives the example of Martha Demientieff, a native Alaskan teacher of Athabaskan Indian students. Martha divides a classroom bulletin board in half. On one side she lists words and phrases taken from student writing that represent what she calls "Our Heritage Language," and on the other side she provides translations into "Formal English." Martha and her students discuss the differences between the two styles. As Delpit points out, "It is possible and desirable to make the actual study of language diversity a part of the curriculum for all students" (p. 253). The Athabaskan students conclude their unit of study with a formal dinner at which they speak only formal English and a picnic where they speak their heritage language. In this way, students begin to understand that different kinds of language are appropriate for different contexts. In Halliday and Hassan's (1976) terms, language is coherent when the kind of language used fits the context. Martha is increasing her students' language proficiency by increasing the range of contexts in which they can use language appropriately. She is not only teaching them language, but also showing them which language varieties to use in different situations.

Cazden (1992) uses the term "concentrated encounter" to describe teaching activities that help students develop the language needed to function in varying social contexts: "By concentrated encounter, we refer to . . . activities like games and role playing in which opportunities for practice in a wide range of language functions can be created at school" (p. 112). In Australia, Brian Gray, working with Aboriginal children, has developed a curriculum approach that employs concentrated encounters to help the children acquire the functions of language required for different social contexts.

For example, in a unit on cattle stations, students develop the language used in the situation. Gray's curriculum sequence includes the following: (1) children have first-hand experience with the real situation; (2) teachers and children role-play the situation and use appropriate language; (3) children talk about the situations as they look at photographs; (4) the teacher helps the children write a group report about the experience; and (5) students do independent writing on the topic. In the cattle station situation, students would first visit the station. Later, in the classroom, they would role-play different aspects of cattle stations, talk about them, and write about them, first as a group and then independently. In this sequence, Gray moves from the concrete to the abstract, from language use with more to less contextual support. Through this process, he helps students add to their repertoire of language functions.

Martha Demientieff and Brian Gray have found ways to help students acquire additional forms of language needed to function in certain social contexts. What seems important is to avoid direct teaching of certain uses of language in ways that suggest that only those uses are valid. It is important that one form of language not simply replace another. Teaching specific language forms may send the message that the language children bring to school is inadequate. Rather than seeing the child's linguistic resources as limited, schools can follow Heath's advice to provide "the greatest possible range of oral and written language uses" (p. 144). By expanding the range of language functions that count, schools can begin with and build on the language that students bring to school.

For this reason, it is critical to bring the home experiences of all the students into the classroom. For example, rather than planning cultural celebrations such as Mexican Independence Day or Hmong New Year and telling students how they will celebrate, teachers might invite in members of cultural communities to discuss cultural holidays, the ways their own family celebrates holidays, how they interact with different people in their families and in their culture groups, what values they hold, and how they see their views as different from mainstream culture in the United States. Demonstrations of crafts and cooking might include discussions with all the students of how individual families do things differently and why they do them. By involving people from the cultures themselves, by recognizing individual differences, and by discussing these differences, teachers can help students expand their language and their cultural understanding.

Finding ways to incorporate the languages and cultures of the community into the school context is one step toward developing an intercultural orientation. We saw in the previous chapter how Yvette encouraged students to reflect on their attitudes and prejudices as they studied different cultural groups. We will now present more examples of ways teachers can use interactive/intercultural teaching to help students examine their cultural backgrounds.

Interactive/Intercultural Teaching

Teachers have found a number of different ways to introduce students' cultures into the classroom. Denette, an elementary teacher, has suggested a way to get students to begin discussion of their own backgrounds by means of a "Find Someone Who . . ." (see Figure 12-1) on genealogy.

Denette begins the activity with the following directions:

Each of you has a "Find Someone Who . . ." sheet. You are going to try to find someone in the class who fits each one of these items. You will ask people in the room, for example, "Do you have a great-great-grandparent still alive?" or "Do you have a family tree?" When you find someone in the class who can answer one of the items "Yes," put that person's name on that item. *You may use someone's name only once.* After we have interviewed each other, we will tally the answers to see what we have learned about each other.

GENEALOGY

Denette Zaninovich

FIND SOMEONE WHO:

1. Has a great-great-grandparent alive.
2. Has a family tree mapped out.
3. Has their mother's and father's last names as their own.
4. Has been to a family reunion before.
5. Lives with a grandparent.
6. Knows what their last name means.
7. Knows what country their grandparents came from.
8. Visited the country that their culture came from.
9. Speaks two languages, one being the language of their grandparents.
10. Has a family picture that includes three generations.
11. Has a photo album of old pictures that includes grandparents, great-aunts, great-uncles, or cousins.

Figure 12-1   Find someone who

Denette has discovered that a "Find Someone Who . . ." is a great way to start a unit by getting students to interact with one another. She has developed a "Find Someone Who . . ." on such varied topics as geology, mythological characters, checking and banking, weather experiences, and environmental practices. Certainly, her genealogy "Find Someone Who . . ." is a good activity to initiate a unit designed to involve students in looking at their own cultural backgrounds.

Earlier we introduced Shelly's unit on "Culture: A Pattern of Civilization," which she planned with her seventh- and eighth-grade social studies ESL students. Shelly stated the following four goals for the unit:

1. To increase student self-esteem/self-awareness.
2. To build mutual respect and self-understanding.
3. To increase an awareness of why we study about others.
4. To learn about the past and to be prepared for the future.

In her rationale statement for her unit, Shelly demonstrates how teachers can help students change their view of themselves in relationship to schools:

> The unit activities are hands-on and accommodate second language students, giving them an opportunity to actively participate in projects. Also, because these activities are centered around validating their culture, it will help make second language students more comfortable with their culture in the classroom. They will develop clear concepts of cultural diversity and a true appreciation and respect of the wonderful differences in people of the world.

TIME LINE AND ORGANIZATION OF UNIT ACTIVITIES

WEEK 1:

Introductory Activity:

1. Physical characteristics—to begin to identify who they are by becoming comfortable with their own physical characteristics. To demonstrate one unique aspect of the individual. (Activity is attached.)

Unit Activities:

2. Home Archaeologists/Introduction to Doing Research—methods and ideas to uncover family history, traits, values, language, and culture.

3. Begin research projects.

WEEK 2:

1. Field trips—library visits, museums, culture centers.

2. Continue working on term projects. Students may compare their findings to other classmates.

WEEK 3–4:

1. Map family's immigration path—each student will do this, and each path will be drawn on a class map.

2. Continue field trips.

3. Begin final projects—choose one aspect of research and develop a project for a final presentation.

WEEK 5:

1. Celebration—a completion and sharing of final projects—"cultural fair" with class presentations, food festival of favorite family recipes, guest speakers, music.

Figure 12-2   Shelly's timeline

Figure 12-2 shows the time line and organization of the unit activities.

Shelly's unit included activities that did just what she hoped for in her rationale. Her five-week plan began by having students study their own physical characteristics and talk about them to recognize their uniqueness. (See Figure 12-3.)

Shelly then discussed with her students the job descriptions for an archaeologist and an anthropologist. Next she told them that *they* would be archaeologists and anthropologists. She shared examples of fossils, artifacts, legends, pieces of art, folk beliefs, and old written documents to give students ideas about how scientists research the past. The students brainstormed what aspects of their own cultural background they would explore during the unit. The following seven items were chosen:

1. Customs/traditions—Discuss five cultural traditions/customs.

2. Religious traditions (if applicable)—Discuss five religious traditions.

3. Recipes/food—Share five favorite family recipes.

WHO AM I? / PHYSICAL CHARACTERISTICS
(Introduction to a Social Studies Unit, which will explore the question:
What's my part in my family and my culture?)

GOAL: To begin to explore the unique physical appearance of each individual.

PURPOSE: Through this process the student will get a grasp of their own physical characteristics. Most students will be able to relate this information if asked, but in this particular context they will begin to realize their uniqueness. In realizing their own dimensions as well as the differences evident in skin, hair, and eye color, we will begin to lay the foundation to getting to know oneself.

OBJECTIVE: To record physical characteristics.

MATERIALS:
  A. Mirror
  B. Yardstick
  C. String
  D. Pencil and paper for each student
  E. List of specific steps posted in classroom:
      1. Look into the mirror and record the color of your skin, eyes, and hair.
      2. Using the string and the yardstick, have your partner measure and record:
          a. the distance around your head and neck.
          b. the length of your right leg and your left arm.
          c. the length from heel to toe of the bottom of your foot.
          d. your height from your heel to the top of your head.

PROCEDURE:
  A. Students will review measuring methods and concepts: inch, foot, yard, metric. Students will be measuring by finding a length with a piece of string, then measuring the length of the string with a yardstick.
  B. Students will be placed into groups of two by numbering off throughout the class.
  C. Students will then take their paper and pencil and with their partner follow the steps listed on the board.
  D. Looking into the mirror the student will record the color of their hair and eyes.
  E. With help from their partner the students will take the required measurements and record the information.
  F. When the students have finished with the required observations and measurements, they will compare and contrast their observations with those of their classmates.
  G. The class will graph the heights of all the students in the class.

EVALUATION: Students are required to participate in the activity and discussion. The instructor will check their recorded information as they work.

SUMMARY: The class will discuss various physical differences in people and the relevance if any to what that person is "really" like . . . what does the "outside" mean?

Figure 12-3   Student characteristics

4. Legends—Record three legends.

5. Music—Share the lyrics of three songs, or list names of musical compositions.

6. Holidays—Discuss five holidays.

7. Values—Discuss family values and important issues.

After each student had picked a topic from the list, they interviewed their families to find out about coming to the United States and California. This information was compiled for a class map so students could compare the migrations of others in their class. In addition, students brought in "artifacts" from their homes and created a class museum of cultural pieces.

Cummins points out that teachers who take an intercultural orientation use alternative forms of assessment rather than standardized tests. Shelly evaluated the students' learning by having them do a project. They were given several choices including making a home video; doing a mural or illustration of their family or culture; compiling a book or report on family myths, legends, traditions, or recipes; producing a family newsletter, including not only history and present-day gossip, but also articles written by family members; creating and performing a drama; or putting together a scrapbook or collection of articles, advertisements, or pictures that displayed aspects of their culture. Shelly explained why this alternative form of assessment was so successful:

> The project was the culmination of the students' self-exploration of their own culture. Most of the students were very eager to do something with the information they had spent four weeks gathering. Since the class had developed particular guidelines that everyone used to explore his/her culture, I could have given them an essay exam based on these questions. In fact, the students were surprised that I did not give them a test. I think that this project worked much better.
>
> The students completed a variety of projects, utilized their talents, and practiced reading, writing, and verbal language skills. They were able to work in groups and share their knowledge. I believe that they learned so much more by sharing than if they had simply studied for a test. Many of them continued to record new information long after I had made my final check of their research notebooks. They were interested in the information.

Examples from two projects demonstrate not only what students learned, but the pride they developed in their own culture. Patricia and Suiem coauthored a bilingual Spanish/English book on Mexican holidays. The title page and dedication pages and a sample holiday description (Figure 12-4) show the importance the two teenagers gave to their work. Two other pages, one on "Héroes de la independencia" ("Heroes of the Independence") and another on "Personajes de la Revolución Mexicana" ("Important Figures of the Mexican Revolution") (Figures 12-5 and 12-6), show what the students learned about the history of their native country.

It is important to note that Shelly allowed her ESL students to use both English and their first languages. This not only validates their first language and culture as Cummins encourages, but it also makes it easier for students to show what they do know and to share that information. In Cummins' (1989) terms, Shelly takes an advocacy-oriented approach to assessment. The students were proud of their work and viewed it as important, as evidenced by Patricia's author's page (Figure 12-7).

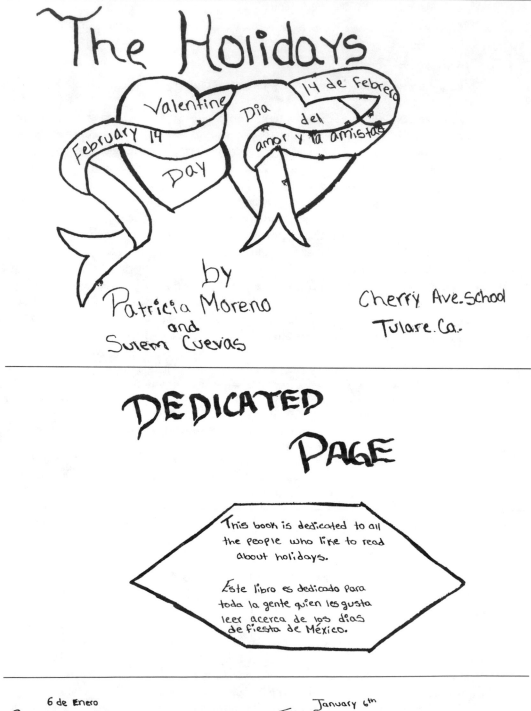

The Holidays

Valentine   Dia   14 de Febrero
February 14   del
Day   amor y la amistad

by
Patricia Moreno
and
Surem Cuevas

Cherry Ave. School
Tulare. Ca.

DEDICATED
PAGE

This book is dedicated to all
the people who like to read
about holidays.

Éste libro es dedicado para
toda la gente quien les gusta
leer acerca de los días
de fiesta de México.

6 de Enero
Se celebra haciendo una rosca de pan dulce
adornado y se le pone 1 o 2 monitos dentro. Y
al que le toque el pedazo con el monito tiene que
hacer una corrida o una fiesta para los invitados.

January 6th
They celebrated by making a ring of sweethbread.
The bread have 1 or 2 dolls hidden in it. If you
get a piece of bread with one doll you have to
made a party for your family and friends.

Figure 12-4   Mexican holidays—title and dedication pages and sample description

Figures 12-5 and 12-6   Heroes of the independence and important figures of the revolution

Patricia Moreno is 13 years 8 months old
and was born Hermosillo Sonora, México
on February 25, 1979.
Patricia has one brother and three sisters,
Her mother's name is Carmen and her father's
name is Francisco.
She enjoys playing volleyball in her spare
time. She has lived in the United States
for a year and a half.

I hope that who read this book
like because are holidays of México
and are importants.

Espero que quien lea este libro
les guste porque son días de fista
de México y son importantes.

Figure 12-7   Patricia's author's page

Valores Familiares en México.	Family Values in Mexico
Son aquellos que nos han venido dejando nuestros antepasados, como nuestros bisabuelos, abuelos, padres y así de generación a generación. Y son primeramente el	They are those that have been passed on to us by our ancestors, such as our great-grandparents, grandparents, parents and so forth from generation to generation and are primarily the following
Respeto a nuestros padres,	Respect for our parents
El respeto a toda persona mayor,	Respect for all older people
El vestir y hablar correctamente o decentemente delante de personas mayores.	Dressing and speaking properly or decently in front of older people
El ~~casar~~ procurar que la mujer siempre vaya virgen al matrimonio.	Being sure that a woman always is a virgin upon getting married
El tener siempre una diciplina rígida tanto para el hombre como para la mujer.	Discipline should be strictly maintained for both men and women
El conservar siempre la dignidad y la honradez delante de todo.	Above all else conserving always dignity and honesty
El seguir siempre el ejemplo familiar.	Always following the example of the family
El ~~saber~~ elegir a nuestras amistades y ~~saber~~ destinguir lo bueno y lo malo.	Knowing how to choose our friends and knowing how to distinguish between good and evil
El tenerle amor y respeto a nuestra Bandera y nuestra patria, Así como a la escuela y nuestros maestros.	Having respect and love for our flag and our country as well as for our school and our teachers

Figure 12-8   Family values in Mexico

One of the most powerful examples of the positive results from this project came from Patricia's book on "My Culture of México." In this book of over twenty neatly handwritten pages in Spanish, Patricia included the national hymn of Mexico, selected pieces of poetry, two legends, summaries of holidays, traditions, religious customs, and values and attitudes of the Mexican people. Her page on "Valores Familiares en México" ("Family Values in Mexico") is a clear demonstration of how a project such as this can help students not only understand their culture but also have pride in what that culture represents. (See Figure 12-8.)

Shelly's unit served to help her students learn through reading, writing, and sharing in several different content areas. In addition, an activity that offers choice can build on what students already know or can discover from their families, assuring success for all students. In fact, Shelly's self-evaluation illustrates why a project such as this one is important for second language learners:

> This project worked exceptionally well in my ESL class since all the students are at so many levels. Although some of the projects may appear to show little work in comparison to others, each student worked very hard. I was able to assess each student's work based on his abilities since the projects were individual.
>
> The class really developed sophisticated concepts about culture. As we have continued to study other cultures it is obvious that they have a framework within

which to work. By having them study their own culture first, they were able to personally define the meaning of custom, tradition, culture, religion, family, values, and perspective. As we continue to study other cultures they are comfortable with the new information. I will definitely continue to use this project and the unit it completed.

Another example of how teachers can take an intercultural orientation comes from Rusty, the sixth-grade teacher who authored the poem in Chapter 10. Rusty's class has many Hispanic as well as Anglo students. In the farming community where the students live, the attitudes that Anglos hold about Hispanics, especially migrant Mexicans, is very negative. The little social interaction that takes place between Anglos and Mexicans is usually hostile.

Rusty has completed a graduate program in reading and is presently working on a bilingual cross-cultural specialist credential. Through this coursework, his creativity, and his dedication to teaching, he has been able to develop a collaborative classroom where all his students work together to explore topics of interest. However, he is continually frustrated with what is happening at his school in general:

> It is really difficult to challenge the status quo at the individual school site, let alone the district's policies. Most principals are (or certainly seem to me) even more ignorant of the principles/concepts that are involved in bilingual education than teachers. And our resource teacher (bless her heart) hasn't taken *any* classes (in reading or bilingual education) since I have been here and that covers fifteen years. The principal has been here for over twenty years. How do you bridge this gap without being very threatening or being seen as a "rebel"? My approach has been an effort to model what I believe are good practices in my own classroom. The problem is that my principal thinks that these things work because Rusty is doing them, and does not wish to extend the principles/concepts to other staff.

Rusty has taken definite steps to try to change the attitudes of the students in his classroom. He uses a resource and activity book, *Portraits of Mexican-Americans: Pathfinders in the Mexican-American Communities* (Pérez 1991), which contains information about the significant Mexican-American contributors in several areas including the history of the Southwest, farm workers, the arts, writers, educators, politicians, and sports figures. The book is designed for cooperative learning activities and includes several in both Spanish and English. Rusty has found these materials to be especially powerful because Hispanic students feel pride in their culture as they read about the history of the Mexican people in the United States. Several exercises involve students in linguistic investigations about the origins of Spanish words. In these, Rusty's Spanish-speaking students serve as experts.

When Anglo students in Rusty's class read about the rights promised Mexicans living in the United States by the Treaty of Guadalupe Hidalgo, the treaty written when the war between Mexico and the United States ended in 1848, they also feel the indignation of their Hispanic classmates over the broken promises. Students study the changing geography of the Southwest between 1810 and 1848, and they begin to understand the strong roots that Spanish-speaking peoples claim in this country. Studying about political activists like Cesar Chávez and Gloria Molina, as well as writers and artists, gives Hispanic students a pride in their culture and people. In discussion about identity and labeling, students read about Chicanos and what that name implies as opposed to "Mexican American."

Rusty works hard to try to meet the needs of all his students, including his language-minority students, but sometimes he admits how overwhelming his students' needs are:

> There is so much to learn/absorb/implement that sometimes I get a headache just thinking about it. I look at what I am doing in my classroom and at the needs of Placido and Nora and Rosalinda and I just become overwhelmed. Sometimes I also get very frustrated at the slow pace at which I seem to be making the changes that I need to make. I'm not berating myself because I know that what I am doing really does make a difference in the lives of my students.

One final example of a teacher who has taken an intercultural orientation comes from Georgia, who teaches international students at a local private school that prepares students for university work by helping them improve their English. Often, these students spend only a brief time in the United States, between three and six months. Georgia, a graduate student, has been studying about language acquisition and current approaches to teaching a second language. She wanted to try some of the things she has been learning.

Georgia has decided that publishing is a good way to get the students writing, so during her month-long sessions with a group of students, she involves them in writers workshop. The students freewrite daily in journals. Georgia responds to each entry but makes no corrections so that students become comfortable with writing their thoughts freely. In addition, the class reads and discusses together *New Kids in Town* (Bode 1989), a book in which different immigrant students tell their own stories about coming to the United States to live. After the reading and discussion, the class brainstorms together the kinds of things they want to write in their autobiographies. The students write drafts, edit their own and each others' writing, Georgia edits, and they type their pieces on the word processor and publish them in a class book.

Since Georgia wants her students to be writing for an audience, she decided to try to have the adult international students visit a local public school and share their autobiographies with American school children. This addition to the writing and publishing has turned out to be especially successful. In the last two sessions, Georgia has taken two different groups of students to classrooms. In Vince's fourth-grade class, the international students sat in the classroom's author's chair and read their autobiographies, while Vince's students took notes to use to ask questions. Both the international students and the fourth graders learned a lot from one another in the exchange.

For the second visit, Georgia went to Kim's sixth-grade classroom. This time Georgia and Kim tried a different organization for the visit. The sixth graders sat in small groups, and the international students went to the groups to read their autobiographies and answer questions. Neither Kim nor Georgia was prepared for the exciting exchanges that took place! The conversation was so lively that the five minutes planned per group took much longer. Finally, Kim's students went out to recess, but the visit did not end there. After recess, Kim's students read books they had published to the international students so that they could ask questions of the sixth graders. It was exciting to see this international/intercultural exchange as both younger and older students warmed up to one another and learned from one another.

One of the most interesting and unexpected benefits that came from this visit was that the international students experienced firsthand the diversity in schools in the

Raed

:-autobiography:-

My name is Raed Al Shayji. I'm from Kuwait. I was born

in 1968. when I was five. I went to kindergarten for two years.

After I finished kindergarten, I went to primary school

for four years. Then middle school for four years and high

school for four years. I went to school for 14 years (12). After

that, the war started in Kuwait with Iraq. The war started

on August. 2. 1991 and finished on February. 26. 1992.

I have three brothers and three sisters. All of my brothers and

sisters finished university. My three brothers finished university

in the U.S.A.

In my country, most of the people wear "Thobe",

Because Kuwait is an islamic country. Thobe is the national

clothes for men.

My country's climate is very hot. Thirty five years ago

But later, when the oil was pumped up in to the air from

the ground all Kuwait changed. Now kuwait has many

beautful hotels and kinds of differently designed buildings.

Most of the touirsts come to Kuwait to see the new Kuwait.

Figure 12-9   Raed's autobiography

United States. Even though they had read *New Kids in Town,* the students really did not think they would meet immigrant students in public schools. The international students were amazed that most of Vince's and Kim's students did not speak English at home, that many had been born in another country, and that they were English language learners, too!

Raed, an international student from Kuwait, found the experience of visiting Kim's sixth-grade class especially moving. He had not been a particularly hard worker in Georgia's sixth-level class (there are twelve levels) until he learned that he would be reading his autobiography to American students. He worked very hard on his autobiography, practiced it, and made notations to himself in his first language, Arabic, over the English on his draft copy (see Figure 12-9).

Once Raed got into the small group and started talking, he was one of the most active and interested participants, asking the students about their native countries, their families, and their struggles with learning English. After this visit his journal entry in English to Georgia was the longest and certainly the most enthusiastic he had written (see Figure 12-10).

Georgia had provided her students with a true intercultural exchange, and in the process Vince's and Kim's students learned about other parts of the world. More importantly, the fourth and sixth graders felt validated because the international students were so interested in them, their backgrounds, and their experiences as immigrants.

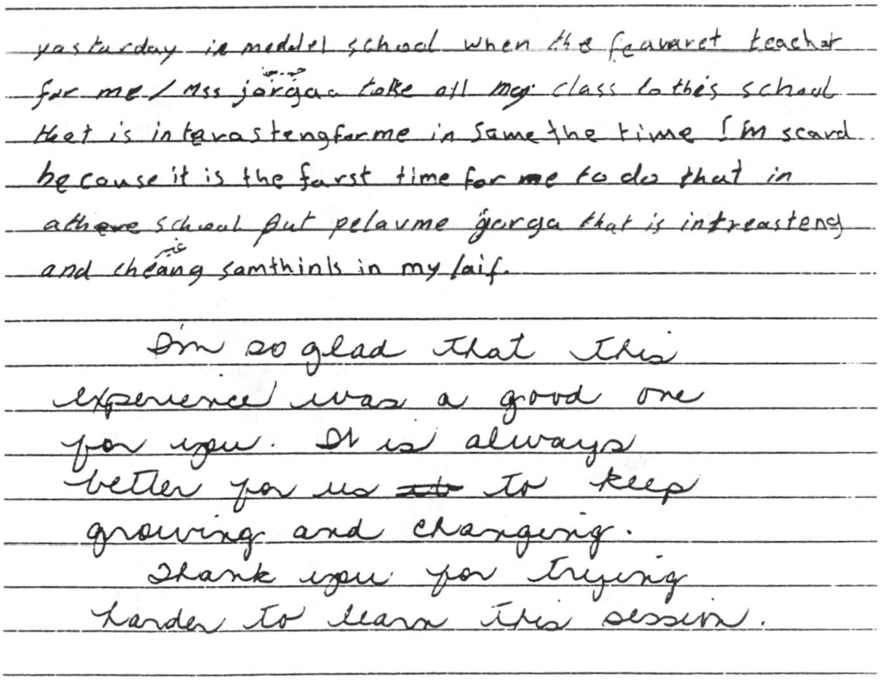
yasterday in meddel school when the feavaret teacher for me / Mss jorgaa take all my class to this school That is intavastengforme in same the time I'm scard because it is the farst time for me to do that in athere school But pelavme jorga that is intreastend and cheang samthinls in my laif.

I'm so glad that this experience was a good one for you. It is always better for us to keep growing and changing. Thank you for trying harder to learn this session.

Yesterday in middle school when the favorite teacher for me/ Miss Georgia take all my class to this school That is interesting for me in same the time I'm scared because it is the first time for me to do that in other school But believe me, Georgia, that is interesting and changing something in my life.

Figure 12-10 Raed's journal entry

Teachers like Shelly, Rusty, and Georgia, who develop curriculum that promotes an intercultural orientation, make a real difference in the education of language-minority students. By incorporating students' cultures and languages into their daily lesson plans, these teachers focus on students' strengths. They help students value their classmates, themselves, and the cultural heritages they share.

Using Literature Studies

In Chapter 10 we described how Charlene used a literature study to explore questions concerning peace and conflict. Literature studies can help students at any stage come to understand other cultures more fully. In addition, during literature studies, teachers and students can raise and discuss important issues that have to do with the relationships between communities and schools. We often think of literature studies being used in elementary or secondary classes, but we have found that they are extremely valuable for older students as well. As part of our graduate ESL Methods class we involve all students in a literature study.

We use literature studies for two reasons. First, we want students to experience a literature study so that they can implement it in their own classrooms. Second, we want them to engage in literature that involves them in the lives, concerns, and feelings of diverse peoples. We begin by giving book talks, short advertisements, for a series of books. Then the teachers each choose one of these pieces of adolescent literature to read and discuss in a literature study group. We generally try to ensure that groups have between three and five students. If only one or two students choose a book, we ask them to make a second choice. If more than five students choose the same book, we divide the readers into two or more groups.

For our literature study we use the model suggested by Bird and Alvarez (1987) and organized into steps by Yvonne Freeman (see Figure 12-11). Teachers read their books for pleasure and then discuss them together. The one stipulation for discussion each time the group meets is that each person has a chance to share without being interrupted before any open discussion takes place. That way everyone has a chance to respond to the reading.

For each group meeting, we ask one of the students to take notes and then summarize their discussion. We then make an assignment for the next meeting. For example, if group members have commented on how well the main character was developed, we ask them to go back through the book and find specific passages that contributed to character development. Another group might be asked to look for passages that foreshadowed the conclusion. The assignments are always based on the particular group's discussion. Therefore, if a groups tells the class how funny their book was, their assignment might be to go back into the book and locate passages they found humorous to share. At the next meeting, students share the passages they have marked. In this way, during the literature study, students become more aware of the author's craft as they return several times to the text itself.

After group members have had opportunities to revisit the book and examine different aspects of the story, they plan a presentation for the whole class that represents their experience with the book. At different times students have performed skits, given dramatic readings, sung songs, and recited poems they created. Often these presentations inspire their classmates to read their books as well.

LITERATURE STUDIES
(Bird and Alvarez, 1987)
organized by Y. Freeman, 1988

I. Teacher or other students do a book talk.

II. Students read the entire book on their own (can write in their literature logs as they go along, can discuss the book with others in their groups).

III. Students meet with the teacher and respond to the book (what they liked/disliked/ found interesting/didn't understand).

IV. Teacher makes an assignment from what the students came up with that has the students go back to the text and find out more about the book and especially the author's craft.

V. Students meet again with the teacher—they respond to their tasks—(might be in writing in their literature logs). From this discussion new tasks are assigned.

VI. This procedure can be repeated until students and teacher feel the book no longer is a source of interest or information.

A literature study:

1. explores the author's craft,

2. involves students in constructing their own meanings,

3. encourages students to read whole texts to increase their understanding of the world.

Literature study is *not:*

1. answering comprehension questions,

2. finding the teacher's main idea,

3. doing skill exercises from the text,

4. testing the students' knowledge of the details of the text.

Figure 12-11   Literature study steps

The choice of books we provide is important because we want the teachers to experience another culture through literature. At various times we have used different books. Appendix G includes books that represent the experiences of young people from a number of different cultures. These are chapter books that could be used with students from about grades four through high school.

The experience of being involved in a literature study for the teachers has been a positive one. Kristene wrote how both the book and the sharing had moved her:

> My first literature study—I'll never forget it! I enjoyed the book talk and couldn't wait to buy *Lupita Mañana*. The excerpt was read so warmly in the book talk, I knew I wanted to get to know the main character, Lupita.
>
> During our first meeting we each got a turn to comment on the book without anyone interrupting. This was a very considerate step and created a sense of quiet respect for each individual's opinion. I did find myself so wanting to respond but held back. I had highlighted parts of the book that moved me, so this was a perfect

opportunity to read them aloud and reflect. One member of our group had LIVED the experience of Lupita and shared her touching story with us. I will never be the same.

Another member of Kristene's group, Mary, a bilingual first-grade teacher, was so moved by the book and the literature study that she read it to her Hispanic children:

> I began using *Lupita Mañana* in my classroom each day after lunch. I paraphrase the book, chapter by chapter. I enjoy changing my voice and jumping up out of my chair to show the moving emotions in the story. My first graders are enthralled with the plights of Lupita and Salvador. We are presently at the point where they attempted to cross the border the first time and were caught and sent back to Tijuana. I interject a Spanish phrase here and there as the author did and some of the LEP students are catching both the English and the Spanish. When we finish the book, I would like to have the kids do something to show their impressions of the book. My students don't let me forget to continue *Lupita Mañana*. I have yet to hear any reactions that might indicate similar experiences from my students' lives, but I may eventually.

Literature Study with Picture Books

Mary read her chapter-length literature study book to her students, but younger children can do literature studies with picture books, too. Bishop and Hickman (1992) define a picture book as "a picture storybook, a fiction book with a dual narrative, in which both the pictures and the text work interdependently to tell a story" (p. 2). Picture books usually have pictures on each page, and the text is usually quite limited.

Laura had the opportunity of doing literature studies in the first-grade classroom where she did her final student teaching. The teacher had four different sets of picture books for the children. Laura describes the procedure she followed:

> On Monday we would introduce the four books with a brief book talk on the rug and let the kids look through all four choices later at their reading table time. The kids would write a big number one and the title of their first choice on one side of a small slip of paper and a two and their second choice on the other side. On Tuesday, the new groups would be announced and in groups we'd read through the stories together. Tuesday night they'd read their book choice books at home with someone special. On Wednesday we'd discuss who they read with and discuss interesting, sad, funny parts and go back into the story to share these places. Wednesday night they read the books at home again and wrote in their literature logs. On Thursday, the students shared their literature logs, going back into the story to illustrate their points. Friday was reserved for sharing journals and talking about anything they wanted concerning their books.

Alicia, the bilingual second-grade teacher mentioned earlier, described still another variation on a literature study that was her own invention:

> This experience (a literature study) was very beneficial to me, so I decided to try it with my Spanish readers. One group chose *Los tres chivos testarudos* (*The Three Stubborn Goats—Three Billy Goats Gruff*) and the second group chose *Los tres cerditos* (*The Three Little Pigs*). First I gave them time to read the book by themselves or with a partner if they wished to do so. Secondly, I met with them and asked them one at a time to tell me what they thought about the book. I had very little response so I asked them to talk together about the book. Third, I had them read the book aloud

Contrast between Literature Study Sessions and "High Level" Reading Comprehension Sessions   Carole Edelsky

Literature Study Session	"High Level" Reading Comprehension Session
General Characterization	General Characterization
Grand conversation	Gentle inquisition
More like an adult book group	More like a classroom reading group
Community of learners	Individual learners
Teacher Activity	Teacher Activity
Teacher participates	Teacher facilitates
Teacher asks questions to increase own comprehension text	Teacher asks questions to check up on students' comprehension
Teacher assumes comprehension	Teacher checks up on comprehension
Role of text	Role of text
Open the book (and let's investigate	Close the book (and see what's remembered)

Figure 12-12 Edelsky checklist

because some of them wanted to do it. Later the same day, they wrote an entry in their journals. The next day they made an accordion book retelling the story in their own words. As a culminating project, they are going to act out the story.

The books Alicia and Laura used with their young students were more traditional picture books. Quite a few picture books are also available that would be especially good for discussion of diverse cultures and customs. If teachers of younger children wanted to try literature studies with some of them, the activity could lead to interesting discussions about how people are the same and how they are different. For example, they could begin by reading *People* (Spier 1980) and *We Are All Alike: We Are All Different* (1991). Then students could choose from any of a number of books. Appendix G includes a number of picture books that are excellent for discussions of diversity.

Picture books can also be used effectively with older second language students. Care should be taken that the content and pictures represent the reality of more mature readers, but many books have been published that meet that criterion. An excellent book that gives suggestions for using these kinds of materials with older students is *Beyond Words: Picture Books for Older Readers and Writers* (Benedict and Carlisle 1992).

Certainly, there are many other books that would help students and teachers develop new perspectives on cultures. For more reading on literature studies we recommend *Grand Conversations* (Peterson and Eeds 1990), and for further reading on teaching multicultural literature, *Teaching Multicultural Literature in Grades K–8* (Harris 1992).

The thing to remember in implementing literature studies is that they are adaptable. The procedure for doing a literature study should not be so routine that it becomes formulaic. In fact, the best thing about a literature study is that students are excited about reading and about discussing what they have read. As they do this, they become more sophisticated readers and learn about the author's craft.

A helpful guide for teachers wanting to do literature studies and make them different from the more traditional way of checking readers' comprehension is the contrast provided by Edelsky (1988) between "Literature Study Sessions and 'High-Level' Reading Comprehension Sessions" (see Figure 12-12). Teachers can use this chart as a checklist for any variations on literature studies that they try with their students.

Conclusion

Teachers who adopt an intercultural orientation find ways to incorporate students' languages and cultures into the school program. They adopt interactive pedagogical approaches and take an advocacy-oriented approach to assessment. An intercultural orientation can open communication between the world of school and the world of the community. In the next chapter we turn to the important issue of working with parents and other community members to promote a positive societal context for education.

Applications

1. Read over the characteristics of successful schools working with Hispanic students. Discuss in small groups where your own school stands in relation to these criteria. Are all of the suggestions in the Lucas study appropriate for your school setting?

2. Sharma and José Luis, Patricia, and Guillermo got support from groups outside of school (church, friends, language classes). Consider your case study student or any second language learner you know. Does that person have support outside of school? What is it? Discuss with a partner or small group.

3. Read over what label quests and meaning quests are. In your teaching in the next week try to be aware when you use these. How do your second language learners respond to them?

4. Heath talks about the importance of four genres: recounts, accounts, eventcasts, and stories. In interest-level groups (elementary, middle school, secondary, adult, EFL) discuss how students in your classes are expected to use these genres.

5. Discuss with three other people a unit and/or materials that would support an intercultural orientation.

6. Bring to class an adult book (fiction or nonfiction) that you have read that informed you about another culture. Do a book talk in a group about your book.

7. Bring a literature book appropriate for your students that supports an intercultural orientation. Share the book with a group.

CHAPTER THIRTEEN

How Can Schools Involve Parents?

T eachers have been heard to say the following:

"The problem is these parents. They just don't care about their child's education."

"There is no parent participation. They don't come to Open House. I know one parent that didn't even come to his son's graduation!"

"The parents don't even want to learn English! No wonder their kids aren't learning. How can I communicate with them?"

"What have the parents been teaching them at home? They don't even know their numbers or colors!"

And the parents respond:

"I only had two years of school in a *pueblo*. How can I tell the teacher anything?"

"In my country the teacher is very respected. In my country teachers don't like parents to interfere."

"I can't understand anything that anyone says anyway. Why should I go to school meetings?"

"We work very hard and long hours to get food on the table. Anyway, we don't have anything to say to the teacher."

"My son asked me not to attend his graduation. He said it was because I wouldn't understand and would be bored, but I know it is because he is ashamed of me."

"Teachers come up to me and shout. They are so rude! I can't understand English. Shouting doesn't help!"

"No quiero que mi hijo hable español en la escuela. Yo quiero que él aprenda hablar inglés bien." ("I don't want my son to speak Spanish in school. I want him to learn to speak English well.")

These quotes are typical, and they reflect the misunderstandings and frustrations of both teachers and parents. However, we know of schools where these kinds of comments are being made less and less frequently. At these schools, teachers, counselors, administrators, and other personnel have adopted an intercultural orientation. They encourage community participation, and they develop effective programs to involve parents of second language students. As Cummins (1989) points out, when schools take an intercultural orientation, they promote positive relationships between the school and the community. By doing this, schools create a supportive societal context for the education of students between worlds. In this chapter we look at some of the ways schools and teachers have been able to work successfully with parents of second language students.

"Second Language Parents Just Don't Care"

Some of the teachers' remarks indicate that parents of bilingual students are indifferent. Why do so many teachers feel that second language parents don't care?

Our basic assumption is that all parents want their children to be successful. However, some parents of second language students are so busy dealing with their own problems that they do not appear to show interest in their children's lives. Juan Medina's parents, for example, are faced with the struggles of everyday living. Their work is not stable, and they have to move frequently, so Juan has attended a number of different schools. The kinds of problems Juan's family faces makes it difficult for them to find the time or energy to involve themselves in his schooling. Tou, the

Hmong student, comes from an immigrant family that has suffered greatly because of the move from Southeast Asia to the United States. Tou's parents have separated, and he lives with his father who cannot find work and does not speak English. His father only came to school for a conference at the request of school personnel. He would probably not voluntarily come to parent meetings. The three teens from El Salvador live by themselves. Their only relative in the United States is an aunt. She is a wife, a graduate student, and teaches Spanish at both the university where she studies and at the local community college. Like Tou's father, she would come to a school meetings, but only if a serious problem arose.

Parents of second language students like Juan and Tou realize that school may be the only road to success for their children. Yet they do not know how to help them succeed, especially if they do not speak English and have had very little schooling themselves. Even if they have had an education, it may have been in a school system very different from the system in this country. Because of their previous experiences, second language parents' expectations of schools and their attitudes toward teachers may differ considerably from the expectations and attitudes of mainstream parents. As a result the parents may give the impression that they don't care even when they really are very concerned.

So it is not surprising when teachers conclude that parents of bilingual students aren't interested in what happens with their children in school. Teachers who criticize parents for not trying to learn English and for not spending more time with their children, however, may not realize how difficult it is for immigrant parents to adjust to life in a new country, to understand our school system, and to comprehend the expectations schools have of parents.

Our own family's experiences while living in Mexico have helped us to more fully appreciate the problems language-minority parents face. When we first moved to Mexico City with two children in elementary school, we did not realize how difficult this change would be for all of us. Everything took longer. Simple errands could never be done easily. Day-to-day living became a real challenge. In addition, even though we are both teacher educators and had quite a bit of travel experience, we were often bewildered by the school system our children were in. Teachers at our children's school must have concluded that we just weren't interested.

Two experiences stand out. About a month after their bilingual Spanish/English school had started, our first grader, Mary, brought home an invitation to her class's Spanish *asemblea* (assembly). Each class gave one asemblea in English and one in Spanish yearly. On the invitation was glued a magazine picture of a Native American in an elaborate buckskin outfit complete with headdress and bow and arrow. Both of us asked Mary about her part in the asemblea. She was a bit confused. She knew her friend Erica was to be a Spanish dancer. Mary said she was going to be a Native American Indian and that she needed a costume. We thought that was a bit strange, but we rummaged around our closets and put together a long colorful skirt and a peasant blouse.

We arranged our schedules to attend the event and thought little more about it until the day before the assembly when we received a telephone call from the director of the school. Mary was in her office in tears. The director coldly asked us about Mary's costume. We explained what we had in mind, but the director said that it would definitely not do. The school had, after all, sent a picture of what the costume must look like several weeks before! We were shocked. To find a costume like that in Mexico

City at this late date was going to be impossible. Besides, we did not consider the expense involved as justified, and we were uncomfortable with the stereotyping of the costume anyway.

The situation did turn out all right for Mary. Fortunately, another child slated to be a Native American Indian was unable to attend, and he loaned Mary his costume. It really did look like the picture. His parents had bought the material and hired a seamstress to make the buckskin outfit. However, the school personnel knew that we hadn't provided the costume ourselves, and they began to think that we were negligent parents.

Another incident with our kindergarten-aged daughter, Ann, convinced them they were correct. We had arrived in Mexico City in December, so just two months later, in February, Valentine's Day was being celebrated. Ann came home at 5:00 P.M. and told us that she needed red velvet paper, glitter, glue, and shiny red paper for school the next day. We could not imagine a teacher asking for all those supplies at the last minute, and anyway, we had no idea where we would get them. Ann was insistent, but we were equally so. The next morning Ann complained that she had a terrible stomachache and could not go to school. When we pursued this with questions, she burst into tears and told us the teacher would get very mad at her if she came without her supplies, and she was scared to go to school. We let her stay home, asked neighbors about where to buy what she needed—we discovered the world of the *papelería* (paper supply store)—and vowed to inform ourselves better in the future.

The only reason that we were not totally labeled as terrible parents by the school personnel and the other parents at that school was that Yvonne began to work at the school the children attended. Because she was there, she could ask questions and see for herself what was needed for our two daughters. However, there were many differences in expectations including uniform requirements, the need for parent signatures on homework, the purchase of many supplies and mandatory gifts for teachers and administrators. Few of the people at the school ever understood our early confusions even when we tried to explain them later. Our worlds were different, and they had trouble accepting that their world was not the only real and reasonable one.

Reaching Out to Parents

Our own experiences have helped us understand the gulf that can exist between parents' beliefs about school and school's expectations of parents. Even when parents really do care, they may do things that lead teachers and other school personnel to conclude that they do not. The community and the school can really be two different worlds. What can teachers and other school personnel do to bridge the gap?

One way teachers can begin to understand the world of their immigrant students is to visit their homes. Several school districts have made it mandatory for teachers to visit their students in their homes either before school starts or at the end of the first grading period.

Kristi was in her first year of teaching when she visited her students' homes at the end of the first grading period. Before she went, she complained about the time and effort it was going to take. Afterwards, however, she realized how much she had learned. Her students' homes were modest, located around the small farming commnity where she teaches. She came away from each visit with respect for both the parents and the children. She saw that many parents were struggling to get food on the table for their children. She found out that many of her first-grade children often took on responsibilities at home, while parents and older siblings worked extra hours to make ends meet. Perhaps what touched her most, however, was the eagerness and respect with which she was received in the homes and the interest, pride, and hope the parents showed for their children's futures.

Even when it is not a school requirement, several teachers we work with have made home visits because this has helped them understand their students and parents so much better. Peter sends an introductory letter to all the children and their parents two weeks before school starts. He tells them in the letter he will be visiting their home to get to know them in the following week. Then he makes short visits to as many homes as possible. Even though he does not speak the first languages of many of his students, he is welcomed into the homes and has a chance to see something of his students' home life. He has found that those visits have made a big difference for students during their first days of school and that parents are much more comfortable with both him and the school. The visits have often given him ideas about how parents can become involved in his class. One parent, for instance, played a musical instrument, and another did wood carving. Peter would never have known this had he not been in the students' homes, and since the parents have met him, they are more responsive to his invitations to come and share their skills. The personal contact before school even starts has made a big difference for Peter in the home-school relationship.

Home visits are one important way for teachers to develop a greater understanding of their students. In addition, teachers can attend community cultural celebrations to learn about the traditions and beliefs of the parents of second language students. Ouk (1993) has suggested other ways that teachers can gain valuable information about their students' backgrounds: One is through the study of traditional proverbs. Ouk has analyzed Cambodian proverbs to show how they help form student and parent attitudes toward "proper" behavior at school. These two Cambodian proverbs with Ouk's commentary provide clear examples of the importance of Ouk's suggestion:

> "When not invited, it is not appropriate to attend; when not asked, it is not proper to answer." Educators need to understand the diversity in the Cambodian community and employ multiple strategies for reaching out and communicating with parents. Some parents may respond to written notices; others may need to receive a follow-up telephone call or a home visit by school staff members. If parents are expected to be at a school event, it is important that they be *invited* to participate. A simple notification may not convey the importance of their attending.

> "Silence is better than speech." Americans believe in freedom of speech; Cambodians believe in freedom of silence. Silence is a sign of humility and deference, a way to show one's respect for others (p. 5).

By making the effort to visit parents at home, to attend cultural celebrations, and to study cultural beliefs, teachers and other school personnel take an intercultural orientation. Rather than trying to change parents, teachers can work with them. This attitude can lead to greater parent involvement in schools.

Working with Parents

Another way to provide a link between the immigrant community and the schools is to offer adult ESL and first language literacy programs to parents. However, even when parents can get to school, it is often difficult for them to concentrate because of the many other concerns and responsibilities they have. In addition, their attendance is often sporadic at best as job opportunities, family illnesses, and child care responsibilities must take priority.

Steve, an adult ESL teacher, was well aware of the fact that his students needed English, but they also needed to cope with many problems as they adjusted to a new country and culture. He decided to adopt a method that would enable his students to learn English in the process of discussing the problems they faced.

Problem Posing

Steve was teaching beginning English to Southeast Asian immigrants living in the inner city when he first read about Freire's idea of problem posing (Freire 1970). Freire had developed this method for teaching reading to peasants in Brazil. Steve also read how Wallerstein (1987) had adapted Freire's idea to teaching adult ESL, and he decided to try it with his students. Steve began by asking the students to list some of their problems. During the course of the discussion, the topic of inadequate housing came up several times. Almost all the Southeast Asian students lived in large apartment complexes, and the apartments had many defects.

When Freire developed problem posing, he brought pictures of peasants' homes into the classroom to get students to talk about their living conditions. The pictures, which Freire calls "codes," serve as a catalyst to help the peasants identify problems. Steve didn't have pictures, so he asked his students to draw a picture of the problems they had and to label the problems in English. Chao's picture shows that a sink with no plug and cockroaches were very serious problems for him and his family (see Figure 13-1). Kong identified many problems including a sink with no plug, children running and yelling, no air conditioner, a broken window, a leaking roof needing a canvas to cover it, a broken door, a stove with a broken burner, a plugged-up shower head, and a broken (extinct!) coil in the oven (see Figure 13-2).

Steve decided his students' drawings could be the codes for class discussion. The discussion was lively, and both Steve and his students began to talk not only about the problems, but also the solutions. Steve then had his students identify one specific complaint, consider why it was troublesome, what caused it, and what could be done about it. Solutions included talking to the landlord, contacting the owner, writing a letter, and as the next example shows, moving. Kia and her husband Txong, Mien people from Laos, wrote about their problem and their solution together (see Figure 13-3). It is interesting that these beginning ESL students with no first language literacy were able to understand and answer the first three questions though they were confused about number four. In addition, their solution is clear.

For Steve's students, problem posing served as a way for them to increase their English and also to solve real-world problems at the same time. The vocabulary they were learning was meaningful and important to them. Problem posing is a method of teaching ESL that is consistent with an intercultural orientation and an explorer image of teaching and learning. Using this method, Steve's students learned English as he

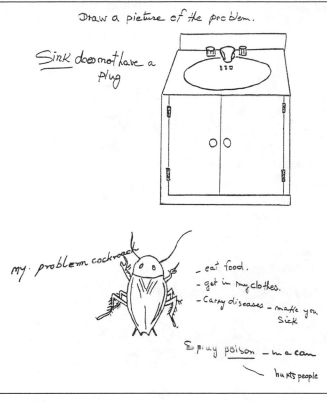

Draw a picture of the problem.

Sink does not have a Plug

my problem cockroach
- eat food.
- get in my clothes.
- Carry diseases - make you sick

Spray poison - in a can
hurts people

Figure 13-1 Chao problem posing

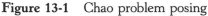

sink does not have plug
children run and yell
"sink"

Very hot air conditioner was broken.

The window broken →
hourse canvas
canvas hourse

The door broken

The stove not good
it broken

The shower head plug

The heating coil extinct
oven

rack
heating coil

Figure 13-2 Kong problem posing

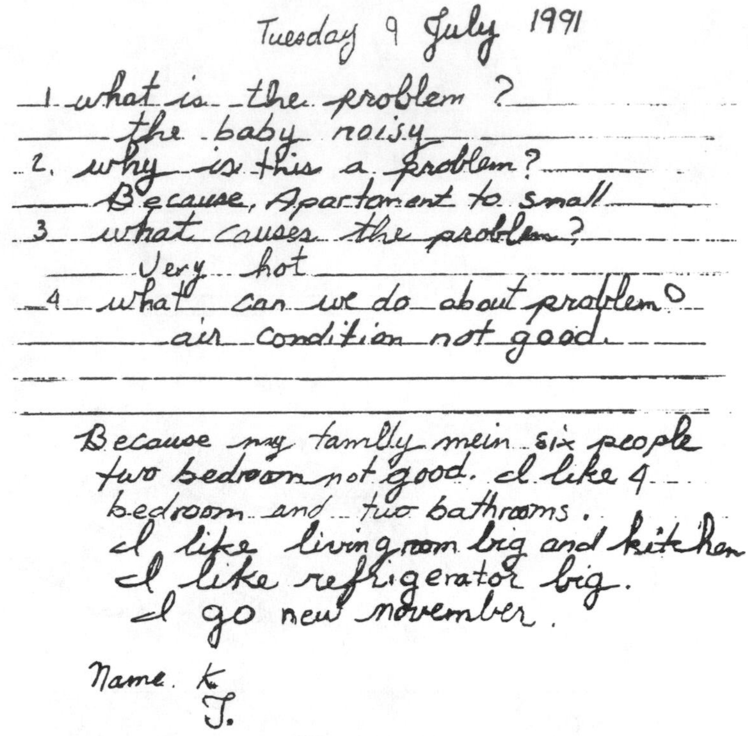

Tuesday 9 July 1991

1 what is the problem ?
    the baby noisy
2. why is this a problem?
    Because, Apartoment to small
3 what causes the problem?
    Very hot
4 what can we do about problem
    air condition not good.

Because my family mein six people
two bedroom not good. I like 4
bedroom and two bathrooms.
I like living room big and kitchen
I like refrigerator big.
I go new november.

Name. K.
      J.

Figure 13-3   Kia and Txong problem and solution

helped them cope with the daily problems of living that they faced as they adjusted to a new culture.

Because of the hardships they face, immigrant parents may find it difficult to attend classes. Some districts have solved this by offering ESL and literacy classes to adults at the same location where their children attend school. Classes may be held either during regular school hours or after school. When they study at their children's school, parents begin to feel more comfortable there and are more willing to participate in classroom activities or attend parent meetings.

In addition, these programs for parents serve two purposes. They not only provide ESL and primary-language literacy to parents, but this education enables parents to help their children with school-related activities. Parents who are not literate themselves can learn how to encourage their children to read and write at home. In the same way that Steve was able to teach English through the meaningful content of daily living problems, these programs teach both English and first language literacy through a focus on parenting skills. Three types of literacy programs are available in California for second language parents.

FELP Programs

The Family English Literacy Program (FELP), funded by Title VII, Office of Bilingual Education and Minority Languages Affairs, U.S. Department of Education, is de-

| | Component | | |
Theme	Adult literacy	Cultural orientation	Family literacy
family	personal information, health, food, housing, safety	family activities, health and nutrition, nuturing environment	family histories, multicultural stories, storytelling
school	schools, day-care centers	school orientation, parent participation, helping with homework	holidays around the world, holiday arts and crafts
community	jobs, post office, telephone, transportation, library, stores and shops	community resources, library, health and social services	field trips to library, reading to children
language of instruction	English, native language support	native language, sheltered content instruction	sheltered content instruction, native language
instructional time	four hours per week	two hours biweekly	two hours biweekly

Figure 13-4   Themed parent program

signed to help language-minority parents acquire language and literacy and, at the same time, learn parenting skills (California 1990). In addition, FELP classes help parents adapt to their new culture with instruction on topics such as nutrition, health and safety, and the U.S. education system. The FELP programs are intergenerational, so students and parents work together during the classes on literacy-related activities. Parents are shown how to encourage their children to talk and write about books and tell stories. In some programs, only English is spoken, and in others, English and the parents' and students' native languages are used.

One especially interesting FELP program in Sacramento City Unified School District has had tremendous success with many different ethnic groups but especially with Southeast Asian parents (Holt 1993). The project was set up to provide six hours per week of classes in English literacy, cultural orientation, and family literacy at two different school sites. One school served only Hmong speakers, and the other served Cantonese, Hmong, Khmer, Mandarin, Mien, Spanish, Ukranian, and Vietnamese parents.

The curriculum for the project was determined by extensive surveying done in native languages. This needs assessment provided the FELP staff with three major themes: home, school, and community. The adult literacy component had parents work together in groups, in pairs, and as individuals to develop both oral and written language related to each theme. In the cultural orientation component, speakers from different agencies, including the county health department and the police department, gave presentations on topics within the three themes. Parents and children participated together in the family literacy component in field trips, arts and crafts, cooking, storytelling, and reading. Figure 13-4 is a chart that outlines the three themes, the topics, the language of instruction, and the instructional time.

The team for the Sacramento project worked hard on parent recruitment, sending out fliers in different languages, presenting school programs in native languages, and making phone calls and home visits. In addition, local media and adult education programs were notified. However, as Holt explained, "Perhaps the most effective recruitment strategy is done by class participants who encourage other family members or friends to attend the classes" (p. 19).

Teachers and teaching assistants for FELP were chosen from people who were already working at the school sites. Staff involved with the project also had to be fluent in one of the native languages of the project participants. Therefore, because teachers were from the school and spoke the participants' first languages, they provided an important bridge between the parents, the school, and the children. The results were worth the effort needed for this project. Ninety-nine families participated in the 1992–93 project, far exceeding the expected sixty!

Even Start Programs

The Even Start Program, funded under Chapter 1, Compensatory Education, U.S. Department of Education, also provides both adult literacy and training for parents (Ramírez 1990). This program is only for parents and children from preschool through second grade. Parents involved in the program must need English and/or basic skills for employment. In the Even Start Program the goals are to help parents (1) become aware of their role as their children's first teacher; (2) help their children practice and develop school/life-related skills; (3) motivate their children; (4) develop ways to support their children's reading; (5) help their children with homework; (6) ensure the basics for learning, including basic nutrition, sleep, and a place to study; (7) strengthen and improve communication with their children and with teachers; and (8) develop parenting skills.

An important feature of the Even Start Program is that training and planning time is also provided for staff and teachers in the school. Teachers are given insights on how to improve parent-teacher communication, how to validate the parents' role as teachers of their children, and how to conduct training and/or meetings for parents. Special emphasis in the program is given to showing nonliterate parents what they can do to support their children by engaging them in extended dialogue, telling them stories, listening to them read, and asking their children questions. In addition to these educational supports, the program offers child care for parents and referral services for other needs.

The Migrant Education Office of Fresno County has involved sixteen rural schools in a Home-School Partnership Kindergarten Readiness Program using Even Start funding (Loya 1993). Four teachers and two instructional assistants provide services to ninety-two children and ninety-six parents. Parents are instructed weekly in English literacy and given parenting strategies including helping their children with reading in Spanish. Under the supervision of project staff, parents practice the strategies with their children at the school site and at home. Loya explains how the program draws on strengths the parents already have: "Parents are encouraged to tell stories to their children and introduce them to literature. Staff emphasize the value of the families' native language and culture in strengthening the children's preparation for school" (p. 30). As Loya points out, programs such as these succeed because educators and parents work together "to improve their respective abilities and to support the children" (p. 29).

Individual District Literacy Programs

Individual school districts have also developed effective plans for developing parent literacy to help children in schools. For example, in San Bernardino, California, Father Ray Rosales worked with Spanish-speaking parents using the Spanish language version of Systematic Training for Effective Parenting (STEP), Padres Eficaces con Entrenamiento Sistemático (PECES) (Naso and Mirande 1990). The STEP program is designed to improve family relationships and help children to become responsible and confident. The Spanish PECES program is meant to help build a bridge "between traditional Latino parenting styles and American, democratic familial norms" (p. 13). Though the main goals of the program were to help Latino parents and children communicate in a foreign culture, other benefits came out of the classes. Because the process of arriving at better communication involved sharing and role playing, parents made new, close friends. They shared information with one another about community services, adult vocational and ESL classes, meeting with teachers, volunteering at school, and seeking employment. Parents' self-esteem was raised as they became more confident and assertive through the mutual support of the others in the classes.

All three types of parent programs strengthen home-school relationships. They help parents develop their own English and literacy skills. In addition, these programs show parents how to help their children in school. Appendix H lists a number of resources for teachers or schools working with parents.

Trust Parents to Help

> Parents from every culture need to know that you care, respect, and value their families and are doing your best to educate their children for success.

This was written by Cándida, Eugenia's bilingual kindergarten teacher. She was responding to her reading and class discussion about parents and how to involve them. A key to involving parents is to trust them to help. This may sound simplistic, but it is too often the case that teachers or other school personnel decide that parents cannot help when they really can.

In fact, a misconception about non-English-speaking parents is that they cannot help their children because they do not speak English. One of the worst recommendations that has come from schools in the past is "Speak English at home." This advice not only negates the value of the students' first languages and the importance of family discussions for building concepts, but it effectively cuts off important family communication to build relationships. Hispanic parents, for example, have been known to feel guilty if they speak to their children in Spanish, so they encourage their children to watch television instead of talking to them. Richard Rodriguez' *Hunger of Memory* is a poignant account of a family silenced and divided as they try to follow school personnel's advice to "speak English."

In Chapters 8 and 9 we stressed the importance of first language support in schools for academic success. Though parents may ask themselves how they can help when they do not speak English, what children need to learn are ideas, concepts, and processes, and it does not matter in which language they learn these things (Cummins 1989; Krashen 1985). Parents should teach their children about the world. Once children understand ideas, form values, and solve problems in their first language, they transfer those basic understandings to their second language. When parents are encouraged to talk to their children and read and write with them in their first language at home, children build important first language background that leads to school success. Parents can support their children's school success in the following ways:

1. Talking—Parents who play with their children and have conversations with them are helping them to think and to explore their world. In this process children learn to use language for a variety of functions.

2. Reading—Parents who read with their children and take them to the library are giving their children experiences with books that they need for school success. If parents are not confident readers, they can ask their children to do the reading, or parents and children can follow a story while listening together to a tape-recorded reading.

3. Writing—Parents who encourage their children to draw and write are beginning to teach their children to express themselves in writing. Parents can also make children aware that adults use writing for a variety of purposes every day, including writing letters, making out checks, jotting notes, and making shopping lists.

Teachers need to trust that parents will engage in talking, reading, and writing with their children. Goldenberg and Gallimore (1991) worked over several years on a project to improve reading achievement of Spanish-speaking children. One of the aspects of the study included parent involvement. The teachers at the school where the research was conducted were very hesitant about parent involvement because they believed that there was no literacy in the home, that parents were not interested in the children's achievements, and that because of their minimal academic background, parents could not help their children. Goldenberg and Gallimore found these assumptions to be false:

> Although literacy did not occupy a prominent place in most homes, it was not entirely absent. Virtually all homes, for example, sent and received letters to Mexico or Central America. All homes received printed flyers or advertisements. . . . Most parents reported (and subsequent studies have confirmed) that children consistently asked about signs, other "environmental print," or the contents of letters to or from relatives. None of this would be possible if literacy did not exist in the homes, at least at some level (pp. 8, 9).

In interviews with parents, Goldenberg and Gallimore found that parents "saw themselves as playing a key role in their children's school success, particularly while their children were young" (p. 9). In addition, when asked, parents expressed great interest in helping their students at home though many "expressed fear of confusing their children" because they were "unfamiliar with 'the system' here" (p. 9).

The researchers found that "although the overall educational levels of parents were indeed low," most of the parents could read books with limited text and several were able to read quite well (p. 8). Despite the doubts of teachers about the parents' ability to help their children, story books and other literacy materials were sent home with the children. Some teachers developed activities for parents to do with their children at home that would reinforce what was being done in the classroom. These activities were similar to the *tarea* (homework) that parents were familiar with from their native countries. Some of the activities were actually quite fragmented. However, the important finding from this study was that parents did get involved. They wanted to help their children at home, and they *could* help them.

Pulling Parents In

Reaching out to parents through activities such as home visits often helps parents develop a positive attitude toward schools. Working with parents through ESL and family literacy programs improves parents' own skills and increases their ability to help their children succeed in school. However, school personnel must take additional steps to pull parents in and involve them actively in school events. Parents of second language students may attend ESL or family literacy classes, but often they do not attend school meetings, school functions, or parent-teacher conferences. This pattern can be changed. Carolina, a bilingual teacher discussed earlier, offered the following:

> As bilingual teachers, we are often frustrated by conditions which we *perceive* as being unchangeable. For instance, our site's Parent/Faculty Club has been frustrated by the fact that our Hispanic parents do not actively participate in the Fall Carnival or in the Spring Chicken Barbecue Sale. Why should parents come when they can't understand the meeting's agenda or when they feel uncomfortable because we're having to whisper our translations? Why not have the meeting conducted in two different languages for part of the time so that both groups can meet and share their results? I believe our English language parents would be surprised as to how our Hispanic parents will respond.

Unfortunately, Carolina's scenario of Hispanic parents feeling uncomfortable and not part of the meeting is not uncommon. Tammy, a relatively new teacher, writes about a parent meeting she attended in another farming community with a high Hispanic population:

> I walked in and took a seat at what would be my first experience at attending a Parent-Teacher Association meeting. As I sat down, I observed the Association president sitting next to last year's president, two white, middle-class women. I watched as three more women of the same type came and took their usual seats. I sat, feeling a little strange to not see any Hispanics, especially since the school is at least 90% Hispanic. Then, four Hispanic women came in escorted by one of our bilingual teachers. What a relief! The four "new" women spoke only Spanish and were looked on by the others as "out of place." In fact, one of the regular attendees (a middle-class Oriental woman) walked in late and turned around to leave because the sight of the Hispanics at the meeting led her to believe that she was in the wrong place.

Fortunately, some districts have found ways to involve parents. In a school district near Tammy's that has an equally high Hispanic population, two different school sites have held bilingual parent meetings in the evening. At both schools, the meetings were well publicized. Emphasis was given to the fact that the presentations would be in both Spanish and English and that the speakers would discuss ways parents could help their students succeed. In both cases, teachers and administrators were overwhelmed by the response of the Hispanic parents. In fact, Hispanic parents outnumbered Anglo parents ten to one. Both meetings were so crowded that there was standing room only. At one site the meeting was held on Back to School Night, and the principal announced it was the best-attended Back to School Night the school had ever had!

Parents get involved when schools take specific actions to include them. Kay is a resource teacher in a district with a high Hispanic population. In the past, the district did little to include minority parents, but recently district administrators have made parent involvement a priority. The district commitment has extended to hiring experienced bilingual teachers like Kay to work with parents. When Kay started working for the district, she observed that Hispanic parents were left out of parent organization events. The Anglo parents complained that "those parents" did not want to help, but the Anglos never made an effort to include them.

Kay initiated an event that she thought would be of particular interest to Hispanic parents. The Mexican-American farmworkers in the small community always celebrated the Cinco de Mayo (Fifth of May), so Kay decided to have an all-school Cinco de Mayo celebration. She called a meeting of Spanish-speaking parents to discuss a Cinco de Mayo school celebration and promised to conduct the meeting bilingually. When only Spanish-speaking parents showed up, she talked about her idea in Spanish and asked them what they thought. They were very enthusiastic. They offered to bring food, to teach the students how to perform traditional dances, and to decorate the school.

Kay admits that she was nervous that first year. Others at the school, including the administration, were skeptical about whether the parents could be counted on to help, but they did agree to set aside a day for the activities once Kay showed them the plans she and the parents had developed. Kay spent long hours coordinating the activities, and the results were fantastic. Hundreds of migrant families attended the all-day celebration, which included dancing, singing, crafts, and a huge lunch. Almost all the parents contributed something, and many took on the role of teachers of their culture as they instructed whole classes in art and music. The day was so successful that it became an annual school and community event.

Lisa helps coordinate the Migrant Education program in a large urban district. Migrant Education helped Southeast Asian parents, who historically had never participated, become empowered and involved. In order to receive Migrant Education funds, the district is mandated to hold at least six council meetings yearly with representatives from each school. The Migrant Education staff organized these school-site meetings. They provided translators so that parents could raise concerns. Having translators at these meetings allowed the Asian parents to gain a stronger voice in district decisions. Further, the Migrant staff encouraged parents to seek solutions by working with school personnel. In just three years, there has been a tremendous difference in parent participation and empowerment. Lisa reports an example of how parents are taking the responsibility for initiating change:

> We are finding more and more parents initiating meetings at their schools without our help or involvement. An example of this was when a Southeast Asian parent typed an invitation to the district superintendent inviting him, administrators, teachers, and parents from his school to a luncheon at his house. The purpose of this meeting was to bring together the diverse cultures at the school (Marasco 1993, p. 17).

An additional benefit of these school-site meetings has been increased communication between Southeast Asians and Hispanics, groups who had previously resisted working together:

> Another positive outcome from this council is that with the help of translators I have also seen the Hispanic and Southeast Asian parents come *together* to brainstorm solutions to their concerns. At the last meeting our Southeast Asian president and Hispanic vice-president expressed a belief that all our children have to learn to live peacefully with one another and their role as parents is to model this (Marasco 1993, p. 17).

Agencies like Migrant Education can provide the resources districts need to develop effective parent programs. Other sources of help are also available. Linda works in a rural school district with a high Hispanic population. Her school wrote a grant that will allow them to reach out to parents more effectively:

> One of our major priorities will be to create a parent center at our school, staffed with a bilingual person who can offer services to parents and provide a place where parents can find out about school policies and make them feel more in touch and in tune with our school.

Teachers and administrators at Linda's school have found additional ways to make parents feel welcome. For Back to School Night all the families were invited to bring a picnic and blankets. In the early evening students, parents, teachers, and administrators had dinner together on the lawn outside. After dinner, parents visited booths where they could find information in English or Spanish about the various programs at the school. Later, the parents met with individual teachers in the classrooms. Linda reported, "It was a huge success and the comment made most often was that the parents felt welcome and at ease at school."

At schools such as the ones we have described here, minority-parent involvement is a priority. Specific events and programs are planned to pull all the parents in, to make them feel welcome, and to give them a voice in decisions that affect their children. These schools send out a clear message to parents: "We want you to help us provide the best possible education for your children."

Getting Parents Involved in the Classroom

Schools can change community attitudes by reaching out to parents, working with parents, and pulling parents in to meetings and other school functions. In addition, a number of teachers have found ways to involve parents even more directly in daily classroom activities. For these teachers, parents of second language students are a valuable resource.

At Fipps Primary School in rural Riverdale, California, teachers instituted a plan to involve parents in their children's reading by starting a program they call "Book Bags." The idea was to find a way to get books into the homes. The teachers first collected a number of books. Then teachers and parent volunteers sewed the book bags using a heavy canvas material. They decorated them with an appliqué to represent each book. (For example, *The Little Red Hen* bag had an appliqué of a hen.) The teachers first shared books in Spanish or English in class and then put them inside one of the book bags for students to take home. They also put storytelling props, when appropriate, into the bags. These props helped the children share their books in different ways with their parents. Rojas (1993) describes the importance of the Book Bags project:

> Teachers decided that the best way to encourage literacy was to send home books that the parents and children could enjoy together on a daily basis. Without the opportunity to take books home daily, many of these students would not read at home due to the lack of materials. Besides the benefits for the kindergarten students, the book bags have also provided the preschool siblings of these students some of their first opportunities with books (p. 8).

Projects such as this one show that parents are interested in improving their children's literacy and that they are willing to help their children when the school provides them with the necessary resources.

Finding ways to involve bilingual parents can be a special challenge for teachers who are not bilingual themselves or who have students from several language backgrounds. Nevertheless, as the following examples show, the effort is well worth it.

Gayleen, a kindergarten teacher, set up a schedule for her bilingual parents to come into her first-grade classroom and participate in class events. She had children whose first languages included Spanish and several Southeast Asian languages. She was especially excited about the involvement of one husband-and-wife team. The father of a Spanish-speaking child agreed to come into the class and read books to Spanish-speaking children in Spanish. Gayleen encouraged the father to read the books in Spanish to the entire class. At first he was reluctant to do this, but when Gayleen let him choose the book ahead of time and take it home to practice first, both the father and the children had a positive experience with reading. The wife was not comfortable reading in Spanish, but she also wanted to do something in the classroom. Gayleen asked her to help with cooking and crafts and encouraged her to speak Spanish with the children as she did this. All of the students in Gayleen's class benefited from these experiences even though only a few spoke Spanish.

Sharon, a first-grade teacher, also wanted more of her parents to participate in the classroom. She knew that many non-English-speaking parents were reluctant to come to school because they did not speak English, and they did not really understand the school system. She decided to have community aides invite parents personally to a meeting, promising to have translators available.

On the night of the meeting, Sharon and the aides, who were able to speak Spanish, Lao, Mien, Hmong, and Khmer, waited anxiously for parents to arrive. Sharon describes what happened:

> The time came for the meeting and only two parents were there so I told the interpreters they could leave. Ten minutes later about ten more parents showed up and there were representatives of every language in my classroom! I visited around the room and discovered there was at least one parent from each different culture represented who could speak English. Each one of these became an interpreter for several new friends. At times you would hear them laughing together at things I said or they interpreted. They all seemed to have a great time sharing and laughing together. At the end of this meeting they decided they wanted to meet together on a regular basis. There were smiles on their faces and new friends made.

Sharon's parent group met about five times that year, working on strategies to help their children at home. Sharon showed them how she used big books, predictable books, journal writing, and themes, and through their sharing, the parents helped teach each other. They became active at school and helped with field trips and class activities. Working with this group was one of the most rewarding experiences Sharon had ever had. Parents from different language and culture groups worked together to learn, and because they helped each other and set the agenda themselves, they felt good about themselves and their involvement in school.

In each of these cases teachers believed that parents could and would help. Rather than accepting negative stereotypes of language-minority parents, these teachers took a positive view and found ways to utilize their talents.

Conclusion

Working effectively with parents has never been easy. When the cultural and linguistic backgrounds of teachers and parents differ, the challenge becomes even greater. Teachers are busy people, and establishing positive relationships with second language parents takes time and effort. The efforts are worthwhile, and individual teachers are greatly helped when the effort is schoolwide, supported by administrators, and often, by outside agencies or by funds and personnel supplied by grants.

Parent involvement fosters a positive relationship between the community and the school and helps create a supportive societal context for the schooling of students who move between worlds. The societal context strongly influences the educational context, and teachers and other school personnel must work to develop a supportive societal context. At the same time, teachers must continually refine their own practices to meet the needs of their students. In our final chapter we turn again to the school context as we consider ways teachers can reflect on and continually improve their educational practices through classroom-based research.

Applications

1. Group yourselves according to the age level of the students you are teaching or plan to teach. How can parents or other community members be involved at your school? If you teach adults in this country, how can you help adults feel more part of the schools their children attend or more part of the community in general? If you plan to teach EFL (English as a foreign language) in a foreign setting, discuss how different school systems affect expectations of what curriculum should look like.

2. Interview the parent or parents of a second language learner. Try to determine the parents' expectations for the student. Do they agree with what the school's goals are?

3. Review the three types of parent ESL/literacy projects described in this chapter. Have you seen any of these programs or programs similar to these used in schools? How did those programs work? Were there problems? Discuss with a small group, and then share your conclusions with the larger group.

BACK
IN
AGAIN

How Can Teachers Improve
Their Practice Through
Classroom-Based Research?

I work through the needs of limited English students a majority of my teaching (and nonteaching) day. The concerns and recommendation of the California Tomorrow report are fought out in the battleground of my classroom with parents, administrators, students, other teachers, and even in the confines of my own consciousness. But because of this, in the last year I have come to understand my best ammunition is in working *with* students, allowing group process/social interaction, increasing and refining comprehensible input for context-reduced academic tasks, letting students come to an understanding that they can achieve in their own way and time—providing a safe environment . . . and wrapping this in a format that celebrates students' personal experiences.

Rhoda, the teacher of our case study student Sharma, reflects here on how she works to improve schooling for her second language students. Teaching for Rhoda, and for many committed explorer teachers, extends well beyond the normal school day. She has read books like *Crossing the Schoolhouse Border* (Olsen 1988), a report put out by the organization California Tomorrow, that help inform her about her immigrant students. Rhoda has adopted an intercultural orientation and an exploratory teaching style. She has studied theories of language, learning, teaching, and curriculum. She has considered factors both inside and outside the school that affect her students who move between worlds. In the process, she has become a teacher researcher who can reflect on and refine her own practice in a continuous attempt to improve learning for all her students.

In this final chapter, we will look more closely at the idea of teacher research as a way to find context-specific solutions to the challenges of teaching English language learners. Teacher researchers are aware that in any situation a number of different factors interact to influence the school performance of second language students. These teachers reject single-cause explanations for the success or failure of their students. Through awareness of the world outside school, the societal context, and through reflection on their own teaching, the world inside school, teacher researchers attempt to discover practices that fit their particular situations and help all their students succeed.

Context-Free Interpretations of School Performance

Sue and Padilla (1986) point out that many explanations for minority group failure are context free. Such explanations are assumed to fit all situations and all students. Here are three context-free interpretations of school performance:

1. genetic inferiority
2. cultural deficit
3. cultural mismatch

Genetic Inferiority

An early context-free interpretation was genetic inferiority. Some people argued that certain minority groups do better than others because of genetic factors. This reason was offered in the past to explain, for example, the poor academic performance of African-American students. Unfortunately, this view has not entirely disappeared.

When a teacher in the teachers' lounge is overheard making a statement about second language students like "What can you expect from *those* students," that teacher is taking a context-free view and assuming that a whole category of students has little potential for success.

This genetic-inferiority perspective blames the minority group and precludes any solution, since hereditary factors can't be changed. While educators now reject such explanations, they may still use materials that were developed on the assumption that certain racial groups are inferior. A good example is Distar, a reading program developed especially for African Americans. For a critique of Distar, see Cummins (1989).

Cultural Deficit

Certain groups are also accused of having a cultural deficit. Comments like "What can you expect if you look at José's background?" or "There's no possibility of support for Mai at home. No one speaks English there, and there are no books or magazines at home" are examples of cultural-deficit attitudes. This puts the blame on students' home life and background rather than the students themselves.

Recently a supervisor wrote an evaluation of a student teacher in which he commended her for working "hard to challenge and reward her pupils, especially those with learning or cultural handicaps." The supervisor's positive comments about the student teacher revealed that he held a cultural-deficit view of her students who were mainly second language students. This is a stance that labels certain cultures as deficient and students who come from those cultures as handicapped.

A possible response to this interpretation of minority-group school performance would be to attempt to change what are regarded as deficient cultural conditions or practices. If, for example, it is assumed that parents in certain cultures don't read to children, then community reading programs might be instituted. Programs such as Headstart have been based on the assumption of a deficit model. These programs do not attempt to build on the strengths that learners and their families bring to the learning situation. Instead, they attempt to "cure" the "problems" that "deprived" students have in order to make them more like the mainstream population.

Cultural Mismatch

At times, rather than speaking of a cultural deficit, researchers have presented the idea of a cultural mismatch. Instead of blaming the culture as deficient, these researchers suggest that some minority groups experience school failure because of some incongruity between school and community. The term "mismatch" may refer to differences in the language of home and school or differences in how cultures typically interact. Sometimes, for example, Asian students are criticized for never speaking up in class and for not participating in school activities. People might say that in the Asian culture (as though there were just one Asian culture) it is a virtue to be quiet around adults and that Asian parents do not think it appropriate for their children to participate in school activities. Therefore, since school success requires students to volunteer answers, the mismatch between cultural and school norms leads to poor school performance.

While the term "cultural mismatch" is more positive than "cultural deficit," the underlying assumptions are usually the same. Something must be done to change the

I'm a Mexican-American
which I proudly exclaim!
I come from two worlds
Mexico and America.

At home, I can speak
Spanish, "¡Sí, como no!"
    or
English, if I please
That's bilingualism.

In my two worlds,
I can choose to eat
tortillas with chorizo
    or
eat white bread with ham.

I can listen to lively mariachi music
    or
listen to some jams.

In my two worlds
I can be a beautiful bronze brown
    or
anything in between!

I can have a name like Enrique
    or Guadalupe
which for the rest
can really be a test.

In my two worlds
I can find teachers,
lawyers, mechanics
and farmworkers.

I can hear many say,
"Get out of the two worlds
and come into one!"

BUT . . .

My worlds are so beautiful
I prefer and love to see
life through BOTH for
as long as I can
cause I'm proud to be who I am!

By Yolanda Shahbazian
Dedicated to Room 19
April 1989

Figure 14-1   Yolanda's poem

community so that students will be better prepared to follow mainstream school practices. For example, if students come from homes where children do not commonly answer known-information questions (label quests), schools may encourage parents to work with children to name objects and give their characteristics.

One example we have seen is when traditional Hispanic parents will not let their children go on school field trips. A possible response to cultural mismatch would be to change practices in both the community and the school rather than just trying to get parents to change. For example, a teacher might go to the home and explain to Hispanic parents the educational importance of the field trip in an effort to get permission for participation. At the same time, schools could invite Hispanic parents to accompany their children on the trips. Afterwards, parents and children could talk about the experience.

Yolanda, a fifth-grade bilingual teacher in a school serving rural students of Hispanic background, provided a still more positive response to the context-free cultural mismatch interpretation. Yolanda was concerned that several of her bilingual students did not want to engage in any activities in Spanish and were constantly saying "Why are we doing this in Spanish? Let's just do it in English." To help her students take pride in their culture and language, she wrote the poem in Figure 14-1.

Yolanda stressed that the difference between the two cultures did not constitute a deficit on the part of Spanish speakers. Further, she did not see the difference as a

Perspectives on Failure to Achieve and Possible Solutions
Sue and Padilla (1986, p. 42)

Perspective	Attribution of blame	Primary solutions
Genetic inferiority. Minorities fail to do well because they are genetically inferior.	The groups themselves, not society, are to blame.	No solutions are possible since little can be done to change heredity.
Cultural deficit. Minorities fail to do well because their culture is viewed as deficient.	The groups themselves, as well as social prejudice and discrimination, are to be blamed.	Train minorities to be less deficient and eliminate prejudice and discrimination.
Cultural mismatch. Minorities fail to achieve because their cultural traits are incompatible with those in the U.S. mainstream.	No one is to blame since cultures just happen to be different.	Change groups so that they can participate in the mainstream, but also change schools so they can better accommodate and ameliorate the mismatch.

Figure 14-2   Perspectives on failure

mismatch. Instead, she encouraged students to develop their potential in both languages and cultures.

A problem with context-free interpretations of school success or failure such as genetic inferiority, cultural deficit, or cultural mismatch is that these are single-cause explanations that are expected to apply to a wide range of situations. In contrast, Cortés' Contextual Interaction Model holds that a number of factors interact in any situation and that single-cause explanations are inadequate. Sue and Padilla (1986) summarize these different perspectives on failure, shown in Figure 14-2.

Context-Specific Interpretations

Díaz, Moll, and Mehan (1986) argue that context-free explanations do not lead to solutions to particular problems. Instead, teachers should look for context-specific answers. They claim that "at the heart of the context-specific approach is the study of the actual process of interaction between individuals and their environment, not just a measure of the products of interaction" (pp. 191–192). In other words, instead of measuring student success or failure by looking at test score results or the quality of papers students produce, Díaz, Moll, and Mehan argue that we should look at the actual interactions inside and, if possible, outside classrooms. As they explain, "In the study of any learning activity, the unit of analysis becomes the act or system of acts by which learning is composed, as seen in the context of the classroom, the school, and the community" (p. 192).

As an example of a context-specific approach, Díaz, Moll, and Mehan describe a case study they conducted involving third- and fourth-grade Spanish-speaking children's reading. They observed these students in two different contexts, a Spanish reading lesson and an English reading lesson. They noted a great discrepancy between the two. The Spanish teacher focused on comprehension, but the English teacher concentrated on having these same students decode sounds. The same students who functioned as proficient readers in one context were perceived as inadequate in the other. The authors use this example to show how student performance is influenced by the situation: "The context-specific view proposes that intelligence displays and language use are dependent on the circumstances and situations of their assessment. They are not general abilities that appear uniformly in all types of situations" (p. 196).

Díaz, Moll, and Mehan reported on how they changed factors in the context to alter the educational outcomes. For example, they assumed that the students' Spanish reading performance was more indicative of their true ability, so they conducted an English reading lesson that focused on comprehension rather than on decoding. Further, they allowed students to respond in Spanish during the discussion of the story they had read in English. These changes resulted in vastly improved English reading performance for the students. In fact, the researchers report that their approach represented "a three-year jump in participation in English reading" (p. 208).

The FELP and Early Start programs described in Chapter 13 are also attempts to find context-specific solutions when working with second language learners. In these programs, instead of the school deciding exactly how students and parents should change to fit into the mainstream mold, families are brought into the educational process. The programs address different factors that affect children's schooling. Parents are brought to school sites and encouraged not only to learn English, but also to enrich their own first language and then to participate in their children's education. Perhaps most important, participants are consulted about what they perceive as their needs, and sincere attempts are made to help them meet those needs.

Programs like FELP and Early Start are not based on the assumption that only one factor determines students' school success. Instead, administrators of these programs recognize that a number of factors come into play and that by changing some of these factors students are more likely to succeed. As a result of programs such as these, parents become more fluent in English. They improve their own first language literacy. They share their culture with their children and each other, and they learn how to help their children in school. Further, within these programs, parents also make new friends, build new support communities, and learn how to help each other. By changing these different factors, programs like FELP and Early Start alter patterns of interaction in an attempt to improve the educational performance of second language students.

A Contextual-Interaction Perspective

We return to a case study from Chapter 1 to make the point that a contextual-interaction perspective provides a more satisfactory analysis than does a context-free perspective. Robert is from a large Hmong family. His parents are refugees who have suffered displacement after the trauma of war. He has not shown any progress in English since entering school in kindergarten. He is extremely quiet in large groups and in small groups where he does not know all the participants.

Robert's academic performance could easily be explained by any of the context-free interpretations. It would not be surprising for his academic failure to be attributed to genetic inferiority ("Those Hmong are really primitive tribal people. You can't expect them to do well in school here. They can't really understand our complex society"), cultural deficit ("Hmong people have strange customs and beliefs. Children are not encouraged to talk much"), or cultural mismatch ("Hmong culture doesn't value school. All Hmong people get married young and have big families. Parents don't encourage education").

However, many factors influence Robert's future success or failure. Choosing one of the context-free perspectives to explain why Robert is not doing well presently would be a simplistic approach to a complex situation. Further, none of those perspectives offers a solution. A context-free interpretation also denies positive factors, such as the fact that Robert's father is literate in both Hmong and Laotian, he teaches his children to read and write Hmong, and both parents are supportive of the schools.

From a contextual-interaction perspective, several factors interact to influence Robert's performance. By changing one or more of these factors, it may be possible to improve his chances for success. Robert's teacher, Sharon, has begun to do this. She has identified strengths he has in art and is drawing him into classroom communication through supportive small groups. She is showing Robert that she believes in him and wants him to do well. By altering these aspects of the context, Sharon is increasing the possibility that Robert will achieve.

Conducting Case Studies to Develop Context-Specific Interpretations

Teachers who wish to understand the complex interaction of factors that affect the performance of their students benefit from conducting case studies such as the one Sharon did of Robert. Such studies take into account factors from both the world of the school and the world of the community outside school. The way that students interact with one another and with teachers, the students' and teachers' attitudes, expectations, and goals, as well as the attitudes and values of the community, all shape the outcomes of learning experiences for students between worlds.

Case studies can reveal possible courses of action teachers can take to change situations in which students are not succeeding. In the process of carrying out these studies, teachers become teacher researchers who analyze the effectiveness of the teaching strategies they use. Teacher research provides insights that enable teachers to modify their practices in ways that result in greater success for their students. Case studies of individual students or studies of classroom practices constitute a context-specific response to educational questions. By conducting classroom research, teachers can gain greater understanding of the different factors that impact student performance. At the same time, this sort of research can help teachers reflect on and make changes in their own daily teaching practice.

To help the teachers in our master's-level language-acquisition and cross-cultural communication class discover the strengths of their immigrant students, we have them read about and discuss second language acquisition and the importance of students' first language and culture. We also study the ways the community context affects schools. Then the teachers choose one second language learner to work with closely.

They read, write, and talk with their student. When the graduate class meets, the teachers share what they are learning from their experiences as they write up their case studies. They read each other's drafts and discuss the students they are studying. Through their research on one student and their interaction with their peers, many of these teachers begin to change the way they view all the language-minority students in their classes, and many begin to change the way they teach.

The case studies our teachers have written provide powerful evidence that, under the right conditions, second language students can succeed. The following excerpts from four of the case studies our students have conducted illustrate how children from different cultural backgrounds have overcome incredible odds in classrooms when others help them to believe in themselves and their own cultural and language heritage. At the same time, these case studies also show that the teachers who wrote them have taken on a new view. This new perspective has allowed them to value and build on their students' strengths (D. Freeman and Y. Freeman 1990).

Luis

For her case study, Mary chose Luis, a student in her bilingual first-grade class. From reading school records and talking with other teachers, Mary discovered that Luis is the middle child in a family of migrant farm laborers who move at least twice during each school year but return to the same schools yearly. When tested for kindergarten, Luis had not responded orally to any of the questions asked in English except for the question about his father's work, which he had answered in detail in Spanish. Mary noted that Luis could give lengthy explanations if allowed to use his first language.

However, Luis had been reluctant to try speaking in English. He had repeated kindergarten. His two monolingual English-speaking kindergarten teachers reported that although Luis had been silent in class, he seemed to enjoy school and participated cheerfully, though silently, in class activities. Mary decided that Luis had been going through what Krashen and Terrell (1983) have termed a "silent period." Such students need a safe environment where they can risk speaking in a new language.

Mary found that there were two places where Luis had broken his silence. He spoke some English on the playground with peers as he played ball. Luis was also motivated to use English to participate in games with his classmates. Mary decided he was developing conversational ability in situations where language was rich in context (Cummins 1989). Luis also began to develop language for academic purposes in a summer school session where he studied with a bilingual teacher who supported him in both Spanish and English.

Mary interviewed Luis' family and found that he communicated freely at home in his first language. When Luis entered Mary's classroom, she observed that he understood English. For example, as she watched him react to two peers at his table, she wrote, "Luis seems to be amused with them as they are a bit naughty." She noticed that Luis took part in whole-class readings of poetry or songs but would not answer or would only whisper a couple of words when called on to speak alone.

Mary decided to create situations in her classroom that were more like the playground situations where Luis would have to communicate to get what he needed or wanted. She made him responsible for asking for sports equipment for his table. She also gave him lots of opportunities for choral work with the class for reading and started conferencing with him individually about his journal entries.

Just when Mary began to see progress, Luis moved. However, a fellow teacher familiar with the family told Mary that Luis' family was expected back in two months. Mary closed her case study with a positive statement concerning her belief in Luis' potential, "This move will provide the experiences and knowledge that I can capitalize on in working with Luis when he returns." Partly as a result of doing the case study, Mary has learned that Luis has potential, and she will draw on his strengths and experiences to help him succeed in school.

Mony

Shortly after her arrival in the United States, Mony, a six-year-old Cambodian refugee, was placed in Katie's prefirst class. Although Mony had attended kindergarten, she needed more support before being placed in first grade. Katie was intrigued by Mony, who "seemed 'deeper' more serious than students who, though 'silent' in English, converse freely with their L1 (first language) peers."

Like Luis, Mony followed directions and participated silently in most activities. Her art work was so advanced that Katie, a veteran teacher of ten years, commented that Mony was "the most advanced six-year-old artist I'd *ever* seen." Socially, Mony avoided eye contact with most people and preferred the company of the one other Cambodian child in the room. In fact, if her peers paid too much attention to her, Mony would stick her tongue out at them, trying to make sure Katie didn't see her do it!

Though Katie could coax Mony to come close to her for cuddling during quiet times and comforted Mony when she would have crying periods, she could not convince her to converse with peers in Khmer or discuss her fears and concerns in her first language.

After only a month with Katie, Mony transferred to another school. Katie quickly scribbled a note "to whom it may concern" at the transfer school, explaining, "I worried that her (Mony's) darting tongue and serious look might get her into unfair trouble, that her lack of oral language would be confused with lack of intelligence, and I wanted someone to know of her treasured artistic ability." She received one brief follow-up call.

Since Katie teaches at a year-round school and went on vacation shortly after Mony left, she chose to do her case study on Mony in her new school setting. She decided to visit Mony in her new classroom, talk, and read with her and continue an interactive journal she had begun with Mony when Mony had been in Katie's class. Katie visited Mony ten times and kept anecdotal records of their reading, writing, and discussions. Katie's reflections on these visits were similar to what the other teachers doing case studies had found. Katie wrote, "I was *amazed* at Mony's proficiency in English and shocked at what I'd *wrongly* perceived it to be when she was in my class." Having looked closely at one student, Katie made this conclusion about second language learners: "It sounds so simple, but if we as teachers put more effort into *who* we're teaching, more of the *what* would take care of itself. When we concentrate on program, or strict time lines, we lose sight of all the important *human* element." Doing the case study helped Katie see that human element anew.

Mo

Mo, a ten-year-old Hmong boy in Charlene's fourth-grade classroom, also was reluctant to talk in English or Hmong except on the playground or with his peers. Over a period of four months, he refused to join in class discussions, even during literature study time. Charlene knew he was reading and enjoying the books his group was reading because he wrote responses to each story in English. Mo not only understood what he was reading, but he also related what he read to his own life. After reading one story, Mo wrote, "If I was a girl I would go and buy me a buetiful dresses so I could win the contest." In her case study, Charlene commented, "It was obvious that Mo was transacting with Eleanor Estes, author of *The Hundred Dresses*. He showed compassion toward the main character who was a fellow ESL learner."

Charlene drew on class readings on research with second language learners (Hudelson 1984; Rigg and Hudelson 1986; Urzúa 1987). She decided that she could draw on Mo's strengths through reading and writing. During writers workshop, when students wrote, revised, edited, and published their own books, Charlene noticed that Mo collaborated freely with peers in both his first and second languages and even risked sharing the stories he was working on. After publishing *Dog*, a ten-page book, Mo began to share orally in different contexts. Charlene observed, "Gaining confidence as a writer helped Mo find his voice in literature conferences and class discussions. He began to share humorous anecdotes he discovered in the books his literature group had chosen to read."

Mo used writing to begin to communicate in the classroom. His teacher recognized this, saw Mo's potential, drew on this strength, and gently pushed him further. When the class did a unit on oceanography, Mo's group became experts on the gray whale. They read about gray whales, wrote about them, drew pictures of gray whales, and made one to scale to hang from the classroom ceiling. When the celebration day came and the groups shared their knowledge with other classes in the school, parents, and administrators, Mo presented his part orally to everyone confidently.

Charlene realized that she had witnessed a transformation. In the process of observing and reflecting on this second language learner, she had found his strengths, encouraged him, and given him opportunities to explore learning with his peers.

Hilda

Sandra is a designated ESL instructor in a farming community. In her case study she described nine-year-old Hilda the first time she saw her:

> She was tall for our K–3 school, skinny with bent-over posture, dull eyes, dirty hair, and dirty clothes. She smelled very strongly of poor hygiene. She had big, black circles under her eyes and no energy. I knew that she was from El Salvador. I didn't know then what "being from El Salvador" could mean.

Sandra soon learned enough about Hilda's past life, filled with poverty and fear of war, to marvel at how quickly Hilda adjusted to her new culture and to school in the United States. Unlike Luis, Mony, and Mo, Hilda participated from the beginning even though she had little past experience with schooling of any kind and knew no English. Perhaps because she was older and physically larger than the others in her classroom, she pushed herself to succeed. Her third-grade teacher, who usually found new immigrants like Hilda a problem, commented to Sandra, "From her appearance, I knew I couldn't expect much of her. What really impressed me was her eagerness to learn and participate."

Sandra worked with Hilda in her pull-out ESL/bilingual classroom. She noticed that Hilda demanded to be pushed as she read and did process writing in both Spanish and English. Sandra explained Hilda's progress by referring to Vygotsky's (1978) discussion of movement within the Zone of Proximal Development:

> I think that by asking for the opportunity to do what others around her are doing, asking for help, for explanations, Hilda herself, is taking charge of making sure she's not sitting alone working at her independent level, but actively engaged in pushing herself toward new accomplishments and expanding her "Zone."

Sandra believes that second language learners need support in subject area material in their first language so that they can keep up academically as they learn their new language (Cummins 1984; Hudelson 1987; Krashen 1985). She provided content books in Spanish for Hilda to read in both her pull-out classroom and in the regular classroom. Sandra was supported in this decision by the regular classroom teacher, even though that teacher didn't read Spanish. In her regular classroom, Hilda read books in Spanish, and during ESL time, Hilda discussed the ideas from these content books in both her first and second languages with her peers and with Sandra.

Sandra realizes the importance of Hilda's first language and supports her enthusiasm for learning English. Although she is concerned that Hilda may not receive enough core curriculum in her first language, she is trying to provide as much support as possible in both Spanish and English. Sandra's concluding comments on Hilda reflect what she has learned as a teacher researcher: "If every immigrant child had such a good prognosis after such bad experiences, our job would be easy." The job of teachers like Sandra is never really easy, but her case study, which focused on the success of a second language learner, helped Sandra maintain a positive view.

Influence of Case Studies

The teachers in our classes agree that the case studies helped them put theory into practice. It is one thing to read about second language learners and to discuss different theories of language acquisition in the setting of a college classroom. It is another thing to work with second language students and try to apply what one has read, especially in large classes with students from many different language and cultural backgrounds. However, when our teachers have taken the time to study one child carefully, they have gained a new perspective on all their second language students. Katie reflected this new attitude when she concluded her case study by listing five ways the case study would influence her teaching.

1. I will expend more effort in getting to know my students personally.
2. I will provide individual time for each student as often as possible.
3. I will never again assume that "what I hear" is "what they know."
4. I will arrange my classroom/curriculum around whole, real, purposeful, meaning-filled experiences.
5. I will find, value, and exploit each student's contributions and talents.

One comment and one question that often arise when we suggest doing case studies to teachers is "That is a marvelous idea. Where will I find the time to do this?"

As we have worked with teachers doing case studies over the past six years, we have seen that time is not so much the issue as that of developing new eyes to see things differently. Teachers conducting a case study must focus in on a student in a way they have not done before. Some teachers keep a notebook by their desk to jot down what they notice as things happen with their case study. Others keep short notes in a folder, and still others take five minutes at the end of the day to summarize what they have seen. They all keep student written work in folders to analyze over time. Those folders are often organized by the students themselves. Even kindergarten students learn to file their own work as they learn to find their name on a file folder.

Once teachers begin to gather information on one child, to notice one child and what that child can do, they begin to look at all their students differently. While the analysis of what they see takes some extra time, it is often less time than a teacher takes agonizing over report card grades. One teacher felt the case study approach helped her move through the difficult process of giving grades much more quickly because she actually knew her students, their strengths, and where they needed to grow. Katie's list of five ways the case study influenced her teaching has proven useful for other teachers as well.

As they conduct case studies of their own students, teachers begin to realize why context-free interpretations of school performance are not satisfactory. Simply saying that a student has a cultural deficit or that the student is failing because of a cultural mismatch is not an answer. Instead, teachers begin to understand that a number of factors interact in any situation. By studying the particular contexts that affect their students, teachers begin to take on new attitudes and to try new teaching strategies to build on the strengths they see in their students.

Models of Teacher Research

Conducting case studies helps teachers understand their students, and it also helps them evaluate their own teaching. The case studies we have described comprise one model of teacher research. Our students work alone in their classrooms as they study a student. Then they share their results and get feedback from peers in their college class. In a second model, all the teachers at a school carry out research in their own classrooms and then share the results with colleagues. This model has proven effective for staff development. A third possibility is for individual teachers to work collaboratively with college researchers.

Action Research

Staff development that involves hiring outside "experts" to come and tell teachers about the latest methods for teaching language-minority students runs the risk of attempting a context-free approach. The experts may have good suggestions, but they often lack knowledge of the specific community and school situations where they are speaking. A better approach is to have the experts spend time in classrooms and the community to develop with teachers possible curricular changes that would be beneficial.

Nunan (1993) has worked extensively on staff-development programs. These programs help teachers do classroom research, particularly in ESL and foreign language classes. He refers to this as action research. Nunan defends action research as "real" research. He defines research as "a systematic process of inquiry consisting of three elements or components: (1) a question, problem, or hypothesis, (2) data, (3) analysis or interpretation of data" (p. 42). He points out that action research meets this definition. Nunan identifies the following steps in an action research cycle:

1. problem identification
2. preliminary investigation
3. hypothesis
4. plan intervention
5. outcome
6. reporting

An action research cycle begins with the teacher identifying a problem or puzzle. For example, a teacher might notice that students don't like working in cooperative groups. The teacher then does some preliminary investigation. This would include making systematic observations. The teacher might tape the class sessions when students are given group tasks. The next step is to form a hypothesis. For example, the teacher might hypothesize that the top students don't feel they learn anything in the groups and that they are doing all the work because they don't want to get a bad grade.

The fourth step in an action research cycle is for the teacher to plan an intervention. An intervention involves some change in practice. The teacher could change the way students are graded on group projects to include both individual and group grades. Or the teacher could change the composition of the groups. This intervention results in some outcome that is then reported. If action research is part of staff development, the report could come at the next staff meeting as teachers share the results of their research.

Though the basic idea is the same, Sumara (1993) defines action research and outlines the steps slightly differently. In accord with Nunan's premises, Sumara insists that practitioners must be the ones to undertake research in order for educational practice to improve. He points out that action research is not new and, in fact, "has its origins in the work of social psychologist Kurt Lewin (1946) who used it in a variety of community development projects in the United States" (p. 134). According to Sumara, educational applications of action research were first applied in a number of teacher-managed research projects by Stephen Corey in 1953.

Sumara points out that in action research it would "be inappropriate for a 'university researcher' to thrust upon a teacher or group of teachers a particular research question and/or agenda" (p. 134). He identifies four stages of action research—planning, acting, observing, and reflecting—that are worked through by groups or by individual educators wishing to improve their practice. Sumara explains the four stages:

> In the planning stage the participant(s) of the action research project try to define the area(s) of their own practice which they want to improve as well as begin to decide how it is they will do this. . . . In the second stage of action research, the participants work to enact their plan—essentially, putting into practice the plan for action that they have developed. Concurrent with this stage is one of observation where the participants monitor the impact of their actions by collecting data pertaining to the results of their actions. The last stage is that of critical reflection where the participants reflect

upon what is happening with their project, developing a revised action plan based upon what they are learning from the process of planning, acting, and observing (p. 134).

We can list Sumara's stages like this for a clearer parallel with Nunan's cycle:

1. Planning: Define area of practice to improve and decide how to improve.
2. Acting: Put into practice the plan for action.
3. Observing (concurrent with acting): Collect data to determine results of actions.
4. Reflecting: Critically reflect on what is happening as the result of actions taken.

Action research has great potential for positive teacher change. Rather than listening to an outside expert who has all the answers, teachers identify puzzles, investigate them, try out new practices, and report the results to a supportive group of colleagues. This approach to staff development encourages teachers to become explorers in their own classrooms. The process is cyclical because the results of one investigation often lead to new questions.

Collaborative Action Research

In some cases, teachers may work with researchers from colleges or universities as they engage in action research. Sumara (1993) has suggested that action research can be collaborative. What differentiates collaborative research from traditional research is that the researcher's "role switches from that of 'external authority' to one of 'internal facilitator/supporter'" (p. 135).

A number of benefits can result from teachers' collaborating with researchers from colleges and universities. The "outsider" can sometimes bring a new perspective and suggest new ideas. In addition, a college researcher may have a fresh perspective, time, and resources a teacher lacks. The college researcher can come into the classroom and view the class with fresh eyes. It often happens that discussion with the teacher afterwards reveals that the researcher saw things that the teacher, distracted by other concerns, never noticed before. It is also possible that a college researcher would have more time or a more flexible schedule to do things like interview parents or other community members. Finally, the researcher can identify books or articles about situations similar to the ones the particular teacher is facing and bring those to the teacher's attention.

Allwright (1993) lists seven major aims for any project for collaborative research involving a teacher and a college researcher:

1. relevance
2. reflection
3. continuity
4. integration
5. collegiality
6. learner and teacher development
7. theory building

Any research proposal should meet all seven aims. Concerning relevance, Allwright states the following:

> The least to hope for from our work is that teachers bringing research into their own teaching will ensure that what they explore is relevant to themselves regardless of what concerns academic researchers, and that it is also relevant to their learners, who may well have interesting puzzles of their own to explore (p. 128).

Allwright is an advocate of exploratory teaching and learning. He sees classroom research as a way that both teachers and students can explore aspects of their situation together with assistance from academic researchers. This call for relevance is particularly important. Too often outside researchers have conducted studies that were not relevant to the teachers and students in the classrooms where they worked. Allwright's call for relevance also points to the need for true collaboration. The academic researcher and the classroom teacher, along with the students, are exploring matters of mutual interest. The outsider is not coming in to offer expert advice or to conduct a study whose only purpose is to advance the researcher's career.

In addition to relevance, Allwright proposes that classroom research should promote reflection by both teachers and learners. He also stresses that integrating research and pedagogy should be a continuous enterprise. If the research is relevant, and if teachers and students reflect on what they are discovering, then the results can be integrated into daily practice. In addition, Allwright feels that integration of research and pedagogy should encourage collegiality among teachers and also bring teachers closer to their students. Finally, Allwright points out that any proposal for integrating research and teaching should have the aims of learner development, teacher development, and theory building.

Allwright notes that certain problems are to be expected. Action research requires time, new skills, and a willingness to change ineffective practices. First, "doing research in the language classroom is time-consuming" (p. 129). Teachers need more time to prepare lessons to try out new ideas, and more time is needed for reflecting on the questions being explored. Our students, for example, took extra time to talk, read, and write with individual students, and then they took time to think and write about what they were learning. However, as we explained earlier, most teachers conclude that this is time well spent.

Teachers involved in action research also need to learn new skills. For example, teachers may need to learn how to develop effective questionnaires or record daily observations. In addition, the research may show that certain practices teachers have been following are not effective, so research can be a threat to a teacher's self-esteem. This threat is minimized when there is true collaboration between the teacher and the researcher. It is maximized when the outside expert comes in to critique the teacher's practices. Despite these potential problems, collaborative research is extremely effective in helping teachers refine their educational practice in ways that benefit all their students.

Yvonne and Sam's Experience

Yvonne spent time working in Sam's combination first- and second-grade bilingual classroom (Freeman and Nofziger 1991). Their work together fits Sumara's stages of action research: planning, acting, observing, and reflecting. Both found that this type of collaboration was not always easy, but that it was very beneficial. The two met through their church and after preliminary discussion they agreed to work together over time to see how curriculum could be organized around themes in Sam's class. Both Yvonne and Sam were a bit nervous at first, and both went through stages of wondering how the collaboration would really work. Yvonne shared her feelings as the project began and the two were in the planning stage:

> On the day of my first visit to Sam's classroom, I was nervous. I worried that my convictions about whole language for second language learners might not really work with these bilingual children. I wasn't certain that I would be able to communicate honestly with Sam. Before the end of the first hour, my fears were being replaced with excitement. Things I noticed about the children and things Sam pointed out to me helped me realize we had similar interests and concerns: We both showed similar interest in student journal responses that were intriguing; we both noticed the same strengths in the children as they interacted; we both had similar concerns about students who were not involved enough in the classroom community. After school that first day, we sat and talked for over two hours discussing our philosophies about learning for bilingual students and considering where we might begin (p. 66).

It was important to both Sam and Yvonne that they decide together the direction the classroom research should take. Yvonne explained how they reached their decision:

> Sam was already using literature in English and Spanish instead of basals, and he had his children doing daily journal writing and also writing stories in the language of their choice. However, he wasn't comfortable with the organization of his classroom and wasn't sure how to begin working on that. After some discussion we decided to see if working with a broad theme that included comparison and contrast would give us a start (p. 66).

Sam reflected on his perspective as he began the project and also on some of the limitations in what he was willing to do with the researcher:

> When Yvonne's visit began, so did our adventure. Although I was using some activities consistent with whole language, I knew that I did not completely understand the philosophy behind whole language and that there was more that needed to be done. . . . While there were parts of our classroom schedule I was anxious to work on, there were areas within the day that Yvonne and I decided not to modify because I felt that these were important times for the students. I was not willing to change the morning opening time, the time spent in small groups with Mrs. Romero, the bilingual aide, or our daily share time. Yvonne supported my decision, reinforcing the idea that I was the teacher and I had to decide what I wanted to change and how I wanted to try to change it (p. 67).

This element of the collaboration was very important. Sam had to feel that he was in charge of his own classroom and that, at any time, he could make decisions. Sam recalled one incident early on where he had to pull back from the new things he was trying to do. He was instituting more choice for his students, but it did not run as smoothly as he would have liked. He was, as Sumara has suggested, acting and observing at the same time:

> Once I began giving students choice, there was stress. That first day with Yvonne's help and the help of the aide, all went quite smoothly even though two or three children could not make their own choices. However, by the third day, I felt myself

losing control. Students in some centers were involved but at others they seemed to get bored quickly, and relied on me to make their choices for them. The more things changed, the more I feared I was losing control. I called Yvonne, telling her I could not do this. She assured me that it was my classroom, and that I should do what I needed to do. At this point in my learning, I realized a very important thing: Too much change too quickly hurts the students as well as the teacher (p. 71).

Sam and Yvonne learned that collaborative classroom research is both challenging and exciting. As they reflected together, they learned about the structure needed for an explorer classroom, they learned what helped bilingual children read and write, they learned that change was hard but worth it. As Sam commented, "We were not 'traditional' teachers anymore. Over the past months, our roles had changed. We liked our new roles better" (p. 83). Sam and Yvonne also followed up with one more step from their research. They wrote a chapter for a book together (Freeman and Nofziger 1991). This practice of classroom teachers and researchers writing and publishing together is one more act of true collaboration.

Despite the potential problems and extra work, collaborative classroom research can benefit academic researchers, teachers, and students. Academic researchers can learn more about the different factors that promote students' academic success. Teachers can learn more about the practices that work for them and their students and also gain a greater understanding of why those practices work. Students can gain insights into their own situation and start to learn more about what they can do to help themselves be more successful learners.

All three models of teacher research we have discussed hold great promise. Teachers from different schools can conduct individual research, such as case studies, and then share their results in graduate classes. Teachers at one school site can work together to conduct and share research as a part of a staff development program. Or teachers can collaborate with college researchers to explore problems and puzzles in their classrooms. The result in each case is a context-specific solution to particular problems that teachers identify. As teachers conduct research, they reflect on their practice and build an integrated theory of language, learning, teaching, and curriculum.

What Makes an Effective Teacher?

We have described various models of classroom research that involve teacher researchers in examining their own practices in an attempt to improve the learning situation for their students. Teachers do want to improve their teaching. Whether or not they are effective in instituting change depends on a number of factors. Erickson (1993) observed and interviewed teachers working with English language learners at different grade levels from elementary through adult. Some followed traditional approaches. Others used an interactive, exploratory approach.

In her interviews, Erickson asked the following questions:

1. What makes teaching second language students difficult for you?
2. What has helped?
3. What would help?

4. What do you like about teaching?
5. What do you think is the most successful thing you've done?
6. Why or how did it come about?
7. What kinds of things would you like to try next? (p. 60)

After discussing these questions, Erickson asked, "What else would you like to comment on?" She was interested to find that teachers had a great deal to talk about. Many teachers are isolated. They are often doing wonderful things, but they may not have anyone who is truly interested in listening to their stories. Perhaps they fear that if they tell about their failures, they will be criticized. If they tell about their successes, they might appear to be bragging. Having someone who was interested but who wasn't directly part of their school ask them to talk provided the teachers with the sounding board they needed. Erickson commented as follows:

> All of these teachers work under different circumstances. Each one faces budget constraints, facility challenges, and scheduling problems. Yet each teacher worked within those constraints to creatively reach the students, and every one in a different way expressed that it was the students themselves who make their job worthwhile (p. 70).

In her conclusions, Erickson listed five characteristics of effective teachers:

1. Teachers are effective when they assume an advocacy role for their students.
2. Teachers are effective when they have an adequate theoretical preparation for working with second language students.
3. Teachers are effective when they have professional support.
4. Teachers are effective when they assume control over their physical environment.
5. Teachers are effective when they have a sense of mission.

In the process of conducting classroom research, teachers often take on these characteristics. The decision to conduct research in their own classrooms is a first step toward taking an advocacy role for students.

Teacher researchers also read about theories of learning and second language acquisition as they attempt to explain what they observe in their classes. Teacher researchers gain support from colleagues or university researchers. As they reflect on their practice, they often begin to take control of the classroom and make changes in the learning environment. Teachers willing to take the time and make the effort to conduct research with their own students do so out of a sense of mission. They are true professionals who do everything they can to improve the chances for school success for all their students.

Throughout the book we have shared examples of how explorer teachers take an intercultural orientation to meet the needs of English language learners. For many of these teachers, this has required a change in their attitudes, assumptions, and daily practices. We close the book with the story of Bunny, a second language teacher who engaged in action research, critically reflected on her traditional teaching and, as a result, changed her practice drastically. Bunny was, in fact, one of the teachers interviewed in the Erickson study and exhibits all the characteristics of an effective teacher.

Change Through Action Research

Bunny became involved in action research when her life circumstances changed, and she decided to return to college for a master's degree. Bunny was a teacher with many years of experience. She used traditional grammar-based lessons with vocabulary lists and spelling lessons with her second language students. Bunny believed students needed the basic building blocks of English before they could hope to communicate either orally or in writing. Activities in Bunny's ESL classes were geared to improve students' linguistic competence, their ability to manipulate linguistic units, rather than their communicative competence (Hymes 1970).

However, when Bunny took her first two graduate courses, Introduction to Reading and Miscue Analysis, she was introduced to a sociopsycholinguistic view of learning. Though she resisted some of the things she was learning and did not institute change in her classes immediately, Bunny began to question whether her traditional methods were really helping her students.

When Bunny was asked to do a case study of one of her students for her graduate Language Acquisition and Cross-Cultural Communication class, she chose an eighteen-year-old Hmong woman who had shown little progress in her class. In fact, at the time of the case study, Pa was in her second year of beginning ESL. Bunny described her impressions of Pa at the beginning of the study:

> When Pa first entered school, she was shy and silent. Although she tried faithfully to do all the work, her comprehension level was very low, requiring much tutorial assistance and translation. She seemed to be withdrawn and uncomfortable. I felt she was not feeling very good about herself, and she appeared lonely and insecure with little evidence of any friends.

Bunny's early impressions of Pa were consistent with the labels Pa brought with her. Based on her reading test scores, Bunny had placed Pa in a low level for reading, and the types of activities that Pa was engaged in reinforced a kind of deficit view of her abilities. Bunny viewed Pa as a student with little self-confidence who required much individual help.

The assignments Bunny gave did not seem to inspire either Pa or Bunny. Figure 14-3 shows a typical assignment of Pa's that Bunny had given her students before doing the case study. Bunny first dictated the spelling list and then asked students to write the words in sentences. The words for the spelling list were chosen because they all contain a short "a" sound. Grading of the sentences was related to grammatical correctness only.

In the graduate language-acquisition class, Bunny read about theories of second language acquisition, including the importance of supporting the first language and lowering the affective filter (Cummins 1981, 1989; Krashen 1982, 1985). As she read and discussed these ideas with other teachers in her graduate class, Bunny started to realize that her spelling assignment not only reinforced a part-to-whole view of learning focusing on accurate forms, but was also inauthentic (Edelsky 1986). Bunny began to introduce activities that would encourage a more exploratory type of learning. She wanted to build her students' independence and increase their self-confidence. The case study assignment provided Bunny with the impetus to begin to make changes.

As she observed Pa closely and carefully examined the work Pa turned in, Bunny began to reflect on Pa's overdependence, loneliness, and insecurity:

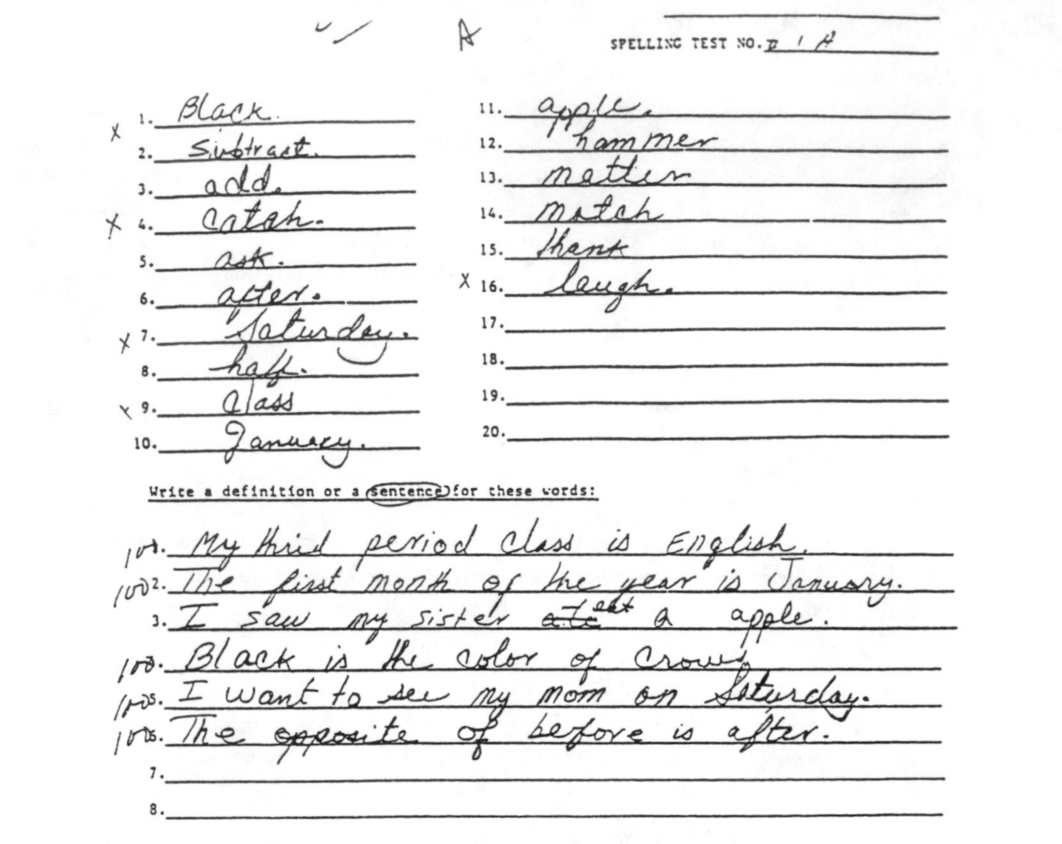

SPELLING TEST NO. _II_ / _A_

1. Black
2. Subtract
3. add
4. catch
5. ask
6. after
7. Saturday
8. half
9. class
10. January
11. apple
12. hammer
13. nettle
14. match
15. thank
16. laugh

Write a definition or a (sentence) for these words:

1. My third period class is English.
2. The first month of the year is January.
3. I saw my sister eat a apple.
4. Black is the color of crows.
5. I want to see my mom on Saturday.
6. The opposite of before is after.
7.
8.

Figure 14-3 Spelling test

She usually was waiting for me when I arrived each morning and seemed to look forward to standing near me chatting haltingly about things that happened last year. Then I noticed little messages she was slipping to me in her written work hinting at her loneliness and homesickness. In a classroom writing assignment on a topic not at all related to personal feelings, Pa wrote, "I am lonely every day."

The writing assignment Bunny is referring to is another set of sentences based on the weekly spelling words. One of the words was "lonely," and that prompted Pa's sentence, "I am lonely every day."

Rather than marking grammatical errors as she might have done in the past, Bunny wrote a personal response to Pa, "I am sorry you are lonely. I want to be your friend." Bunny was beginning to see Pa not simply as a student needing lots of assistance to improve her language, but also as a person with human needs.

When Bunny asked Pa if she could be her case study subject, Pa was "delighted and very cooperative." Bunny decided she wanted to reduce Pa's anxiety and increase her self-confidence and sense of self-worth through personal attention and encouragement. Because Bunny had been reading about the importance of first language support, she asked the primary-language tutor to encourage Pa to use her native-language skills to help other Hmong students in group settings. Over time, this led to a change in Pa's self-perception and interactions with all her peers, including those of different language backgrounds. In one of her anecdotal notations, Bunny described how Pa was changing as the result of this new role:

> She has assumed a leadership role in tutoring and translating for other students. . . . Interestingly, I have noticed her moving out of her seat to help not only girls of other cultural backgrounds, but boys with a different first language as well, unusual for a Hmong girl.

These interactions in class led to the building of friendships that Bunny noticed extended outside the classroom. "Another change is her happiness with her new friends. I now see her almost daily sitting in the hall studying with them before class instead of sitting silently by herself."

Pa's use of her first language had other advantages. Bunny became more aware of Pa's academic competence:

> She knew more than I assumed. Recently, as I began reading a Hmong folktale to the class, Pa volunteered to read the Hmong translation as I read the English, and did so with ease and enjoyment. My surprise shamefully revealed a serious judgment error on my part by supposing that because Pa had not developed fluency in English, she lacked cognitive proficiency in her first language.

In addition to encouraging Pa to use her first language, Bunny initiated authentic writing activities with all her students. She began with a dialogue journal (Peyton 1990) and was particularly pleased with Pa's responses. "Immediately, she responded by writing a whole paragraph in comprehensible English. Subsequently, she began to share with me more information about herself and her background." Figure 14-4 shows one of Pa's entries and Bunny's response.

The dialogue journal writing freed Pa from having to use the week's spelling words. In the journal, Pa was able to create a coherent text with related sentences. She reminded her teacher of a picture Bunny had given her last year and explained that she kept the picture at home. In her response, Bunny recalled the present Pa had given her last year at Christmas and pointed out that she had displayed it in the classroom. She did not comment on or mark the grammatical errors in Pa's journal as she had done with the spelling tests. Instead she focused on the content and established rapport with Pa.

Bunny's work with Pa was a catalyst that led her to change her teaching practices with all of her students. An early anecdotal record for this case study reflects how impressed Bunny was by the effect of personal attention on Pa:

> Due, I think, to the effect of the special attention focused on her by this study, I have noticed in recent weeks some changes in Pa's classroom behavior and progress. Most evident is her willingness to participate in all activities. She now volunteers information and comments regularly.

In addition to implementing authentic writing activities, Bunny made changes in her reading program. She found that the difficulties Pa experienced with reading were a reflection of the "very poorly condensed and difficult version" of the novel she had asked her class to read. In other words, Bunny began to critically examine reading materials rather than blaming the students. She asked Pa to read a complete short story

Wednesday, Oct. 5

I Today I'm feel good and nice time
Because I happy something to do now.
Or you will be my friend teacher
in last year and this year.
Can you remember last year you gave
year a picture to me?
But, now I keep your picture in
my home. And Sometime I miss you
I take your in my forther to see.
Okay thank you Mrs. H.

Thank you. It will be fun doing this
project with you. Yes, I remember last year.
You were one of my best students and
You gave me a present at Christmas. I
have it on the flags in this room. Thank
you.

Figure 14-4   Pa's journal entry

and retell it. Bunny found that Pa made very few significant miscues in her reading and "in the retelling she covered all of the important details adequately and clearly."

Encouraging the use of the first language, beginning a dialogue journal, using complete stories, and responding to Pa personally were all steps toward more effective teaching for Bunny. She was willing to begin making changes in her classroom practices because she could see the difference these practices were making for Pa. She concluded, "At this point Pa seems to be feeling pretty good about herself and her progress. . . . I believe Pa is well on her way to developing adequacy, perhaps even fluency, in English rather soon."

Using dialogue journals instead of spelling lists was a big first step for both Bunny and her students. When we saw Bunny and several students at Back to School Night the next fall, we were delighted to find that they had taken a new step. Her high school ESL students had put together a collection of their personal stories around the theme of "The Big Experience." They wrote about coming to the United States, their first days at school here, or things they had experienced previously, such as the Mexico City earthquake. They typed the stories, planned the artwork, and designed a cover for their "published" book. The class book is now a reading resource for all the ESL classes in the school, and students take their copies of the book home to read to family and friends.

Authentic writing activities such as the publishing of their own stories as a book also led the students to other kinds of authentic language-development activities. Once the students decided to publish their book, they realized they needed money to do so. Bunny allowed the class to decide what they wanted to do. They elected to put on a spaghetti dinner to make money. The students planned the menu, sought out recipes, calculated ingredients, figured out how much money was required in advance to buy what they needed, arranged to use the school facilities, made the advertisements, and put on the dinner. Bunny's enthusiasm for this activity could hardly be contained as she observed not only the varied language students were using as they planned and worked, but also the students' enthusiasm as they completed a project in which they used English for real purposes.

An Explorer Teacher

We end this book with one final example of how an explorer teacher supports English language learners. Ever since Bunny began to involve her students in authentic reading, writing, and learning activities, she has seen the difference her new orientation makes. And she continues to reflect on her practice as it evolves. She has begun to write about her experiences and recently published an article in *California English* (Rogers 1992) describing a unit she did with one high school ESL class that tended to be rowdy and had students who were frequently absent. The students were "mostly tenth graders who had been speaking English for two years or less, representing five different languages" (p. 8).

In the second semester Bunny decided to introduce a unit on the history of World War II and Hiroshima. The topic of war was meaningful to her students since so many of them were refugees. Bunny brought into the class a variety of resources about the war including magazine articles, pictures, and poetry. She also brought in a piece of trinite from New Mexico, where the first atomic bomb was exploded. The trinite had been given to her by a relative who was a retired scientist and a Fellow of the Los Alamos National Laboratory.

After the students had had time to examine what she had brought, Bunny put them into groups and asked them to record their understanding and impressions of these different resources through brainstorming and note taking. Then she asked the students to produce some kind of poster that represented what they thought was interesting and important. In this way, she was able to focus on the learner, provide choice, and encourage social interaction. Bunny described the scene:

> I observed substantial language development and historical learning taking place. . . .
> Some groups used as many as three languages at once. . . . In spite of the noise—I'll
> be honest, it was bedlam!—good things were happening. Creative ideas were being
> shared. The kids were doing a good job and they knew it (p. 8).

When the students presented their posters, Bunny was impressed by the understandings they showed, but she wanted to try to make the investigations into questions about war even more meaningful. Since she was going to visit the retired scientist, she told the class she would bring their posters to share with him and would be glad to deliver any letters students would want to write. Bunny was amazed at the students' responses:

Offering the students the possibility of an authentic audience was the magic wand that turned the class around in ways beyond my wildest imagination. Even the stragglers completed their posters on time, with improved quality. More surprisingly, the quietest boy in the class, Kee Y., came through with a brief note, which I hand-delivered along with all their posters (p. 8).

Bunny's scientist relative was impressed with both the posters and the letter and promised to respond. While the class awaited an answer, they began to read *The Thousand Paper Cranes* (Coerr 1977) for a literature study that encouraged reading, writing, and discussion on the topic of the effects of war.

Finally the letter arrived. Bunny anticipated that the letter opening would be special, so she asked the television class at the school to record the event on video. The scientist responded personally to each student and ended the letter by saying "I think many of you know more about war than I do, but have you stopped to think how wars *cause* wars?" He went on to ask twelve questions including "If nobody ever wins a war, why do people kill other people?" and "If our blood is the same, we can't be very different, can we?"

Bunny summarized the scientist's questions and made the summary available to all the students. Then she left it up to them to decide if they wanted to respond, and if so, how they would answer. At this point, as at other points in the unit, Bunny showed her respect for her students. She kept the focus on the learners but still provided direction and guidance. After much discussion, the students decided not to write answers but to make a video!

During the weeks that followed, the former pattern of absenteeism changed. Nobody missed class as the students worked together on the project, reading, writing, editing, coaching, and rehearsing daily. Students took interest and pride in their work as they researched answers to the scientist's questions. They set up individual appointments on their own time with the video production studio on campus to record for the scientist what they had learned. Kee, for example, wrote out careful notes and recorded his answer in flawless English. Bunny explained the importance of this project to her students:

One girl who stayed with it was almost full term in pregnancy. She finished her piece perfectly, dropped out, had her baby a few days later, and reenrolled before the end of the year! Suddenly, one hundred percent of my raucous, low-achieving class had become stars (p. 9)!

Bunny concluded her description of the class project by noting that "the students gained in self-confidence, self-esteem, language development, and historical knowledge" (p. 25).

Bunny takes an explorer approach to teaching. All the characteristics of an explorer classroom were present in her class during this unit. She showed respect for her students by valuing their opinions. She provided them with access to both English and academic content by starting with the whole, with big questions, and moving toward the parts. She focused on her students and built on their strengths by providing choice, building curriculum around their questions, making learning meaningful, encouraging collaborative learning, and allowing students to learn and express their learning through different modalities, including their first language.

Bunny's teaching has changed dramatically. She has moved from traditional vocabulary lists and spelling tests to dialogue journals, meaningful literature, and content area units. Bunny considers many different factors that influence her students. When Bunny really looked at Pa through a case study, she realized the complexity of Pa as a person. She started to take into account both academic and social factors as she worked with Pa. This experience has led Bunny to view all her students in a new way.

We see Bunny frequently and every time we see her, she is excitedly talking about the latest projects she and her students are involved in. For example, Bunny and her students invited an author/illustrator of adolescent books to their classroom. Not only did the students interview him and show him both their writing and artwork, but the students and author are considering a joint project that might result in a published book about the students themselves.

Bunny has come to understand the importance of working and sharing ideas with other teachers. She is now part of a team of teachers at her school who work together creating curriculum and exchanging ideas for working effectively with their immigrant students. Their collaboration and joint projects have led to the creation of a "graffiti-free zone" in the hall where ESL classes are held. Instead of grafitti, students and teachers put up writing, artwork, photos, and posters that are related to their classwork. The grafitti-free zone has attracted other students and teachers to the ESL area of this large high school. The second language students' work is drawing attention and being appreciated.

While other teachers Bunny's age dream of upcoming retirement and freedom from the tedium of teaching students they do not like or understand, Bunny continually plans new projects and gets involved wherever she can to improve her teaching and to help her students. Her sense of mission led her to become a member of the California Literature Portfolio Assessment Project for high school ESL assessment. This work contributed to her master's thesis project on portfolio assessment for second language learners. When she graduated with her master's degree, she received the Dean's Award as the Outstanding Master's Student not only because of her thesis but because of her involvement and dedication. Bunny told us afterwards that she was surprised by the award, that she was "overwhelmed," and that she still had much to do. She plans to write a book on secondary ESL teaching, outlining the projects she and her colleagues are working on with their students.

Bunny is a classic example of Erickson's five characteristics of an effective teacher.

1. Beginning with the case study and her close look at Pa, Bunny has begun to advocate for her students. She sees them as having potential and is as excited as they are when they succeed.
2. Bunny's graduate work has provided her with a theoretical base that supports the successful practices she is implementing in the classroom.
3. Through friends she made in the graduate classes, an encouraging school administration, and the team she works with at her school, Bunny finds support for what she is doing.
4. Despite the fact that Bunny works in a large inner-city high school that is poorly maintained and often dangerous, she and her colleagues are making an attempt to improve the physical conditions in which they work with projects like the graffiti-free zone.
5. Certainly, Bunny has a sense of mission. This is shown by her dedication to and enthusiasm for her work and her students.

Some Final Words

In this book we have examined the different factors inside and outside of classrooms that affect the second language acquisition and academic development of students caught between worlds. We have based our analysis on Cortés' Contextual Interaction Model. Cortés argues that the societal context affects the educational context in a number of ways. Effective teaching requires an understanding of both social and school factors that influence second language acquisition and academic development.

We have proposed an orientation to teaching, learning, language, and curriculum that is interactive and exploratory. Throughout the book we have provided examples of explorer teachers who take an intercultural orientation. In this last chapter, we have suggested that classroom-based research, which results in context-specific solutions and takes into account factors from both worlds—the school world and the societal world—offers the best possibility for creating meaningful and effective classrooms for English language learners. Effective teachers, as Erickson points out, are advocates for their students, they have a knowledge of theory, they have support, and they have a sense of mission. Teaching, and especially teaching second language students, does require a sense of mission. It's a changing profession in a changing atmosphere as student populations and the community contexts both shift rapidly.

We see teachers meeting the challenges of the ever-changing contexts daily. They are proof of Bruner's (1985) observation that "learning is indeed context sensitive, but that human beings, given their peculiarly human competence, are capable of adapting their approach to the demands of different contexts" (p. 6). These teachers effectively promote optimal learning situations for second language students. It is exciting to see the kind of work they are doing, and it is our hope that their examples can provide support and inspiration for other teachers of English language learners. We hope that other teachers will conduct research in their classrooms and share their results so that all of us can continue to grow in our understanding of how best to promote educational success for all our students and especially for our students between worlds.

Applications

1. Three context-free interpretations for the school performance of second language students are genetic inferiority, cultural deficit, and cultural mismatch. In a small group share any experiences you have had where minority students' failure has been interpreted in one of these ways. What would you now say to the person who took this perspective?

2. Look back at the case studies in Chapter 1, or look at the case study of a second language learner that you have done. What context-free interpretations could be given for the success or failure of the student on which you are focusing? How could a contextual-interaction perspective better account for the student's performance?

3. Different models of teacher research are discussed in this chapter. Have you ever been part of any of these models? In a group share your teacher research experiences and/or how you see yourself doing teacher research in the future.

4. Allwright states three potential problems with teacher collaborative research. Have you or any of your peers ever experienced these problems? Discuss.

5. Erickson's research suggests five characteristics of successful teachers. Do you agree with her conclusions? Would you add others? Discuss.

APPENDIX A

Methods of Teaching a Second Language

Overview of Methods

Blair, R. 1982. *Innovative Approaches to Language Teaching*. Rowley, MA: Newbury House.

Chastain, K. 1976. *Developing Second Language Skills: Theory to Practice*. 2d ed. Boston: Houghton Mifflin.

Diller, K. 1978. *The Language Teaching Controversy*. Rowley, MA: Newbury House.

Larsen-Freeman, D. 1986. *Techniques and Principles in Language Teaching*. New York: Oxford University Press.

Richards, J., and T. Rodgers. 1986. *Approaches and Methods in Language Teaching: A Description and Analysis*. New York: Cambridge University Press.

Stevick, E. 1980. *Teaching Languages: A Way and Ways*. Rowley, MA: Newbury House.

Stevick, E. W. 1976. *Memory, Meaning and Method*. Rowley, MA: Newbury House.

Total Physical Response

Asher, J. 1977. *Learning Another Language Through Actions: The Complete Teacher's Guide*. Los Gatos, CA: Sky Oaks Publications.

Romijn, E., and C. Seely. 1979. *Live Action English*. San Francisco: Alemany Press.

Segal, B. 1983. *Teaching English Through Action*. Brea, CA: Berty Segal, Inc.

The Natural Approach

Krashen, S., and T. Terrell. 1983. *The Natural Approach: Language Acquisition in the Classroom*. Hayward, CA: Alemany Press.

Communicative Language Teaching

Brumfit, C. J., and K. Johnson. (Eds.). 1979. *The Communicative Approach to Language Teaching*. Oxford: Oxford University Press.

Enright, D. S., and M. L. McCloskey. 1988. *Integrating English: Developing English Language and Literacy in the Multilingual Classroom*. Reading, MA: Addison-Wesley Publishing Co.

Rivers, W. 1983. *Communicating Naturally in a Second Language: Theory and Practice in Language Teaching*. New York: Cambridge University Press.

Rivers, W. 1987. *Interactive Language Teaching*. New York: Cambridge University Press.

Widdowson, H. 1978. *Teaching Language as Communication*. Oxford: Oxford University Press.

Wilkins, D. A. 1976. *Notional Syllabuses*. Oxford: Oxford University Press.

Suggestopedia

Lozanov, G. 1982. Suggestology and Suggestopedy. In *Innovative Approaches to Language Teaching*, edited by R. Blair. Rowley, MA: Newbury House.

Community Language Learning

Curran, C. 1982. Community Language Learning. In *Innovative Approaches to Language Teaching*, edited by R. Blair. Rowley, MA: Newbury House.

Sheltered English

Freeman, D., and Y. Freeman. 1988. "Sheltered English Instruction." *ERIC Digest*. October. Washington, DC: Center for Applied Linguistics.

Freeman, Y., and D. Freeman. 1991. "Using Sheltered English to Teach Second Language Learners." *California English* 27(1): 6–7, 26.

Cognitive Academic Language Learning Approach

Chamot, A., and M. O'Malley. 1989. "The Cognitive Academic Language Learning Approach." In *When They Don't All Speak English: Integrating the ESL Student into the Regular Classroom*, edited by P. Rigg and V. Allen. Urbana, IL: NCTE.

Chamot, A., and M. O'Malley. 1987. "The Cognitive Academic Language Learning Approach: A Bridge to the Mainstream." *TESOL Quarterly* 21(2): 227–249.

Problem Posing

Freeman, Y. S., and D. E. Freeman. 1991. "Doing Social Studies: Whole Language Lessons to Promote Social Action." *Social Education* 55(1): 29–32, 66.

Wallerstein, N. 1987. Problem Posing Education: Freire's Method for Transformation. In *Freire for the Classroom*, edited by I. Shor. Portsmouth, NH: Heinemann.

APPENDIX B

Readings on Second Language Acquisition

Beebe, L. 1987. *Issues in Second Language Acquisition: Multiple Perspectives.* New York: Newbury House.

Brown, H. D. 1980. *Principles of Language Learning and Teaching.* Englewood Cliffs, NJ: Prentice Hall.

Chastain, K. 1976. *Developing Second Language Skills: Theory to Practice.* 2d ed. Boston: Houghton Mifflin.

Collier, V. 1989. "How Long? A Synthesis of Research on Academic Achievement in a Second Language." *TESOL Quarterly* 23(3): 509–532.

Elley, W. 1991. "Acquiring Literacy in a Second Language: The Effect of Book-based Programs." *Language Learning* 41(2): 403–439.

Ellis, R. 1986. *Understanding Second Language Acquisition.* Oxford: Oxford University Press.

Ferreiro, E., and A. Teberosky. 1982. *Literacy Before Schooling.* Portsmouth, NH: Heinemann.

Gass, S., and J. Schacter. (Eds.). 1989. *Linguistic Perspectives on Second Language Acquisition.* New York: Cambridge University Press.

Heath, S. B. 1983. *Ways with Words: Language, Life, and Work in Communities and Classrooms.* Cambridge, England: Cambridge University Press.

Holt, D. 1986. *Beyond Language: Social and Cultural Factors in Schooling Language Minority Students.* Evaluation, Dissemination, and Assessment Center, California State University, Los Angeles.

Krashen, S. 1982. *Principles and Practice in Second Language Acquisition.* New York: Pergamon Press.

Larsen-Freeman, D., and M. Long. 1991. *An Introduction to Second Language Acquisition Research.* New York: Longman.

Lindfors, J. 1987. *Children's Language and Learning.* 2d ed. Englewood Cliffs, NJ: Prentice Hall.

McLaughlin, B. 1987. *Theories of Second Language Learning.* London: Edward Arnold.

Scarcella, R. 1990. *Teaching Language Minority Students in the Multicultural Classroom.* Englewood Cliffs, NJ: Prentice Hall Regents.

APPENDIX C

Books Used in Unit About Plants

Ada, A. F. 1990. *Just One Seed.* Carmel, CA: Hampton Brown Books.

Ada, A. F. 1990. *Una semilla nada más.* Carmel, CA: Hampton Brown Books.

Bolton, F., and D. Snowball. 1986. *Growing Radishes and Carrots.* New York: Scholastic.

Cumpiano, I. 1992a. *Hugo Hogget.* Carmel, CA: Hampton Brown Books.

Cumpiano, I. 1992b. *Ton-tón el gigantón.* Carmel: Hampton Brown Books.

Darlington, A. 1983. *Un jardín en tu dormitorio (A Garden in Your Room).* Barcelona, Spain: Ediciones Toray.

Flores, G. S. 1988. *Pon una semilla a germinar.* Mexico, D. F.: Trillas.

Holloway, J., and C. Harper. 1990. *¿Animal o planta?* Cleveland, OH: Modern Curriculum Press.

Holloway, J., and C. Harper. 1990. *¿Plant or Animal?* Cleveland, OH: Modern Curriculum Press.

Krauss, R. 1945. *The Carrot Seed.* New York: Scholastic, Inc.

Krauss, R. 1978. *La semilla de zanahoria.* New York: Scholastic, Inc.

Madrigal, S. 1992a. *Farms.* Carmel, CA: Hampton Brown Books.

Madrigal, S. 1992b. *Granjas,* Carmel, CA: Hampton Brown Books.

Montenegro Bourne, P. 1992. *Things Change.* Carmel, CA: Hampton Brown Books.

Montenegro-Bourne, P. 1992. *Las cosas cambian.* Carmel, CA: Hampton Brown Books.

Murphy, B. 1979. *Jaw-Jar and Saucer Gardens: A Garden in Your Bedroom.* London: Transworld Publishers.

Murphy, B. 1983. *Un jardín en tu dormitorio,* from *El niño quiere saber* series. Barcelona, Spain: Ediciones Toray.

Puncel, M. 1993. *El prado del tío Pedro.* Orlando: Harcourt, Brace, Jovanovich.

Rhodes, D. 1993. *The Corn Grows Ripe.* New York: Puffin Books.

Scholastic News Staff. "Los niños hacen un jardín." *Scholastic News* 49(6) (March 1993).

Walker, C. 1990. *Plants Grow Everywhere.* Cleveland, OH: Modern Curriculum Press.

Walker, C. 1990. *Las plantas crecen dondequiera.* Cleveland, OH: Modern Curriculum Press.

Walker, C. 1990. *How New Plants Grow.* Cleveland, OH: Modern Curriculum Press.

Walker, C. 1990. *Cómo crecen las plantas nuevas.* Cleveland, OH: Modern Curriculum Press.

Walker, C. 1990. *Gardening Is Fun.* Cleveland, OH: Modern Curriculum Press.

Walker, C. 1990. *La jardinería es divertida.* Cleveland, OH: Modern Curriculum Press.

Walker, C. 1990. *Alimentos que obtenemos de las plantas.* Cleveland, OH: Modern Curriculum Press.

Walker, C. 1990. *Foods That We Get From Plants.* Cleveland, OH: Modern Curriculum Press.

Walker, C. 1990. *Las diferentes cosas que vienen de las plantas.* Cleveland, OH: Modern Curriculum Press.

Walker, C. 1990. *Different Things We Get from Plants.* Cleveland, OH: Modern Curriculum Press.

APPENDIX D

Spanish and Asian Resources

Spanish Literature Resources

California

Mariuccia Iaconi
    Book Imports
1110 Mariposa
San Francisco, CA 94107
(800) 955-9577
(415) 255-8193
FAX (415) 255-8742

Edumate
2231 Morena Blvd.
San Diego, CA 92110
(619) 275-7117
FAX (619) 275-7120

Ateneo Booksellers
5505 N. Figueroa
Los Angeles, CA 90040
(213) 259-8850
FAX (213) 258-2909

Hampton Brown Books
PO Box 223220
Carmel, CA 93922
(800) 333-3510

Santillana (World of
    Literature catalog)
924 South Gerhart Avenue
Los Angeles, CA 90022
(800) 526-0107

Bilingual Educational Services
2514 South Grand Avenue
Los Angeles, CA 90007
(800) 448-6032
FAX (213) 749-1820

Basics Plus
Whole Language Spanish
    Big Books
97 Cresta Verde Drive
Rolling Hills Estates, CA 90274
(213) 325-7100
FAX (213) 534-0312

Children's Book Press
1339 61st Street
Emeryville, CA 94608
(415) 655-3395
FAX (415) 428-2861

Outside of California

The Bilingual Publications Co.
270 Lafayette Street
Suite 705
New York, NY 10012
(212) 431-3500
FAX (212) 431-3567

Lectorum Publications, Inc.
137 West 14th Street
New York, NY 10011
(212) 929-2833
FAX (212) 727-3035

Modern Curriculum Press
13900 Prospect Road
Cleveland, OH 44136
(800) 321-3106

Perma-Bound
1100 Libros en español
Vandalia Road
Jacksonville, IL 62650
(800) 637-6581
FAX (800) 551-1169

AIMS International Books, Inc.
7709 Hamilton Avenue
Cincinnati, OH 45231
(513) 521-5590
FAX (513) 521-5592

Santillana
257 Union Street
Northvale, NJ 07647
(800) 526-0107

D.D.L. Books
6521 N.W. 87 Avenue
Miami, FL 33166
(800) 635-4276

Hispanic Book Distributors
(Libros para niños y
    jóvenes catalog)
1665 West Grant Road
Tucson, AZ 85745
(602) 882-9484
FAX (602) 882-7696

Children's Press
(Libros en español
    para niños)
1224 West Van Buren Street
Chicago, IL 60607

T.R. Books
PO Box 310279
New Braunfels, TX 78131
(512) 625-2666
FAX (512) 620-0470

Libros Sin Fronteras
PO Box 2085
Olympia, WA 98507-2085
(206) 357-4332

Direct from Mexico
(Can call collect for orders—
orders sent air freight.)
Puvill-División México
c/o Carmen de Garcia Morena
English spoken
Empresa 109, Mixcoac
México, D.F. 03910
1-011-52-5-598-0991 or
1-011-52-5-598-4379

Puerto Rico
Publicaciones Yuguiyu
Av. Cesar González 407 Urb.
    Roosevelt
Hato Rey, Puerto Rico 00918
(809) 767-2963
FAX (809) 763-4690

Magazines About Hispanics

Más
PO Box 1928
Marion, OH 43305-1928

Hispanic (English and Spanish)
111 Massachusetts Avenue N.W.
Suite 200
Washington, DC 20077-2053

Comic Books in Spanish

Diamond Comics
PO Box 1196
Costa Mesa, CA 92628

Spanish-Language Classroom Newspapers

Mi Globo (Available in
    three levels.)
11320 Meadow Flower Place
San Diego, CA 92127-9965
(800) 777-0929

Scholastic News (Available in
    English and Spanish.)
Scholastic supplement includes
    bilingual posters
Scholastic Inc.
PO Box 3710
Jefferson City, MO 65102-3710
(800) 631-1586

Perspectiva
    (Upper grades)
Educational News Service
PO Box 177
South Hadley, MA 01075
(413) 538-7127

Bookclubs in Spanish

Alegría Book Corner
    Club and Fair
Mara Iaconi
PO Box 26806
Los Angeles, CA 90026
(213) 482-3633

Leer es Poder
PO Box 3447
Seal Beach, CA 90740-2447
(213) 594-4141

Libros Rodríguez
2160 Olga Street
Oxnard, CA 93030
(805) 981-9504

El Correo de Cuentos
PO Box 6652
Pico Rivera, CA 90661

Videos and Films

Madera Cinevideo
525 E. Yosemite Avenue
Madera, CA 93638
(209) 661-6000
FAX (209) 674-3650

AIMS películas y videos en español
9710 De Soto Avenue
Chatsworth, CA 91311
(800) 367-2467
FAX (818) 341-6700

Asian Resources

Shen's Books and Supplies
821 S. First Avenue, Suite A
Arcadia, CA 91006-3918
(818) 445-6958
FAX (818) 445-6940

Greenshower Corp.
Asia Children's Books
10937 Klingerman Street
S. El Montem, CA 91733
(818) 443-4020
(800) LEP-HELP

Multicultural Distributing Center
Asian Indian Languages
800 N. Grand Avenue
Covina, CA 91724
(818) 859-3133
FAX (818) 859-3136

National Asian Center for Bilingual
    Education
Institute for Intercultural Studies
11729 Gateway Blvd.
Los Angeles, CA 90064
(213) 479-6045

Pan Asian Publications: Books for
    Children
29564 Union City Blvd.
Union City, CA 94587
(415) 475-1185

A Resource Guide for Asian and
    Pacific American Students, K–12
ARC Associates, Inc.
310 Eighth Street
Suite 220
Oakland, CA 94607
(510) 834-9455

Children's Books in Korean
3030 W. Olympic Blvd. #111
Los Angeles, CA 90006
(213) 387-4082

Heian International, Inc.
1260 Pacific Street
PO Box 1013
Union City, CA 94587
(415) 471-8440

Pacific Rim Connections, Inc.
Source for Asian Language Software
3030 Atwater Drive
Burlingame, CA 94010
(415) 697-9439
FAX (415) 697-9439

Claudia's Caravan
Multicultural Multilingual Materials
PO Box 1582
Alameda, CA 94501
(415) 521-7871

Dong-A Book Plaza (Korean books
    and materials)
3460 West 8th Street
Los Angeles, CA 90005
(213) 382-7100
FAX (213) 382-2819

Global Village
2210 Wilshire Blvd.
PO Box 262
Santa Monica, CA 90403
(213) 549-5188

Cheng & Tsui Company
25 West Street
Boston, MA 02111
(617) 426-6074

Xuan Thu Publishing (Vietnamese
    books)
PO Box 97
Los Alamitos, CA 90720

The Bess Press (Hawaii's
    multicultural publisher)
PO Box 22388
Honolulu, HI 96823
(808) 734-7159
FAX (808) 732-3627

APPENDIX E
Bilingual Education

Selected Readings on Bilingual Education Theory and Research

Collier, V. 1992. "A Synthesis of Studies Examining Long-Term Language-Minority Student Data on Academic Achievement." *Bilingual Research Journal* 16(1 & 2): 187–212.

Cummins, J. 1981. "The Role of Primary Language Development in Promoting Educational Success for Language Minority Students." *Schooling and Language Minority Students: A Theoretical Framework.* Evaluation, Dissemination, and Assessment Center, California State University, Los Angeles.

Cummins, J. 1984. "Language Proficiency and Academic Achievement Revisited: A Response." In *Language Proficiency and Academic Achievement,* edited by C. Rivera. Clevedon, England: Multilingual Matters Ltd.

Hakuta, K. 1986. *Mirror of Language: The Debate on Bilingualism.* New York: Basic Books.

Hudelson, S. 1987. "The Role of Native Language Literacy in the Education of Language Minority Children." *Language Arts.* 64(8): 827–840.

Krashen, S. 1985. *Inquiries and Insights.* Haywood, CA: Alemany Press.

Krashen, S. 1991. "Bilingual education: A focus on current research." National Clearinghouse for Bilingual Education, Occasional Papers in *Bilingual Education,* Spring, 1991k, number 3.

Krashen, S., and D. Biber. 1988. *On Course: Bilingual Education's Success in California.* Sacramento, CA: California Association of Bilingual Education.

Ovando, C., and V. Collier. 1985. *Bilingual and ESL Classrooms: Teaching in Multicultural Contexts.* New York: McGraw-Hill.

Skutnabb-Kangas, T. 1983. *Bilingualism or Not: The Education of Minorities.* Clevedon, England: Multilingual Matters.

Willig, A. 1985. "A Meta-analysis of Selected Studies on the Effectiveness of Bilingual Education." *Review of Educational Research* 55: 269–317.

Bilingual Education and English Only

Baker, C. 1993. *Foundations of Bilingual Education and Bilingualism.* Philadelphia: Multilingual Matters.

Cazden, C., and C. Snow. 1990. *English Plus: Issues in Bilingual Education.* Newbury Park, CA: Sage Publications.

Crawford, J. 1989. *Bilingual Education: History, Politics, Theory and Practice.* Trenton, NJ: Crane.

Crawford, J. 1992. *Language Loyalties: A Source Book on the Official English Controversy.* Chicago: The University of Chicago Press.

Cummins, J. 1989. *Empowering Minority Students.* Sacramento: CABE.

Daniels, H. 1990. *Not Only English: Affirming America's Multilingual Heritage.* Urbana, IL: National Council of Teachers of English.

Judd, E. 1987. "The English Language Amendment: A Case Study of Language and Politics." *TESOL Quarterly* 21(1): 113–135.

Porter, R. 1990. *Forked Tongue: The Politics of Bilingual Education.* New York: Basic Books.

Stein, C. B. 1986. *Sink or Swim: The Politics of Bilingual Education.* New York: Praeger.

Trueba, H., and C. Barnett-Mizrahi. 1979. *Bilingual Multicultural Education and the Professional.* Rowley, MA: Newbury House.

APPENDIX F

Language Varieties and Functions

Cazden, C. 1988. *Classroom Discourse: The Language of Teaching and Learning*. Portsmouth, NH: Heinemann.

Delpit, L. 1990. "Language Diversity and Learning." In *Perspectives on Talk and Learning*, edited by S. Hynds and D. Rubin. Urbana, IL: National Council of Teachers of English.

Edelsky, C. 1989. "Putting Language Variation to Work for You." In *When They Don't All Speak English: Integrating the ESL Student into the Regular Classroom*, edited by P. Rigg and V. Allen. Urbana, IL: National Council of Teachers of English.

Heath, S. B. 1983. *Ways with Words: Language, Life, and Work in Communities and Classrooms*. Cambridge, England: Cambridge University Press.

Phillips, S. 1972. "Participant Structures and Communicative Competence: Warm Spring Children in Community and Classroom." In *Functions of Language in the Classroom*, edited by C. Cazden, V. John, and D. Hymes. New York: Teachers College Press.

Wallace, C. 1988. *Learning to Read in a Multicultural Society: The Social Context of Second Language Literacy*. New York: Prentice Hall.

Wigginton, E. 1985. *Sometimes a Shining Moment: The Foxfire Experience*. New York: Doubleday.

Wolfram, W. 1991. *Dialects and American English*. Englewood Cliffs, NJ: Prentice Hall Regents.

Wolfram, W., and D. Christian. 1989. *Dialects and Education: Issues and Answers*. Englewood Cliffs, NJ: Prentice Hall Regents.

APPENDIX G

Literature Study Books

Beatty, P. 1981. *Lupita mañana*. New York: William Morrow and Company.

Buss, F. L., and D. Cubias. 1993. *Journey of the Sparrows*. New York: Dell Publishing.

Coerr, E. 1979. *The Thousand Paper Cranes*. New York: Dell Publishing.

Crew, L. 1989. *Children of the River*. New York: Dell Publishing.

Fisher-Staples, S. 1989. *Shabanu*. New York: Alfred A. Knopf.

Garland, S. 1992. *Song of the Buffalo Boy*. San Diego, CA: Harcourt Brace Jovanovich.

Gilson, J. 1966. *Hello, My Name Is Scrambled Eggs*. New York: Pocket Books.

Ho, M. 1991. *The Clay Marble*. New York: Farrar Straus Giroux.

Kidd, D. 1989. *Onion Tears*. New York: Orchard Books.

Lord, B. B. 1984. *In the Year of the Boar and Jackie Robinson*. New York: The Trumpet Club.

Miklowitz, G. 1985. *War Between the Classes*. New York: Dell Publishing.

Milton, J. 1987. *Marching to Freedom: The Story of Martin Luther King, Jr.* New York: Scholastic.

Namioka, L. 1992. *Yang the Youngest and His Terrible Ear*. Boston: Little, Brown.

Nhoung, H. Q. 1982. *The Land I Lost*. New York: Harper & Row.

Patterson, K. 1988. *Park's Quest*. New York: Harper & Row.

Pettit, J. 1992. *My Name is San Ho*. New York: Scholastic.

Rhodes, D. 1993. *The Corn Grows Ripe*. New York: Puffin Books.

Taylor, M. 1976. *Roll of Thunder, Hear My Cry*. New York: Dial Press.

Taylor, T. 1973. *The Maldonado Miracle*. New York: Avon Camelot.

Taylor, T. 1992. *María: A Christmas Story*. San Diego: Harcourt Brace Jovanovich.

Tsuchiya, Y. 1988. *Faithful Elephants*. Boston: Houghton Mifflin.

Turner, A. 1987. *Nettie's Trip South*. New York: MacMillan.

Uchida, Y. 1976. *Journey to Topaz*. Fairfield, PA: Atheneum.

Uchida, Y. 1978. *Journey Home*. Fairfield, PA: Atheneum.

Uchida, Y. 1983. *The Best Bad Thing*. New York: Aladdin Books.

Whelan, G. 1992. *Goodbye, Vietnam*. New York: Alfred A. Knopf.

Williams, V. 1982. *A Chair for My Mother*. New York: Scholastic.

Yep, L. 1977. *The Child of the Owl*. New York: HarperCollins.

Picture Books for Intercultural Discussion

Ashley, B. 1991. *Cleversticks*. New York: Crown.

Bunting, E. 1988. *How Many Days to America?* Boston: Clarion Books.

Cohen, B. 1983. *Molly's Pilgrim*. New York: Lothrop, Lee & Shepard Books.

Coutant, H. 1974. *First Snow*. New York: Alfred A. Knopf.

Dorros, A. 1991. *Abuela*. New York: Dutton.

Friedman, I. 1984. *How My Parents Learned to Eat*. Boston: Houghton Mifflin.

Kindergartners, C. E. S. 1991. *We Are All Alike: We Are All Different*. New York: Scholastic.

Levine, E. 1989. *I Hate English*. New York: Scholastic.

Levinson, R. 1985. *Watch the Stars Come Out*. New York: Dutton.

Levinson, R. 1987. *Mira, cómo salen las estrellas*. Madrid, Spain: Ediciones Altea.

Mayled, J. 1986. *Feasting and Fasting*. Morristown, NJ: Silver Burdett Press.

Mayled, J. 1986. *Religious Customs*. Morristown, NJ: Silver Burdett Press.

Morris, A. 1989. *Hats, Hats, Hats*. New York: Lothrop, Lee & Shepard Books.

Morris, A. 1992. *Houses and Homes*. New York: Lothrop, Lee & Shepard Books.

Most, B. 1990. *The Cow that Went Oink*. San Diego, CA: Harcourt Brace Jovanovich.

Spier, P. 1980. *People*. New York: The Trumpet Club.

Stanek, M. 1989. *I Speak English for My Mom*. Niles, IL: Albert Whitman & Co.

Surat, M. M. 1983. *Angel Child, Dragon Child*. New York: Scholastic, Inc.

Waters, K. 1989. *Sara Morton's Day: A Day in the Life of a Pilgrim*. New York: Scholastic.

Xiong, B. 1988. *Nine in One Grr Grr*. San Francisco, CA: Children's Press.

Yang, M., P. Thao, and S. Yang. 1981. *Yer and Tiger*. St. Paul, MN: Ava-Dale Johnson.

Yashima, T. 1965. *Crow Boy*. New York: Scholastic.

APPENDIX H

Resources for Working with Parents

Professional Organizations to Contact

National Association of Bilingual Education
1220 L Street, NW, Suite 605
Washington, DC 20005-4018
(202) 898-1829
Ask for publications for parents, including publications in languages other than English.

National Council of Teachers of English
1111 Kenyon Road, Urbana, Illinois 61801
Ask for publications for parents in languages other than English.

National Clearinghouse for Bilingual Education
1118 22nd Street, NW, Washington, DC 20037
Ask for publications for parents in languages other than English.

Bilingual and Multicultural Office
William Dean Howells Building
4016 Woodbine Avenue, Salón 137
Cleveland, Ohio 44113
Ask for materials for parents in languages other than English.

California Association of Bilingual Education
926 J Street, #810
Sacramento, CA 95814
(916) 447-3986
Ask for publications for parents, including publications in languages other than English. They have parent membership in the organization and offer bilingual workshops and conferences for parents.

California Department of Education
P.O. Box 271
Sacramento, CA 95802-0271
(916) 445-1260
Ask for publications for parents in languages other than English, including "Parents are Teachers Too."

California Teachers Association
1705 Murchison Drive
Burlingame, CA 94010
Ask for publications for parents in languages other than English.

California Literature Project
University of California, San Diego
9500 Gilman Drive
San Diego, CA 92093-0415
Ask for information for language minority parents, especially concerning The California Learning Record (portfolio assessment).

Center for the Study of Books in Spanish for Children and Adolescents
California State University
San Marcos, CA 92096-0001
Write for listing of resources and activities.

Books and Guides of Possible Interest

The Changing Language Arts Curriculum: A Booklet for Parents.
California State Department of Education #0-8011-0867-5, California State Department of Education, P.O. Box 271, Sacramento, CA 95802-0271 (10 for $5)

Nicolau, S., and C. L. Ramos. 1990. *Together is Better: Building Strong Partnerships between Schools and Hispanic Parents* and *La Escuela es Neustra También.* Write Hispanic Policy Development Project, 1001 Connecticut Avenue, NW, Suite 538, Washington, DC 20036. Ask about other publications for parents.

"52 Ways to Help Your Child Learn," published by the California Teachers Association, has been translated into Spanish. Vietnamese, Khmer, Laotian, Chinese, and Korean. For translations, write Santa Clara County Office of Education, 100 Skyport Drive, San José, CA 95115.

Recommended Readings in Spanish Literature, Kindergarten Through Grade Eight. California State Department of Education #0-8011-0895-0, California State Department of Education, P.O. Box 271, Sacramento, CA 95802-0271 ($3.25 each).

Parenting Curriculum for Language Minority Parents. Available in Spanish. Contact Cross Cultural Resource Center, California State University, Sacramento, CA (916) 929-3708.

Freeman, Y., and C. Cervantes. *Literature Books* en español *for Whole Language.* Occasional Papers, Program in Language and Literacy, 504 College of Education, University of Arizona, Tucson, AZ 85721 ($3.50 each—available in Spanish).

Education Books about Language Learning *en español*

For purchase contact Mr. Gustavo Blankenburg
EDUMATE
2231 Morena Blvd.
San Diego, CA 92110
(619) 275-7117
FAX (619) 275-7120

Goodman, K. 1989. *Lenguaje Integral.* Mérida, Venezuela: Editorial Venezolana.

Gomez del Manzano, Mercedes. *El protagonista-niño en la literatura infantil del siglo XX.* Madrid, España: Notigrat.

Ferreiro, E., and A. Teberosky. 1982. *Literacy Before Schooling.* Portsmouth, NH: Heinemann. (Contact Heinemann for publication in Spanish.)

Graves, D. 1991. *Didática de la escritura.* Madrid, España: Ediciones Morata.

Osuna, Adelina Arellano. 1991. *El lengaje integral: Una alternativa para la educación.* Mérida, Venezuela: Editorial Venezolana.

Barron, M. 1993. *Aprendo a leer y a escribir de la manera en que aprendo a hablar: Mi primer libro acerca del lenguaje integrado.* Write Richard C. Owen, 135 Katonah Avenue, Katonah, NY 10536.

REFERENCES

Allwright, Dick. 1993. "Integrating 'Research' and 'Pedagogy': Appropriate Criteria and Practical Possibilities." In *Teachers Develop Teachers Research: Papers on Classroom Research and Teacher Development,* edited by J. Edge and K. Richards. Oxford: Heinemann International.

Anthony, Edward. 1965. "Approach, Method, and Technique." In *Teaching English as a Second Language: A Book of Readings,* edited by H. Allen and R. Campbell. New York: McGraw-Hill.

Atkin, Susan. 1993. *Voices from the Fields: Children of Migrant Farmworkers Tell Their Stories.* Boston: Little, Brown and Company.

Auerbach, Elsa. 1993. "Reexamining English Only in the ESL Classroom." *TESOL Quarterly* 27(1): 9–32.

Barnes, Douglas, 1990. "Oral Language and Learning." In *Perspectives on Talk and Learning,* edited by Susan Hynds and Donald Rubin. Urbana, IL: National Council of Teachers of English.

Beebe, Leslie. 1987. "Introduction." In *Issues in Second Language Acquisition: Multiple Perspectives,* edited by L. Beebe. New York: Newbury House.

Benedict, Susan, and Lenore Carlisle (Eds.). 1992. *Beyond Words: Picture Books for Older Readers and Writers.* Portsmouth, NH: Heinemann.

Bennett, William. 1985. "The Bilingual Education Act: A Failed Path." Press release of address to Association for a Better New York. New York. September 26.

Berman, Paul. 1992. *Meeting the Challenge of Language Diversity: An Evaluation of Programs for Pupils with Limited Proficiency in English.* BW Associates. NTIS, R-119/1.

Bird, Lois, and Linda Alvarez. 1987. "Beyond Comprehension: The Power of Literature Study for Language Minority Students." *ESOL Newsletter* 10(1): 1–3.

Bishop, Rudine, and Janet Hickman. 1992. "Four or Fourteen or Forty: Picture Books Are for Everyone." In *Beyond Words: Picture Books for Older Readers and Writers,* edited by Susan Benedict and Lenore Carlisle. Portsmouth, NH: Heinemann.

Bliatout, B. T., B. T. Downing, J. Lewis, and D. Yang. 1988. *Handbook for Teaching Hmong-speaking Students.* Folsom, CA: Folsom Cordova Unified School District.

Blum, R. 1991. "America as Seen Through Daddy's Eyes." *The Fresno Bee.* January 13: H1, H4.

Bode, J. 1989. *New Kids in Town.* New York: Scholastic.

Brimner, L. D. 1992. *A Migrant Family.* Minneapolis: Lerner Publications Company.

Brisk, Maria, and A. Bou-Zeineddine. 1993. "It Feels So Good": *Native Language Use in ESL.* Paper presented at the meeting of Teachers to Speakers of Other Languages, Atlanta, GA. April 20.

Brown, H. Douglas. 1980. *Principles of Language Learning and Teaching.* Englewood Cliffs, NJ: Prentice Hall.

Bruner, Jerome. 1985. "Models of the Learner." *Educational Researcher* 14(6): 5–8.

Bunting, Eve. 1988. *How Many Days to America?* Boston: Clarion Books.

California. 1992. Language Census Report for California Public Schools.

California, Department of Education. 1990. "Efforts to Help Parents of LEP Students Take Many Forms." *BEOutreach* 1(3): 1, 8.

California, Department of Education. 1991a. *Recommended Readings in Spanish Literature: Kindergarten Through Grade Eight.* Curriculum, Instruction and Assessment Division.

California, Department of Education. 1991b. *Remedying the Shortage of Teachers for Limited-English Proficient Students.* Bilingual Education Office.

Cambourne, Brian, and Jan Turbill. 1988. *Coping with Chaos.* Portsmouth, NH: Heinemann.

Canale, Michael, and Merril Swain. 1980. Theoretical Bases of Communicative Approaches to Second Language Teaching and Testing. *Applied Linguistics* 1(1): 1–47.

Cazden, Courtney. 1992. *Whole Language Plus: Essays on Literacy in the United States and New Zealand.* New York: Teachers College Press.

Celce-Murcia, Marianne. 1991. *Teaching English as a Second or Foreign Language.* 2d ed. Boston: Heinle and Heinle.

Chavez, K. 1993. "Wilson Advertisements Target Illegal Immigrants." [Letter to the editor]. *The Fresno Bee.* August 9: A1, A8.

Chomsky, Noam. 1959. "Review of Verbal Learning." *Language* 35: 26–58.

Claassen, Roxanne. 1993. "Discipline that Restores." Fresno Pacific College: The Center for Conflict Studies and Peacemaking: A Report of the First Three Years. Fresno, CA.

Clark, Edward. 1988. "The Search for a New Educational Paradigm: Implications of New Assumptions About Thinking and Learning." *Holistic Education Review* 1(1): 18–30.

Clay, Marie. 1973. *A Diagnostic Survey: Concepts about Print Test.* Auckland, New Zealand: Heinemann Educational Books.

Cochrane, Orin, Donna Cochrane, Sharen Scalena, and Ethel Buchanan. 1984. *Reading, Writing, and Caring.* Winnipeg: Whole Language Consultants Ltd.

Cohen, Andrew, and Elite Olshtain. 1993. "The Production of Speech Acts by ESL Learners." *TESOL Quarterly* 27(1):33–56.

Cohen, Barbara. 1983. *Molly's Pilgrim.* New York: Lothrop, Lee & Shepard Books.

Collier, Virginia. 1989. "How Long? A Synthesis of Research on Academic Achievement in a Second Language." *TESOL Quarterly* 23(3): 509–532.

———. 1992. "A Synthesis of Studies Examining Long-term Language-minority Student Data on Academic Achievement." *Bilingual Research Journal* 16(1 & 2): 187–212.

Cortés, Carlos. 1986. "The Education of Language Minority Students: A Contextual Interaction Model." In *Beyond Language: Social and Cultural Factors in Schooling Language Minority Students,* edited by D. Holt. Evaluation, Dissemination, and Assessment Center, California State University, Los Angeles.

Crawford, James. 1989. *Bilingual Education: History, Politics, Theory and Practice.* Trenton, NJ: Crane.

———. 1992. *Language Loyalties: A Source Book on the Official English Controversy.* Chicago: The University of Chicago Press.

Criddle, Joan, and T. B. Mam. 1987. *To Destroy You Is No Loss: The Odyssey of a Cambodian Family.* New York: The Atlantic Monthly Press.

Crowley, Paul. 1993. "Perceptions of the Reading Process and Reading Instruction by Selected Students in Five Whole Language Classrooms." Unpublished doctoral dissertation. Columbia: University of Missouri.

Cummins, Jim. 1981. "The Role of Primary Language Development in Promoting Educational Success for Language Minority Students." In *Schooling and Language Minority Students: A Theoretical Framework*. Evaluation, Dissemination, and Assessment Center, California State University, Los Angeles.

————. 1984. *Bilingualism and Special Education: Issues in Assessment and Pedagogy*. Clevedon, England: Multilingual Matters.

————. 1989. *Empowering Minority Students*. Sacramento: CABE.

Davidson, M. 1988. *The Story of Jackie Robinson, Bravest Man in Baseball*. New York: Dell Publishing.

Delpit, Lisa. 1988. "The Silenced Dialogue: Power and Pedagogy in Educating Other People's Children." *Harvard Education Review* 58: 280–298.

————. 1990. "Language Diversity and Learning." In *Perspectives on Talk and Learning*, edited by Susan Hynds and Donald Rubin. Urbana, IL: National Council of Teachers of English.

Dewey, John. 1929. *My Pedagogic Creed*. Washington, DC: The Progressive Education Association.

Dewey, John, and A. F. Bentley. 1949. *Knowing and the Known*. Boston: Beacon Press.

Díaz, Stephen, Luis Moll, and Hugh Mehan. 1986. "Sociocultural resources in instruction: A context-specific approach." *Beyond Language: Social and Cultural Factors in Schooling Language Minority Students*. Los Angeles: Evaluation, Dissemination and Assessment Center, California State University, Los Angeles.

Dolson, David, and Jan Mayer. 1992. "A Longitudinal Study of Three Program Models for Language Minority Students: A Critical Examination of Reported Findings." *Bilingual Research Journal*, 16(1 & 2), 105–157.

East, David. 1993. "Metta, Bridging Technology, Whole Language and Bilingual Education." Unpublished master's project, Fresno Pacific College.

Edelsky, Carole. 1986. *Writing in a Bilingual Program: Había una vez*. Norwood, NJ: Albex.

————. 1988. "Living in the Author's World: Analyzing the Author's Craft." *California Reader* 21: 14–17.

Edelsky, Carole, Bess Altwerger, and Barbara Flores. 1991. *Whole Language: What's the Difference?* Portsmouth, NH: Heinemann.

Enright, D. Scott, and Mary Lou McCloskey. 1985. "Yes, Talking!: Organizing the Classroom to Promote Second Language Acquisition." *TESOL Quarterly* 19(3): 431–453.

————. 1988. *Integrating English: Developing English Language and Literacy in the Multilingual Classroom*. Reading, MA: Addison-Wesley Publishing Co.

Erickson, Jeannette. 1993. "Teachers' Voices: An Interview Project." Unpublished master's thesis, Fresno Pacific College.

Fennacy, Jean, and Debbie Manning. 1993. "Respect for Language and Learners in the Whole Language Classroom." In *Whole Language: History, Philosophy, Practice*, edited by S. K. Bradley and T. Sills. Dubuque, IA: Kendall/Hunt Publishing Co.

Ferreiro, Emilia, and Anna Teberosky. 1982. *Literacy Before Schooling*. Translated by Karen Goodman Castro. Portsmouth, NH: Heinemann.

Fitzgerald, Jill. 1993. "Literacy and Students Who Are Learning English as a Second Language." *The Reading Teacher* 46(8): 638–647.

Flores, Barbara. 1982. Language Interference or Influence: Toward a Theory of Hispanic Bilingualism. Unpublished doctoral dissertation, University of Arizona, Tucson, AZ.

Freeman, David, and Yvonne Freeman. 1990. "Case Studies: Viewing New Students in New Ways." *California English* 26(3):8–9, 26–27.

———. 1992a. "Is Whole Language Teaching Compatible with Content-based Instruction?" *The Catesol Journal* 5(1): 103–108.

———. 1992b. "Enriching Classroom Resources: Primary Language Student Publications." *CABE Newsletter* 15(2): 12–13.

———. 1993. "Strategies for Promoting the Primary Languages of All Students." *The Reading Teacher* 46(7): 552–558.

Freeman, Yvonne, and Carolina Cervantes. 1991a. "*Literature Books en Español for Whole Language.*" In *Occasional Papers: Program in Language and Literacy,* edited by K. S. Goodman and Y. M. Goodman. Tucson: University of Arizona.

———. 1991b. "Literature Books en Español for Whole Language Classrooms." In *The Whole Language Catalog,* edited by K. Goodman, L. Bird, and Y. Goodman. Santa Rosa, CA: American School Publishers.

———. 1993. "Libros de Literatura en Español para el Lenguaje Integral: Una Bibliografía Comentada." Translated by Marisela and Jesús Serra. In *Occasional Papers: Program in Language and Literacy,* edited by K. S. Goodman and Y. M. Goodman. Tucson: University of Arizona.

Freeman, Yvonne, and David Freeman. 1989. "Bilingual Learners: How Our Assumptions Limit Their World." *Holistic Education Review* 2(4): 33–39.

———. 1990. "New Attitudes for New Students." *Holistic Education Review.* 3(2): 25–30.

———. 1992a. *Whole Language for Second Language Learners.* Portsmouth, NH: Heinemann.

———. 1992b. "The Questioning Lesson Plan." In *The Whole Language Catalog: Supplement on Authentic Assessment,* edited by K. Goodman, Y. Goodman, and L. B. Bird. Santa Rosa, CA: American School Publishers.

———. 1993. "Celebrating diversity: Whole language with bilingual learners." In *Whole Language: History, Philosophy, Practice,* edited by S. Brady and T. Sills. Dubuque, IA: Kendall/Hunt Publishing Co.

———. 1994. "Whole Language Learning and Teaching for Second Language Learners." In *Reading Process and Practice: From Socio-psycholinguistics to Whole Language,* edited by C. Weaver. Portsmouth, NH: Heinemann.

Freeman, Yvonne, and Yetta Goodman. 1993. "Revaluing the Bilingual Learner Through a Literature Reading Program." *Reading and Writing Quarterly: Overcoming Learning Difficulties,* 9:163–182.

Freeman, Yvonne, and Sam Nofziger. 1991. "WalkuM to RnM 33: Vien Vinidos al cualTo 33." In *Organizing for Whole Language,* edited by K. Goodman, Y. Goodman, and W. Hood. Portsmouth, NH: Heinemann.

Freeman, Yvonne S., and Lynn Whitesell. 1985. "What Preschoolers Already Know about Print." *Educational Horizons* 64(1): 22–25.

Freire, Paulo. 1970. *Pedagogy of the Oppressed.* Translated by Myra Ramos. New York: Continuum.

Freire, Paulo, and Donaldo Macedo. 1987. *Literacy: Reading the Word and the World.* South Hadley, MA: Bergin and Garvey.

Gardner, Howard. 1984. *Frames of Mind.* New York: Basic Books.

Gee, James. 1988. "Count Dracula, the Vampire Lestat, and TESOL." *TESOL Quarterly* 22: 201–205.

————. 1990. *Social Linguistics and Literacies: Ideology in Discourses.* Bristol, PA: Falmer Press.

————. 1992. *The Social Mind: Language, Ideology, and Social Practice.* Edited by D. Macedo. Language and Ideology. New York: Bergin and Garvey.

Goldenberg, Claude. 1991. *Instructional Conversations and Their Classroom Application.* National Center for Research on Cultural Diversity and Second Language Learning. Santa Cruz, CA.

Goldenberg, Claude, and Ronald Gallimore. 1991. "Local Knowledge, Research Knowledge, and Educational Change: A Case Study of Early Spanish Reading Improvement." *Educational Researcher* 20(8): 2–14.

Goodman, Kenneth, E. B. Smith, R. Meredith, and Yetta Goodman. 1987. *Language and Thinking in School: A Whole Language Curriculum.* 3d ed. New York: Richard C. Owen.

Goodman, Kenneth S., Yetta M. Goodman, and Barbara Flores. 1979. *Reading in the Bilingual Classroom: Literacy and Biliteracy.* Rosslyn, VA: National Clearinghouse for Bilingual Education.

Goodman, Yetta M., Bess Altwerger, and Ann Marek. 1989. "Print Awareness in Preschool Children." In *Occasional Papers: Program in Language and Literacy,* edited by K. Goodman and Y. Goodman. Tucson: University of Arizona.

Goodman, Yetta M., and Kenneth S. Goodman. 1990. "Vygotsky in a Whole Language Perspective." In *Vygotsky and Education: Instructional Implications and Applications of Sociohistorical Psychology,* edited by L. Moll. Cambridge, England: Cambridge University Press.

Goss, J. L., and Jerome C. Harste. 1985. *It Didn't Frighten Me.* Worthington, OH: Willowisp Press.

Graham, Carolyn. 1979. *Jazz Chants for Children.* New York: Oxford University Press.

Hakuta, Kenji. 1986. *Mirror of Language: The Debate on Bilingualism.* New York: Basic Books.

Halliday, M. A. K. 1975. *Learning How to Mean.* London: Edward Arnold.

————. 1984. "Three Aspects of Children's Language Development: Learning Language, Learning Through Language, and Learning About Language." In *Oral and Written Language Development Research: Impact on the Schools,* edited by Y. Goodman, M. Haussler, and D. Strickland. Urbana, IL: National Council of Teachers of English.

Halliday, M. A. K., and R. Hassan. 1976. *Cohesion in English.* London: Longman Group, Ltd.

Hamayan, Else. 1989. *Teach Your Children Well.* Twelfth annual statewide conference for teachers of limited English proficient students. Oak Brook, IL. Speech at the conference.

Harman, Susan, and Carole Edelsky. 1989. "The Risks of Whole Language Literacy: Alienation and Connection." *Language Arts* 66: 392–406.

Harris, Violet. 1992. *Teaching Multicultural Literature in Grades K–8.* Norwood, MA: Christopher-Gordon Publishers, Inc.

Harste, Jerome, Virginia Woodward, and Carolyn Burke. 1984. *Language Stories and Literacy Lessons.* Portsmouth, NH: Heinemann.

Hatch, Evelyn. 1983. *Psycholinguistics: A Second Language Perspective.* Rowley, MA: Newbury House.

Heath, Shirley. 1986. "Sociocultural Contexts of Language Development." In *Beyond Language: Social and Cultural Factors in Schooling Language Minority Students,* edited by D. Holt. Evaluation, Dissemination, and Assessment Center, California State University, Los Angeles.

————. 1983. *Ways with Words: Language, Life, and Work in Communities and Classrooms.* Cambridge, England: Cambridge University Press.

Holmes, D. 1993. "IATEFL 1993: Are Politicians Seized by Linguistic Panic?" *TESOL Matters* 3(3): 1, 8.

Holt, Dan (Ed.). 1993. *Cooperative Learning: A Response to Linguistic and Cultural Diversity.* Washington, DC: Center for Applied Linguistics.

Holt, Grace D. 1993. "Family English Literacy Project Uses Thematic Approach to Instruction in Sacramento Unified." *BEOutreach* 4(2): 19–21.

Hudelson, Sarah. 1984. "Kan Yu Ret an Rayt en Ingles: Children Become Literature in English as a Second Language." *TESOL Quarterly* 18(2): 221–237.

————. 1986. "ESL Children's Writing: What We've Learned, What We're Learning." In *Children and ESL: Integrating Perspectives,* edited by P. Rigg and D. S. Enright. Washington, DC: Teachers of English to Speakers of Other Languages.

————. 1987. "The Role of Native Language Literacy in the Education of Language Minority Children." *Language Arts* 64(8): 827–840.

Hymes, Del. 1970. "On Communicative Competence." In *Directions in Sociolinguistics,* edited by J. Gumperz and D. Hymes. New York: Holt, Rinehart and Winston.

Jones, Ron. 1976. *The Acorn People.* New York: Bantam.

Kagan, Spencer. 1986. "Cooperative Learning and Sociocultural Factors in Schooling." In *Beyond Language: Social and Cultural Factors in Schooling Language Minority Students,* Los Angeles: Evaluation, Dissemination, and Assessment Center, California State University, Los Angeles.

————. 1988. *Cooperative Learning: Resources for Teachers.* Riverside, CA: University of California, Riverside.

Kitagawa, Mary. 1989. "Letting Ourselves Be Taught." In *Richness in Writing: Empowering ESL Students,* edited by D. Johnson and D. Roen. New York: Longman.

Klassen, Charlene. (In press.) "Content Area Literature Discussions: Exploring 'The Color of Peace.'" In *Cycles of Meaning: Conversation, Story, and Dialogue in Learning Communities,* edited by K. Mitchell Pierce and C. Gilles. Portsmouth, NH: Heinemann Educational Books.

Kozol, Jonathan. 1991. *Savage Inequalities.* New York: Harper.

Krashen, Stephen. 1982. *Principles and Practice in Second Language Acquisition.* New York: Pergamon Press.

————. 1985. *Inquiries and Insights.* Haywood, CA: Alemany Press.

————. 1990. "How Reading and Writing Make You Smarter, or How Smart People Read and Write." Georgetown University Round Table on Languages and Linguistics. Washington, DC: Georgetown University Press.

Krashen, S., and D. Biber. 1988. *On Course: Bilingual Education's Success in California.* Sacramento, CA: California Association of Bilingual Education.

Krashen, Stephen, and Tracy Terrell. 1983. *The Natural Approach: Language Acquisition in the Classroom.* Hayward, CA: Alemany Press.

Larsen-Freeman, Diane. 1986. *Techniques and Principles in Language Teaching.* Oxford: Oxford University Press.

Larsen-Freeman, Diane, and Michael Long. 1991. *An Introduction to Second Language Acquisition Research,* New York: Longman.

Levinson, Riki. 1985. *Watch the Stars Come Out.* New York: E. P. Dutton.

Lindfors, Judith, 1982. "Exploring In and Through Language." In *On TESOL '82: Pacific Perspectives on Language Learning and Teaching*, edited by M. Clarke and J. Handscombe. Washington, DC: Teachers of English to Speakers of Other Languages.

Lindfors, Judith. 1987. *Children's Language and Learning*. Englewood Cliffs, NJ: Prentice Hall.

————. 1989. "The Classroom: A Good Environment for Language Learning." In *When They Don't All Speak English: Integrating the ESL Student into the Regular Classroom*, edited by P. Rigg and V. Allen. Urbana, IL: National Council of Teachers of English.

Long, Michael. 1983. "Does Second Language Instruction Make a Difference? A Review of the Research." *TESOL Quarterly* 14: 378–390.

Loya, Oscar. 1993. "Success in School Begins Before Kindergarten." *BEOutreach* 4(2): 29, 30.

Lucas, Tamara, R. Henze, and R. Donato. 1990. "Promoting the Success of Latino Language-minority Students: An Exploratory Study of Six High Schools." *Harvard Educational Review* 60(3): 315–340.

Marasco, Lisa. 1993. "Parent Empowerment through Involvement." *T.I.P.S. Teacher-Inspired Practical Strategies, NCTE/ESL Assembly Newsletter* 2(1): 16–17.

McCormick, E. 1993. "Wilson's Immigration Plan Won't Get Anywhere, Critics Say" [Letter to the editor]. *The Fresno Bee*. August 11: A3.

McGroarty, Mary. 1993. "Cooperative Learning and Second Language Acquisition." In *Cooperative Learning: A Response to Linguistic and Cultural Diversity*, edited by D. Holt. Washington, DC: Center for Applied Linguistics.

Moll, Luis. 1989. "Teaching Second Language Students: A Vygotskian Perspective." In *Richness in Writing: Empowering ESL Students*, edited by D. Johnson and D. Roen. New York: Longman.

Murphy, Sharon. 1991. "The Code, Connectionism, and Basals." *Language Arts* 68(3): 199-205.

Naso, M., and E. Mirande. 1990. "PECES: A District-supported Parent Training Program." *BEOutreach* 1(3): 12–14.

Navarrette, R. 1993. "Latinos for immigration reform" [Letter to the editor]. *The Fresno Bee*. August 15: B6.

Novak, M. 1971. *Ascent of the Mountain, Flight of the Dove: An Invitation to Religious Studies*. New York: Harper and Row.

Nunan, David. 1993. "Action Research in Language Education." In *Teachers Research Teachers Develop: Papers on Classroom Research and Teacher Development*, edited by J. Edge and K. Richards. Oxford: Heinemann International.

Ogbu, John. 1991. "Immigrant and Involuntary Minorities in Comparative Perspective." In *Minority Status and Schooling: A Comparative Study of Immigrant and Involuntary Minorities*, edited by M. Gibson and J. Ogbu. New York: Garland Publishing Co.

Ogbu, John, and Maria Matute-Bianchi. 1986. *"Understanding Sociocultural Factors: Knowledge, Identity and School Adjustment."* In *Beyond Language: Social and Cultural Factors in Schooling Language Minority Students*, edited by D. Holt. Evaluation, Dissemination, and Assessment Center, California State University, Los Angeles.

Olsen, Laurie. 1988. *Crossing the Schoolhouse Border: Immigrant Students and the California Public Schools*. San Francisco: California Tomorrow.

Olsen, Laurie, and N. Mullen. 1990. *Embracing Diversity: Teacher's Voices from California Classrooms*. San Francisco: California Tomorrow.

Olsen, Roger. 1991. "Results of a K–12 and Adult ESL Survey—1991." *TESOL Quarterly* 1(5): 4.

Onore, Cynthia. 1990. "Negotiation, Language, and Inquiry: Building Collaboratively in the Classroom." In *Perspectives on Talk and Learning,* edited by S. Hynds and D. Rubin. Urbana, IL: National Council of Teachers of English.

Ouk, Mory. 1993. "Cambodian Proverbs Help U.S. Educators Understand and Respond to Children and Their Parents." *BEOutreach* 4(2): 5, 6.

Ouk, Mory, F. E. Huffman, and J. Lewis. 1988. *Handbook for Teaching Khmer-Speaking Students.* Folsom, CA: Folsom Cordova Unified School District.

Palinscar, A. S. 1986. "The Role of Dialogue in Providing Scaffolded Instruction." *Educational Psychologist* 21: 73–98.

Peterson, Ralph, and Mary Ann Eeds. 1990. *Grand Conversations.* New York: Scholastic.

Pérez, T. 1991. *Portraits of Mexican-Americans: Pathfinders in the Mexican-American Communities.* Carthage, IL: Good Apple.

Peyton, Joy. 1990. *Students and Teachers Writing Together: Perspectives on Journal Writing.* Alexandria, VA: Teachers of English to Speakers of Other Languages.

Phillips, Susan. 1972. "Participant Structures and Communicative Competence: Warm Spring Children in Community and Classroom." In *Functions of Language in the Classroom,* edited by C. Cazden, V. John, and D. Hymes. New York: Teachers College Press.

Piaget, Jean. 1955. *The Language and Thought of the Child.* New York: Meridian Publishers.

Pienemann, M., and M. Johnston. 1987. "Factors Influencing the Development of Language Proficiency." In *Applying Second Language Acquisition Research,* edited by D. Nunan. Adelaide: National Curriculum Research Centre.

Pinker, S., and A. Prince. 1988. "On Language and Connectionism: Analysis of a Parallel Distributed Processing Model of Language Acquisition." *Cognition* 28 (1–2): 73–193.

Radford, Andrew. 1981. *Transformational Syntax: A Student's Guide to Chomsky's Extended Standard Theory.* Cambridge: Cambridge University Press.

Ramírez, D. 1990. "Even Start Program Promotes Family-centered Education." *BEOutreach* 1(3): 10–12.

Ramírez, J. David. 1991. "Final Report: Longitudinal Study of Structured English Immersion Strategy, Early-exit and Late-exit Bilingual Education Programs." U.S. Department of Education. NTIS, 300-87-0156.

Rigg, Pat, and Virginia Allen. 1989. "Introduction." In *When They Don't All Speak English,* edited by P. Rigg and V. Allen. Urbana, IL: National Council of Teachers of English.

Rigg, Pat, and D. Scott Enright. 1986. *Children and ESL: Integrating Perspectives.* Washington, DC: Teachers of English to Speakers of Other Languages.

Rigg, Pat, and Sarah Hudelson. 1986. "One Child Doesn't Speak English." *Australian Journal of Reading* 9(3): 116–125.

Roberts, Michael. 1993. *"Theories and Practices in Empowering Latino Students."* Unpublished master's thesis. Fresno, CA: Fresno Pacific College.

Robinson-Flint, Manilton, Kirka, Rense, and White. 1992. "Stereotyping Habit: Young People Try to Fight It." *The Los Angeles Times* Nov. 30:33.

Rodíguez, Richard. 1982. *Hunger of Memory: The Education of Richard Rodríguez.* Boston: David R. Godine.

Rogers, Bunny. 1992. "Integrating ESL Listening and Speaking Through an Authentic Audience." *California English* 27(1): 8, 9, 25.

Rojas, Jill. 1993. "Book Bags: Literacy at Home." *T.I.P.S. Teacher-Inspired Practical Strategies, NCTE/ESL Assembly Newsletter* 2(1): 8.

Romero, Guadalupe. 1983. "Print Awareness of the Pre-school Bilingual Spanish-English Speaking Child." Unpublished doctoral dissertation. Tucson: University of Arizona.

Rosenblatt, Louise. 1978. *The Reader, the Text, the Poem: The Transactional Theory of the Literary Work.* Carbondale, IL: Southern Illinois University Press.

Scarcella, Robin. 1990. *Teaching Language Minority Students in the Multicultural Classroom.* Englewood Cliffs, NJ: Prentice Hall Regents.

Scarcella, Robin, and Rebeccah Oxford. 1992. *The Tapestry of Language Learning: The Individual in the Communicative Classroom.* Boston: Heinle & Heinle.

Scholastic News Staff. 1993. "¡Nuestro Nuevo Presidente!" *Scholastic News* 49(4): 1–4.

Schon, Isabel. 1992. "Center for the Study of Books in Spanish for Children and Adolescents." *CABE Newsletter* 14(4): 34.

Schumann, J. 1978. *The Pidginization Process: A Model for Second Language Acquisition.* Rowley, MA: Newbury House.

Searle, Dennis. 1984. "Who's Building Whose Building?" *Language Arts* 61(5): 480–483.

Seliger, Herbert. 1988. "Psycholinguistic Issues in Second Language Acquisition." In *Issues in Second Language Acquisition: Multiple Perspectives,* edited by L. Beebe. New York: Newbury House.

Short, Kathy G., and Charlene Klassen. (In press.) "Literature Circles: Hearing Children's Voices." In *Literature Across the Curriculum: Making It Happen,* edited by B. Cullinan. Newark, DE: International Reading Association.

Silver. 1992. "The New Discipline Program." *The Fresno Bee.* April 25: B3.

Sizer, Theodore. 1990. *Student as Worker, Teacher as Coach.* Viewer's guide to teleconference. New York: Simon and Schuster.

Skinner, B. F. 1957. *Verbal Behavior.* New York: Appleton.

Skutnabb-Kangas, Tove. 1983. *Bilingualism or Not: The Education of Minorities.* Clevedon, England: Multilingual Matters.

Smith, Frank. 1983. *Essays into Literacy: Selected Papers and Some Afterthoughts.* Portsmouth, NH: Heinemann.

———. 1988. *Joining the Literacy Club: Further Essays into Literacy.* Portsmouth, NH: Heinemann.

Spier, Peter. 1980. *People.* New York: The Trumpet Club.

Sue, Stanley, and Amado Padilla. 1986. "Ethnic Minority Issues in the United States: Challenges for the Educational System." In *Beyond Language: Social and Cultural Factors in Schooling Language Minority Students.* Bilingual Center, School of Education. California State University, Los Angeles.

Sumara, Dennis. 1993. "Living Between Theory and Practice: Professional Development of Whole Language Teachers Through Collaborative Action Research." In *Whole Language: History, Philosophy, Practice,* edited by Sandra Brady and Toni Sills. Dubuque, Iowa: Kendall/Hunt Publishing Co..

Swain, Merrill. 1985. "Communicative Competence: Some Roles of Comprehensible Output in Its Development." In *Input in Second Language Acquisition,* edited by S. Gass and C. Madden. Rowley, MA: Newbury House.

Urzúa, Carole. 1987. "You Stopped Too Soon: Second Language Children Composing and Revising." *TESOL Quarterly* 21(2): 279–297.

Van Lier, Leo. 1988. *The Classroom and the Language Learner.* New York: Longman.

Villaseñor, Victor. 1991. *Rain of Gold.* New York: Dell Publishing.

Vygotsky, Lev. 1978. *Mind in Society: The Development of Higher Psychological Processes.* Cambridge, MA: Harvard University Press.

Vygotsky, Lev S. 1981. The Genesis of Higher Mental Functions. In *The Concept of Activity in Soviet Psychology,* edited by J. V. Wertsch. Armonk, NY: M. E. Sharpe.

Wallerstein, Nina. 1987. "Problem Posing Education: Freire's Method for Transformation." In *Freire for the Classroom,* edited by I. Shor. Portsmouth, NH: Heinemann.

Waters, K. 1989. *Sara Morton's Day: A Day in the Life of a Pilgrim.* New York: Scholastic.

Watson, Dorothy. 1994. "Whole Language: Why Bother?" *The Reading Teacher.* 47:(8) 600–607.

Weaver, Constance, and Linda Henke (Eds.) 1992. *Supporting Whole Language: Stories of Teacher and Institutional Change.* Portsmouth, NH: Heinemann.

Wells, Gordon, and Gen Chang-Wells. 1992. *Constructing Knowledge Together.* Portsmouth, NH: Heinemann.

Wertsch, James. 1991. *Voices of the Mind.* Cambridge, MA: Harvard University Press.

White, L. 1987. "Markedness and Second Language Acquisition: The Question of Transfer." *Studies in Second Language Acquisition* 9: 261–85.

Whorf, Benjamin. 1956. "Science and Linguistics." In Brown 1987.

Widdowson, Henry. 1978. *Teaching Language as Communication.* Oxford: Oxford University Press.

Wilkinson, T., and S. Chavez. 1992. "Cadillac Jim—Homage to an L.A. Homeboy." *Los Angeles Times.* April 26.

Willet, Jerri. 1987. "Contrasting Acculturation Patterns of Two Non-English-speaking Preschoolers." In *Success or Failure? Learning and the Language Minority Student,* edited by H. T. Trueba. New York: Newbury House.

Wink, Joan. 1993. "Labels Often Reflect Educators' Beliefs and Practices." *BEOutreach* 4(2): 28–29.

Wolfram, Walt. 1991. *Dialects and American English.* Englewood Cliffs. NJ: Prentice Hall Regents.

Wolfram, Walt, and Donna Christian. 1989. *Dialects and Education: Issues and Answers.* Englewood Cliffs, NJ: Prentice Hall Regents.

INDEX